Democracy and
Social Change in India

Democracy and Social Change in India

A Cross-sectional Analysis of the National Electorate

Subrata K. Mitra
V.B. Singh

Sage Publications
New Delhi ■ Thousand Oaks ■ London

Copyright © Subrata K. Mitra, V.B. Singh, 1999

All rights reserved. No part of this book may be reproduced or utilised in any form or by any means, electronic or mechanical, including photocopying, recording or by any information storage or retrieval system, without permission in writing from the publisher.

First published in 1999 by

Sage Publications India Pvt Ltd
M–32, Greater Kailash, Part–I
New Delhi–110 048

Sage Publications Inc.
2455 Teller Road
Thousand Oaks, California 91320

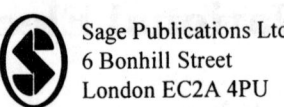

Sage Publications Ltd
6 Bonhill Street
London EC2A 4PU

Published by Tejeshwar Singh for Sage Publications India Pvt Ltd, lasertypeset by Asian Telelinks, New Delhi and printed at Chaman Enterprises, Delhi.

Library of Congress Cataloging-in-Publication Data

Mitra, Subrata Kumar, 1949–
    Democracy and social change in India: A cross-sectional analysis of the national electorate/Subrata K. Mitra and V.B. Singh.
       p. cm.   (cl.)
    Includes bibliographical references and index.
    1. Elections—India. 2. Public opinion—India. 3. Social change—India. 4. India—Politics and government—1977– 5. India—Social conditions—1947– I. Singh, V.B., 1941–. II. Title.
    JQ294. M58 320.954'09'045—dc21   1999   99–26780

ISBN: 81-7036-809-X (India-HB)
       0-7619-9344-4 (US-HB)

Sage Production Team: Lt Col Dhiren Bahl (retd), Abantika Chatterji, O.P. Bhasin and Santosh Rawat

This book is dedicated to the memory of
Bashiruddin Ahmed
and
G. Rama Reddy
whose contributions constitute
major milestones of empirical research
in Indian politics

Contents

	List of Tables	8
	List of Figures	12
	Preface and Acknowledgements	13
1	Introduction: Competing Paradigms of Politics and Social Change in India	17
2	Continuity and Change in Indian Politics: A Cohort Analysis of the Electorate	56
3	The Limits of Consensus: A Profile of the Electorate	86
4	Political Competition, Social Change and Transformation of the Party System	118
5	The Dialectics of Nation and Region in Indian Politics	155
6	Poverty, Economic Policy and Social Opportunity in India	179
7	Community, Conflict and Local Democracy: Patterns of Regional Variation	209
8	Conclusion: Social Change and the Resilience of Democracy in India	250
	Appendix 1 Note on Methodology	283
	Appendix 2 Construction of Scales and Variables	296
	Appendix 3 Questionnaire	302
	Bibliography	324
	Index	336
	About the Authors	342

List of Tables

1.1	Competing Paradigms of State–Society Interaction: A Classificatory Scheme	28
1.2	Election Data, Indian Parliamentary Elections, 1952–98	40
1.3	Participation Trends in Major Assembly Elections, 1952–95	41
1.4	Percentage Turnout in Assembly Elections, 1984–95	41
2.1	Level of Political Information by Generation	68
2.2	Level of Education by Generation	69
2.3	Effect of Vote by Generation	69
2.4	Parties' Attention to People by Generation	70
2.5	Importance of Elections by Generation	70
2.6	Trust in Institutions by Generation	71
2.7	Attitudes towards Ayodhya Incident by Generation	72
2.8	Policy towards Pakistan by Generation	73
2.9	Resolution of Kashmir Issue by Generation	73
2.10	'No Need for Atomic Bomb' by Generation	73
2.11	Separate Civil Code by Generation	74
2.12	Reservation for Women by Generation	74
2.13	'Needs of Muslims Neglected' by Generation	75
2.14	Economic Satisfaction by Generation	76
2.15	Privatisation by Generation	76
2.16	No Free Trade to Foreign Companies by Generation	77
2.17	Limited Ownership by Generation	77
2.18	Government Better without Parties by Generation	78
2.19	Party Support by Generation	78
3.1	Distribution of Respondents by Background Characteristics	89
3.2	Timing of Voting Preference	91

3.3	Interest in Election Campaign	92
3.4	Attendance of Election Meetings during Campaign	93
3.5	Campaign Exposure	94
3.6	Visit by Candidate, Party Worker, Canvasser	96
3.7	Guided in Voting Decision	97
3.8	Distribution of Voters and Non-Voters	100
3.9	Reason for Not Voting	100
3.10	Information about Local MP	103
3.11	Correct Naming of Prime Minister	104
3.12	Correct Naming of Chief Minister	105
3.13	Index of Political Information	106
3.14	Major Problems Facing the Country	108
3.15	Main Issues in the 1996 Election	109
3.16	Financial Situation during the Last Few Years	110
3.17	Present Financial Situation	111
3.18	Future Financial Situation	112
3.19	Better Opportunities for Children	113
3.20	Financial Satisfaction	114
4.1	Summary of Lok Sabha Elections, 1952–71 (Seats and per cent of Vote)	128
4.2	Summary of Lok Sabha Elections, 1977–98 (Seats and per cent of Vote)	131
4.3	Social Bases of Political Parties (1996 and 1998)	134
4.4	Efficacy of Vote	141
4.5	Usefulness of Political Parties	142
4.6	Better Government without Parties, Assemblies and Elections?	144
4.7	Partisan Response to the Demolition of Babri Mosque	146
4.8	Partisan Opinion on Resolution of Kashmir Problem	147
4.9	India should Develop Friendly Relations with Pakistan	149
4.10	Need for Separate Civil Code for Every Community by Party Support	150
5.1	National Parties in Lok Sabha Elections: Seats and Votes	159
5.2	Concern about Central and State Government	161
5.3	Loyalty to Region First and Then to India	161
5.4	Regional Parties Provide Better Government	162

5.5	Loyalty to Region by 'Regional Parties Provide Better Government'	163
5.6	Trust in Local/State/Central Government	163
5.7	Loyalty to Region by Trust in Different Levels of Government	163
5.8	Regionalists by Caste	165
5.9	Regionalists by Religion	166
5.10	Regionalists by Level of Education	166
5.11	Sense of Political Efficacy of Regionalists	167
5.12	Sense of Financial Satisfaction of Regionalists	168
5.13	Regionalists and their Attitudes towards Communal Accommodation	169
5.14	Regionalists' Attitudes towards Kashmir Issue and Friendship with Pakistan	170
5.15	Regionalists and Partisan Preference	171
5.16	Regionalists and Partisan Preference: Assam	171
5.17	Regionalists and Partisan Stability	172
6.1	Cross-tabulation of Class with Caste	189
6.2	Cross-tabulation of Class with Education	190
6.3	Perception of Financial Satisfaction by Socio-demographic Groups	191
6.4	Multiple Correlation of the Indicators of Relative Deprivation	194
6.5	Social Profile of the Most and Least Deprived	195
6.6	Limit of Ownership by Social Background	198
6.7	No Free Trade for Foreign Companies	200
6.8	Privatise Government Companies	202
6.9	Deprivation and Attitudes towards Policy	204
7.1	Population, Literacy, Urbanisation, Turnout and per capita Net Domestic Product by States	218
7.2	Performance of Select States on Various Indices	219
7.3	Perception of Conflict and Social Change by State	222
7.4	Regional Variation in Trust in Central, State and Local Government	227
7.5	Trust in Local Government across Regions and Socio-economic Strata	237
7.6	Social Construction of Elite Status	240
7.7	Great Deal of Trust in Different Levels of Government	240

7.8	Great Deal of Trust in Local Government by Region	241
8.1	Multiple Correlation of the Components of Democracy and Social Change	255
8.2	Evaluation of Different Institutions and Actors	260
8.3	Cross-tabulation of Efficacy and Legitimacy	262
8.4	Caste and Political Competition	270
8.5	The Politics of Community Formation	270
8.6	Mean and Standard Deviation on the Accommodation Scale	275
A1.1	State-wise Distribution of Sampled Units and Respondents	285
A1.2	Comparable Figures for the Sample and the Universe	286
A1.3	List of Sampled Constituencies: Lok Sabha and Vidhan Sabha	287
A2.1	*Do you think your vote has effect on how things are run in this country, or do you think your vote makes no difference?*	297
A2.2	*Are you a member of a political party?*	297
A2.3	(If not a member of a party at the moment) *Were you ever a member of a political party?*	297
A2.4	Place of Residence	298
A2.5	Construction of Deprivation Scale	298
A2.6	Frequencies of Deprivation Scale	298
A2.7	Questions for Accommodation Scale	299
A2.8	Multiple Correlation of Questions for Accommodation Scale	300

List of Figures

1.1	The *Jajmani* System	**44**
1.2	The Breakdown of the Pyramid of Social Dominance	**44**
4.1	Percentage of Votes of the Congress relative to the Largest Non-Congress Party or Coalition	129
4.2	Shift in OBC Vote for Congress and BJP+ (1967–98)	138
4.3	Shift in Upper Caste Vote for Congress and BJP+ (1967–98)	138
4.4	Shift in Scheduled Caste Vote for Congress and BJP+ (1967–98)	139
4.5	Shift in Scheduled Tribe Vote for Congress and BJP+ (1967–98)	139
5.1	Votes and Seats Share of National Parties in Lok Sabha, 1952–98	160
6.1	The Polarisation Model	184
A2.1	Distribution of Accommodation Variable by Age	301
A2.2	Distribution of Accommodation Variable by Party Voted for	301

Preface and Acknowledgements

General elections provide a benchmark to measure the movement of social cleavages along the political topography of a country over consecutive electoral periods. Each election is a still picture of the larger process of social change, mediated by the electoral articulation and political aggregation of interests. As such, a post-poll analysis of public opinion focussed on political attitudes and perceptions is a crucial instrument for the study of the nature and course of social change. In the aftermath of a general election, once the heat of the campaign, the deals made by leaders and aspirants and the casting of the vote by a mass electorate are over and the body politic returns to its normal shape, a critical analysis of the opinions and attitudes of a cross-section of the national electorate can provide the ideal vantage point from where to review the process of power-sharing and social change. Typically, such questions go beyond issues of who won and who lost. Instead, they raise deeper issues of the legitimacy of the political process itself, its efficacy in meeting the expectations of the mass electorate, and the depth and spread of the concept of popular democracy across social cleavages.

The post-election survey of 1996, which provides the backdrop to this book, forms part of a genre of empirical studies of Indian politics. Some of the basic issues of democracy and social change, perception of the main issues facing the country, and the interaction of democratic rights and political order formed part of the National Election Study 1996 (NES '96) undertaken by the Centre for the Study of Developing Societies shortly after the 11th Parliamentary elections in India. Thanks to growing interest in quantification of social and political phenomena in India, and growing demand for them from the media, the public and the academic establishment, such studies have proliferated greatly in recent times. This has been facilitated by greater availability of financial support for empirical research, and by easier access to quantitative instruments. Particularly noteworthy is the availability of detailed constituency-level data on voting for national and regional elections. However, accessible and comprehensive data on social and political attitudes are less readily available. Since such data can be collected only through elaborate and expensive surveys, to the extent such data exist, it is important to communicate the findings as directly and rapidly as possible to a larger audience. The main objective of this book is, thus, to present the values, beliefs, attitudes, political preferences and information which underpin the choices of the electorate to the students of Indian politics. To that extent, the statistical treatment has been kept to a minimum in the main tables.

It is, of course, not possible to state political facts merely as facts, much less so in the context of a society where mass participation and state policy have transformed the nature of the political system in a relatively short span. The facts reported in this book are responses to questions which are, themselves, informed by the theories about interactions of the society and electoral politics. Since the social facts that describe the mass perception of change are ensconced within a body of social policies, we have decided to state our assumptions and concepts that underpin these facts somewhat explicitly, but only as a guide to the quantitative material. In this sense, this is not a book about the theory of social change in India. Nor is this conceived as a book on Indian politics as such. Instead, our objective is to present some interesting empirical findings in an accessible way, in order to assist those engaged in theory building, the verification of current hypotheses or formulation of new conjectures with regard to politics and social change in India.

The book is a testimony to the support and fellowship that our colleagues at the Department of Political Science of the South Asia Institute (SAI) of Heidelberg and the Centre for the Study of Developing Societies (CSDS), Delhi, have extended to us. The CSDS, a pioneer of quantitative research in Indian politics since its inception in 1963, has a long tradition of large-scale surveys. The latter include two major surveys conducted in 1967 and 1971. In recognition of its contributions and capacity, the Indian Council for Social Science Research extended substantial support to the CSDS for the purpose of the National Election Study of 1996, for which we owe a deep debt of gratitude. We are equally grateful to the Konrad Adenauer Foundation, which provided a major research grant to study the impact of democratisation on social change and political order in India on the basis of the perception of the mass electorate. But for the combined financial strength of the two projects, a study of this magnitude would not have been possible. We are deeply indebted to the representatives of the Konrad Adenauer Foundation in St. Augustin and Delhi for their unstinted cooperation to advance the study, and to submit its findings to experts and the interested public in India as well as in Germany.

The project required, from the outset, close coordination between the authors, based respectively in Heidelberg and Delhi. This was greatly facilitated by a fellowship of the German Academic Exchange Service (Deutscher Akademischer Austauschdienst [DAAD]) which made it possible for V.B. Singh to join Subrata Mitra at the South Asia Institute of Heidelberg from December 1996 to January 1997 for the preliminary analysis of the data. Similarly, while Subrata Mitra's visits during the preparatory phase of the survey were financed from the original grant of the Konrad Adenauer Foundation, his visit to Delhi during the final stage of the preparation of the manuscript was made possible thanks to a generous grant of the German Research Council (DFG). The computer analysis, review of the literature and preparation of the diagrams have been greatly facilitated by the excellent research assistance of Mike Enskat. This was made possible by a publication grant from the Konrad Adenauer Foundation.

Though the book as a whole is addressed to the interweaving themes of modernisation and democratisation, its narrative strategy focuses on specific puzzles for each chapter. As such, the respective chapters can also be read as relatively self-contained pieces. Several of these were written in response to specific challenges, and in their second incarnation, carry the atmosphere of the debate that first brought them to life. Parts of the introductory chapter were first presented by Subrata Mitra in Bangalore in a Ford Foundation conference on the terms of political discourse in India in 1990. The second chapter is largely derived from a paper on Midnight's Children presented by Subrata Mitra to a conference on Fifty Years of India's Independence held in Hull in 1997. Chapter 3 is mainly based on an article by V.B. Singh published in the *Economic and Political Weekly* in 1996, as well as on a presentation given by the two authors to the Konrad Adenauer Foundation in St Augustin in January 1997. The ideas for chapter 4 were first presented by Subrata Mitra at the annual meeting of the International Political Science Association in Seoul in 1997. Some of the findings presented in chapter 5 were published in Mitra (1997b), and a paper laying down the basic framework for chapter 7 was presented in a conference entitled 'Against all Odds' held at Princeton in 1997.

A study of this kind was made possible only by the generous help extended to the project by Bashiruddin Ahmed who, despite his busy schedule as Vice Chancellor of the Jamia Millia Islamia, spent hours together in the conceptualisation and framing of the survey instruments. Sadly, he passed away before the completion of the study. We are also greatly indebted to Rajni Kothari, Ashis Nandy, D.L. Sheth, Ghanshyam Shah, R.K. Hebsur, Yogendra Yadav and Shankar Bose for their advice on many crucial aspects of the survey. We would also like to take this opportunity to thank the members of the all-India network who have greatly facilitated this research project. Several colleagues volunteered to take charge of coordinating the study in their respective states and played a pivotal role in carrying out this survey. Without willing cooperation from Prakash Sarangi (Andhra Pradesh), Apurba K. Baruah (Assam and the North-East), Sanjay Kumar (Bihar and Delhi), Peter R. D'Souza (Goa), P.M. Patel (Gujarat), Sandeep Shastri (Karnataka), Gopa Kumar (Kerala), Ram Shankar (Madhya Pradesh), Suhas Palshikar and Rajendra Vora (Maharashtra), S.N. Misra (Orissa), T.R. Sharma (Punjab, Haryana and Himachal Pradesh), S.N. Singh (Rajasthan), G. Koteswar Prasad (Tamil Nadu), V.K. Rai (east Uttar Pradesh), Mohammad Aslam (central Uttar Pradesh), Pradeep Kumar (west Uttar Pradesh) and Sajal Basu (West Bengal), this research could not have been accomplished. Likewise, we are indebted to Sujit Deb, Vinita Sinha, Chandrika Parmer, Sanjay Kumar, Aditya Nigam and Kanchan Malhotra for their help at various stages of the project, to Himanshu Bhattacharya and Peter Lehr for their unstinting and expert help with data processing and interpretation, and to Clemens Spiess and Kansten Frey for critical research assistance, Yifang Tang for her meticulous work on the bibliography. We are grateful to Harihar Bhattacharyya, Baden-Württemberg Fellow, 1998, and Pervaiz Iqbal Cheema, Iqbal Professorial Fellow, South Asia Institute, for their valuable comments on an earlier draft of the manuscript.

Finally, we are thankful to our respondents who spoke willingly to strangers and supplied information vital for the study. But for their cooperation—a glowing testimony to the viability of survey research in India—a study of this nature would not have been possible at all. The opinions expressed here and the conclusions drawn on the basis of them are our own and do not necessarily represent the opinions of the South Asia Institute, Heidelberg, the Centre for the Study of Developing Societies, Delhi, or of the organisations which have extended financial support to the study.

Heidelberg and Delhi
July 1998

Subrata K. Mitra
V.B. Singh

1

Introduction: Competing Paradigms of Politics and Social Change in India

Jawaharlal Nehru, ensconced in the Constituent Assembly on the eve of the attainment of Independence, comes closest to a Prometheus in India. Nehru's speech on the 'Tryst with Destiny', delivered in his capacity as the recently anointed Prime Minister, 50 years into time, still appears as both a masterpiece of rhetoric and prescience.

> Long years ago we made a tryst with destiny, and now the time comes when we shall redeem our pledge, not wholly or in full measure, but very substantially. At the stroke of the midnight hour, when the world sleeps, India will awake to life and freedom. A moment comes, which comes but rarely in history, when we step out from the old to the new, when an age ends, and when the soul of a nation, long suppressed, finds utterance. It is fitting that at this solemn moment we take the pledge of dedication to the service of India and her people and to the still larger cause of humanity.[1]

Nehru continued:

> We end today a period of ill fortune and India discovers herself again. The achievement we celebrate today is but a step, an opening of opportunity, to the greater triumphs and achievement that await us. Are we brave enough and wise enough to grasp this opportunity and

accept the challenge of the future? The future is not one of ease or resting but of incessant striving so that we may fulfil the pledges we have so often taken and the one we shall take today. The service of India means the service of the millions who suffer. It means the ending of poverty and ignorance and disease and inequality of opportunity. The ambition of the greatest man of our generation has been to wipe every tear from every eye. That may be beyond us, but as long as there are tears and suffering, so long our work will not be over.... To the people of India, whose representatives we are, we make an appeal to join us with faith and confidence in this great adventure. This is no time for petty and destructive criticism, no time for ill will or blaming others. We have to build the noble mansion of free India where all her children dwell.

Nehru spoke of the background of the carnage of India's Partition, and also of the urgency of a concerted effort to remove mass poverty and ignorance. Democracy, a sense of community and modernisation were the fire that would lead the way. The fact that these principles originated mostly in cultures foreign to India, did not matter at that moment of euphoria. For India had already been exposed to some of them for the better part of the duration of colonial rule, at least in the form of ideals to wish for. The most radical of them, namely, the principle of universal adult franchise as the basic principle of legitimacy and popular accountability, was very much in the air, at least since the 1937 elections. The six decades that preceded Independence had witnessed a steady, incremental extension of the right to vote under the overall hegemony of British colonial rule.[2] While these limited experiments had already planted the seeds of mass democracy, the extension of franchise to the entire adult population in one fateful moment was a bold leap, particularly when one takes into consideration the fact that the Constituent Assembly, which decided on this momentous step, was itself the product of restricted franchise. But the measure was in keeping with the spirit of popular sovereignty, which was the guiding principle of India's freedom movement and whose essence Nehru described in his famous oration on 'Freedom at Midnight'.

In the event, after five decades of application of universal adult franchise as the main ideology of the state, and as such, the preferred instrument of social and political change, and democratic accountability as a critical ingredient of the principle of governance, India continues to offer hope, but with a lingering sense of doubt. The reasons for hope become clear as one browses through the record of its achievements since Independence.

Regular, free and fair elections have been held to the legislatures at national and regional levels from 1952 onwards. Participation in these elections has been respectable, in comparison with the United States, if not with continental Europe. The locus of political power has changed as a result of elections. Political prominence and control of resources by social groups to which power was transferred by the British in 1947 has been successfully challenged by subaltern groups in many regions and localities of India. Though the state has, in many cases, initiated these changes through legislation, the incentive has often come from the anticipated electoral dividends. There have also been occasions when the beneficiaries have themselves forced the hands of the government through protest movements and electoral mobilisation.[3] The main consequence of these multiple modes of politics has been that five decades after Independence, India can with some justification claim to have achieved a minimum of welfare and food security. In the same vein are the records on inflation and social inequalities, the extremes of which have been tamed. And now, with the liberalisation of India's economy, international business confidence in India has increased considerably compared to the recent past.[4]

If Nehru's bold vision has been borne out by the overall success of India's democratic record, it has had to contend with persistent mass poverty and illiteracy, communal conflagrations and political insurgency.[5] Democracy itself has wilted from time to time, but only to bounce back eventually with renewed vigour. In the meantime, structural change of the society and the economy has continued to progress, though at an uneven pace. This book examines the basis of this resilience by drawing on the opinions and attitudes of a representative cross-section of India's electorate.

The empirical evidence that underpins the narrative is, by its very nature, both limited and static in character, whereas the story it illustrates is vast in its dimensions and dynamic in nature. In order to link the facts with the larger structure they are intended to give concrete shape to, this introductory chapter will first establish the historical context that provides the backdrop to the study, concentrating particularly on the possibilities that Independence presented, the alternatives that were available to the leadership, and the perils and predicaments of the choices made. Reading this book is an exercise in looking backwards from the vantage point of a successful democratic transition, speculating about the reasons that might have facilitated this transition. To this context are added the public opinion data from a post-poll survey held shortly after the Parliamentary elections of 1996, supplemented by aggregate electoral statistics and public opinion data from 1998. This empirical base is drawn upon in order to look for evidence that might give plausibility to some of these hypotheses about why democratic transitions sometimes succeed.

The Historical Context

The faith that the fathers of the Indian Constitution reposed in the wisdom of the masses in 1947 was symptomatic of the spirit of the times. To the triumphant Allies at the end of the Second World War, the defeat of Fascism implied the victory of democracy. The principle led to the founding of the United Nations, and the elevation of the principle of the Rights of Man as the minimal basis of civilised government. The same principles influenced the idealism that underpinned the constitution of many newly independent countries. The doubters—unreconstructed imperialists and conservatives on one side and the proponents of authoritarian modernisation on the other—surfaced later.[6] Since then, the improbable mix of democracy, mass illiteracy, hunger, and, of late, criminalisation of politics, has been much commented on.[7] But Indian politics as a whole, with the important exception of the Emergency of 1975–77, has remained steadfast in its commitment to electoral democracy.

The record is not, of course, positive in its entirety. Ethnic conflict and violence are routinely reported in the media.[8] A rough calculation would put the number of Indians living under informal army rule anywhere between 40 and 50 million people.[9] Even at the national level, political democracy all but collapsed in 1975 when Indira Gandhi imposed Emergency rule. But then, familiar patterns of electoral politics did bounce back in testimony to the resilience of India's democracy once the Emergency came to an end.[10] After a brief authoritarian interlude, India became once again the functioning democracy, based on elections and mass participation, that it used to be. Thus, on balance, particularly if we compare the past half-century with the preceding century-and-a-half, the quickening of the pace of India's democracy, in terms of increased political awareness and efficacy, becomes quite clear. The message of democracy has spread far and wide, pervading the English-language as well as vernacular press. The changed political backdrop to social and economic life has increasingly become a major theme of discourse outside the narrow circle of the specialist.

The sense of this political innovation and resilience of popular democracy can be seen in V.S. Naipaul's *A Million Mutinies Now*, which, coming after such dark and pessimistic renderings of the Indian scene as *India: An Area of Darkness*, and *India: A Wounded Civilization*, spelt out India's achievements in terms of millions of people standing up for their rights, and, in the process, changing their destiny and that of their nation. Naipaul captures the consequences of the process through which society impinges on politics, and political competition creates new social forces in a memorable passage:

> ... the idea of freedom has gone everywhere in India. Independence was worked for by people more or less at the top; the freedom it brought has worked its way down. People everywhere have ideas now of who they are and what they owe themselves. The process quickened with the economic development that came after independence; what was hidden in 1962, or not easy to see, what perhaps was only in a state of becoming, has become clearer. The liberation of spirit that has come to India could not come as release alone. In India, with its layer below layer of distress and cruelty, it had to come as disturbance. It had to come as rage and revolt. India was now a country of a million little mutinies (Naipaul 1990: 517).[11]

Naipaul's observations point to the two faces of electoral democracy in India. As a post-colonial society, where power was transferred in a relatively peaceful manner to a national movement which thereafter became the ruling elite, India belongs to a category of states which, at the time of Independence, had not made the economic transition that preceded the introduction of universal adult franchise in contemporary stable democracies. The new rulers of the post-Independence state, nevertheless, committed themselves to generate the legitimacy of the regime from popular participation through elections based on universal adult franchise. Seen through the eyes of the long suppressed and the exploited, representative democracy is plain and simple logic of numbers, of the cumulation of voting strength through short-term alliances and its aggressive use for the promotion of sectional interests. But political majorities can function most effectively and meaningfully only in the context of respect for individual rights and tolerance of minority values. These are the essential principles of democracy, which often appear to be the victims of the logic of numbers.

The process of accelerated interaction of politics and society, of which mass elections are the main intermediaries, is thus fraught with contradictions, appearing occasionally to run into the cul-de-sac of populist rhetoric and electoral consecration into political power of rogues and scoundrels. Democratisation can thus appear to gnaw at the roots of governance and civility; the quickening and deepening of the pace of politicisation, characteristically releasing into the political arena social forces that are capable of pulverising the very basis of stable government and norm-bound institutions.

The Constitutional Design

This fear of popular politics getting out of elite control, or worse, the elites themselves, labouring under the pressure of intra-elite competition, engaging in activities detrimental to orderly politics, always underpinned the thinking of the Congress High Command during the days of the freedom movement.[12] The spectre of India breaking apart under the cumulative weight of such politics became a refrain of commentaries on Indian politics in the early years after Independence.[13] The full fury of this phenomenon would, however, not be released until the 1980s, growing in its frenzy until it reached a climax in the terrorist violence, communal clashes and political disorder, poignantly symbolised by the destruction of the Babri mosque on 6 December 1992. Early pointers to these developments had already caught the critical eye of Rajni Kothari:

> In India, the legacy of a long tradition, the integrity of an historical culture and the great solidarities that were built through religious and social movements that were characteristically Indian had for long acted as buffers against an inherently fissiparous situation. The social system provided a key to political stability. Now this very social system is undergoing profound changes and has entered a process of continuous fluidity and fragmentation (Kothari 1970: 3).

It is interesting to note here that, coming from a different ideological angle, Huntington (1968: 55) makes the same negative prognosis about the relationship of popular mobilisation and the prospects of orderly rule. While Western students of the democratic transition in the societies freed from colonial rule after the Second World War have seen little prospect for internal resolution of the conflict between the logic of numbers and the principles of democracy, Indian scholarship, however, from the early years after Independence has steadily accumulated arguments and evidence which point towards the deepening of the roots of democracy in the social fabric of India.[14]

The constitutional design and the structure of institutions that were intended to give concrete shape to the idealistic goals of the Republic, enshrined in the preamble, adopted methodological individualism as the cutting edge of social change. However, such principles as individual rights, representation based not on group identities but individual interests and structured along the lines of political majorities, seen in the context of a society based on hierarchy and tightly-knit social groups, could only lead to conflicts based on values and interests of everyday politics. How these conflicts are aggregated, articulated and eventually incorporated within the structure of the political system in a post-colonial state, through the fusion of endogenous political norms and alien political institutions, is the main theme of Indian politics.[15] Before we move in the direction of outlining the features of the Indian 'model' of democracy and social change, it is important to make an excursion into the competing models of which the political actors of India, facing the challenge of social change, have had a reasonably free choice at the outset.

Competing Models of Social Change

Though elections were intended to be a necessary feature of Indian politics after Independence by the makers of the Constitution, the electoral process on its own could not have constituted a sufficient basis for its functioning. An effective electoral process requires a specific political culture for its functioning. The existence of such cultural attributes and political structures could not be taken for granted at the outset. There was no unanimity about the objectives of social change at that time, as indeed there was no single hegemonic idea that dominated the national movement to the exclusion of other shades of ideology. The issue, therefore, is how India developed the high degree of instrumental attitude towards politics, and a basic minimum of trust in the institutions which facilitate the functioning of a democratic system.

At the point of departure, we shall look at a society based on the core value of hierarchy of status, assigned to the individual at birth on the basis of the primordial identity, juxtaposed with legal and institutional structures whose mainstay are individual rights and their justiciability in a court of law. Right from the outset, there have been advocates of different paths in order to achieve these values. Since some of those early speculations about the desirable goals of social change voiced just after Independence have surfaced regularly since then, and endow India's political space with its richness and complexity, an attempt would be made in this section to provide a brief sketch of the theoretical relations between competitive politics and social change in the context of a poor, post-colonial state,[16] living check by jowl with a society where traditional values of hierarchy and primordial identities still prevail.

The very concept of social change is the starting point of this attempt to classify the competing notions of social transformation at the attainment of Independence and the political process that gave legitimacy to the plurality that characterised the discourse about change. As a point of departure, one can refer to a conventional view of social change: 'Social change is the significant alteration of social structures (that is, of patterns of social action and interaction), including consequences and manifestations of such structures embodied in norms (rules of conduct), values, and cultural practices and symbols.'[17] Social change refers to directly observable phenomena such as status, roles, norms, patterns of interaction, as well as non-tangibles which can be 'measured' (if at all) indirectly, by their implications and consequences. Talking about social change, Clifford Geertz, the American anthropologist, advocates a 'distinction between observable social interactions and the web of meanings that those actions have for the participants'.[18]

To the students of the political process in the early years after Independence, these normative aspects of social change come across as competing programmes, voiced by different social groups of India, guided by their different interests born out of their location in the social matrix and their perception of the opportunity structure. Thanks to Nehru's uplifting rhetoric and the delicate balance of crass materialism and noble idealism that characterised the six decades of competitive politics that preceded Independence, the Indian voter knew that the essence of politics consisted in both the distribution of resources (of politics as a game of 'who gets what and how'), and its more transcendental implications for enduring considerations (of politics as an 'authoritative allocation of values'), that frame everyday politics. The line-up of political groups with different social agendas provides a good approximation of the spread of opinion in the country with regard to social change. It ranges between the Communist Party of India on the left, with its internal cleavages between the advocates of revolutionary campaigns as opposed to the votaries of

Parliamentary transition into socialism occasionally surfacing in public, and the Bharatiya Jan Sangh on the right, the ambiguity of its approach to the secular democratic state anticipating later developments. Ranged between them were various shades of social democrats and centrists, all competing for votes in the first general election.

The question that arises here is why this potent mixture of pent-up demands from the lower social orders, and sudden empowerment through universal adult franchise, kept simmering but did not boil over. Sharp differences were articulated, but mostly in terms of the orderly discourse of ideological leanings, neatly ranged within the paradigm of modernisation rather than the violent clashes that account for the stillborn majority of post-colonial democracies. This issue, which provides the overall theoretical backdrop to this book, would be addressed in different ways in each of the chapters. In this section, we would provide a bare sketch of the early ideological voices of the electorate, and the modernisation paradigm within which they articulated themselves.

The modernisation paradigm is typically summed up in terms of a transition from an agrarian society to the industrial world. The former is typically associated with the predominance of ascriptive, particularistic and diffuse patterns, multiplex social relations, stable local groups and limited spatial mobility, relatively simple and stable occupational differentiation, and a stratification system based on social hierarchy. The modern industrial society, on the other hand, is characterised by the predominance of universalistic, specific and achievement norms, a high degree of social mobility, both vertical and horizontal, well-developed occupational systems insulated from other social structures, 'egalitarian' class systems based on generalised patterns of occupational achievement and the prevalence of 'associations', i.e., functionally specific, non-ascriptive structures.

One of the main themes of contemporary research on social and political change in India is marked by a growing scepticism of the cultural assumptions on which some of these earlier models of development, economic growth, and modernisation were based. The shift in emphasis is not confined only to scholarship in India. It is also evident in the contrast between the positions taken by some of the leading scholars of development during the halcyon years of post-War modernisation with their subsequent 'rethinking'.[19] As the assumption of nineteenth century European thinkers about the eventual spread of 'universal' rationality has come under critical examination, the demand has grown for the creation of 'theoretical frameworks that combine a demystified, rationalist world-view with an understanding of the phenomenology in societies where the gods have not yet died' (Rudolph and Rudolph 1987: 742). The debate, which has moved beyond the narrowly political, now affects the broader issues of identity and the high politics of the state. The new interest in indigenous values, identity, and culture closely parallel developments in the real world of politics. Today, in India as in other parts of the world, the appeal of ethnicity and religion has overtaken the post-war emphasis on economic development and class conflict as the dominant modes of political perception. This uncertainty of the terms of discourse is the predominant theme of Indian politics in the latter half of the post-Independence phase, as compared to the overall stability of the first two decades following the end of British colonial rule.

Some 'Flawed' Paradigms

A growing rift between a society and its intellectuals, and the absence of institutions which provide for their continuous interaction is the recipe for a serious epistemological and political crisis. The implications of this intellectual malaise should be familiar to those who acquired their knowledge of Indian politics during the early decades of the Republic, when universal adult franchise and competitive elections were introduced with much euphoria, and who now look askance at rising ethnic conflict and the plethora of the new vocabulary of political discourse in India today.[20]

The difficulty of explaining substantive political problems is further compounded by terminological confusion. Running in parallel with established concepts as democracy, participation and development, are such unofficial concepts of indeterminate legality as *gherao, dharna*, boycott, *rasta roko, chakka jam, jail bharo*.[21] Larger structural changes within Indian society have produced these new concepts of resistance to the authority of the state and the encroachment by the market on the lifestyles and traditional means of livelihood of victims of rapid change. In their counter-strategy to neutralise these terms of struggle, both the state and the market have devised new concepts such as *loan melas* and *garibi hatao*, further enriching the vocabulary of Indian politics.[22] This extraordinary range and richness of the conceptual and empirical material does not, however, appear to have affected the conceptual framework with which one seeks to understand it.

One explanation for this relative lack of synchronisation can be found in the 'derivative' nature of Indian political science and its relatively narrow institutional focus.[23] Those with long memories will remember a failure on a similar scale on the part of the social sciences during the freedom struggle, when millions were moved by *swaraj* and *swadeshi*, while the political scientist was restricted to the narrow empirical range of British constitutionalism applied to India, or to the ethereal spheres of philosophical speculation. Indian reactions against this conceptual inadequacy have been articulated in terms of the call for a rejection of the universal categories, and a return to authentic indigenous categories, a solution which is not without problems of its own.[24] The importance of the underlying problem can be seen from the debate that has surfaced intermittently in national as well as international fora, articulated mostly but not exclusively by students of sociology[25] and political science,[26] and in the more specific context of the historiography of colonial rule in British India.[27]

Two epistemological puzzles that arise out of this crisis are of interest to us. First, how meaningful are the terms of academic discourse such as *democracy* and *secularism* to society at large? Second, to what extent is it possible to map the terms of academic discourse that have arisen from methods of direct action such as *gherao, dharna*, boycott, *chamcha, zulam shahi*, without a significant loss of meaning in the categories of political analysis? Effective empirical data analysis is not possible without an understanding of the meaning and significance of the key categories of political discourse. This section attempts to approach this larger debate through an analysis of Western scholarship on Indian politics in order to set the stage for the survey data to follow. While it specifically focuses on the literature which has its origins in the intellectual community in the West, the larger implications that the book seeks to draw are also applicable to Indian academics who have based their work on the methods and substantive conclusions of Western scholars. The intention behind the survey of this literature is not to evaluate critically their substantive findings as such, but rather to identify the key concepts with which scholars drawing on concepts that originated in the West have sought to represent the Indian reality, to examine their internal variation and differentiation, and to explore the grounds of commensurability between their general approaches.

Four parameters underlie the classificatory scheme of the political process that characterises state–society relations suggested here. The first is the social vision, namely, the desired shape of the future which constitutes the objective of social transformation. The preferred values are to be realised through a set of instrumental values. These are: perception of the role of the state, perception of society, and the institutional process through which social change is achieved. These, which constitute the other three parameters, specify the nature of the state structure and society, as they occur at the start of play, and the institutional process that is intended to suitably transform them for the realisation of the social vision. Using these criteria, the body of writings can be grouped into three broad streams, namely, developmental, functional, and revolutionary. The positions they adopt on the key parameters are indicated in Table 1.1. The respective paradigms and their interconnectedness are discussed below.

Table 1.1
Competing Paradigms of State–Society Interaction: A Classificatory Scheme

Paradigms	State	Society	Institutional Process
Developmental	Hegemonic leader	Object of transformation	Bureaucracy, rational planning
Functional	Non-exclusive initiator	Object and initiator of transformation	Interpenetration, mutual accommodation of state/social system
Revolutionary	Epiphenomenon/ source of opposition	Epiphenomenon/ source of resistance	Class struggle/ revolutionary movement

The Developmental Paradigm

Basic to this approach is a dichotomous view of the universe. On one side is to be found the world of tradition, woven together in the intricate web of reciprocal obligations into an organic community, where life is ascription-oriented, particularistic, and functionally diffuse. On the other side is the brave new world of functionally specific, universalistic, achievement-oriented society. The movement from one pole to the other is seen by the proponents of this paradigm as both a historical process and a moral imperative for those societies which are not yet modern.

The developmental paradigm which aims to achieve modernisation for traditional societies involves not only a change in psychological attitudes and the structure of social organisation, but also implies a radical change in the political process and economic organisation of society. Rapid economic growth, to be followed by political participation, are related concepts that provide the necessary linkage between the largely sociological writing on modernisation, and the authors who address themselves essentially to development.

During the post-war period, it is the writings of Rostow that have been identified with the idea of economic growth as representing the quintessence of development. In the somewhat sparsely populated world of development 'theories', which have achieved broad acceptance by the non-economists, Rostow (1960) must certainly constitute an ideal exemplar. For evidence of acceptance of this framework, one needs only to consider such concepts as 'economic take-off', 'sustained growth', and 'preconditions for economic development', among others, which have now found their way into the everyday language of planners, captains of industry, as well as the taxpayer. In this much publicised work, Rostow defines the sweep of modern history as a set of stages of growth essential for the process of transformation that a traditional society undergoes in order to reach modernity.

Though it is presented only as 'an economic historian's way of generalising', as one proceeds through the great five-fold scheme of the stages of growth through traditional society, the preconditions for take-off, take-off to sustained growth, drive to maturity, and eventually, the age of high mass consumption, it gradually becomes clear that the formulations add up to more than mere description of a historical sequence. For what is being suggested here is not only the historical sequence of past events, but a developmental scheme with universal spatio-temporal dimensions. To generate the necessary momentum for this analytical descriptive scheme that alone can impart to it the character of the 'sweep to modern history', and thus reinforce its claim to be cross-culturally valid, Rostow identifies in the culture and social and political structure of societies that are fairly advanced in the scheme of the stages of growth, as well as those that are still groping their way towards it, certain forces that possess qualities akin to the forces that drive human beings towards a predetermined goal.

This goal, as indicated in the scheme, is the attainment of mastery over one's environment, which, besides the immediate natural surroundings, eventually comes to include other people and also their natural surroundings. Political power in the hands of modernisers, with the state serving as the catalytic agent, is among the chief means towards the attainment of this goal. The modernising goal is achieved through the process of nation-building and economic growth, both of which involve the transformation of the production system towards greater productivity. These processes are complemented by the diffusion of entrepreneurial spirit and socio-cultural attributes, collectively referred to as modernisation.[28]

Thus, viewed from the perspective of the developmental paradigm, political power in the hands of a modernising elite becomes a critical 'bridge' concept that links the international state system and the developing world, whose members would secure full membership once their elites have succeeded in the political, economic, and cultural transformation of their respective societies. It is this spirit that provides a unifying bond to such core writings on the developmental/modernisation paradigm as Huntington (1968), Myrdal (1968), as well as the influential series of volumes on Political Development brought out by the Social Science Research Council (New York).[29] In each of these works, India played the role of a critical empirical case for the concerned scientific paradigm, both as a source of supportive evidence, as well as a target of necessary advice in the form of policy implications for countries more or less in the position of India.

The vast majority of American scholars in the behavioural tradition, doing empirical work on India, placed themselves within the world-view of modernisation, either explicitly or implicitly. The application of this paradigm to Indian politics has been made in a significant way by Shils (1961) and Weiner (1962b, 1967, 1983), who extended the developmental paradigm to the field of electoral analysis.[30] Those writing in this vein have examined the relationship between modernisation and consolidation of democracy in India (Field 1980), diffusion of the norms of participatory democracy, and institutionalisation of political competition and bargaining (Hardgrave and Kochanek 1993), and electoral competition and party politics (Eldersveld and Ahmed 1978; Palmer 1975; Weiner 1978, 1983), modernisation of religion (Smith 1963), interest groups and pressure groups (Weiner 1962b).

The 'pattern variables' of Parsons (reminiscent in many ways of the formulation of the course of modernisation by Toennies as the transition from *Gemeinschaft* to *Gesellschaft*), such as ascription/achievement, particularism/universalism, diffuseness/specificity, collectivity orientation/self-orientation and affectivity/neutrality, constituted the key parameters of the developmentalist paradigm. Though Parsons himself was cautious enough to admit the 'identification' of the universalistic-achievement pattern with the 'dominant American ethic',[31] the same cannot be said of those who sought to apply this paradigm to India. In the brave new modern world envisioned by the developmentalists, they predicted 'a future in which caste as well as other "primordial" collectives would be superseded by individualistic modern associations' (Frankel and Rao 1989/90: 14).

Growing economic differentiation and urbanisation, it was thought during the first decades following Independence, would lead to a decline of caste solidarity, resulting in a greater secularisation of the political culture. According to Hardgrave:

> The differentiated political culture represents, perhaps most accurately, simply a foundation for the emergence of a political culture reflecting identities based on economic interests and growing political awareness (Hardgrave 1969: 105).

Research on the consequences of modernisation has, however, shown a different picture. Exposure to modern methods of communication, growing affluence, and the spread of literacy and migration to urban areas, have in many cases led to the spread of Sanskritic ideas and values (Beteille 1969). Singer (1980) has argued similarly that the spread of urbanisation, literacy, education and expansion of the mass media represented a technical modernisation that was exploited in order to democratise the 'Great Tradition' and make it more accessible. These anomalous aspects of modernisation, marked by the spread of participation and political consciousness, have been pointed out by several authors including Madan (1987) and Nelson (1987).

The developments within Indian politics have witnessed both the spread of the norms of liberal democracy and its opposite, particularly methods of coercion and collective protest, to a degree where participation theory could not be explained within the paradigm of development. There were other anomalies as well. Whereas modernisation theory had confidently predicted the decline of the political saliency of religion and the supersession of primordial identities by civil loyalties, the politics of the 1980s and since have been, if anything, dominated by religion, communal and caste conflict, and attempts by ethnic groups to carve out political territories for exclusive dominance.

Faced with these anomalies, the current version of the modernisation paradigm has found an explanation for India's problems in the 'theory' of deinstitutionalisation and criminalisation of politics, which suggests the moral case for the resurrection of the institutions of state to their original stature, which they are presumed to have enjoyed during the Nehru era.[32] Once again, devoid of its empirical and theoretical arguments, the latest version of the modernisation paradigm can rely only on its moral core.[33] Being descriptive and essentially prescriptive in nature, the deinstitutionalisation thesis can only describe but fails to explain.

It does not have the requisite theoretical depth to pose the all important question of the *cause* of the structural discontinuity, the symptoms of which are being referred to as deinstitutionalization. To the extent that any attempts are made in this direction, its proponents are able to offer explanations only in terms of political styles and motives of key actors. Nor is the issue of the state's ability to regenerate itself raised with any degree of seriousness (Mitra 1988: 333).

The Functional Paradigm

The relative autonomy of politics from the social process and its ability to reformulate the rules of social transaction are the determining factors that we can use in our efforts to identify authors who can be placed within this paradigm. Though identified widely with the work of Dumont (1966), who specifies an hierarchical social structure with the abstract values of *dharma* at the apex as the fundamental basis of Indian society, other major conceptual contributions to this approach include Bailey's notion of the peasant society as a multiplex of relations that selectively and rationally incorporates elements of modern life (Bailey 1970), Morris-Jones' concept of the three idioms of politics in India (Morris-Jones 1963, 1987), and the notion of the modernity of tradition put forward by Rudolph and Rudolph (1967). Bailey's theoretical formulations on a model of Indian politics, based as it is on excellent fieldwork, deserves careful attention. He describes the Indian political system as the aggregation of a set of interlocking and 'nested' arenas at the locality, district, and regional levels. Each arena operates according to rules specific to it, which is why there is no homogeneity across the larger political system. Therefore, issues of cross-systemic significance have to be 'translated into something else at constituency level and have to be translated yet again at village level' (Bailey 1970: 232). However, overall, while functionalist arguments are effective in explaining the mutual accommodation of traditional social institutions and modern political processes, they are on weaker ground with regard to political discontinuities and cases of system failure such as India has witnessed the past two decades.

The Paradigm of Revolution

A Marxist revolution whose ultimate objective is to place Prometheus in the service of the toiling masses has provided a rallying point for those dissatisfied with the inadequacies of the developmental and functional paradigms. Such influential works as pre-war Dutt (1940) and post-war Moore (1966), as well as more recent writers like Frankel (1978)[34] and Kohli (1987) broadly share some of the humanist and politically radical sympathies embodied in the Marxist paradigm. Kohli questions the incrementalism of developmental models by referring to the unbroken exercise of power 'by an alliance of a nationalist political elite with entrepreneurial classes, capable of stimulating economic growth' (Kohli 1987: 8), placed within a 'state supported capitalist economy' (Kohli 1987: 80).

Those without property or other means of contributing to the process of production—which presumably provides the bonding principle for the rather different groups collectively referred to as India's ruling classes—can expect very little out of the political system. Mass poverty in India is therefore neither an accidental nor an incidental feature of the Indian political system, but its logical concomitant. The failure to mitigate even the worst of India's poverty is a consequence of the institutionalised patterns of dominance within India (Kohli 1987: 8).

These themes find further reinforcement in Byres (1988), Harris (1982), and a wide variety of writers both within and outside India. The wide-ranging nature of Marxist scholarship on the state and political discourse can be seen in the impact it has exercised on other aspects of Indian life. An impressive range of contributions, originally inspired by Guha, but which has increasingly been recognised as a distinct mode of analysis under the collective appellation of the 'subaltern' school, has sought to overcome, in a more promising way, some of the limitations of what we have earlier referred to as Marxist political formulations on the state in India. These writers have attempted to incorporate indigenous political idioms within the Marxist paradigm in their efforts to locate collective protest in India within a revolutionary agenda.[35]

Rooted in a Marxist understanding of political change and evolution, but reinforced nevertheless 'with a wealth of empirical material and hard evidence', and drawing freely on a range of social sciences, Guha has succeeded in placing the specific historical conjuncture of colonial rule within a broader framework, in a manner where the categories of the actor and his political experience converge. As a result, subaltern research has extended the scope of social research into previously unexplored areas. However, having unleashed a rich stock of evidence at the level of individual consciousness, subaltern historiography demonstrates a tendency to slip back into orthodox Marxist political formulations when it seeks to place it within the context of macro-theory. The difficulty arises when attempts are made to impart a dynamic aspect to the analysis of the specific situation, almost to the extent that description of the political negotiations and transactions that mark the post-insurrectionary situation is not possible without reintroducing the dreaded concept of false consciousness all over again.[36]

This brief and synoptic survey of the leading paradigms of discourse on Indian politics demonstrates two sets of difficulties. The first refers to those that characterise the normal functioning of a paradigm which serves to suggest an agenda, identifies a community of scientists, specifies the puzzles, and lays down the criteria of acceptable rules of evidence. In the case of each of the paradigms examined here, we have identified its key concepts and parameters, its major puzzles and the degree of success it may have achieved in suggesting solutions to them. The inability of each of these 'flawed' paradigms to give a satisfactory account of reality, it is suggested here, is explained by the fact that the root concepts around which they are organised are not germane to the experience that comes under their domain.

One possible explanation for this intellectual shortcoming of the paradigms of politics might lie in their essential character as extensions of a 'Western' *problematique* and a paradigm with which men and women sought to order their universe in post-Enlightenment Europe. The consequence is a fatal dissociation between belief and practice, categories and experience, and, most alarmingly, society and its intellectuals. Institutions, which provide the political context within which the dialectical interaction of ideas and experience takes place, are under considerable and increasing strain. The ironical consequence of this confusion is the rich abundance of terms of political discourse where terms of discourse, jostling for public recognition, are engaged in competition. The exercise undertaken in this chapter is intended to facilitate the search for a more effective paradigm, set within terms of discourse derived from Indian political experience and articulated in endogenous political vocabulary.[37]

We have argued so far that the interaction of electoral democracy and social change is a complex process. Its significance and inherent contradictions are not always obvious even to those in daily and intimate touch with politics and social change. This renders the communication of the meaning, the potential resources and the failings of India's democracy an uphill task, not only abroad in the context of a Western audience, but also at home. Something gets lost in the communication of the specialists' knowledge of the statistical and technical aspects of elections and democracy in India to the public. Commentators in India and stable Western democracies who are happy to celebrate the success of the democratic form of government in India, are often not able to understand how best to view its aberrations. Western students of Indian politics have a special problem of cognition. At the level of their general publics, two powerful obstacles interpose themselves between the Indian universe and its perception. The Indian world is seen alternately either as organic or morally anomic. They are two complementary myths. Whether it is seen in a well-meaning way—the Little Buddha syndrome—or as organically cohesive, bounded, collective identities, the Indian mind is seen as incapable of individual rationality, a necessary prerequisite for sustaining the complex political institutions of democracy. Alternately, when mass politics in India is conceptualised in terms of individual calculations of interest, its limits are seen as restricted to the family, caste and tribe. The sum of these individual calculations could obviously not sustain democratic politics. From this follows the scepticism about the character of electoral democracy in India and the unreality—and unreliability—of elections. Western audiences, like sections of India's urban elite without close links to the electoral process, sometimes find it difficult to think of Indians as skilful political actors, with goals and strategies, and enough information about others against whom they are pitted in order to manoeuvre their way through choices they have to make.

This book reports some of the findings of a study which discusses precisely these details of Indian politics. They have been collected from a national survey, based on a random sample of about 10,000 men and women representing the Indian electorate conducted during May–June 1996, in the aftermath of the 11th Parliamentary elections. The next section presents some introductory observations about the model of politics and social change which India followed since Independence. It provides the theoretical backdrop to our discussion of survey data. The main assumptions of this model are drawn from rational choice. They suggest that the peasant (like the businessman) is also an optimiser, and both respond to changes in the institutional context which underpins their daily lives. Electoral information, just like participation, is a political resource. Politicians, as well as electors, are engaged in purposive action, and their choices are based on a cost-benefit calculus. The implications arising from these assumptions will be looked at with the help of data emerging from the survey. It is our hope to be able to share with students of Indian politics our field experience of the electoral process and the keen interest that Indians take in politics. The concluding chapter will raise the issue, once again, of how, in the hands of ordinary men and women, politics has become the cutting edge of social change in India. It has become like that fire which Prometheus stole from the gods to give to men so that through politics, they can give themselves what their gods have not given them![38]

The Indian Model

A convergence of many of the broader conjectures arising out of the paradigms discussed here has gradually taken the shape of what we may term as the 'Indian' model that underpins much of the empirically grounded theories of Indian politics. The basic parameters of this model are political participation, the ability of the political system to give shape to many of the initiatives from below and ideas from above in the shape of new institutions or to reinforce existing institutions and finally, the ability of the political actors of India to engage in 'two-track strategies' that combine normal political action with rational protest.[39] Many of the strands of these empirically grounded theories are drawn from Kothari's pioneering contributions to the empirical study of politics and social change, which provided both the paradigmatic groundwork for an analytical context, and the methodology to juxtapose fragments of India's political discourse with general concepts of political theory. One can see further maturing of these traditions in *Citizens and Parties* (Sheth 1975), which introduced in an effective way the concept of hypothesis verification by drawing on empirical data, both ecological and attitudinal. By undertaking multivariate analysis of attitudinal and statistical data, Sheth and his co-authors made it possible to isolate the effects of social status from other aspects of the political universe, such as education, age, gender, political networks and social class. In the second place, the regional focus made it possible to measure the variations within India's federal polity, where regional and subregional identities have increasingly emerged as important influences on the voter.[40] The latter theme has been developed further in subsequent texts such as Frankel and Rao (1989/90) which, within a theoretical framework that represents the triangular relation of caste, class and dominance, was able to show the variation across regions. In their efforts to generate a general explanation for the triangular relationship of caste, class and dominance within different regional arenas, Frankel and Rao and their co-authors drew deeply on political economy, as a consequence of which they did not relate collective outcomes to strategic choices of individuals. Mitra and Lewis (1996) have shown the impact of the strategic thinking of leaders and ordinary political actors on their alliances. This has been particularly useful in explaining political coalitions of castes that are conventionally held to be so far apart in status, that no alliances would appear feasible. These powerful models of sophisticated rational choice and short-term maximisation of interests have become an important heuristic device to explain political behaviour, and thus, a useful complement to survey research.

Thanks to the salience of the themes of ethnicity and identity in the literature of comparative politics, bringing the individual and the subjective back in again appears to have been one of the main themes in recent scholarship. Attempts to draw on the contextual-individual linkage, vigorously argued in general literature[41] have also found their representation within the writings of India.[42] In sum, the cumulative impact of the writings over the past decades has been to constitute an analytical and empirical context for the study of politics and social change that draws on a range of factors, including the strategic perception of the individual, his ability to mobilise the collective political resources, and his ability to connect himself to his political universe at the local, regional and national levels. At the heart of this expanding body of literature, which we have only briefly drawn on in order to illustrate the evolution of its theoretical stretch and empirical depth, is a model of politics and social change which informs much electoral analysis. Before looking at the specific results obtained from the survey, we need to take this model of state–society relations, institutions and structure of policy making that underpins the political process in India, and, as such, provides the theoretical backdrop to the statistical data, into account.

Convergence of Competing Paradigms

It is rather commonplace in ordinary political discourse in India to use the concepts of social change and democratic change interchangeably. While this may very well be the case in practice in some historical contexts, as we learn from the social history of great transformations, such as the British enclosure movement (Moore 1966), it need not necessarily be so. Hence, it is important to define the two key concepts in order to show what a convergence of competing paradigms connotes, and then to test empirically if this is indeed the case in India.

The concept of social change generally indicates a process of transition from a social order based on one set of core values to a different social order, based on a different set of values. The most important of these values is social hierarchy, as opposed to equality of status. But the other values that distinguish different social orders, such as the self-definition of ordinary people, is just as important. The salient criteria in this respect are the identity of the individual in terms of subjecthood or citizenship, and his definition of the boundaries of his political universe, seen either as restricted to his locality within which he has face-to-face contact with a definite group of people as compared to a more complex web of concentric circles, composed of locality, region and nation or even beyond, reaching out to the community of all nations. Democratic social change is a special case where the society changes from an order organised around unequal status and social hierarchy, to one where equality of legal status becomes the norm. Democratic social change, at the level of individual beliefs and attitudes, is, therefore, the transformation of *homo hierarchicus* (Dumont 1966) to *homo aequalis* (Dumont 1985).

In terms of these definitions, the Indian model has two objectives. It wishes to promote social change of a kind that promotes the spread of democratic values of equality, citizenship and federalism within the context of national unity. Second, it intends to bring about these changes in a democratic manner. This, according to a number of specialists, is logically impossible and empirically improbable.[43] The arguments would be familiar to those who have drawn on the literature of economic development for an analysis of politics and social change in India.

We learn from the literature of industrialisation and the transformation of societies based on subsistence agriculture to those where the full range of economic activities came under modern technology, that structural change preceded the extension of franchise.[44] This, as specialists like Moore (1966) inform us, is how the course of development took place in Europe. Structural change took place in the form of crushing of the poor and the marginal; the crushing took place in the sweatshops that produced the Industrial Revolution, as well as in the brutal suppression of riots and risings by the poor and hungry. Large-scale participation became a reality only when the main structure of the economy and society were in place. The painful history of this crushing of the poor and the marginal in the West has only recently been recognised as a scholarly area of study, thanks to the efforts of historians like Gilmour (1992), Tilly (1975), Hobsbawm and Rudé (1968), to name only a few. In India, the introduction of mass democracy, rather than following structural change, preceded it. When

Nehru, in his famous speech on Freedom at Midnight engaged the state to this objective, he was not being entirely rhetorical or metaphorical. Universal adult franchise was introduced in 1952, and both the non-democratic left and non-democratic right were invited to compete equally with the centre and moderate left and right for political power through elections.

Indian politics, in the wake of Independence, consisted of an enormously large, national, mass electorate, parts of which had not even experienced direct British rule, and were stepping out of feudalism straight into popular democracy. The electorate comprised a majority of Hindus, still recovering from the trauma of Partition, who were being asked to become citizens of a country which did not recognise any official religion; of poor, marginal, land-hungry peasantry, who would be the eventual victims of the economy of scale; of manual labourers, who would have to choose between eventual redundancy and replacement through more productive, skilled and necessarily fewer workers. What should have followed is described by several specialists. One of the most cited is Harrison (1960), who spelt out a future of communal conflict, disharmony and Balkanisation. Huntington (1968) predicted structural discontinuity in the face of popular mobilisation. State theorists like Gunnar Myrdal came up with the formulation of the 'soft state' based on popular consent, which would necessarily be lacking in the authority with which to tackle basic problems of structural change. Weaving all these strands into a unified and comparative perspective, these theoretical writings predicted in the case of India a state of peaceful paralysis in the years to come.

But, as the record shows, elections and democracy have kept pace with one another (Table 1.2). On all aggregate indicators, as the data show, India has kept up steady progress. True, the level of electoral participation has not reached the level of national elections in Europe, but the national average of India certainly compares favourably with that of the United States. Statistical data on the participation of women, former untouchables and tribals do not lag far behind that of the national average. Finally, levels of electoral participation in some regions of India are as high as in continental Europe.

The relatively modest rate of participation in the first General Election should be seen in the context of its relative novelty to the Indian electorate, for this was the first ever General Election where universal adult franchise became the norm. This was applied to the whole of India, including former princely states which had not known the incremental growth in representation, and was introduced in steady degrees in those parts of India which

Table 1.2
Election Data, Indian Parliamentary Elections, 1952–98

Year	Seats	Candidates	Polling Stations	Electorate (in millions)	Votes Polled (in millions)	Turnout (%)
1952	489	1,874	132,560	173.2	79.1	45.7
1957	494	1,519	220,478	193.7	92.4	47.7
1962	494	1,985	238,355	217.7	120.6	55.4
1967	520	2,369	267,555	250.6	153.6	61.3
1971	518	2,784	342,944	274.1	151.6	55.3
1977	542	2,439	373,908	321.2	194.3	60.5
1980	529	4,629	434,742	363.9	202.7	56.9
1984	542	5,493	479,214	400.1	256.5	64.1
1989	529	6,160	579,810	498.9	309.1	62.0
1991	534	8,780	588,714	511.5	285.9	55.9
1996	543	13,952	767,462	592.6	343.3	57.9
1998	539	4,708	765,473	602.3	373.7	62.0

Source: Data Unit, CSDS, Delhi.

were ruled directly by the British. Added to this was the problem of the relative lack of political linkages between voters and candidates, normally mediated by party machines which were not yet effectively organised at the constituency level. But, as the figures show, the level of participation has grown over the years, occasionally declining to the relatively low mid-1950s, but generally hovering around 60 per cent. Unlike the United States, where the responsibility of registration with the electoral authorities lies with the voter, in India the state takes the necessary steps. A number of measures, such as close proximity of the polling booth (of which there is more than one on the average for each of India's half-million villages), their location in schools and such public places where access is relatively free for people of all walks of life, and an electoral machinery specially mobilised for the occasion, make sure that voters can exercise their franchise without fear and without inordinate delay.

If participation in national elections on the average is respectable by world standards, then participation in regional Assembly elections is truly remarkable. As the figures in Table 1.3 show, the level of participation has not only kept pace with the national figures, but in some instances, has been at an even higher level.

Finally, the detailed voting figures from Table 1.4 bring to our attention the tremendous variation of the levels of voting in India at the State level. In States with high education and political consciousness, participation has reached levels one normally finds in national elections in continental Europe. Kerala is an outstanding example of this. But equally significant

Table 1.3
Participation Trends in Major Assembly Elections, 1952–95

Year of Election	States	Total Seats	Turnout (%)	Total Contestants	Contestants per Seat Total	Contestants per Seat Independents
1952	22	3,283	45	15,361	4.7	1.9
1957	13	2,906	48	10,176	3.5	1.4
1960–62	15	3,196	58	13,665	4.3	1.3
1967	20	3,487	61	16,507	4.7	1.9
1971–72	21	3,131	60	13,768	4.4	1.6
1977–78	24	3,723	59	22,396	6.0	2.2
1979–80	16	2,589	54	17,826	6.9	3.2
1984–85	18	3,131	58	26,963	8.6	5.4
1989–90	18	3,028	60	35,187	11.6	7.0
1993–95	16	2,770	64	40,773	14.7	9.1

Source: 'Reconfiguration in Indian Politics: State Assembly Elections, 1993–95', *Economic and Political Weekly of India*, 2–3, 13–20 January 1996.
Note: A 'major' round of Assembly elections is defined here as one which involved, within a year or two, elections to at least 2,000 Assembly constituencies.

Table 1.4
Percentage Turnout in Assembly Elections, 1984–95

States	1984–85	1989–90	1993–95	Increase (%)
Andhra Pradesh	66.7	67.6	71.1	3.5
Arunachal Pradesh	76.3	68.9	81.4	12.3
Bihar	55.1	62.2	61.8	- 0.4
Delhi	55.6	54.3	61.8	7.5
Gujarat	47.4	51.1	64.7	13.6
Goa	71.9	68.7	71.7	3.0
Himachal Pradesh	69.6	66.7	71.7	5.0
Karnataka	66.3	63.8	68.8	5.0
Madhya Pradesh	48.6	52.8	59.0	6.2
Manipur	87.3	80.6	88.8	8.2
Maharashtra	58.3	61.1	72.0	10.9
Mizoram	70.6	80.4	80.8	0.4
Orissa	51.4	55.5	73.8	18.3
Rajasthan	54.0	56.5	60.6	4.1
Sikkim	62.6	69.5	81.0	11.5
Uttar Pradesh	44.8	48.5	57.1	8.6
Total	55.3	60.3	64.2	3.9

Source: Yogendra Yadav, 'Reconfiguration in Indian Politics: State Assembly Elections, 1993–95', *Economic and Political Weekly of India*, 2–3, 13–20 January 1996.
Notes:
1. Table entries in the last column are for percentage of turnout in the 1993–95 Assembly elections as compared to the previous Assembly election in 1989–90.
2. Table entries for 1984 and 1989 in the case of Delhi are for turnout in Lok Sabha elections; Delhi did not have an Assembly then.
3. Turnout in the 1991 election to UP Assembly was 47.1 per cent.

is the very high level of participation in the small hill States, long thought to be outside the pale of national democratic politics. The figures of 1993–95, with Arunachal Pradesh at 81.4 per cent, Manipur at 88.8 per cent, Mizoram at 80.8 per cent and Sikkim at 81 per cent, show how important political participation has become even for regions that are normally far removed from the mainstream of India's high politics.

Students of comparative electoral sociology, familiar with the history of the slow and tortuous development of franchise and participation in contemporary stable democracies might wonder as to how this came about in India. By drawing on the rational calculus of participation[45] which basically suggests that people vote because they consider it worthwhile for them, particularly because the act of voting furthers their interest, we can construct a general hypothesis.

Voting behaviour in India in the immediate aftermath of Independence is often described in terms of 'vote banks'. A vote bank is a complex concept in the sense that unlike people voting as a group, in this situation, though the bulk of the voters in a particular village or locality might vote a particular way, the decision is not really a group decision. Members of a vote bank are guided towards the polling booth by the 'banker', possibly the head of a local family of high social status, owning land, and wielding political influence. The Rudolphs have described this as *vertical mobilisation*, which implies

> the marshalling of political support by traditional notables in local societies that are organised and integrated by rank, mutual dependence and the legitimacy of traditional authority. Notables reach vertically into such social systems by attaching dependants and socially inferior groups to themselves through their interests and deference (Rudolph and Rudolph 1967: 24).[46]

But even here, voting remains an individual decision, except that the basis of the act is not grounded on the explorations of the limits of what is politically possible. Rather, it is the expression of a pre-existing social bond.

The vote bank describes a cluster of exchange relations which runs parallel to the social system based on *jajmani*. However, the hold of the *jajmani*-vote bank system began to decline as people at the bottom of the social pyramid gradually dispensed with some of the intermediaries and started negotiating the terms of exchange directly with politicians from outside seeking support. In the more successful cases of this transformation, new forms of mobilisation, described by the Rudolphs as the *differential* and *horizontal* patterns of mobilisation, gradually replaced *vertical* mobilisation.

> Horizontal mobilization involves the marshalling of popular political support by class or community leaders and their specialized organizations. Ignoring the leaders and members of natural associations or little platoons, they make direct ideological appeals to classes or communities. Horizontal mobilization of solidiarities among class or community equals introduces a new pattern of cleavage by challenging the vertical solidarities and structures of traditional societies (Rudolph and Rudolph 1967: 25).

In a typical case of transition, however, both horizontal and differential mobilisations are likely to take place within the same political arena, creating what the Rudolphs have described as differential mobilisation, which involves

> the marshalling of direct and indirect political support by political parties (and other integrative structures) from viable, but internally differentiated communities through parallel appeals to ideology, sentiment, and interest. The agent of mobilization in this case is the political party rather than the local notable or community association, and its strategies of mobilization vary (Rudolph and Rudolph 1967: 26).

This transition from social hierarchy to egalitarianism can be presented in terms of two diagrams. We shall define the baseline in terms of the reciprocal bonds of obligation known as the *jajmani* system (Srinivas 1987), and the political implications arising out of it as a 'pyramid of dominance' (Frankel and Rao 1989/90; see Figures 1.1 and 1.2).

The circle depicting the *jajmani* system describes the reciprocal relations between the centre where the groups owning land and disposing of higher status are located, and the periphery, where the service groups are situated. In the ideal type situation, at the centre are groups which derive their dominant status from their control over force and the means of production. Politically, these groups and families form the local elite. Once again, since the bond that thus binds the 'elite' and the 'non-elite' is deeply ingrained, the social pyramid looks like a natural rather than a political construction.

Figure 1.1
The Jajmani System

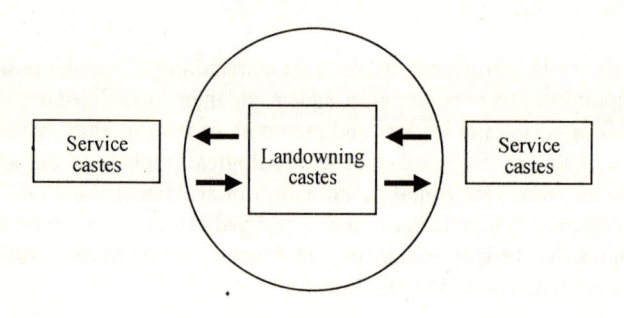

Figure 1.2
The Breakdown of the Pyramid of Social Dominance

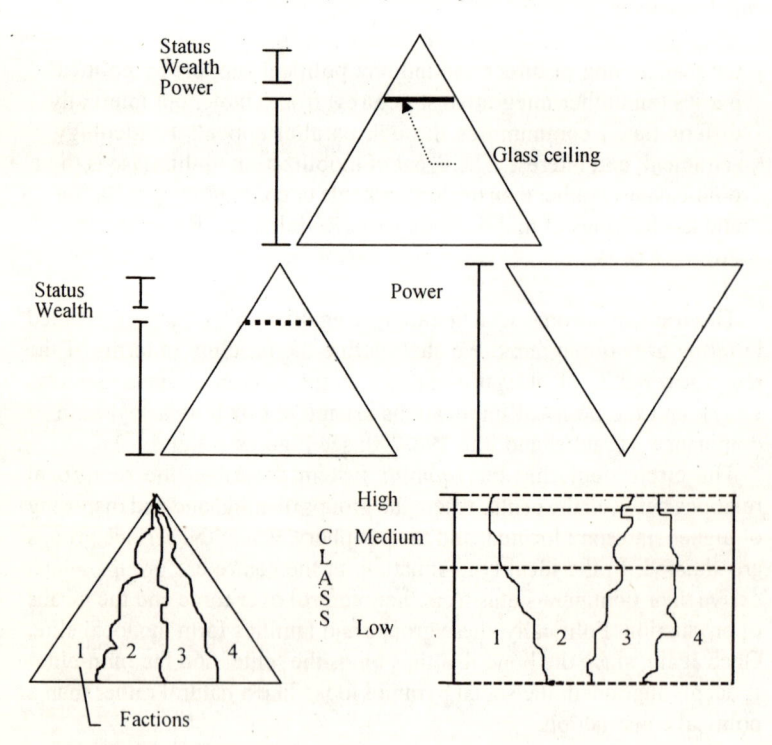

The representation of the *jajmani* system in Figure 1.1 follows the patterns of domination that one considers natural from within the framework of the caste system. The bonds that bind the members of this system are reciprocal, though neither the obligations nor the rights are by any means equal. The landowning groups around which the system is organised possess the bulk of the means of production, in most cases land, which forms the main source of economic activity in the village. The others, with their specialised occupations that form part of the process of cultivation, or of the other functions necessary for the purposes of ritual or social interaction, form the large and unspecified group of service castes. The complex social relationships with their political and economic implications constitute the standard *jajmani* system in its ideal form. Since domination is not perceived as such, it is more appropriate to use the concept of social notables rather than an organised and self-conscious elite, located at the core of the system and dominating the non-elite relegated to the periphery.

All this, however, changes with the coming of political consciousness and organisation, creating political tension and conflict. The process is depicted in Figure 1.2. Thus, in the ideal world of the *jajmani* system, which can be presented as a pyramid of dominance, based on status, power and wealth which accumulate in the families of the social notables, a form of social closure creates a low upper-threshold which defines the limits of social aspirations on the part of the peripheral groups in the village.

The convergence of the different forms of power in society gives a certain stability and rigidity to the system. However, the extension of franchise brings an additional political resource. Since the constitutional right to vote does not respect status, power or wealth, their conglomeration at the lower levels of the pyramid upsets the pattern of dominance inherent in the traditional social structure. Metaphorically, the pyramid breaks as the bottom is empowered through elections. Since the literature (particularly Huntington 1968) warns against the ensuing disorder, the question that we need to raise here is why the social pyramid in India as a whole did not break chaotically.

The tensions that are implicit within any form of social domination become explicit ones; legislation and economic change bring about a sense of empowerment to the peripheral social groups. The two pyramids in Figure 1.2, depicting respectively different forms of power, show how status and wealth might continue to inhere in the social notables though the enfranchisement and political mobilisation of the erstwhile peripheral social groups generally more numerous than the social notables reverses the direction of power, where the tiny base of the pyramid is dominated by the poor and low-status groups who vastly outnumber them. When these divergent forms of power are superimposed on one another, the result is the fracturing of the cohesive life of the *jajmani* system, which now splits into several factions. Figure 1.2 represents factions, first in the form of their own leadership, and the followers who are more numerous. The same concept is presented in the second graph in the bottom row of Figure 1.2, which shows how the factions intersect the established class patterns of the village, with some members of each social group of the village finding themselves within every faction, though, in most cases, one would find a radically different percentage from different social classes within each faction.

The empowerment of the lower social orders through elections has been described by the Rudolphs as the transformation of *vertical* mobilisation into *differential* and *horizontal* mobilisation. Typically, as the social groups located at the periphery discovered the negotiable value of the vote, they started participating directly in the political trade that matches electoral power to material resources. Established *jajmani* systems break down to create new groupings, based more directly on initiative from below, formation of coalitions among disparate interests, and, finally, creation of caste associations among groups with horizontal social and economic interests.

The state structure in India has institutionalised these ideological and social changes from below in the form of institutional innovations. Federalism, consociationalism and elite policy initiatives linking social power to political and economic change have created in the hands of national, regional and local elites, a useful 'room to manoeuvre in the middle'.[47]

These innovations have been possible in India because of four factors. First, the Gandhian legacy, which gave the first formal shape to a 'two-track' strategy where political actors seek to use the tactics of conventional political participation and recourse to protest movements, as part of the same strategy.[48] Politics after Independence gave formal acknowledgement to this development. The second factor is the ability of the national and regional elites to transfer knowledge from one arena to another. Panchayati raj is a good example. The third was the availability of the Congress system and the elite consensus that defined it during the formative years after Independence. Last, though India, unlike the stable Western democracies, lacked a tradition of liberal political movements or institutions, its feudal past, nevertheless, did not lead to the re-emergence of authoritarian tendencies, as in post-Meiji Japan. What provides a bedrock to India's ability to sustain her democratic polity is its ethos of toleration, accommodation and infinite patience. In contrast, the military-authoritarian tendencies of Tokugawa Japan (1603–1868) resurfaced and subverted the democratic experiments of the 1920s and 1930s.

In sum, the successful transition of a traditional society based on hierarchy to one which is egalitarian and participatory requires, first and foremost, the institutional basis for a participatory democracy. But these institutions would not be effective if they were not underpinned by an electorate that is conscious of its rights and, in consequence, feels efficacious. However, while efficacy is a necessary condition, it is not sufficient by itself because, without the restraint of institutions, a sense of empowerment derived from efficacy can quickly degenerate into anarchy, inviting non-democratic forces to intervene and take over in public interest. Thus, the best conditions of transition are provided by a situation where a conscious, participatory mass electorate is ensconced within the context of an elite consensus about the core values of the political system and a basic commitment to the political institutions.

The Context of the 1996 Parliamentary Election and the Post-poll Survey

Corresponding to the picture of going from a traditional social hierarchy to modern social egalitarianism is the transformation of the political process from the one-party-dominance period from 1952 to 1967 to the stable multi-party democracy that we have today. The hegemonic dominance of the Congress party broke down by the fourth General Election of 1967, when the first grand coalitions of parties of the left and right took place. After this, the Congress started gradually alternating with other political parties and coalitions, very much like any other political party. Under the leadership of Indira Gandhi, the party took the path of popular authoritarianism which brought the party great electoral success in 1971, but led to the corrosion of its organisational links with the society. One consequence was the Emergency of 1975–77, which, ending in the General Election of 1977, saw the Congress party out of power in Delhi at the Union level for the first time. Since then, Indian politics has entered a period of broad-based coalitions forming part of an unstable multi-party system.

Has this unstable party system already acquired the political resilience essential to high governance? Some macro-level evidence of resilience can be seen in Narasimha Rao's minority government, which lasted its full term; Deve Gowda's government (in spite of its coalitional character and minority status), successfully undertaking elections in Kashmir, Uttar Pradesh and Punjab and, mediation in regional conflicts; developing and forcefully defending a coherent position on the Comprehensive Test Ban Treaty in the face of opposition from the superpowers; and keeping the pace on reservations, empowerment of women, and liberalisation. The Gujral government, despite the outer signs of internal stress, appeared to have continued the momentum in the major areas of public policy, including, most notably, relations with India's South Asian neighbours. After the 12th General Election, an unprecedented coalition of the BJP and several regional parties continued the task of democratic governance at the Centre. These developments indicate a certain degree of resilience of the political system, which has been able to strike a dynamic balance between the perils of mass participation with all its potential for exorbitant political demands and the rewards of popular legitimacy, which alone can sustain long-term trends of nation and state formation, growth of citizenship and the growth of regional identity in the context of a cooperative federation. These are important themes in their own right, with research agendas that go beyond the scope of this book. Our main concern here is with the analysis of the interaction of electoral politics and social change in India, for which the main sources of evidence are the opinions and attitudes of the electorate, which would be analysed in depth in the subsequent chapters.

The Scheme of the Book

The broad conjectures about the nature and course of the interaction of electoral politics and democratic social change presented in the first chapter give rise to a number of hypothetical expectations with regard to the opinions of individuals concerning citizenship, the sense of efficacy and legitimacy of the system, their sense of involvement in the electoral process, and the level of political information that goes into the making of electoral decisions. These indicators of social change are pitted against a background of a traditional society and a post-colonial state, both struggling to come to terms with the radically new ideas of democracy and national sovereignty, and what the Nehruvian elite saw as the imperatives of modernisation. Since Independence came as a result of a transfer of power rather than a revolutionary break, the issue that arises here is to what extent the *ancien régime* survived in the post-Independence era in the form of the attitudes and opinions of the pre-Independence generation. Chapter 2 examines this theme of 'continuity and change' on the basis of a cohort analysis of the two generations: the pre-Independence generation, and the generation of the Midnight's Children.

The analysis of historical continuity is followed by a sociological profile of the Indian electorate in Chapter 3. It undertakes a broad overview of the findings of the survey to identify the limits of the consensus on all aspects of state–society interaction in India. It also provides a very broad overview of the responses of individuals when queried about where they stand on these issues. The strands of the specific arguments are then elaborated in a deeper analysis in the chapters that follow.

Since the interaction of traditional society and the post-colonial state takes place primarily in the electoral arena where political parties are the main actors, Chapter 4 continues the theme of the social bases of parties and the transformation of the party system of India that has come about with the broadening and deepening of democracy. Though electoral politics is conceptualised as the main instrument of democratic social change in this book, our understanding of the inner dynamic of this process would be incomplete without exploration of the organisational context in which electoral participation takes place. The nature of India's party system has changed radically since the days of the one-dominant-party system, and the hegemonic role of the Congress party as the fulcrum of the political system. Some of these ideas, presented in an embryonic form in Chapter 1, are further developed in Chapter 4. The transformation of the party system is analysed in the latter chapter on the basis of electoral statistics regarding partisan voting in national elections since Independence. The chapter then identifies the supporters of the main political parties and analyses their social bases. The intention here is to show to what extent there is a resonance of the electoral rhetoric of leaders, be it *dalit* (downtrodden: a political label used by activists among former untouchables as a means of contesting their social marginality) power or cultural nationalism, at the level of supporters. The results show that individual voters generally make the connections between their positions and those of the leaders, and that electoral choice is influenced by this connection. Individuals' abilities to establish these connections have important implications, both for their own sense of efficacy, as well as their evaluation of democratic politics as compared to the politics of movements, riots, terrorism and insurgency for achieving their political demands. The chapter also reports how, at the level of party supporters, there exists a great measure of consensus on major national issues, despite the fiery rhetoric of their leaders. That perhaps explains why, once parties are voted into the legislature, they have little difficulty in seeking out potential coalition partners and actually coming up with legislation with far-reaching implications for social and economic change.

The issue of regionalism, which recalls the fear of *Balkanisation* that underpinned much writing on Indian politics during the early decades after Independence, is the main theme of Chapter 5. This chapter, devoted to the nature of 'nation and region in India', raises the question of the inclusive character of identity in India where the loyalties to the nation and the region are not seen as *conflicting*, but rather as *converging* categories. The spatial boundaries of the political arena that define the limits of the political world of the individual, and the relationship of his political universe with the larger bodies of which it is a part, is also an important aspect of social change in India. Does the insular individual, for long confined to the limited world of the locality, simply reject it in favour of the world beyond the village once he is given the knowledge of the potential it holds for him and the opportunity to exercise a choice? Does locality simply dissolve itself in favour of the region, and the region for the creation of the nation? Or does the assertion of local and regional identities act to the detriment of the nation? Chapter 5 answers these questions in terms of the opinions and attitudes of 'regionalists', who are found to use their identification with the region more as a tool of transactional politics, rather than as exclusive territorial categories, promoted as a necessary contradiction of the 'idea of India'.[49]

The economy of independent India, from the outset, has remained an integral part of her politics, in striking contrast to that of developmental states where the authority to direct the course of growth and distribution was entrusted to an elite immune to political control by the masses. Despite the ubiquitous bureaucracy and the Planning Commission which controlled the 'commanding heights of the economy', ultimate authority for regulating the direction of the economy always remained in the hands of the elected executive, ever sensitive to the political demands of the masses. Successive governments of India have sought, over the last few years, to change the role of the government in regulating growth and redistribution through the policies of liberalisation and deregulation. The issue of popular perception of these policies, the overall perception of growth and welfare, and the linkages between class and perception of economic change, are examined in detail in Chapter 6, which examines 'poverty, economic policy and social opportunity in India'.

Drawing on the previous analysis, Chapter 7 on 'community, conflict and local democracy', examines the relationship between socio-economic change and political conflict in India, and illustrates the main argument by drawing on a regional comparison. Based on conventional theories of relative deprivation, the chapter first examines the relationship between the socio-economic status of the individual and his perception of his welfare and that of his children over the past, at the present moment, and his views about what the future holds for him. These findings provide interesting insights into the existence of slow growth combined with stable democracy in India. This global picture, constructed on the basis of the full sample, is then decomposed into regions, and the pictures emerging from a selected set of regions are compared in order to arrive at more specific formulations of the relationships between socio-economic change and political conflict.

Finally, Chapter 8, which examines the theme of the resilience of India's democratic political system, moves in the direction of drawing some general inferences about the underlying strengths and vulnerabilities of democratic social change in India. Important in this respect is the survey finding regarding the high trust that individuals repose in the political system as a whole and their general distrust of the people who run it, particularly politicians and the police.

Since many of the attitudes reported in this book are politically sensitive and difficult to measure in a survey situation in a consistent manner, it is important to discuss the background to the survey, particularly the methods of sampling and the training of investigators, as closely as possible. A detailed methodological appendix and the questionnaire used in the survey, make this background information available to the reader.

Notes

1. Jawaharlal Nehru, *Tryst with Destiny*, in Rushdie and West (1997: 1–2).
2. See Chiriyankandath (1992).
3. See Omvedt (1992) for a compilation of social movements in India; see Mitra (1991) for an attempt to derive the rationale for political movements from actors' strategies.
4. India is not alone in facing these teething problems of state formation. It may be remembered that post-1688, Britain or Wilhelmian Germany also went through similar uncertainties before the modern state took shape. Hobsbawm takes a more balanced view of the Indian experience: 'India of course remains at the time of writing by far

the most impressive example of a Third World state that has both maintained an unbroken civilian supremacy and an unbroken succession of government by a regular and relatively honest popular elections though whether this justifies the label "the world's greatest democracy" depends on how precisely we define Lincoln's "Government of the people, for the people and by the people" (Hobsbawm: 1995: 348).

5. The leading voice of Cassandra from the early decades after Independence was that of Harrison (1960). Less widely cited but no less trenchant was Naipaul (1964).
6. Harrison's (1960) was the first major statement of the difficulties that the Indian experiment with democracy had to face. Later, Moore (1966) gave a theoretical shape to some of these political problems. See, especially, Chapter 6, 'Democracy and Peaceful Change in India'.
7. One of the most recent examples of writing in this genre is Khilnani (1997).
8. Kohli's (1990) data show a rising trend of violence. Anecdotal evidence reinforces it further.
9. This figure is given by Cohen (1988).
10. See Mitra (1979) for a discussion of the resurgence of representative democracy in a micro-arena.
11. Here, Naipaul has further extended his message by putting the five decades since Independence in the context of the historical *longue durée*. He traces the slow recovery of North India to the establishment of the twin principles of orderly rule and representation, which he singles out as the main historical significance of British rule in India. The past five decades have seen a broadening and deepening of the latter, though their significance for the former remains a theme of further exploration.
12. Nanda (1995) reports faction fights and rowdy behaviour in national sessions of the Congress party long before the party got into real power, indicative of more recent happenings.
13. See Harrison (1960).
14. For representative exemplars of the former, see Huntington (1968) and Moore (1966). Sheth (1975) was one of the earliest landmark studies of the social base of political democracy in India.
15. We shall discuss below a body of consistent and cohesive literature that has grown around the theme of democracy and social change in India. The specific reference here is to Sheth (1975).
16. See Mitra (1999) for a detailed discussion of the theoretical and institutional implications of social change in the context of a post-colonial state. Though both volumes draw on the logic of competing paradigms and their convergence through competitive politics, the main arguments of the two volumes are expressed in different forms, drawing on case study and historical data in the former, and survey data in tha latter. The research findings based on analysis of the survey data are complementary to the case studies presented in *Culture and Rationality*.
17. Wilbert Moore, 'Social Change', in *International Encyclopaedia of the Social Sciences*, vol. 14 (1968: 366).
18. *Encyclopaedia Britannica*, vol. 16 (1974).
19. See, for example, Apter (1971, 1987); Kothari (1970, 1988); and Long (1977, 1989).
20. In the epilogue to the 1987 edition of *The Government and Politics of India*, Morris-Jones talks about a major change in the tone and content of Indian politics during the last two decades. The 'peaceful interpenetration of tradition and modernity'

which characterised the first two decades after Independence has given way to a political context that is much more violent. The political landscape is increasingly being taken over by local protest movements, even internal war. The loss of coherence and internal vitality that has affected the party system which had functioned remarkably well as an intermediary between the state and society, has grave implications for the political system as a whole. 'This is the basic loss suffered by the political system in the last two decades; it is this loss which has largely removed the nation-wide stabilising element, without whose management capacity to contain particularist thrusts the system continually falls apart, with a centre which does not effectively hold' (Morris-Jones 1987: 266).

21. *Gherao:* (in Hindi) surrounding a decision maker and pressurising him to negotiate.
    Dharna: literally, to sprawl one's self publicly on the ground, to bring pressure to bear on a decision maker.
    Rasta roko: stopping traffic on main roads.
    Chakka jam: to seize crossroads and thus, stop traffic.
    Jail bharo: filling up jails by protesters to bring pressure to bear on the government.

22. Thus, Sathyamurthy (1989: 3) suggests: 'At the same time, a large number of economic and sociological terms are used to describe aspects of the political process which pertain to the subterranean reaches of politics rather than strictly to the sphere of formal institutional mechanisms (e.g., *dalal, mamul,* Permit-Quota-Licence-Raj in discussions of corruption; *loan melas* in discussions of partisan favours in the economic sphere; and *chacha, dada, mastaan, Aayaa Ram Gayaa Ram* and *Garibi Hatao* in discussions about the manipulations of political and economic processes). These represent only a thin cross-section of the enormous range of concepts of differing vitality and import that have arisen in discussions of Indian politics.'

23. For comments on the 'derivative' discourse on politics in India, see Sathyamurthy (1989: 5). Commenting on the philosophical origins of Western scholarship on South Asia, he suggests: 'Weber's work was used as the intellectual inspiration for functionalism and positivist sociology in post-war America, mainly by such scholars as Parsons and Shils and Merton and their students. Behaviourist, positivist and functionalism approaches to the study of society went hand in hand in the generation of "comparative" studies purporting to provide typologies of different social and political systems based on common criteria.... Over the years, the two broad perspectives—Marxist and Weberian, interpenetrated to varying degrees in the approaches adopted by social science researchers, although this may have led to a certain degree of eclecticism rather than to attempts at generating a third general alternative approach' (Sathyamurthy 1986: 463).

24. Though the language is extreme and rather deliberately provocative, Naipaul's (1977: 18) comments on the perils of 'endogenous' models are not without justification. '...[I]ndependent India, with its five-year plans, its industrialisation, its practice of democracy, has invested in change. There always was a contradiction between the archaism of national pride and the promise of the new; and the contradiction has at last cracked the civilisation open. The turbulence in India this time hasn't come from foreign invasion or conquest; it has been generated from within. India cannot respond in her old way, by a further retreat into archaism. Her borrowed institutions have worked like borrowed institutions; but archaic India can provide no substitutes for press, parliament, and courts. The crisis of India is not only political or economic. The larger crisis is of a wounded old civilisation that has at last become aware of its inadequacies and is without the intellectual means to move ahead.'

25. See Bailey (1957).
26. See Mehta (1987); also Sathyamurthy (1971, 1986).
27. See Guha (1983); also Hardiman (1987).
28. Rostow (1960) contains the most definitive, though not exclusive, statement of this position.
29. The reference here is to the Princeton series on political development which became a paradigmatic statement of the field in the 1960s. See, in particular, Pye and Verba (1965).
30. In a purely technical sense, Indian applications of electoral forecasts have gone beyond the predictive accuracy achieved by their original Western inventors. The reference here is to the phenomenal success of electoral forecasts on the eve of the 1989 Indian parliamentary election.
31. The point has been made in Verney (1986).
32. The deinstitutionalisation thesis enjoys wide support among some leading students of Indian politics. See, for example, Manor (1983). Kothari (1982, 1983b) offers a similar explanation in elaborating his concept of the 'criminalization of politics'.
33. The moral argument comes out rather strongly in the 'explanation' of state degeneration given by Rudolph and Rudolph (1987).
34. In her recent work, Frankel has changed her methodological stance significantly. Instead of suggesting that the momentum for change could come only from a movement from below, she suggests interaction between the state and society as a more feasible source of radical change in India. See Frankel and Rao (1989/90).
35. The findings of the subaltern school, in six volumes under Guha's general editorship, are published by Oxford University Press. For critical comments on their methodology, see Sathyamurthy (1990). A seventh volume (1992) has been added.
36. Thus, Hardiman (1987) concludes his analysis by attributing a consciously anti-bourgeois stance to the Adivasi uprising described in his work.
37. In a personal communication, Saberwal has indicated that this search would lead to a congruence between the observer's categories with the insider's 'lived-in' terms.
38. 'Prometheus symbolises the revolt of man against the gods. In his hands, ingenuity and treachery were powerful weapons. He managed to deceive Zeus himself and to bring humanity (it is claimed he was its very creator) all the good things refused it by the gods. All this was not achieved, however, without a price' (Comte 1991: 168).
39. For a preliminary discussion of this model, see Mitra (1997a). The parameters of the model are discussed in Mitra (1997a: 36–38).
40. Ahmed and Singh (1975: 165) refer to this as 'structural consolidation'.
41. As in Anderson (1991).
42. Mitra (1994a) and Mitra and Lewis (1996) emphasise the actor's attitudes towards risk and the strategic calculations that go with it.
43. Wittfogel (1957) was an early exponent of this view.
44. See, for example, Rostow (1960).
45. In accordance with theories of utility maximisation as proposed by Downs (1957) and Riker and Ordeshook (1973).
46. Also see Rudolph and Rudolph (1960: 5–22).
47. See Lijphart (1996) for an application of the logic of consociational type power-sharing as a corrective to Indian federalism and as a general explanation of the stability and legitimacy of India's democracy. The 'room to manoeuvre in the middle'

applies to the tendency of India's political elite to interpose themselves between traditional society and the modern state.
48. See Mitra (1992) for a detailed discussion of this argument.
49. See, for instance, Khilnani's (1997) interesting book with the same title.

2

Continuity and Change in Indian Politics: A Cohort Analysis of the Electorate

Many post-colonial states start their independent existences with a brave programme of social change. But some regimes eventually collapse because of lack of support from important entrenched social groups. The depth and breadth of the political consensus that lies behind the programme of social change with which the ruling groups are identified is thus crucial for the stability and legitimacy of the new order. Further, it is not enough for the consensus to have popular support at a given point of time. Yet another feature of a robust political system is one which produces a consensus that not only captures the imagination of the people at a given point of time, but one that anticipates future demands and straddles the gap between the generation in power and generations to come. Some of these points, which were briefly mentioned in the introduction, would be examined further in this chapter.

Not surprisingly, as we have already seen in Chapter 1, debates on the nature and pace of social change deeply divide people in post-colonial states. The political articulation of these divisions, and their further transformation into violent conflict, hold the potential for disastrous consequences for the state. As such, in a context such as that of India in the wake of Independence, one could expect the debate on social change to be of great intensity, drawing both on the politics *within* the system, as well as the politics *of* the system.

We have already seen in the previous chapter how these issues are addressed in the literature on modernisation and social change. Of particular interest to us here is the relationship between the manner of articulation, and aggregation of the normative and material conflicts that social change necessarily gives rise to on the one hand, and the stability and legitimacy of the system on the other. In a situation where the competing parties to the conflict systematically talk past one another, violence and civil war are the most likely outcomes. However, when normative conflicts give rise to an inter-paradigmatic debate and the electoral process becomes a means through which these are articulated, the political system moves rapidly in the direction of a crisis. The political system can gain further legitimacy and momentum as it unfolds only if the conflicting sides share a meta-language in which to express their differences. In brief, a synergetic debate among conflicting paradigms is possible if, and only if, the interface of the competing paradigms is not absent. In operational terms, this is possible if the paradigmatic conflict is not coterminous with an inter-generational conflict, and, if there is a substantial popular base—measured on the conventional criteria of gender, caste, generation and class—that shares the main values and norms of the political system.

These two assertions constitute, respectively, the main themes of Chapters 2 and 3. It could be argued here that age is a social indicator like any other, and in that respect, does not call for a separate analysis. The main reason for singling out the issue of the generational conflict for detailed analysis is derived from the fact that, unlike gender, caste and class, generation, particularly in a post-colonial context, often represents a radical break with history. The younger cohort in the population, whether it is in the form of angry students or younger officers and soldiers in the armed forces, the generation that came to maturity after Independence in many post-colonial states, is often the main source of challenge to the basic values and institutions that the generation to which power was transferred at Independence stands for.

The double failure of the generation that fought for Independence, and, having won power, set up a constitution in the image of the ideals that underpinned the freedom movement, to gain acceptance of the political system by the post-Independence generation, to achieve a smooth succession to power, has been the cause of the undoing of many post-independence states. In the light of these examples, India's ability to sustain the main structure of its Parliamentary democracy and federal state in spite of the passing away of the generation of Independence constitutes a puzzle. In order to explain this puzzle, this chapter would first specify the potential conflict of generations in terms of radically different concepts of nation and state, then elaborate some of the specific ideas that constitute the concrete, substantive themes of India's governance and its statehood and nationhood, and, finally, compare the attitudes of the two generations of Indians on the grid of these issues. By comparing the attitudes and values of the generation that was born after Independence with the ones of those born before, the chapter will ask if a distinctive political idiom has evolved in India, and, will draw on survey data to understand the challenge of political and social change.

A Literary and Political Etymology of the 'Midnight's Children'

Indian political discourse refers to the generational conflict in terms of the values and attitudes of the 'Midnight's Children', a concept that gained popular currency after Salman Rushdie's work of fiction of the same title.[1] The method that we shall follow in this chapter in order to evaluate the generational attitudes towards the achievements of India during the five decades since Independence will draw on these usages and operationalise them by truncating the sample of our survey into two groups. Those who are 45 years or less would be treated as the representatives of the post-Independence generation, to be compared with those who are older.

Since the epithet 'Midnight's Children' bears the unmistakable stamp of the genius of Salman Rushdie, we should start our analysis of the Indian case with a brief reference to the origin of the concept and its use in the text, both as a literary and political device. Rushdie begins his book with a reference to the fateful moment when the birth of the promised Independence is coupled with the tragedy of the Partition of India and Pakistan.

> I was born in Doctor Narlikar's Nursing Home on August 15th, 1947. And the time? The time matters, too. Well then: at night.... On the stroke of midnight, as a matter of fact. Clock-hands joined palms in respectful greeting as I came...at the precise instant of India's arrival at independence, I tumbled forth into the world.... A few seconds later, my father broke his big toe; but his accident was a mere trifle when set beside what had befallen me in that benighted moment, because thanks to the occult tyrannies of those blandly saluting clocks

I had been mysteriously handcuffed to history, my destinies indissolubly chained to those of my country (Rushdie 1982: 9).

The fictive life of Rushdie's protagonist is, of course, only a literary device for the depiction of the career of the post-colonial state and the promise of nationhood with which it was launched. As the story unfolds, we find the youthful dreams of Naseem, the prototype post-colonial figure, entitled by his own reckoning to joy and fulfilment, turning sour. Rushdie's narrative ends with an agonising admission of the defeat of an ideal, of a botched project of nation-building in South Asia. The promised nation, pure and pristine in its potential form, underpinning the rhetoric of the leaders of the freedom movement, turning into mere *chutney*—an eclectic collection of bits casually thrown together. Rushdie's indictment of those responsible for it is laced with rage and disenchantment.

What is required for *chutnification*? Raw materials, obviously—fruit, vegetables, fish, vinegar, spices. Daily visits from Koli women with their saris hitched up between their legs. Cucumbers, aubergines, mint. But also: eyes, blue as ice, which are undeceived by the superficial blandishments of fruit—which can see corruption beneath citrus-skin; fingers which, with featheriest touch, can probe the secret inconstant hearts of green tomatoes; and above all a nose capable of discerning the hidden languages of what-must-be-pickled, its humours and messages and emotions ... at Braganza Pickles, I supervise the production of Mary's legendary recipes; but there are also my special blends, in which, thanks to the powers of my drained nasal passages, I am able to include memories, dreams, ideas, so that once they enter mass-production all who consume them will know what pepperpots achieved in Pakistan, or how it felt to be in the Sundarbans ... believe don't believe but it is true. Thirty jars stand upon a shelf, waiting to be unleashed upon the amnesiac nation (Rushdie 1982: 460).

Rushdie's is clearly a search for a *Kulturnation*, which, four decades since Independence (at the time of his writing) continued to be a chimera. But, is the *Kulturnation* the only kind possible? Is a multicultural nation, drawing on a plural society sharing a common geographic space, merely an *Ersatznation*—far from the real thing—and not an organic entity in its own right, a robust political construct that is capable of drawing on the contradictions of pre-colonial and colonial histories, religious diversity and the plurality of regional and local traditions? In order to answer this question, we need to analyse the perceptions of the 'nation and its fragments' by the people who constitute it. Since these perceptions are constrained by the institutions that form their backdrop, we should first consider the post-colonial state and the project of nation-building as conceptualised by Jawaharlal Nehru, the generally acknowledged author of both the post-colonial state, and the ambitious programme of social change through the agency of the political process and institutions.

Nehru and Freedom at Midnight

The Republic of India which is the backdrop of this book, was to a great extent the creation of Jawaharlal Nehru, the first Prime Minister of India and one of the founding fathers of the Constitution. The institutions of parliamentary democracy, federalism, a written Constitution that guaranteed basic human rights protected by a Supreme Court, and a scheme of nation-building and economic development through five-year plans were intended by Jawaharlal Nehru to serve as the bases of the larger project of nation-building. Nehru described the launching of this project in his famous speech called the 'Tryst with Destiny', from which we have cited at the beginning of this book.

Nehru's rhetoric and the institutions of the post-Independence state have created the expectations that define the Indian agenda of social change. Posing the question that Rushdie attributed to the Midnight's Children, we might ask: How successful has India been in fulfilling Nehru's dreams about democracy, national identity, social change, welfare of the masses and orderly government, and how do the two generations view it? Or, in establishing order and unity in a country of continental proportions with significant numbers of Hindus, Muslims, Sikhs, Christians, Buddhists, Jains, Jews, Parsis and Muslims, speaking 15 major languages divided into 800 dialects, where people live most of their social lives within localised castes, of which there are more than 3,000? Thus framed, the question opens up conflicting answers. The Midnight's Children, who, unlike their elders, have a clearer notion of what they are entitled to, and have the means to compare results both within India and across countries of Asia and Europe, are, to go by the accounts of informed observers, disillusioned.[2]

Since the basis of these expectations is also what has come to be known as distinctive of India's political culture, the following section examines its salient aspects before moving on to a statistical comparison of the views of the pre-Independence generation with that of the voters who are 45 years old or younger.

Some Salient Elements of Political Culture

The way forward in this exploration of the views of the post-Independence generation with regard to state, society and change consists of a basic definition of India's political culture. These attitudes have evolved in response to the issues which serve as reference points for two generations of India's voting population. However, the listing of the main components of India's political culture for the purpose of this comparison is not easy, partly because, being a relatively open society, the debate on India and within India is vast and also because the very nature of India's political discourse, while generating a rich body of ideas, never shies away from casting doubts on those very ideas themselves.[3] Since the research on India carried out over the past five decades has produced a rich body of information on these questions, the list below is necessarily selective.

Institutionalisation of Authority in a Post-colonial Setting

Institutionalisation is one of the most important criteria to measure the success that a post-colonial society has in achieving and sustaining statehood, one where India has been relatively more successful than the majority of post-colonial societies. Political power is wielded by democratically elected governments. In the beginning, the Indian National Congress, which had functioned as an umbrella organisation for the coordination of the anti-colonial movement against British rule, won power at the federal as well as the regional levels all across India. That hegemonic role of the Congress party was over within 20 years of the founding of the Republic. Opposition parties of the left and right as well as centre started coming to power, first at the level of regions, and eventually at the federal level. However, in spite of this change, the major institutions of the state have survived. Even before the French put the concept of cohabitation into the language of politics, Indians have been practising it in terms of the sharing of power by elected governments of the right, left and centre at the regional level, with the Central Government being controlled by the Indian National Congress. The territorial state has seen many changes, particularly at the level of the regions. New regions have been created to give more salience to regional identity, language and economic needs. But, unlike in neighbouring Pakistan, which, mainly as a result of regional imbalance, split into two in 1971, the territorial integrity of India continues to be stable.

India's institutions are not mere artificial constructions devoid of essence. For proof, we need only look at the Supreme Court of India, which, at its own initiative, ordered the Central Bureau of Investigation (a government agency), to speed up the investigations into illegal money changing and other forms of corruption by highly placed politicians and civil servants. Fifty years after Independence, it is no longer possible to lay the credit or the blame for the state of things in India at the door of the British. The responsibility belongs now squarely to the Midnight's Children. As we look at the record in the light of the indicators, we need therefore to ask: How could this sense of accountability be achieved in a relatively short span of time?

At Independence, the electorate consisted of large numbers of voters who had not experienced direct British rule, and were stepping out of princely rule straight into popular democracy. Hindus and Muslims, still recovering from the trauma of Partition, were being asked to become citizens of a country which did not recognise any official religion. Millions of poor, marginal, land-hungry peasantry radicalised through Communist agitations, and unorganised manual labourers and unionised industrial workers were all being asked to repose their faith in multi-party democracy. What should have followed is described by several specialists. One of the most cited is Selig Harrison, whose *India: The Most Dangerous Decades* spelt out a future of communal conflict, disharmony and Balkanisation. Huntington's *Political Order in Changing Societies* predicted structural discontinuity in the face of popular mobilisation. State theorists like Gunnar Myrdal in his *Asian Drama* came up with the formulation of the 'soft state' based on popular consent which would necessarily be lacking in the authority with which to tackle basic problems of structural change. Weaving all these strands into a unified and comparative theory, Moore (1966), in his *Social Origins of Dictatorship and Democracy*, predicted a state of peaceful paralysis for India in the years following Independence. In order to answer this question, we need to turn to political participation, responsible both for the diffusion of institutional norms and the generation of legitimacy, without which mere order can easily degenerate into autocratic rule.

Political Participation

Political power in India originates through the consent of the governed, expressed through regular elections at the level of the federal parliament, regional assemblies, or *gram panchayats* (village councils).[4] Elections are supervised by an Election Commission, with guaranteed autonomy by constitutional design, which maintains fairness and efficiency. Participation in elections was in the region of 40 per cent of those eligible to vote in the first elections after Independence, but that has gone up to about 60. Elections are crucial to the exercise of power in legislative bodies at all levels of the system; they are essential to the functioning of any public or private body which receives public money.[5] Micro-studies in Indian villages show how deep the roots of the electoral principle are. Electoral campaigns are conducted routinely not only to the Parliament, State Assembly and *gram panchayat*—the three legislative layers of the country—but also elections to the cooperative societies, the youth groups, the women's association, the committees of the high school, the minor school and the primary school, as well as an association for the welfare of the former untouchables and tribals.

Universal adult franchise was introduced in India in 1952, and both the non-democratic left and non-democratic right were authorised to compete equally with the centre and moderate left and right for political power through elections. Participating in the first general elections after Independence were the Communist Party of India, which only three years earlier had risen in a violent peasant revolution against the nascent Indian state, as well as the Hindu right-wing party Jan Sangh joining the electoral fray in the background of the assassination of Mahatma Gandhi by a former member of the Rashtriya Swayamsevak Sangh, a Hindu extremist group closely allied to the Hindu nationalist party. This bold gamble on the part of Jawaharlal Nehru appears to have paid rich dividends, by encouraging attitudes favourable to multi-party democracy within these extremist groups.

As the data with regard to electoral participation at the central and regional levels presented in Chapter 1 show, India's record is comparable to stable Western democracies. Major policy initiatives have been taken by elected governments. Parties have alternated in power as a result of elections. On all aggregate indicators of participation, India has kept up steady progress. The level of electoral participation has gone up steadily, reaching the levels of continental European voting in some parts of the country. Participation is widely spread. We learn from survey data that now there is no significant variation in participation along gender, age, occupation, caste, religion and residence.

Citizenship

Using the Constitution as the main instrument, the Republic of India sought to establish individual rights to equality—irrespective of religion, race, caste, creed, gender, age or place of birth—as the cornerstone of the political and social processes. In a country where society was traditionally organised on the principle of hierarchy of gender and status, the introduction of the principle of equality was nothing short of revolutionary. The effect of this radical juxtaposition of social inequality and legal equality first manifested itself in a public way in the 1960s, when political parties, set up by backward castes, who had traditionally worked for landowners from upper castes as tenants or as small and marginal farmers, started exercising power in their own right. The 1980s saw the next wave of this revolutionary process when the former untouchables—beneficiaries of legislative quotas and other methods of affirmative social action—acquired independent political status as key components of national and regional political formations. The stories of great political mobility in spite of social disadvantages are many, but none so impressive as among the new breed of assertive political leaders who have, in the span of one generation, overcome the disadvantages of gender, class, caste and minority religious status.

The subsequent chapters of this book will provide further evidence of the growth of citizenship in India. It is useful at this stage to refer to the historical context in which this has occurred. Since the recent prominence of the Bharatiya Janata Party, which many identify with Hindu nationalism, has drawn worldwide attention to the conditions of Muslims in India, our discussion of the condition of Muslims and other non-Hindus who form about 18 per cent of the population is an important part of the growth of equal citizenship in India. At Independence, when British India was partitioned and Pakistan was created as a homeland for the Muslims of the subcontinent, about a third of India's Muslims nevertheless chose to stay on in the country of their birth. Rather than following the politics of separation, the electoral choice of India's Muslims follows multiple considerations, rather like their non-Hindu neighbours. That should reassure those who already see the polarisation of India's political community on the lines of religion. The point is also proved from the presence of a large number of Muslims in India's legislatures. Except for the former untouchables and tribals who get guaranteed representation in India's legislatures, there is no method of proportional representation in India. However, the total percentage of Muslims in India's legislatures is not very different from their share of the population. In addition, Muslims are found in such high offices as India's President, the national Supreme Court and the High Courts in the states, the bureaucracy and the military, and in the arena of competitive sports.

Growth and Redistribution

Welfare is our fourth important criterion, because without an acceptable standard of living for the masses, no provision of institutions, participation or legal equality would make sense. As always, economists disagree about specific figures. But the percentage of people living below the poverty line has come down from about 50 per cent in 1977 to about 20 per cent by 1994.[6] Reports from the field show that a large majority of people have experienced significant improvement in their conditions of living in the span of one generation. Those with long memories would recall the famous Bengal famine of 1943 and the Bihar famine of the 1960s, and Indian leaders going with the begging bowl to the capitals of rich countries. Thanks to the dramatic rise in agrarian productivity and a competent public distribution system based on a network of food reserves linked to a system of fair price shops, these images have become a thing of the past. During 150 years of colonial rule, India's GNP per capita hardly registered any growth at all. Since Independence, the economy has grown on an average at the rate of 4 per cent per year. There is considerable excitement and activity on the economic front since 1991, when India started liberalising the economy, accelerating the pace of the integration of India's economy with the international market. This has, on the whole, improved international confidence in India's economic potential.

Law and Order

Compared to many anti-colonial movements, India's struggle for Independence was largely peaceful in character. Politics after Independence has continued this trend. The alternative of violent class struggle has had its advocates. Following the split of the Communist Party of India (Marxist), the Maoist CPI (M-L) had briefly emerged as a powerful challenger to the state, and had enjoyed a period of intense support from sections of students. However, the movement has remained geographically limited to pockets of strength, and is not seen as a party specific to the youth. Overall, while the violent mass insurgencies of Punjab, Kashmir and the North-East have attracted worldwide attention, on the whole, India continues to be relatively orderly. Rather than violent conflict, a widely dispersed belief in the rationality of protest movements and their acceptance as a legitimate political resource is an integral part of India's political culture.

There are, of course, other indicators, and not all of them are positive. The important point to note here is, however, that a lot of this data are drawn from the English language press and from the political science literature specifically addressed to India. This leaves out two other important sources of knowledge of politics in India after Independence. The Indian discourse on India—most of which is now carried out in India's own vernacular press—and writings on politics which are not expressed in a self-consciously political language. Some of this debate, important for our purposes, is very critical, and the image of India that emerges from it is poignant, tragic and violent. Since survey data provides an important window to the totality of political discourse, we need briefly to examine the deeper meaning of political culture in its social context, before we can compare the views of the Midnight's Children with those of the older generation.

India's vernacular political discourse is rich, diverse, and complex. We do not have the space to go into it at length. Our intention is to select a few examples in order to complete the picture of Indian politics we get from the foreign-language press. The first example comes from Kalahandi, the district in Orissa where according to the vernacular press death from starvation takes place but is not included in the official statistics; where hunger drives people into desperate acts of inner violence like selling their children. How do the artistic riches of Orissa coexist with such great poverty and deprivation? In the same vein, we can consider the case of Surat, a port city in Gujarat which has known capitalism for at least 300 years, having been on the trade route of the European powers before British colonial rule, but which recently witnessed communal riots accompanied by acts of unspeakable cruelty. In these incidents, we are no longer in the realm of the politics of elections and parliamentary lobbying. The incident at Ayodhya, where a 400-year-old mosque (situated at a place that has been the scene of long dispute between Hindus and Muslims of the area) was torn apart by a Hindu mob is well known. But the debate, mostly condemnatory in its tone, in the English press provides a contrast to the vernacular press which is more ambivalent. This gives us a new dimension on such conflict. Clearly, democracy, which has brought power to the hands of ordinary people, has also revived historical memories of Islamic invasion, forced mass conversion, loot and violence on women. The fear and anxiety translate themselves through political mobilisation into social and communal conflict.

The coexistence of a main framework of cultural traits integral to stable democracies and an undercurrent of social attitudes that indicate their negation, resulting in violent riots and occasional collapse of democratic rule must come across as confusing to the observer. At issue is: Why do the structures of representative democracy function in spite of the contradictions that underpin the political discourse? Survey data provides an opportunity to dissect these apparent contradictions, and move in the direction of identifying their interconnection. The contradiction of civic virtues and uncivil attitudes is caused by social cleavages, such as caste, class, gender, religion, and in many post-colonial societies, the political incompatibility of generations. The analysis undertaken below will concentrate on the generational conflict of attitudes and values.

The Post-Independence Generation: Self-conscious and Polarised

The main components of India's political culture, and the doubts that underpin them, provide some concrete issues where we can compare the views of the generations. In this section we shall present some statistical information on these issues.

Level of Information and Education

Crucial to the functioning of democratic institutions is the information available to the citizens. While this in its own right is a broad theme, we have selected the correct naming of elected representatives as an indicator of political information. Table 2.1 shows that the post-Independence generation is generally better informed than its elders.

Correct naming of the:

- Prime Minister (PM)
- Chief Minister (CM)
- Member of Parliament from own constituency (MP).

Table 2.1
Level of Political Information by Generation (in per cent)

	PM	CM	MP
Up to 45 years	42.8	55.9	57.1
46 years or more	33.8	47.9	49.1
All	**40.3**	**53.7**	**54.9**

The best scores for both generations are in the naming of the recently elected Member of Parliament. The MP, in a single-member constituency with majority voting rules, is the focus of the electoral process. Not surprisingly, both generations fare better as compared to the score for the Prime Minister or the Chief Minister. The Chief Minister of the state is usually one of the most visible figures in the campaign, besides being a major source of jobs, contracts and the other munificence that a welfare state provides to its citizens. The second ranking of the Chief Minister on the correct naming indicator can be understood in this light. The Prime Minister's low score can come across as a surprise, but is understandable in the context in which the survey was conducted. Deve Gowda, occupant of this office at the time of the survey, was something of an 'accidental' Prime Minister, a consequence of the internal manoeuvres of the minority National Front coalition that formed the government after the end of the 13-day rule of the BJP government headed by Atal Bihari Vajpayee. Gowda was not a well-known figure outside his home state (Karnataka) when he was appointed to the highest office of the land. It is not a surprise, therefore, that the scores in this case are as low as they are. It should be noticed, nonetheless, that on all three indicators of level of information, we find the post-Independence generation ahead of those born before Independence.

Level of Education

There are very interesting differences between the two generations in terms of formal education. While the number of the illiterates among the Midnight's Children is still disconcertingly high, it is significantly lower than their elders, where a large majority are illiterate. At the upper level, however, about 45 per cent have formal education at the level of middle school or above, a figure that is twice as high as that of the elders.

Table 2.2
Level of Education by Generation (in per cent)

	Illiterate	Up to Primary	Middle School	Higher Secondary	College and Above
Up to 45 years	36.9	18.1	14.7	23.5	6.9
46 years or more	54.9	21.3	9.0	11.5	3.3
All	**41.9**	**18.9**	**13.1**	**20.2**	**5.9**

Institutionalisation and Participation

Now that we have established that the Midnight's Children are both better informed and better educated than their elders, one could expect political attitudes and a sense of their own worth at variance with the pre-Independence generation. Astoundingly, that does not appear to be the case. There is a process of levelling that is built into India's political discourse, so much so that when it comes to the crucial question of efficacy, generational differences do not appear to be radically at variance.

The following question was asked in order to measure the perception of the sense of efficacy of the voters: *Do you think your vote has an effect on how things are run in this country, or do you think your vote makes no difference?* Over 60 per cent of the post-Independence generation consider their vote to have effect, compared to about 54 per cent of the pre-Independence generation. While the score for the younger generation is several points higher with regard to the sense of efficacy, it should be noted here that even though a majority of them are illiterate, the majority of the older generation *does* think of its participation as both meaningful and efficacious.

Table 2.3
Effect of Vote by Generation (in per cent)

	No Difference	DK*	Has Effect
Up to 45 years	20.9	17.5	60.7
46 years or more	22.6	22.9	53.7
All	**21.4**	**18.9**	**58.8**

* Do not know.

When asked about the instrumental efficacy of political parties, *How much in your opinion do political parties help to make government pay attention to the people—a good deal, somewhat or not much?* no great difference emerged between the two generations. It is interesting to note that when we aggregate the 'somewhat' and 'great deal' scores, more of both generations find parties instrumentally efficacious than the opposite. The close to 40 per cent score of 'not at all', indicating a very low level of trust in political parties (where the two generations draw level), however, gives indications of an underlying fragility within the political system.

Table 2.4
Parties' Attention to People by Generation (in per cent)

	Not at All	Somewhat	Great Deal
Up to 45 years	38.5	43.8	17.1
46 years or more	38.5	42.5	18.3
All	**38.5**	**43.5**	**17.4**

In the same vein, when asked, *How much does having elections from time to time make the government pay attention to the people—a good deal, somewhat or not much?* we find a quarter, in both generations, having rather a low opinion of the instrumental efficacy of the electoral process in terms of its impact on the policies of the government. The aggregation of the moderate to highly positive evaluation of the efficacy of the electoral process indicates a higher score for the younger generation than the older, indicating a more optimistic and positive view of the capacity of the electoral process in influencing government.

Table 2.5
Importance of Elections by Generation (in per cent)

	Not Much	Somewhat	Good Deal
Up to 45 years	25.6	35.3	12.2
46 years or more	25.3	30.8	10.9
All	**25.5**	**34.0**	**11.9**

The process of political participation and the sense of efficacy both assume government as the main reference point, because influencing government is the overall objective of both. In order to measure the perception of government in its various institutional expressions, including the two institutions whose function is to ensure fair and legal government, we have developed a general indicator by aggregating a number of measures of trust. The responses to the various measures of trust were added up to produce a composite index. The items included in this battery were as follows.

- Trust in the Central Government.
- Trust in the State Government.
- Trust in the Local Government.
- Trust in the Judiciary.
- Trust in the Election Commission.

The results, presented in Table 2.6, show over three-quarters of the post-Independence generation exhibiting medium or high trust in institutions, slightly more than the generation born before Independence. This is significant in view of the fact that these institutions are the very ones with which the Republic of India started its career. Manifestly, contrary to the impression created in the media, trust in institutions stays reasonably high, actually higher among the Midnight's Children than the generation that witnessed the birth of the Republic.

Table 2.6
Trust in Institutions by Generation (in per cent)

	Low	Medium	High
Up to 45 years	24.9	45.3	29.7
46 years or more	26.7	42.6	30.7
All	**25.4**	**44.6**	**30.0**

We next take up the attitudes towards the main political, religious and moral issues of the day. It will be noticed from the data presented below that in practically all cases, the post-Independence generation is more sure about its attitudes (i.e., there are fewer of them who do not profess an opinion); and their opinion is polarised, i.e., there is more support for the syncretic, multicultural, accommodative position, but also, marginally more support for the hard, cultural-nationalist position.

Attitudes Towards Social Conflict and Discrimination

The demolition of the Babri mosque on 6 December 1992 marks a watershed in Indian politics. In one powerful and poignant move, this single incident reopened the confessional character of the state in India as a contested issue, challenging those who were so far content to leave the ambiguous character of the Constitution with regard to religion relatively undisturbed. It simultaneously showed the high price of non-action in terms of direct, anarchic mass outbursts. It also indicated the need for concerted action by those who consider tolerance and minority rights to be important elements of Indian politics, making it imperative for mainstream Hindu nationalism to moderate its tone and to seek electoral allies outside the Bharatiya Janata Party and its partners.

The data presented in Table 2.7 capture the political consequences of the incident at Ayodhya four years later. About two-fifths of the national electorate disapproves of the demolition; the level of disapproval among the younger generation is significantly higher than among the older generation. Interestingly, however, while only a small minority of about a fifth of the electorate approves of the demolition, the percentage is marginally higher among the younger people as well. The question was formulated in the following way: *Some people say that the demolition (of the disputed building in Ayodhya [Babri masjid]) was justified while others say it was not justified. What would you say, was it justified or not justified?*

Table 2.7
Attitudes towards Ayodhya Incident by Generation (in per cent)

	Unjustified	Justified	Can't Say	Not Heard About Demolition
Up to 45 years	39.2	23.0	10.2	27.6
46 years or more	34.5	22.4	9.9	44.2
All	37.9	22.8	10.1	29.2

The attitude of accommodation and tolerance towards minorities that the largest number of respondents in Table 2.7 express, finds an echo in further questions that tap the same dimension. On the issue of an approach of accommodation towards Pakistan, we notice, in Table 2.8, a greater agreement towards accommodation from both generations. This position, which became accepted Indian policy in the aftermath of the survey, indicated a departure from the line developed by Indira Gandhi first in the late sixties and put to practice in the eighties through a number of tactical moves, particularly against Pakistan. However, responses to the survey question, *India should make more efforts to develop friendly relations with Pakistan. Do you agree or disagree?* does reveal some support for the continuation of a policy of domination of the smaller neighbours by India. Significantly, support for this policy is higher among the younger generation than the older people.

Table 2.8
Policy towards Pakistan by Generation (in per cent)

	Disagree	Can't Say	Agree
Up to 45 years	18.3	36.1	45.2
46 years or more	15.3	41.7	42.6
All	**17.5**	**37.7**	**44.5**

The policy options towards the militant insurgency in Kashmir evokes a comparable picture, with generally more people opting for negotiation than suppression of the insurgency by force. The lower 'can't say' indicates a comparably higher readiness of the younger generation to pronounce itself—and they do tend to express stronger views on both options (Table 2.9). *People's opinions are divided on the issue of the Kashmir problem—some people say that the government should suppress the agitation by any means, while others say that this problem should be resolved by negotiations. What would you say, should the agitation be suppressed or should it be resolved by negotiation?*

Table 2.9
Resolution of Kashmir Issue by Generation (in per cent)

	Negotiation	Can't Say	Suppression
Up to 45 years	34.7	30.8	11.5
46 years or more	29.8	35.7	10.6
All	**33.3**	**32.1**	**11.2**

On the issue of nuclear weapons, however, we have greater willingness from both generations to keep that option open. We asked: *There is no need for India to make the atomic bomb. Do you agree or disagree with this?* Here the younger lead the elder, just as in the other option of foreclosing the nuclear option. The higher responses on both options among the post-Independence generation apparently comes from the fact that the rate of the 'can't say' option is about 7 per cent lower among them than is the case with the older generation (Table 2.10).

Table 2.10
No Need for Atomic Bomb by Generation (in per cent)

	Agree	DK/NA	Disagree
Up to 45 years	26.9	35.9	36.8
46 years or more	22.9	43.3	33.5
All	**25.8**	**37.9**	**35.9**

The problem of personal law has been an emotive issue since the Shah Bano incident,[7] where an attempt to equalise the law of divorce and alimony for all women (regardless of religion) through judicial interpretation was defeated by an amendment of the Constitution which retained the status quo in favour of the practice of polygamy among Muslims. Responses to the question *Every community should be allowed to have its own laws to govern marriage and property rights. Do you agree or disagree?* show a greater degree of toleration for different personal laws in the country, than the opposition to such plurality, and higher among the younger generation than the older people (Table 2.11).

Table 2.11
Separate Civil Code by Generation (in per cent)

	Disagree	DK	Agree
Up to 45 years	31.4	23.7	44.5
46 years or more	26.9	28.5	44.3
All	**30.1**	**25.0**	**44.5**

Setting up quotas for underprivileged sections of the population in public services and admissions to educational institutions is one of the instruments with which the state in India has sought to combat the historical weight of social discrimination. In this vein, the reservation of 30 per cent of all elected places in village councils has already been written into the basic law of the land through the 73rd Amendment to the Constitution in 1993.[8] The extension of similar reservations for women to legislatures at higher levels has been suggested as the next logical step forward. The responses to this question have been overwhelmingly in favour for the electorate as a whole, with three-quarters of the post-Independence generation supporting the measure, about 5 per cent higher than the older people (Table 2.12). *Like gram panchayats, there should be reservations for women in Assemblies and Parliament. Do you agree or disagree?*

Table 2.12
Reservation for Women by Generation (in per cent)

	Disagree	DK	Agree
Up to 45 years	9.6	14.1	75.9
46 years or more	10.1	18.9	70.5
All	**9.7**	**15.5**	**74.4**

Unlike women, lower classes and former untouchables and backward classes, there is no provision in the Constitution for quotas for religious minorities. Should the practice of reservations be further extended to Muslims? The issue remains implicit, but deeply divisive. To the extent that Muslim electors are perceived to vote as a bloc, political parties see the logic of conceptualising their interests in terms of their religious character as a minority rather than in the conventional categories of caste, class, gender and age. Since the Constitution prohibits discrimination on the basis of religion, and the Election Commission has stringent rules against the use of religion for electoral purposes, explicit statements of this strategy would be possibly against the law of the country/land. Parties, therefore, often resort to informal quotas for Muslim candidates, just as the government often appoints Muslims to high positions in the government as a token of its commitment to the welfare of the minorities. The practice has been vigorously criticised by the Hindu nationalists as 'pseudo-secularism', which actually traps a part of the population into vote banks—conveniently designed political boxes which are deftly manipulated by vote-hungry politicians at election time. The controversial character of the issue can be seen from the responses in Table 2.13, where less than a fifth of the electorate agrees with the assertion that the needs and problems of Muslims have been neglected. Of particular interest to us is the difference between the responses of the generations: the older generation which has lived through the trauma of Partition has a greater rate of non-response compared to the younger, who are more polarised than the older people, with more of them perceiving Muslims as a neglected minority, but also more of the post-Independence generation suggesting that the needs of Muslims have not been neglected. *The needs and problems of Muslims have been neglected in India. Do you agree or disagree?*

Table 2.13
Needs of Muslims Neglected by Generation (in per cent)

	Disagree	Can't Say	Agree
Up to 45 years	43.7	36.3	19.6
46 years or more	40.0	43.3	16.3
All	**42.7**	**38.2**	**18.7**

Age Cohorts and the Economy

When it comes to attitudes towards the economy, the post-Independence generation distinguishes itself with a robust and buoyant attitude. Four questions were asked to measure the level of satisfaction with the economy in the past and the present, as well as the expectations about the economic future. The answers to these are reported in Table 2.14.[9]

Table 2.14
Economic Satisfaction by Generation (in per cent)

	Past	Present	Future	Children	Average
Up to 45 years	30.4	28.4	49.5	54.7	40.8
46 years or more	24.8	28.0	43.1	54.0	37.5
All	**28.9**	**28.3**	**47.7**	**54.5**	**39.9**

On each score, the post-Independence generation is ahead of its seniors. Significantly, on the two items relating to the future, whether it is about the personal future of the respondent, or that of the children, attitudes tend to be more optimistic for both generations than their respective evaluations of the past and the present.

Age Cohorts and Liberalisation of the Economy

When it comes to the specific issue of liberalisation, for which two questions have been asked, the first point to note is the large extent of non-response, much larger among older respondents than among the post-Independence generation. However, with regard to the evaluation of the measures being undertaken to liberalise the economy, whether through privatisation of public sector undertakings or through closer integration with the world market, opinions of the post-Independence generation tends to be polarised, i.e., some are more enthusiastic and others are more sceptical. *Government companies should be given to private hands. Do you agree or disagree?*

Table 2.15
Privatisation by Generation (in per cent)

	Disagree	DK	Agree
Up to 45 years	35.6	40.0	24.0
46 years or more	29.9	47.6	22.0
All	**34.0**	**42.1**	**23.5**

Foreign companies should not be allowed free trade in India. Do you agree or disagree?

Table 2.16
No Free Trade to Foreign Companies by Generation (in per cent)

	Disagree	DK	Agree
Up to 45 years	22.2	38.8	38.6
46 years or more	19.3	46.5	33.8
All	**21.4**	**40.9**	**37.3**

The opinions and attitudes towards liberalisation should be seen in the context of a relatively strong commitment to egalitarianism, which, thanks to the democratic ethos propagated by India's leaders since Independence, has become a part of the core values of the system. This can be seen from the answers to the question regarding the legitimate upper limits to wealth. *Some people say that the government should pass legislation so that people are not allowed to own and possess a large amount of land and property. Others say that people should be allowed to own as much property and land as they can make/acquire. What would you say?*

Table 2.17
Limited Ownership by Generation (in per cent)

	No Ceiling	DK	Ceiling
Up to 45 years	17.9	10.1	69.4
46 years or more	17.5	11.1	67.6
All	**17.8**	**10.3**	**68.9**

Participation and Partisanship

A similarly deeply-held value is of the necessity of parties and elections for the viability of the political system. So strong is the belief, indeed, that their hypothetical abolition, advocated from time to time and practised for a period of 18 months during the Emergency regime of Indira Gandhi (1975–77), is seen as a solution that is unlikely to lead to better government. While this opinion is advocated by a vast majority of about 69 per cent of the population as a whole, the proportion is even higher among the Midnight's Children. *Suppose there were no parties or assemblies and elections were not held, do you think that the government in this country can [then] be run better?* (see Table 2.18)

Finally, the data on partisan preferences give us an explanation of the tendency of the political and social attitudes of the Midnight's Children to polarise at the extremes. Table 2.19 shows that they have a lower probability of supporting the Congress party than the older generation, and significantly more likelihood of supporting the BJP. Interestingly, however, they do not appear to be more likely to support the Left parties and the National Front.

Table 2.18
Government Better without Parties by Generation (in per cent)

	No	Yes	Can't Say
Up to 45 years	70.2	11.0	18.0
46 years or more	65.2	12.5	21.7
All	**68.8**	**11.4**	**19.0**

Table 2.19
Party Support by Generation (in per cent)

	INC+	BJP+	NF	LF	BSP	IND	Others
Up to 45 years	27.0	25.9	9.8	7.5	3.4	1.1	11.8
46 years or more	28.6	22.3	10.5	7.4	3.1	1.4	12.6
All	**27.5**	**24.6**	**10.0**	**7.5**	**3.3**	**1.2**	**12.0**

Political Change in the Context of Structural Continuity

The data analysed in this chapter help put in context the main puzzle that underpins this section of the book. The issue refers to the juxtaposition of several quantitative indicators of the growth of attitudes supportive towards a participatory democracy with phenomena that appear to contradict them. The preceding section, which intended to account for some of these contradictions by drawing on the generational divide (which is sometimes seen as the cause of such apparent contradictions in attitudes at the aggregate level), has found little evidence of any radical, significant differences in the attitudes of the generation to which the British transferred power, and the next generation which came to maturity along with the new Republic.

The data presented above lend support to the picture of post-Independence India when seen in juxtaposition with the British rule that preceded it. The structure of British institutions—parliamentary democracy, rule of law, a professional and politically neutral army and bureaucracy—remains pretty much intact. But the political and cultural essence of this constitutional structure has somehow become quintessentially Indian. This remarkable achievement belongs mostly to the political vision and experience of the generation that fought for independence and the political skills of the next generation—the Midnight's Children—who have smoothly (though sometimes with more than a little nudge) stepped into the shoes of the previous generation.

This comfortable generalisation of a smooth transition from colonial rule to democratic politics is sharply and poignantly called into question with alarming regularity by acts of political carnage, involving religious communities, conflicts in which the state itself has occasionally become embroiled. These anomalies of political transition in India form part of a larger phenomenon which, for lack of a better analytical category, is simply described as ethnic conflict. This points to a deeper theoretical dilemma which splits comparative politics into two camps—of instrumentalists who describe such violence as yet another manifestation of social mobilisation for political purposes, and of primordialists who, on the other hand, draw upon the cases of ethnic violence to paint a picture of the failure of the process of modernisation and the revival of pre-modern social cleavages, reinforced with modern methods of communication and warfare. Based upon these conjectures, Huntington (1996) hints at a general threat to Western liberalism from fundamentalist movements.

Regardless of the theoretical or ideological stance one takes on the picture of liberal, Western civilisation, which faces a rising tide of fundamentalism, as Huntington and others report, there is no denying the descriptive accuracy of some of the intense conflicts. The modernisation theory, in the heyday of the decade of development following the Second World War, would have explained such events simply as the failure to internalise modern values, and would have, therefore, recommended that the efforts to educate and inculcate civic virtues should be doubled. This paradigm stands discredited today, thanks to the tireless efforts of the disciples of Said, Foucault and Inden, who have exposed the political intent behind such 'Orientalist' discourses. The postmodern attempt to correct for the excesses of modernisation theorists by accepting attitudes and values not consistent with modernity as authentic (an approach which can perhaps be summarised as 'ethnic is beautiful') does not help a general understanding either. From the point of view of the political science of ethnic conflict, the main problem is epistemological and theoretical. Thus, for example, in Kalahandi, Surat, Ayodhya or Kashmir as discussed in the introductory chapter, the problem is not as much poverty, bestiality, religious violence or terrorism, but the difficulty of the actors on both sides of the divide of welfare bureaucracy, state, law and civil liberties as ordained in the Constitution to define one another.[10]

Conclusion: The Convergence of India's *Million Mutinies*

The data discussed in this chapter show that generational difference do not account for the surprisingly high support for democracy in India nor for its contradictions. That puts the onus for explanation on the individual as the main source of the ambivalence with regard to the foundations of liberal democracy. Rushdie's metaphors—*chutneyfication* and pickled nation—both allude to some hard, indissoluble core in the cognitive and ontological make-up of the generation that successive doses of modernisation are not able to reconstitute completely. These positions are contested by the data presented in this chapter, and, will be further analysed in subsequent chapters.

Some of our early doubts about the general applicability of the modernisation theory had attracted us to rational choice theory and its application of an actor-centred, rational choice approach to the analysis of Indian politics. The approach is based on the assumption that social outcomes are the result of the summation of individual preferences. When they are faced with a situation that demands a choice, individuals weigh the costs and benefits of each alternative and make a choice that, in their opinion, is the best for them, or, rather, to use the categories of rational choice theory, increases their expected utility. One can, of course, wonder if an approach based on utility calculations by an abstract individual is applicable to the Indian situation. The most useful way to start is to put specific events in a time-space context. Thus, looked at over time, and in interregional comparison, it can be seen that Indian peasants have reacted rationally and positively to price incentives and to optimal conditions of production. Those used to seeing the former untouchables of India as a suppressed minority with little education and less access to power, would marvel at the political sophistication with which they have engaged in political bargaining in the course of the campaign for Parliamentary elections. Once again, however, if rational choice helps us understand the success stories of Indian politics, for the sake of consistency, we have to try to explain the apparently irrational aspects of Indian politics by drawing on the same paradigm. How can we explain the 'rationality' of the kind of violent frenzy that takes over whole communities at the time of riots between Hindus and Muslims; of the destruction of the Babri mosque; of the mass political violence and terrorism that continues to affect politics in Kashmir and North-East India while the rest of the country is deeply engaged in a largely peaceful and intense election process; or, how, while, following the end of the Cold War, as the West is scaling down its nuclear arsenal, much poorer and traditionally peaceful India refuses to sign the Nuclear Non-Proliferation Treaty and continues with its nuclear programme?

The empirical analysis to be undertaken in the subsequent chapters would examine some of these basic issues by applying the logic of individual rationality and goal-oriented, purposive action. Rather than falling back upon Indian culture as an explanation of these phenomena, the main focus of our research on politics in India after Independence in this book will be to first document them accurately, and look at them in their historical context and then ask: If political actors are rational, then how does the pursuit of individual strategies lead to such outcomes that are not collectively rational? This approach—which we would like to call critical traditionalism—helps us find new meaning in the history of India's institutions, leading to policy recommendations for the improvement of individual welfare. The approach and its application suggests that political actors draw on all possible resources available to them—institutional participation, protest movements, culture and ritual—and help create a dialectical synthesis of tradition and modernity.

Nowhere is the conflict of paradigms more apparent than in the ubiquitous Indian usage of the concept of communalism. What interests us with regard to such conflicts in general is, however, not so much the substantial issues involved, but the ontological and the epistemological conflicts involved. For, if we are to take an actor-centred approach, who is to decide whether the mosque-breakers were criminals, or political actors involved in the transcendental act of recovering their collective identity through a symbolic act, or, for that matter, whether the police is the legitimate instrument of a legitimate state, or an occupying army, representing, as the British police once did, a distant and estranged state whose authority is coterminous only with the force at its command?

These issues belong to the grey area of Indian politics, manifest in every act of public disorder dubbed as a communal incident and analysed no further. Is the stone-throwing, traffic-stopping crowd composed of rational actors, or is it merely an irrational mob, out of its political mind? To put it rhetorically, as the Ayodhya discourse did, should a man, bearing a brick with the inscription 'Ram' etched on it and feeling a few inches taller as a consequence, have his head looked at by a professional, or be taken seriously by the political analyst? Liberalism, under the double bind of methodological individualism which enjoins the analyst to respect both the actor's preferences and existing political institutions, faces a moral dilemma when faced with this kind of conceptual problem. Our solution in this book is to look at the problem empirically through the eyes of the actor, and, based on a firm understanding of individual opinions, examine the further implications for political institutions.

Going back once again to Nehru announcing the birth of the Indian state in August 1947, one can visualise a partnership between the modern state, based on individual rights, the rule of law and secularism, and a traditional society, composed around the concepts of organic identities, custom and a religious basis of social life. Nehru spoke in the name of the nation, but the institutions through which he intended to build this nation were not entirely endogenous. In one stroke, Nehru's modern India wished to move from an authoritarian colonial state to a democratic one ensconced within a liberal society, in which every individual had the right to participate. In the process, he inducted into India's political mainstream the little man, lock stock and barrel, along with his traditional values and lifestyle. Unlike their counterparts in Europe, pulverised by the state, nation and the market, India's little men and women first became bit players in the drama of nation- and state-formation during the freedom struggle, and within a generation of Independence, its main protagonists.

In India, which offers a stark contrast to the European case, a modern state, modern economy and a nation had to be built from a fragmented society with very large numbers of marginal, impoverished peasants, obliged to eke out a living through begging, scavenging, stealing, semi-slavery, and mostly through working for those who had control over land. In addition there was the trauma of Partition, with 15 million people killed, maimed for life, raped, burnt, separated from kin and uprooted from the land of their birth—all on the basis of their religion. And yet, Nehru's brave determination to conduct the high politics of the state as if religion did not matter, and the enthusiastic endorsement of that determination by the new generation of Indians in election after election.

For the student of Indian politics, then, the main difference with European history lies in the fact that in Europe, the nation often preceded the state, the institutions of state were the products of endogenous history and culture. In India, the modern state was born through decolonisation and had to create a nation around it; the state was based on concepts and values that were not germane to society, but had to be inculcated. But, most important of all, the state had to appeal to the marginal man to gain legitimacy for its institutions, and some of those institutions had as their main task the destruction of the lifestyle and identity of some of the same people.

It is this dialectical combination of tradition and modernity, state and society, politics of institutions and politics of protest, ritual of politics and social rituals, which is responsible for the resilience of India's democracy. In those parts of India where it has succeeded, the process of politics goes on. In some parts, for historical reasons, such as Kashmir or the North-East, this has been less successful. But the core of the state is still big enough, and the representation of the elite of the disaffected areas strong enough, for a dialogue between them and New Delhi to be still possible.

Finally, post-Independence India is bound to disappoint to the extent one holds on to the ideal of a homogeneous nation ensconced within an exclusive territorial space as the only ideal of nation- and state-building. The empirical analysis undertaken here shows, both through manifest behaviour and attitudinal survey, that India has actually achieved a different ideal in the form of an inclusive nationalism based on communal accommodation and relentless political negotiation. Perhaps 50 years is too soon to tell, and surely there are many more aspects that need to be examined to give this conjecture the status of theory. But there is no denying the fact that Indian experience and the nature of debate within India, both about its achievements and its aberrations, has certainly produced an interesting counter-example to conventional models of nation and state-formation.

In the light of this experience, we can look at Rushdie's disappointment and Huntington's fears as complementary images of a model of nation and state formation that is not supported by the experience of India and the attitudes of the post-Independence generation. The Rushdie–Huntington model of nation- and state-building is based on the expectation of an exclusive, culturally and religiously homogeneous population occupying a territory which is exclusively theirs. Such rhetoric is not uncommon in India. But, in translating itself into reality, it gets diluted to the point of becoming indistinguishable from its opposite. Contemporary India neither denies its pre-colonial Hindu past, nor the colonial political institutions of law, egalitarianism, citizenship and creation of a public space through intense political negotiation. Political attitudes, with the maturing of democracy, gets both clearer and polarised, but still share enough commonality in order to be able to sustain common, legitimate institutions which continue to be the ultimate arbiter of the good of the whole of society. In the words of Naipaul, it is a million mutinies, converging on a common theme, of a wounded civilisation, restoring its ruptured links with its ancient roots through politics.

In the 130 years or so since the Mutiny—the last 90 years of the British Raj and the first 40 years of Independence begin increasingly to appear as part of the same historical period—the idea of freedom has gone everywhere in India. Independence was worked for by people more or less at the top; the freedom it brought has worked its way down. People everywhere have ideas now of who they are and what they owe themselves. The process quickened with the economic development that came after Independence; what perhaps was only in a state of becoming, has become clearer. The liberation of spirit that has come to India could not come as release alone. In India, with its layers below layer of distress and cruelty, it had to come as disturbance. It had to come as rage and revolt. India was now a country of a million little mutinies (Naipaul 1990: 517).

Five decades after Independence, Nehru's bold vision appears to have found concrete shape, albeit in ways that might have surprised Nehru somewhat. The available indications strongly suggest that the post-Independence generation remains committed to the legacy of constitutional democracy. However, it has found the necessary space to explore the pre-colonial roots of Indian nationalism, to involve those sections of Indian society that have stayed outside the pale of India's political mainstream, and to take a bold step towards political accommodation with India's neighbours. As the analysis undertaken in the next chapter will show, there are plenty of sources of conflict. But overall, the prognosis of a deepening democracy in India remains positive. Perhaps the next decades would see similar developments in the region as a whole, so that the Indian experiment would become part of a larger, South Asian project of democracy and civil society.

Notes

1. References to the concept are many. See, for example, Sen Gupta (1996), where he raises the issue of the continuity in basic values between the Midnight's Children and their elders as a main parameter of the legitimacy of the post-colonial state. their elders as a main parameter of the legitimacy of the post-colonial state.
2. Khilnani (1997) gives voice to some of these sentiments. The recent writings of Rushdie, however, are close to a recantation of his earlier doubts. The convergence with the older Naipaul is both remarkable and uncanny.
3. For the writings of an early doubter, see Krishna (1979).
4. For a detailed discussion of the successful implementation of local-level democracy, see Bhattacharyya (1998).

5. See Mitra (1979). The electoral principal which has already been institutionalised as the most important basis of legitimacy in India came bouncing back following the lifting of the Emergency.
6. Figures as reported in *The Economist* (London), 13 April 1996.
7. The Shah Bano case, filed in the Supreme Court, became one of the main political issues in the 1980s. The judgement in this case, which sought to establish the rights of divorced Muslim women as comparable to those of Hindu women under similar conditions, was ultimately overturned by an amendment of the Constitution. The measure, brought about by Rajiv Gandhi, who hoped, perhaps through this gesture, to retain the loyalty of Indian Muslims, also created a major point for mobilisation in the hands of the Bharatiya Janata Party. The Muslim Women (Protection of Rights on Divorce) Bill, passed on 5 May 1986 'only by dint of a stringent three-line whip to enforce Congress Party discipline' provided a temporary reprieve, but indicated a deeper political crisis on the issue. See Rudolph and Rudolph (1987: 45).
8. For more details on the 73rd Amendment, see Bhattacharyya (1997: 106, 138).
9. The questions asked and the abbreviations used for reporting the answers are as follows.
   (a) *During the past few years, has your financial situation improved, worsened, or has it stayed the same? (Past—improved.)*
   (b) *In whatever financial condition you are placed today, on the whole, are you satisfied with your present financial situation, somehow satisfied or not satisfied? (Present—satisfied.)*
   (c) *Now looking ahead and thinking about the next few years, do you expect that your financial situation will stay the way it is now, get better or get worse? (Future—get better.)*
   (d) *Do you think your children have better opportunities in life than you had? (Children—yes, better opportunities.)*
10. The problem of mutual incomprehension when the observer, representing the modern state, and the actor, deeply steeped in traditional society confront one another is brought out by Wagner (1991).

3

The Limits of Consensus: A Profile of the Electorate

This chapter continues the exploration of the contradictory themes of the norms of representative democracy and communal conflict that have become typical of the political arena in many parts of India. The importance of the theme can hardly be overstated. Despite the occurrence of militant violence and caste conflict in parts of India with a regularity that challenges India's democratic image, the rhetoric of its leaders presents the legitimacy of the process of institution-building and democratic transition as the main facts of political life in India. The eagerness to present a consensual view of Indian society has some pre-Independence precedents. At the height of India's freedom movement, just as 'divide and rule' had become the main political basis of colonial rule, 'unite and oppose' was the main strategy through which the Congress party sought to channel the energy of the Indian people in its efforts to accelerate the achievement of Independence. The mantle of united struggle under the banner of a few core values and the organisational framework of a national movement, as we shall see later in this book, have been the main political capital of the Congress party after Independence. However, as the memory of the hegemonic rule of the Congress rapidly recedes into history and India enters the era of coalitional politics, it becomes increasingly important to ask as to how far and deep the support is for the core values and institutional norms that constitute the Indian political system and the process of democratic transition. This chapter, which continues the exploration started earlier, draws on the main components of the survey in order to explore the impact of the problem of modernisation and democratisation, and identify obstacles that society at large poses for them.

Political Aggregation in the Context of Social Diversity

India's daunting diversity was a challenge for the process of democratisation and modernisation to which Nehru committed himself. It is also a challenge for survey research, through which we intend to analyse the process. The social choice, in order to be legitimate, needs to emerge out of a summation of a bewildering range of arenas, communities and social cleavages. At the same time, in order to be effective, it needs to be reasonably rapid and cohesive. In order to study the process of the formation of social choice and the results of the aggregation of the articulate voices emerging from the populace in a statistically manageable manner, one needs some form of sampling of this diverse and large population, distributed over a continental geographic spread. The specific techniques of sampling are discussed in the methodological appendix. The chapter provides a basic description of the electorate in terms of the main variables that describe its attitudes and perceptions.

Inhabited by more than 846 million people spread across 25 States and seven Union Territories, India presents a very diverse society. Topographical divisions, which kept the multiplicity of cultural and ethnic groups apart, make the country still more diverse. People are distributed in 16 major language groups. The smaller languages and local dialects are about 1,000. Similarly, thousands of castes and sub-castes distinguishing themselves in terms of pursuit of occupations, ritual practices, lifestyles, food habits, divide the people in very many ways. Though Hindus constitute the vast majority (82.4 per cent), India is home to almost all the major religions of the world. Divided as they are into many racial and linguistic categories, the very concept of the Hindu as a distinctive, exclusive and homogeneous category is more a term of political discourse than a fact of social life. With about 100 million comprising 11.9 per cent Muslims, India has the second-largest number of Muslims in the world. Though less markedly so, the disjunction between the Islamic identity as a political concept and as a fact of social life provides an ironic parallel between India's Hindus and Muslims. In addition, there is a sizeable number of Christians (2.3 per cent), Sikhs (1.9 per cent), Buddhists (0.8 per cent) and others (0.5 per cent) who do not enjoy equality only, but several minority safeguards are also granted to them.

These are, at best, the glimpses of social diversities that Indian democracy is coping with. But more than these social diversities, economic inequality and its resultant effects constitute greater cause of concern for the legitimacy of the system. Problems of relative deprivation, regional imbalances, poor means of transport and communication, lack of literacy (as high as 47.8 per cent illiterate), and over one-third of its population living below the poverty line, are all on the negative side of any democratic experiment. However, belying all popular myths about conditions hindering or helping a democratic experiment,[1] India has not only ventured to defy these notions, but has also succeeded, to a great extent, to integrate and unify them all through its democratic processes.

The Indian electorate, which has often been described by such derogatory epithets as a 'herd of voters', has established its credentials as a rational and discriminating body. An *ex post facto* analysis of results of previous elections would show that the peoples' verdicts under the prevailing conditions were by far the best, rational choice one would have expected from them. A socio-demographic profile of Indian voters, as generated from a national representative sample (see the note on methodology in Appendix 1) along with their interest and involvement in politics, level of political information and their views on some of the salient socio-political issues which are being presented here, would certainly help to devise and/or revise one's own objective assessment of the Indian electorate.

The socio-economic and demographic attributes of any survey-based finding, claiming to speak in the name of an underlying population, should establish its representative character at the outset. The national representative sample as presented in Table 3.1 would show a great degree of resemblance with the general population of the country. For example, as against 48.1 per cent females in the population, there are 49.4 per cent in the sample. Similarly, proportions of the Scheduled Castes, Scheduled Tribes, rural/urban dwellers and Muslims in the sample are, more or less, the same as in the total population. In a survey of this nature, a difference of 1–2 per cent between the sample and the universe can be regarded as statistically insignificant.[2]

Apart from these basic attributes (comparable to the 1991 Census figures), other background information, like respondents' level of education, main occupation, and caste and community groups presented in Table 3.1 complement the representative character of the sample and its wider coverage. There are 559 respondents (5.8 per cent) with graduation and above degree of education, 11.2 per cent belonging to professional

Table 3.1
Distribution of Respondents by Background Characteristics (in per cent)

Background Characteristic	Sample	Census
Gender		
Female	49.4	48.1
Male	50.6	51.9
Locality		
Rural	76.1	73.9
Urban	23.9	26.1
Age		
Upto 25 years	24.6	—
26–35 years	27.9	—
36–45 years	20.0	—
46–55 years	12.6	—
56 years and above	14.8	—
Education		
Illiterate	41.9	47.8
Up to middle	31.9	—
College, no degree	20.1	—
Graduate and above	5.8	—
Not ascertained	0.2	—
Occupation		
Unskilled worker	13.5	—
Agricultural and allied worker	18.6	—
Artisan and skilled worker	16.3	—
Cultivator with less than 5 acres	15.5	—
Cultivator with more than 5 acres	10.6	—
Business	10.9	—
White collar and professional	11.2	—
Not ascertained	3.3	—
Caste		
Scheduled Caste	18.7	16.7
Scheduled Tribe	9.5	8.0
Other Backward Caste	37.1	—
Other caste	34.8	—
Religion		
Hindu	84.0	82.4
Muslim	10.7	12.1
Christian	3.1	2.3
Sikh	1.3	1.9
Other	0.9	1.3
Economic Class[3]		
Very poor	30.6	—
Poor	31.0	—
Middle	25.2	—
Upper	13.2	—

and white collar jobs, 37.1 per cent from Other Backward Classes (OBC) communities, 3.1 per cent Christians and 1.3 per cent Sikhs in the sample. It may be noted that even the lowest number, i.e., 126 Sikhs, is good enough for an inter-group analysis.

Against this background, we intend to discuss some of the main findings of the survey depicting the nature and character of the Indian electorate, its political participation, its own hopes and fears vis-à-vis the system, and of course, its views on some salient issues confronting the society and the system as a whole. The presentation would be done both in terms of the responses of the whole sample, as well as in terms of socio-economic groups in the case of salient questions. Since some questions were intended to tap underlying dimensions, the responses would also be presented in an aggregate form.

Political Participation

Voting Decision

One of the first questions that arises in connection with the electoral process is as to what extent the campaign has an impact on electoral choice. We see from the data presented in Table 3.2 that the percentage of people who make up their minds once the election campaign starts is far more than those who had decided their partisan choice before the process of campaigning began. Clearly, campaigns affect the majority of the electorate; they affect more people now than in 1971, and having come to a considered decision, people have more of a tendency to remain more stable now (i.e., fewer people make up their minds on the polling day) than in 1971.

Polling day decision-takers largely belong to the group of people who are less informed, i.e., women, older people, rural people, and the illiterates. Contrary to this people belonging to urban areas, highly educated and males, tend to take decisions at quite an early stage, that is, before the campaign starts. Interestingly, quite a few Muslims and Scheduled Castes have also taken their voting decisions before the start of the campaign. Both these groups are known for their group voting in the past.[4] Characterised as traditional Congress voters, the shift of their support away from the Congress was largely caused by two factors, specially in the Hindi heartland. While the Scheduled Castes (*dalits*) gradually moved towards the Bahujan Samaj Party after its formation in the late 1980s, the Muslims, after the 1992 Ayodhya episode, felt more confident with

Table 3.2
Timing of Voting Preference (in per cent)

	1971	1996
On polling day	26.3	19.6
During the campaign	23.0	38.6
Before the campaign	27.3	22.2
Can't say	1.8	7.0
Not applicable (did not vote)	21.7	12.7

Timing of Voting Decision	Polling Day (%)	Before the Campaign (%)
College and above	7.0	27.2
Urban	13.6	25.4
Upper caste	15.3	27.1
Male	15.6	25.9
Upper class	16.9	23.1
Muslim	17.5	24.6
Scheduled Caste	18.2	23.5
All India	19.6	22.2
Aged less than 25 years	19.9	20.2
Hindu	20.1	21.8
Aged more than 56 years	21.2	22.6
OBC	21.3	18.6
Rural	21.4	21.2
Female	23.6	18.3
Very poor	24.9	20.5
Illiterate	26.2	17.9
Scheduled Tribe	31.3	15.4

Mulayam Singh Yadav's Samajwadi Party and Laloo Prasad Yadav's Janata Dal respectively. This kind of group affinity seems to have spurred Janata Dal respectively. This kind of group affinity seems to have spurred these communities and their leaders to take a position quite in advance. That is why, despite belonging to a group of less informed and less educated people, a sizeable number of them have been able to make up their minds about their voting choice prior to the actual campaign process.

Interest in Campaign

Contrary to popular belief that frequent elections produce voting-fatigue leading to apathy, our data suggest otherwise. The percentage of people interested in the campaign has gone up from 27.9 in 1971 to 35.3 in 1996. But overall, roughly two-thirds of electors do not take any interest in the campaign. When it comes to the disadvantaged sections of society, such as women, the illiterates and Scheduled Tribes, the proportion of non-interested people crosses three-quarters, compared to two-thirds for the population as a whole. Similarly, older people, rural voters, the poor and the Scheduled Castes also have larger shares of the non-interested people among them. The reverse is true as well. Educated people belong to the highly interested group. Muslims and Christians both show an above-average level of interest in the campaign. The distribution of cases in the 'interested' and 'not interested' categories and the relationship with different social groups clearly indicate that people belonging to informed groups tend to take greater interest in campaigns. Moreover, the interest in the campaign is not merely determined by knowledge: it is also influenced by one's level of partisanship (Sheth 1975: 111–33).

Table 3.3
Interest in Election Campaign

	1971		1996	
Great deal	11.1		10.5	
		$\Sigma=27.9$		$\Sigma=35.2$
Somewhat	16.8		24.7	
Not at all		71.5		64.8

Took Interest in Campaign	
Illiterate	21.8
Scheduled Tribe	22.3
Female	25.2
Very poor	30.3
56 years or above	32.0
Rural	34.1
Scheduled Caste	34.8
Hindu	35.2
All India	35.2
Muslim	35.9
OBC	36.5
Upper caste	37.7
25 years or less	37.9
Urban	38.9
Upper class	40.2
Male	45.0
College and above	52.3

Attending Election Meetings

Related to the above findings, greater interest in the campaign has led to greater participation in election meetings, going up from about 12 per cent in 1971 to over 16 per cent in 1996. About nine out of 10 from among women, poor and the Scheduled Tribes have no exposure to election meetings whatsoever. Older people (86.9 per cent) and Christians (88.4 per cent) also do not seem to have any interest in attending political meetings. However, Muslims and the Scheduled Castes join the group of young, educated and well-to-do people who form the larger contingent of those attending election meetings.

We do not have comparable data from 1971, but the 1996 data show that participation in meetings is not just passive. About 9 per cent of all those who have been interviewed admit having taken an active part in organising election meetings, joining processions, raising funds, etc., to help parties and candidates during the election campaign.

Participation in election campaigns presupposes a minimum level of involvement or motivation in politics for one reason or the other. Since very few people have any such motivation, we find such a low (9.2 per cent) level of participation in campaign activities. Women, older people, the illiterates, along with the Scheduled Tribes form the group of non-participants. In the male-dominated society of India, one is not surprised

Table 3.4
Attendance of Election Meetings during Campaign (in per cent)

	1971	1996
None	87.9	83.2
Some (one or two)	9.9	12.0
Many (more than two)	2.2	4.2
Female		7.7
Illiterate		9.5
Scheduled Tribe		9.9
Very poor		12.8
56 years or above		13.1
Rural		15.9
All India		16.3
Hindu		16.4
Upper caste		16.6
Upper class		16.7
OBC		16.8
Muslim		16.9
Urban		17.4
Scheduled Caste		17.7
25 years or less		18.3
College and above		20.2
Male		24.6

to find that about 80 per cent of campaign participants are men, which is roughly four times the rate for women. Participation in campaigning positively correlates with income and level of education, but then those struggling hard for their livelihood would hardly find time to campaign for any party or candidate.

Index of Campaign Exposure

Peoples' orientation in election politics can be judged better by combining together the individual responses about one's interest in the campaign, attendance in political meetings and participation in campaign activities to construct a composite index of 'Campaign Exposure'.[5] The distribution of cases on the scale thus constructed and its relationship with different socio-demographic groups are presented in Table 3.5.

Table 3.5
Campaign Exposure (in per cent)

1. Interest in Campaign
2. Attending Political Meetings
3. Participation in Campaign Activities

Campaign Exposure	1996
No exposure	60.3
Low exposure	24.9
High exposure	14.8

	No Exposure	High Exposure
College and above	42.2	19.1
Male	49.5	23.0
Upper class	55.6	15.5
Urban	56.1	16.2
Upper caste	57.7	15.5
25 years or less	58.2	17.3
OBC	59.0	15.0
Muslim	59.7	14.9
Hindu	60.3	15.0
All India	60.3	14.8
Scheduled Caste	60.4	16.8
Rural	61.7	14.4
56 years or above	64.3	11.6
Very poor	65.4	10.9
Female	71.4	6.4
Illiterate	74.7	7.6
Scheduled Tribe	74.8	7.8

The detailed figures in Table 3.5 need to be seen relative to the column averages. Thus, whereas 60.3 per cent of the sample had no campaign exposure at all, the figure was lower among particular sub-populations, e.g., 42.2 per cent among college graduates and 49.5 per cent for men. The same groups had higher than average exposure as well when compared to the illiterate or to women. The latter and the Scheduled Tribes form the major contingent of people having no exposure at all. Three-fourths of the Scheduled Tribes (74.8 per cent), the illiterates (74.7 per cent) and women (71.4 per cent) belong to the category of no exposure. Similarly, about two-thirds of the aged people (64.3 per cent) do not have any exposure to campaigns. Contrary to this, while males dominate the group of highly exposed (78.5 per cent of the highly exposed are men) the educated people, the majority of whom belong to the younger age group, have greater exposure to campaigns. The Scheduled Castes and Muslims both belong to the above-average group. Interestingly, the former, with 16.8 per cent of them belonging to the highly exposed group, top the list *of all the social categories*, indicating thereby the importance they have begun to attach to politics, particularly elections, through which, they feel, they might hasten the process of overcoming their other disabilities. To most of them, the fight for a share in political power appears to be easier than empowering themselves in other spheres of socio-economic life. In this perspective, there hardly appears any sign of such realisation among the Scheduled Tribes, who lag far behind all other social groups on this indicator.

House-to-House Contact

Finally, we have the obverse aspect of campaigns where, instead of the voter seeking out the candidates, they themselves are contacted by party workers in the course of an election campaign. An impressive number of electors are contacted by party workers. Despite the fact that the mobility of campaign workers was restricted in 1996 because of strict implementation of a 'model code of conduct for the candidates', especially in the number of four-wheeled motorised vehicles being used in the campaign as compared to the 1971 elections, the percentage of electors contacted by the campaigner has not declined. On the contrary, it has increased from 40.6 per cent in 1971 to 42.4 per cent in 1996.

We asked the following question: *Did any candidate, party worker, or canvasser come to your house during the campaign to ask for your votes?*

Table 3.6
Visit by Candidate, Party Worker, Canvasser (in per cent)

	1971	1996
Yes	40.6	42.4
No	59.4	57.6

	1996
Scheduled Tribe	16.2
Illiterate	34.2
Female	38.7
Rural	40.7
Very poor	41.0
Hindu	41.6
All India	42.4
Upper caste	43.2
Upper class	44.0
Male	46.1
OBC	46.4
Scheduled Caste	46.5
Urban	47.9
Muslim	48.5
College and above	48.8

Scheduled Tribes, who are yet to be fully assimilated in the mainstream of national political life, are being subjected to utter neglect by political leaders and party activists. Leave aside the period between two elections, no special measures are taken to mobilise them even during the election campaign. As the data suggest, they are the least exposed group insofar as campaign coverage is concerned. Neither do they have an interest in the campaign (77.7 per cent), nor do they take part in election meetings (90.1 per cent). Over and above these, they are not approached by party workers and canvassers either. Only 16.2 per cent of them (compared to 42.4 per cent for the total population as a whole) have been contacted by any party worker. Interestingly, the Muslims and the Scheduled Castes, along with highly educated people, form parts of the chosen few who have been contacted by campaigners the most, the rates going up to 48.5 per cent, 46.5 per cent and 48.8 per cent respectively. Considering the greater propensity of group voting among Muslims and the Scheduled Castes, special attention was paid to them by the parties and candidates to mobilise their support. However, the highly educated people enjoying special status in their respective communities, and, by and large, performing the role of opinion makers in society, turn out to be the most favoured lot to be contacted first, not merely for their vote, but also for support.

Advice on Vote

Notwithstanding the lack of exposure to campaign activities, for a large part of ordinary voters the period of an election campaign provides occasion for political discussion and mutual consultation, leading to formation of opinions on various socio-political issues. Even people having no interest whatsoever in politics suddenly become receptive and curious to know, at least, about the major contestants in their area. From dictating one's own political preference to others, to seeking advice to arrive at a decision, all activities go on side by side during the campaign to influence voters' choices.

To what extent is the voting decision made by the voter himself, as compared to the decision made by others on his behalf? An astoundingly high percentage of three-quarters of the population claim that the decision was an individual one, when they were asked: *In deciding whom to vote for, were you guided by anyone?* As for those who sought advice or in any case, were advised by others, the interesting point here is that the bulk of such people were advised by the members of their family, and *not by people from outside*—a finding which strongly questions the existence of vote banks and those who engage in the buying and selling of votes.

Table 3.7
Guided in Voting Decision (in per cent)

	1996
Yes	25.3
No	74.7
College and above	13.2
Male	16.2
Scheduled Tribe	16.3
Upper class	23.4
Upper caste	24.1
All India	25.3
OBC	26.9
Muslim	28.2
Scheduled Caste	29.2
Very poor	29.5
Illiterate	31.2
Female	34.7

As expected, women top the list in seeking advice from others. More than one-third of them admit to having been advised, as against only 16.2

per cent of the men. Similarly, 31.2 per cent of the illiterate, 29.2 per cent Scheduled Castes, 28.2 per cent Muslims and 29.5 per cent from the very poor section of the society turn out to be advice-seekers more than the population as a whole, where the relevant figure is 25.3 per cent. Interestingly, the Scheduled Tribes (16.2 per cent) and the highly educated (13.2 per cent) have markedly lower tendency to seek advice in this matter, but, of course, for different reasons. Lack of campaign exposure and lesser interest in politics may be attributed as the debilitating factor in promoting discussion and consultation among the tribal electorate, while educated people, who are known for their independent thinking, tend to decide on their own.

Information regarding sources of such advice was also obtained, and one may be surprised to note that the majority of people restricted their consultations to the family only. More than two-thirds of the total advice seekers admitted to having taken advice from family members. Interestingly, only 7.2 per cent of advice seekers sought advice from the caste and community leaders, as against 69.7 per cent from the family. Negating the vote bank theory, generally construed to explain voting behaviour in India, our data suggest that voting decisions are made, by and large, by the voters themselves. Since this observation appears to fly directly in the face of what one observes in the everyday life of the politics of the nation, this finding needs to be explained at some length.

A simple perusal of politics from India's local and regional arenas shows how powerful leaders are constantly pandering to their own constituencies, where political coalitions based on caste and community constitute the main component of politics, and where caste and religion dominate the discourse on politics. Does this not signify that electoral logic is group-oriented, and that the political calculations of the voters as well as candidates are based on group affiliations rather than 'rational' individual maximisation of expected utility? Two points need to be noted here. In the first place, while the rhetoric of caste and community is the consequence of voters' strategic thinking, the process of reasoning is nevertheless based on the individual's perception of where his interests lie. Caste affiliation, in this mode of thinking, is a convenient tool with which to pool one's political resources. The mapping of caste or religion into political support is thus sophisticated, rather than mechanical or completely manipulated by the elite. Caste is thus an important consideration in the voter's choice, but is a good predictor of partisanship only if the party is perceived by the community to be representing its collective interest. Setting up a candidate from a given caste is, therefore, no guarantee that she/he would be able to deliver the votes of the caste in question. The second important point here is that the articulation of individual interest in the rhetoric of the caste or community has long-term consequences for the idiom of politics, because the perceived salience of the categories of discourse become important fixtures of the political process. As such, the expectation that with growing politicisation, caste and community would lose their relevance as instruments of political mobilisation and would be superseded by class and ideological polarisation, can turn out to be a neo-socialist utopia.

Seen in the light of the above, the data reported in Table 3.7 appear to suggest a complex process. It is possible to argue that the college educated and above might make up their minds on the basis of the information that they have, and their heightened perception of the instrumentality of the vote compared to the illiterate. Similarly, men are less likely to be guided by someone as compared to women, or the upper classes as compared to the very poor. However, the Other Backward Classes, Muslims and Scheduled Castes, given to a track record for pooling their votes in collective interest, admit having been guided by someone in their voting preference. That the Scheduled Tribes do not appear to require external prompting for voting is not necessarily indicative of greater individual political consciousness, but to less political mobilisation, indicative of their late incorporation into the rough and tumble of competitive politics. Caste and community leaders enjoy slightly better reputations among Muslims and Scheduled Castes, where 14.2 per cent and 12.2 per cent respectively of the advice seekers followed their advice. Considering the rather closely-knit character of these communities on one hand, and special emphasis on sectional appeal by the parties and candidates to win over their support on the other, the hold of caste and community leaders, even in these groups, seems to be inconsequential as far as obedience to their advice on vote preference is concerned.

Act of Voting

Passing through the period of intensive political upheaval during the campaign, when it comes to the actual exercise of one's franchise, we find that some turn up to cast their vote and others do not. Who votes and who does not? What is the reason for not voting? And are non-voters significantly different from those who vote? Answers to these questions are sought from the data presented in Tables 3.8 and 3.9.

Table 3.8
Distribution of Voters and Non-voters (in per cent)

	Voter	Non-voter
College and above	82.5	17.5
Urban	84.0	16.0
Female	85.1	14.9
Aged less than 25 years	85.6	14.4
Upper caste	85.6	14.4
Aged more than 56 years	85.8	14.2
Muslim	86.3	13.7
Scheduled Tribe	86.5	13.5
Hindu	87.3	12.7
All India	87.3	12.7
Illiterate	87.6	12.4
OBC	88.2	11.8
Rural	88.3	11.7
Scheduled Caste	89.2	10.8
Male	89.5	10.5

Table 3.9
Reason for not Voting (in per cent)

	1971	1996
Did not know I was a voter	1.3	0.2
Out of station or not well	15.3	8.0
Have no interest	1.1	1.7
Prevented from voting/fear of violence	0.4	0.3
Somebody had already voted before I went to vote	1.6	0.3
Any other	1.6	2.2
Not applicable	78.4	87.3

An astoundingly high percentage of 87.3 turnout in our sample as against the actual figure of 57.9 is not only surprisingly high, but also raises doubt about the authenticity of our survey findings as a whole. It is, therefore, imperative on our part to clear this doubt first. Since voting is generally considered an act of responsive citizenry, there is a tendency of slight over-reporting in all such surveys. However, the wide gap of about 30 per cent in the present survey can be explained largely by two factors. First, the span of the survey period in a given locality was restricted to about 30 hours only, including the night falling in between the two days. Therefore, only those present during this period (barring refusals) were interviewed. The people thus interviewed distinguish themselves as generally present in the locality, and so more likely to vote than others. Fully aware of this problem, the interviewers were asked to ascertain, at least, voting/non-voting information about 'not interviewed' respondents as well. Interestingly, only 36.9 per cent of the 'not interviewed' respondents were found to have voted. This brings down the turnout figure from 87.3 per cent to 70.6 per cent. Finally, as a by-product of this survey, we also came to know that as many as 12.7 per cent of the names in the voter list were of non-eligible voters. That is, either they had died, had permanently migrated, working and residing far away from their native place, or were untraceable to the extent that they could be characterised as ghost voters. If these non-eligible voters too are excluded from the potential list of voters the actual turnout figure goes up from 57.9 per cent to 66.2 per cent, which is very close to the revised survey figure of 70.6 per cent.

Going back to non-voters and their attributes, as Table 3.8 suggests, one is surprised to note that highly educated, urban dwellers and people belonging to upper castes—supposedly more informed and enlightened segments of society—constitute a larger share of non-voters. Greater mobility among the educated and urban voters notwithstanding, significantly low turnout in these groups reflects a streak of apathy that might go against the system in the long run. Lower turnout among the upper-caste group might be attributed to significantly low voting participation in their womenfolk.

Women as a group constitute the larger contingent among non-voters. In the case of the upper castes, their non-participation in voting is 16.9 per cent, as against 14.9 per cent for women as a whole. This explains the below-average voting turnout among upper caste women. The voting of Muslim women is not significantly different from that of their male counterparts. Age-wise analysis of voters and non-voters distinguishes middle-aged people as more likely to vote than those belonging to younger or older age groups. The mobility factor seems to be the main cause in both cases. Greater mobility among younger people, either because of work-related migration, or because of their studies leading to their absence from the place of voting, caused non-voting, while the older people's mobility being restricted because of their age and fear of being stranded in the long queue at the polling booth, explains lower participation among them.

In brief, even though the non-voters appear to be evenly distributed across different socio-economic categories, above-average contribution from some of the groups casts aspersions on the system. Leave aside higher forms of political participation, women as a group have failed to come at par with their counterparts in an activity like turning to the polling booth to cast their votes. Similarly, lower turnout among the so-called better informed and opinionated sections of society appears to be more serious. And, finally, lower turnout among the Scheduled Tribes deserves special attention, specially in the context of their being ignored by parties and candidates during the campaign.

Answers to the question, *What was the main reason you could not vote in this election?* as summarised in Table 3.9 are quite revealing. It is often said by those unfamiliar with Indian elections that voters are forced to vote one way or the other, and sometimes, they are even prevented by powerful interests from coming to the polling booth to cast their vote. As the data suggest, the main reason for non-voting was either being temporarily away or ill-health, rather than intimidation. The proportion of bogus voting has gone down considerably from 1.6 per cent in 1971 to merely 0.3 per cent in 1996.[6]

Political Information: Who Governs?

Related to electors' interest in and exposure to election campaign and their participation in voting is the level of political information which is very crucial to the functioning of a democracy. In order to measure how informed the voters are, several questions were asked. Comparing the answers to the question regarding the identification of the Member of Parliament from their constituency, one can see that already by 1971, a majority of Indians were able to name their representatives correctly. It is interesting to note that while 54.7 per cent could identify the recently elected MP, only 41.6 per cent could identify the outgoing MP. This can be explained by the fact that the mechanisms available in older democracies such as the constituency party organisations and the regular 'surgeries' that the British MPs hold, the ever-present fear of 'deselection' of the British MP, or the phenomenal resources and staff available to American Congressmen and senators to stay in touch with their constituents, and above all, the multiplicity of interest organisations available at the local level that prefer to work through local representatives, rather than going straight to the minister, are not available in India.

The questions, *Who won from this parliamentary constituency in this election?* and *Who was your previous MP from this constituency?* were asked to assess voters' knowledge about their local Member of Parliament (present and previous respectively), and the results thus obtained are presented in Table 3.10.

Table 3.10
Information about Local MP (in per cent)

Present Member	1971	1996
Correct	55.1	54.7
Incorrect	43.8	45.3

Previous Member	1971	1996
Correct	—	41.6
Incorrect	—	58.4

Correct Naming of Previous Local MP	1996
Illiterate	20.1
Female	24.8
Very poor	25.4
Scheduled Tribe	27.3
OBC	36.9
Rural	37.7
Muslim	38.1
Scheduled Caste	38.3
All India	41.6
Hindu	41.9
Upper class	51.0
Upper caste	53.8
Urban	54.0
Male	58.0
College and above	78.3

Comparison of the correct identification of the Prime Minister (*Who is the Prime Minister of our country?*) in 1971 and 1996 helps contextualise the findings. Whereas about 56.5 per cent could correctly place Indira Gandhi after the Parliamentary elections of 1971, Atal Bihari Vajpayee or Deve Gowda as Prime Minister score about 16 per cent less. The difference can be explained by the fact that Indira Gandhi in 1971 represented not only the legacy of a famous name, she was in her own right a mover and shaker of Indian politics, having split the Congress party in 1969 and led a rejuvenated and radicalised Congress (Requisitionist) to a resounding electoral victory in 1971. In addition, she had already enjoyed national prominence as, first, the Congress president in the 1950s, member of the cabinet under Lal Bahadur Shastri, and as Prime Minister since 1966. Compared to such a reference point, Vajpayee occupied this position for 13 days and Deve Gowda, who was inducted into the leadership of the United Front in May 1996 as the 'least objectionable' of the many aspirants for the top job among the contenders, had no national profile at all. That, in spite of it all, as high as 40 per cent of correct identification shows the prominence of the institution of the Prime Minister and people's concern for who holds this office.

Table 3.11
Correct Naming of Prime Minister (in per cent)

	1971	1996
Correct	56.5	40.2
Incorrect	42.6	59.8

	1996
Illiterate	12.8
Scheduled Tribe	16.6
Very poor	21.1
Female	24.4
Scheduled Caste	32.3
Rural	33.7
OBC	37.0
Hindu	40.0
All India	40.2
Muslim	42.7
Upper class	50.1
Male	55.8
Upper caste	56.5
Urban	61.3
College and above	92.0

The point made above is greatly reinforced by the findings about the correct identification of the Chief Minister in 1996 as compared to 1971. At 53.6 per cent, it is practically twice as much as the score in 1971, indicating the importance that the regional level has gained in Indian politics, as well as the legitimacy and prominence of the office of the Chief Minister. It is an important departure from the phase of Indian politics under the Prime Ministership of Indira Gandhi, when the Chief Ministers in Congress-ruled states were central appointees more than regional leaders, ruling in their own right. The rise of the regional arenas in terms of their salience to national politics with regional parties deeply entrenched in the social system is a comparatively new phenomenon in Indian politics. The emergence of the Telugu Desam party in Andhra Pradesh provides an excellent example of such a development.

Table 3.12
Correct Naming of Chief Minister (in per cent)

	1971	1996
Correct	29.4	53.6
Incorrect	69.6	46.4

	1996
Scheduled Tribe	26.3
Illiterate	30.2
Female	39.5
Very poor	42.5
Scheduled Caste	50.5
Rural	50.5
OBC	52.6
Hindu	53.2
All India	53.6
Muslim	57.0
Upper class	60.9
Urban	63.8
Upper caste	66.6
Male	67.6
College and above	89.5

Index of Political Information

Considering the answers to the four questions measuring voters' knowledge about the PM, CM and local MP (present and previous), a composite index of 'Political Information' was generated.[7] The distribution of respondents in different categories of levels of information and its relationships with relevant socio-demographic groups are presented in Table 3.13.

The evil of illiteracy and the meagre means of communication are very well reflected when we find as high as 28.5 per cent of the Indian electorate failing to correctly identify any one of the four important political functionaries. As against this, 40 per cent of them are fairly well-informed. Both these extreme categories, 'no information' and 'high level of information', by and large represent two different sets of people. But then, the knowledge, be it political or otherwise, is the function of exposure to the outside world which, in turn, depends largely on one's hierarchical position in society. That is why education and wealth, the two resultant attributes of one's socio-economic position, have found strongest positive relationship with all the items measuring one's political knowledge. The illiterates

Table 3.13
Index of Political Information (in per cent)

1. Information about the Prime Minister
2. Information about the Chief Minister
3. Information about the current Member of Parliament
4. Information about the previous Member of Parliament

	1996
No information	28.5
Low information	31.5
High information	40.0

	No Information	High Information
College and above	1.4	84.3
Male	14.8	57.1
Urban	16.3	54.8
Upper caste	18.8	52.3
Upper class	20.5	50.6
25 years or less	24.7	42.6
Muslim	27.5	39.1
All India	28.5	40.0
Hindu	28.7	40.1
Scheduled Caste	29.8	33.7
OBC	31.9	36.8
Rural	32.3	35.4
56 years or above	38.3	31.7
Female	42.5	22.5
Very poor	44.6	20.6
Scheduled Tribe	48.4	19.9
Illiterate	51.1	14.8

and the poor represent the bulk of the uninformed people. An item-wise analysis of the data (not presented in the tables) shows that only 12.8 per cent of the illiterate could identify the Prime Minister of the country correctly, as against 92 per cent of the graduates and above. On other items too, only 20, 30 and 33.3 per cent of them respectively were correct in identifying their previous local MP, the Chief Minister of the state and the MP who recently got elected from their constituency, respectively. More or less the same is the case with most poor sections of society. In addition to these two disadvantaged groups, the Scheduled Tribes are the third who too are very ill-informed. Except for their present MP (43.5 per cent), on none of the indicators did they fare well. For example, only 16.2 per cent of them were correct in identifying the Prime Minister. The

Chief Minister was correctly identified by 25.2 per cent, and the previous MP by 26.5 per cent.

Who possesses more political information, however, can be understood better by examining the data on the composite index. As Table 3.13 shows, literacy is the most powerful indicator determining the level of information. In addition to this, only those characteristics show a strong relationship (positive or negative) with information which act either as facilitators or as hindrances in one's education, respectively. Interestingly, ascriptive attributes like religion and caste do not seem to be singularly important. For example, the Scheduled Castes and Muslims are both quite close to the national average. Falling prey to a disadvantage syndrome, the illiterates, the Scheduled Tribes and women all constitute the largest proportions of uninformed people. Roughly half of them have a zero level of knowledge as far as the composite index of political information is concerned.

Another method of measuring the level of information of the public is to ask questions about problems and specific issues facing the country that were debated during the campaign. Two techniques have been used in the survey. The first was the method of the top-of-the-mind score, where the respondent is asked to name problems and election issues as she/he perceives them. The second method compared to the 'spontaneous' answers, is the assisted method, where the respondent is asked to respond to preconceived and pre-coded questions.

Answers to both were ascertained through open-ended questions, where the respondents were allowed to mention three important problems or issues that come to their minds spontaneously. Tables 3.14 and 3.15 present the top 10 problems and the issues thus mentioned, respectively.

Problems Facing the Country

As the list of reported problems (Table 3.14) shows, unemployment, poverty and price rise which hit the common people most, get prominence as national problems as well. While naming national problems, people generally look back either at their own problems or the problems confronting the people in their vicinity, and when asked to name national problems, they tend to visualise the same as problems facing the country. Next in order come problems of an institutional character, such as corruption and bribery, which might have not been experienced by most of them directly, but since these have been very widely discussed and debated during the campaign, they acquire significance. Problems like drinking water, education and health, transport and communication and electricity, are the other types of problems bothering the people. Similarly, law and order problems and the problems concerning agriculture are mentioned as national problems only by a small number of people (6.8 per cent and 4.0 per cent respectively) but nevertheless, the fact that they found place in the list of the top 10 problems of the country speaks for their significance.

Table 3.14
Major Problems Facing the Country (in per cent)

Unemployment	25.1
Poverty and low wages	19.4
Price rise and inflation	16.5
Corruption	15.0
Drinking water	11.1
Education and health	8.5
Transport and communication	7.7
Law and order, violence, etc.	6.8
Electricity	6.6
Agricultural problems	4.0

Analysing these problems by socio-demographic groups yields the following results. While the younger, educated and urbanites referred to the problem of unemployment, agricultural problems and water scarcity got prominence among the rural and older people. Interestingly, poverty does not appear to be the problem merely of poor people. More than the material condition, it is perhaps the frame of mind and one's subjective assessment, largely guided by the feeling of relative deprivation, that force one to name poverty as the main problem.[8]

Apart from the Scheduled Castes, no other group generally considered as deprived, such as the Scheduled Tribes, rural people, Muslims, the illiterates and OBCs, have come overwhelmingly to mention poverty as a national problem. On the contrary, urbanites, college educated, upper castes and the Sikhs have mentioned this problem more frequently than others. Such relationships actually refer to relative poverty, and not to the actual state of poverty under which a large number of people live, and yet do not feel the brunt of it. It seems that other sufferings, which might be only the result of poverty, become more painful than the cause itself. That is why while the real poor tend to refer to resultant sufferings, the people living in slightly better economic conditions, like urban dwellers, and Sikhs, etc., have mentioned poverty in a relative sense. Similarly, the problems of corruption and caste and communal problems have been mentioned more by urbanites, the educated, Sikhs, upper castes, and, of course, Muslims. Maximum reference to communal problems has come from the Muslims, followed by the Sikhs, urban and upper castes in that order.

Main Issues During the Election

Among the issues spontaneously mentioned by the respondents, as Table 3.15 shows, corruption, *hawala* and scams come to the fore as the most important issues around which the 1996 Lok Sabha elections were fought. Unlike problems, issues concerning poverty, price-rise and unemployment are relegated to lower-order preferences. That is why the issue of stability and good governance comes as the second-most important issue during the campaign, and make the debate more political. Despite media hype, the issues of the Babri mosque and *Hindutva* could not become the main issues as far as the people's perception is concerned. Similarly, infrastructural facilities and basic needs like housing, and water, etc., failed to attract the attention of the local contestants to the extent that they have been mentioned by a very small fraction of the population.[9]

Table 3.15
Main Issues in the 1996 Election (in per cent)

Corruption, hawala and scams	20.9
Stability and good governance	10.4
Inflation and price rise	7.0
Unemployment	5.9
Poverty	5.1
Infrastructural facilities, viz., roads, electricity, schools, etc.	4.2
Caste and communalism	4.0
Basic needs, viz., shelter, drinking water, etc.	3.5
Babri masjid	3.1
Law and order, violence, etc.	2.2

Such discrepancy between the problems and the issues can be explained by the fact that issues are formulated by the political elites, whereas problems are perceived by the mass electorate, in the context of its everyday reality. Compared to the 1970s, political conflict today is not on issues of poverty and redistribution, but with the sole objective of achieving power, of which the leaders of the subaltern classes have already had sufficient direct experience. It may be noted that while in the 1971 elections, the most important issues were the removal of poverty on the one side and removal of Indira Gandhi on the other, issues like corruption and stability, which have acquired prominence in the 1980s and the 1990s, had no significance whatsoever.

Perception of Economic Conditions

One of the most important conditions determining the prospects of any democratic system is its economic condition. A relatively prosperous nation, with an equitable distribution of societal resources, provides the best milieu for democracy. Studies on the subject show that 'the more well-to-do nations have a greater chance of sustaining democratic governments than those with widespread poverty' (Thorson 1962: 143). Any reservation expressed against the sustainability of Indian democracy is largely guided by such considerations only. Those who put forth this viewpoint perhaps have little knowledge of Indian culture, which derives its strength from the theory of rebirth, wherein, for most of their sufferings, people blame themselves (the *karma* of previous births) and not the system. Moreover, they have a tendency to judge their present in comparison to their own recent pasts. Rather than material conditions, it is generally the subjective feeling of a person with regard to his own economic condition which shapes his view and/or attitude towards the system.

A battery of four questions measuring voters' perceptions of their own economic conditions was asked in order to investigate the associated aspects of the financial question.[10] Since the issues would be analysed in detail later in this book, we shall confine ourselves to the main themes here.

Improvement in Financial Situation

First of all, voters were asked whether their financial situation had improved during the last few years. The data presented in Table 3.16 suggest an improvement. Compared to 1971, more people report an improvement in their financial situation, going up from 20.2 per cent to 29.2 per cent in 1996. Similarly, the percentage of those who feel that their financial situation has worsened also has gone down from 39.7 to 17 per cent.

Table 3.16
Financial Situation During the Last Few Years (in per cent)

	1971	1996
Improved	20.2	29.2
Same	40.1	53.8
Worsened	39.7	17.0

Since the perception of improvement in one's financial situation largely depends on his or her own satisfaction in life, people having done well would automatically feel an improvement. This may well be the reason why people belonging to the upper-income groups, upper castes, higher occupations and, of course, urban dwellers, constitute larger shares of those who feel improvement in their conditions. Contrary to them, the Scheduled Tribes, along with the Scheduled Castes, OBCs and Muslims, constitute lesser shares of those perceiving improvement. The illiterates are the worst placed people in this respect, accounting for the bulk (54.8 per cent) of those who feel that their financial situation has worsened. They have only 22.3 per cent who feel otherwise.

Satisfaction with Present Financial Situation

Similarly, when it comes to a sense of satisfaction with one's present financial conditions, we find a remarkable improvement between 1971 and 1996. The share of satisfied people has gone up to 28.4 per cent in 1996 from merely 10.7 per cent in 1971.

Table 3.17
Present Financial Situation (in per cent)

	1971	1996
Satisfied	10.7	28.4
Somewhat satisfied	28.6	41.2
Not satisfied	60.7	30.4

A sharp decline in the proportion of 'not satisfied' people (from 60.7 per cent in 1971 to 30.4 per cent in 1996) is quite revealing. More than two-thirds of the Indian population feeling satisfied or somewhat satisfied with their present financial situation may appear a bit unrealistic, but reflects people's state of mind. That is, in whatever situations they are placed today, to most of them, their present looks better than their miserable past, and hence the satisfaction. Since behavioural manifestations are largely guided by one's subjective feelings, it is this state of mind which prevents people from directing their resentment against others, specially the system, for their own sufferings and/or failures. Thus, it acts as a shock absorber not for the toiling masses alone, but also provides sustenance to Indian democracy by containing resentment against the system.

Like the perception of improvement in financial condition, satisfaction with one's own present financial situation also reflects similar relationships. The Scheduled Castes (21.2 per cent), Scheduled Tribes (23.5 per cent), the illiterates (22.0 per cent) and, of course, the people belonging to the 'very poor class' (15.6 per cent) have the smallest proportions of satisfied people among them. Women (as usual) have shown reservations vis-à-vis men, the proportions of satisfied being 25.7 per cent for women as compared to 31.0 per cent for men.

Financial Prospects

The assessment of the present is a function of relative judgement wherein people place their present vis-à-vis their immediate past and the promise of the future. Even if the improvement over their recent past is not very satisfactory, a strong optimism about the future acts as a solace to moderate their feelings about present hardships. Moved by this, people's perception about their future prospects was also ascertained; relevant data are presented in Table 3.18.

Table 3.18
Future Financial Situation (in per cent)

	1971	1996
Get better	38.6	47.9
Remain the same	20.9	27.0
Get worse	18.8	8.9
Don't know	21.7	16.2

Following the pattern as already seen in the two preceding tables, the responses presented here too show noticeable improvement over the 1971 situations. The percentage of those who think that their financial situation would get better has gone up from 38.6 per cent in 1971 to 47.9 per cent in 1996. If one excludes the 'don't know' cases, the proportion of optimistic people goes to as high as 57.2 per cent. Compared to this, the proportion of those who apprehend worsening of their future financial situation has gone down from 18.8 per cent in 1971 to merely 8.9 per cent in 1996. In a country like ours, where more than one-third of its population still falls below the poverty line, there cannot be a better situation than this as far as containing grievances against the system for one's own economic hardship is concerned.

Women are marginally more apprehensive about the future. Compared to men, 50.5 per cent of whom expect a promising future, only 45.3 per cent of women have similar expectations. Those who are educated (college and above), distinguish themselves with as high as 69.4 per cent, who foresee better prospects for themselves. Similarly, urbanites (56.9 per cent), white collar and professionals (59.2 per cent), upper class (54.1 per cent), Christians (59.1 per cent), and, of course, younger people below 25 years of age (52.5 per cent) also show a larger share of people who perceive the future to be more promising. The pitiable condition of the poor (36.9 per cent), the illiterates (39.5 per cent) and older people (40.1 per cent) have once again been reflected when a large number of them fail to visualise a better future.

Opportunities for Children

Probing future prospects further, people were asked to assess opportunities for their children vis-à-vis their own. As the data in Table 3.19 show, a majority of the Indian population today expects its children to have better opportunities in life than they themselves had. In the absence of similar data from the 1971 survey, a comparison is not possible, but the fact that 54.5 per cent of the total population (and 71.4 per cent of the opinion holders) feel that their children enjoy better opportunities goes heavily in favour of the Indian political system. That is, it enjoys credibility to the extent that opportunities for the younger generation are there to better their future.

Table 3.19
Better Opportunities for Children (in per cent)

	1996
Yes	54.5
No	21.8
Don't know	23.6

A comparison across different socio-demographic groups, more or less, suggests a similar pattern as in the case of the other three questions. As usual, the disadvantaged sections of society who themselves have suffered also fail to visualise better opportunities for their younger generation. While the privileged, like the educated, rich and urbanites top the list of the hopeful, the disadvantaged, like the illiterates, the poor, the Scheduled Castes and ruralites constitute lesser shares of such people in them. The only encouraging feature one may notice here is that the gap between different groups is not as wide as it has been in the case of other indicators, such as evaluation of the present and the past.

Index of Financial Satisfaction

Individually, these questions have shed light on four different aspects of one's economic life, viz., improvement over the past, satisfaction with the present, prospects for the future and opportunities for children. However, a composite picture is possible only if we construct a scale by using the responses to all these questions together. An index, 'Financial Satisfaction'[11] has accordingly been constructed, and the distribution of responses in different categories of the level of satisfaction and identification of 'high satisfaction' and 'low satisfaction' in terms of socio-demographic groups is presented in Table 3.20.

Table 3.20
Financial Satisfaction (in per cent)

1. Improvement in financial situation.
3. Satisfaction with present financial situation.
2. Financial prospects.
3. Better opportunities for children.

	1996
Low satisfaction	26.6
Medium satisfaction	50.1
High satisfaction	23.3

	Low Satisfaction	High Satisfaction
College and above	12.0	44.0
Christian	15.3	32.2
Sikh	16.7	34.9
Urban	17.0	32.5
Upper class	18.7	30.2
Upper caste	21.3	30.2
Male	24.7	25.1
25 years or below	25.0	24.5
All India	26.6	23.3
Hindu	26.7	23.1
OBC	27.9	21.2
Female	28.5	21.5
Scheduled Tribe	28.6	20.4
Muslim	29.4	21.8
Rural	29.6	20.4
56 years or above	31.4	20.6
Scheduled Caste	32.7	16.1
Illiterate	34.6	15.6
Very poor	40.0	10.3

The distribution of cases on the satisfaction scale presents more or less a balanced picture, where half of the population falls in the middle, i.e., a medium level of satisfaction. It is balanced by 26.6 and 23.3 per cent on the negative and positive sides respectively. The low satisfaction group also includes cases who fail to perceive any improvement/satisfaction on any of the four indicators measuring financial satisfaction. It is a matter of some comfort that there are very few cases in this category. That is, only 1.7 per cent belong to this extreme group who have not perceived any improvement during the last few years; they are not satisfied with their present condition; they do not find their future any better; above all, they also fail to visualise any better opportunity for their children. Placed in a broader context, they present a cause for serious concern. Notwithstanding their size, it is the degree of frustration which may become problematic both for society and the political system in the long run.

Except these rather extreme cases, the data presented in Table 3.20 weighs quite heavily in favour of satisfaction. That is about three quarters of the respondents, except 1.7 per cent, all others show some level of material satisfaction. The category of 'medium satisfaction' includes cases who are satisfied at least on two indicators, and have no negative response on the remaining two. Similarly, 'high satisfaction' includes only those who are satisfied on all the four indicators, or at least on three, but none from the dissatisfied on any of the four indicators. Both these categories put together account for 73.4 per cent of the Indian population who are moderately or highly satisfied with their financial condition. Since two of the four indicators focus on future prospects (i.e., will the financial situation get better, worse or remain the same and do children have better opportunities in life), the moderately and highly satisfied categories also tell us about the confidence and hope people generally repose in the system. Such a feeling, while saving people from getting frustrated in their personal and family lives, minimises dissent against the system. As discussed earlier, it is this deeply-rooted feeling which might be responsible for holding Indian democracy together, notwithstanding its poor economic performance.

Low aspirations and the concept of *karma* (destiny) seem to be major factors in producing such a high level of satisfaction among the Indian electorate with regard to its own material conditions. But how long will it remain unaffected by the modernising influences of expanding education, communication and rational thinking, is a question that continues to puzzle. Rising economic disparities, regional imbalances and decline of public morality, particularly among public figures, will certainly pose questions in the minds of common people. The moment people begin to aspire for more (the signs of which we have already seen in the political world) and stop blaming the *karma* of previous lives for all their present sufferings, they will begin to judge their present more objectively, and objective conditions being what they are, the satisfaction scale presented here will not remain so positive.

Seen in this perspective, the positive relationship between socio-economic status and satisfaction sends signals in two directions. First, the well-to-do sections of society (having larger proportions of satisfied people among them), may, with their opinion-making abilities, be able to provide sustenance to the system and contain the natural growth of dissatisfaction germinating from the material conditions of the toiling masses. Second, the concentration of less satisfied people in the select group of people like the illiterates, Scheduled Castes, Scheduled Tribes, Muslims and the very poor, may suddenly erupt to pose threats to the system. Therefore, even though the distribution of people in categories of various levels of satisfaction presents a satisfactory picture, the data need to be read with caution.

The dimension of the main survey findings undertaken in this chapter shows how there is hardly any section of the Indian population which remains entirely untouched by the process of democratisation. The overall picture questions the images of vote banks and a herd mentality with which the Indian electorate has been described in the past. Far from being the victim of clientelist manipulations by social notables, the electorate is politically conscious and engages actively in campaigns. These findings, which will be discussed at length in subsequent chapters with reference to specific themes, shall, however, not be seen as an absolute and uncritical endorsement of Indian democracy.

The impact of social disadvantages on participation and levels of personal efficacy indicated in a number of parameters discussed above is a cause of concern and calls for more detailed analysis. In the preceding discussions we have noticed certain groups, basically from the disadvantaged sections of society, who are either less informed or insufficiently motivated, for which they are not to be blamed, but for which the system and the actors therein are responsible.

In this context, the role of political parties comes in for bitter criticism, most of whom have reduced themselves merely to a state of an election machinery. They emerge on the scene during elections, only to be seen again in the next election. The exclusion of large parts of the Scheduled Tribe population from the ambit of campaigns on the one hand, and more than average attention to others on the other hand (Table 3.6) illustrates this point better. Since political parties in a democracy are the main agents of the articulation and aggregation of demands, and as watchdogs responsible for disciplining the government, the next chapter will put the party system in the context of political competition and social mobility in India.

Notes

1. See, for example, the conditions of democratic government as discussed in Burns and Peltason (1963: 22–26).
2. However, a difference of about 6 per cent in the share of the illiterates (41.9 per cent in the sample as against 47.8 per cent in the population) can very well be justified by the increase in the overall literacy rate during the period 1991 to 1996. The overall close resemblance of attributes between the sample and that of the total population, while making the sample a truly representative one, also raises confidence to generalise on the data thus collected.
3. See Appendix 2 for the construction of the 'Economic Class' variable.
4. See V.B. Singh, 'Party Fortune in the Uttar Pradesh Election: A Case of Azamgarh', *Economic and Political Weekly*, Annual Number, February 1974 and 'Harijans and their Influence on the Elections in Uttar Pradesh' in Mitra and Chiriyankandath (1992).
5. See Appendix 2 for the construction of the 'Campaign Exposure' variable.
6. Another interesting observation that flows from Table 3.9 is the steep decline in the share of 'temporarily away' cases from the 1971 to the 1996 surveys. As already mentioned earlier, it is largely due to the shorter span of fieldwork during the present survey. That is, the 1996 survey in a sampled locality was completed in 30 hours as against a three-day period during the 1971 survey, which allowed greater coverage of the mobile population.
7. See Appendix 2 for the construction of the 'Political Information' variable.
8. In the survey we asked: *Now let us talk about the problems facing this country. What in your opinion are some of the major problems facing our country?*
9. The question was posed as follows: *Talking about the election just completed, what do you think was the main issue around which the election was fought this time?*
10. For the exact phrasing of these four questions, please refer note 9 in Chapter 2.
11. See Appendix 2 for the construction of the 'Financial Satisfaction' variable.

4

Political Competition, Social Change and Transformation of the Party System

Institutions, whether explicitly political or with implicit political functions are the interface between the individual and the state.[1] As such, the norms and values around which institutions are often the main targets of political reformers and radical revolutionaries. Political institutions play a crucial double role, both for modernisation and democratisation in a post-colonial context. Since such institutions as parties, pressure groups and elections underpin the process of interest articulation and aggregation, they become the main influences on the nature and course of social change. They also become targets of the process of social change. As such, a society can claim to have become institutionalised when its institutions achieve the autonomy to become self-sustaining. The political elites are, therefore, constantly weary of the process getting a little out of hand. But in a democracy, their hands are tied by the constitution which requires public approval to be the main basis of legitimacy. The practical problem of eliciting consent through public participation and regular elections makes it necessary for the elites to keep the door of entry for new social elites sufficiently open. As such, the old elites remain beholden to a party system which is both an instrument of their will, and by the very nature of organisation, a check on the arbitrary use of power by the executive. In some post-colonial societies, in the process of democratisation, political institutions collapse under the contradictory pressures of new elites knocking at the door, and old notables opposed to any power sharing. How India's party system has managed to cope with social change and gained legitimacy in the process is the main theme of this chapter.

By the very nature of their interaction, the structure of institutions, their stability and legitimacy, become important windows of the process of social change. In a post-colonial context, however, the institutions of the state are an important impetus for social change as well.[2] In turn, since the state is not insulated from society, social change deeply affects the institutional structure of politics as well. No democracy permits its elites to believe that consent, once achieved, could be taken for granted in perpetuity as a source of legitimacy. On the other hand, the perpetual threat of intervention by an electorate could deprive the elites of the time and the space to amass the necessary institutional capital which could guide the very process of political aggregation itself. A dynamic and self-reinforcing party system which would facilitate both elite decision-making and democratic accountability is the implicit ideal that underpins democratic theory. An analysis of this interaction between the party system and the emergence of new groups of social elites (as reflected in the aggregate statistics and survey data) provides some insights into this complex process.

While all institutions are in a way affected by social change, it is the party system which is, properly speaking, 'in the eye of the storm'. Parties are the first line of contact between the individual and the state, and, as such, they are the first to register the change in the tone and content of social demands. The continuing strength and legitimacy of institutions, or their fragmentation, are important indicators of democratisation, particularly in the context of a post-colonial state. Of course, other institutions of state, such as the bureaucracy, judiciary or the army and police, are also important institutions that deserve close study. But considering the breadth and complexity of institutions in a diverse state of continental proportions, the party system is perhaps the most effective instrument to measure the nature and course of social change in India.

As the political backdrop to the social process, the party system has long been the focus of analysis by specialists on politics in India. The question, as to how secure is the future of multi-party democracy and civil society in India, however, has gained a new salience. The question first gained currency in the 1950s when India, following Independence from British colonial rule, was rocked by separatist movements based on language, region and religion. The issue has come to the fore from time to time. It gained salience in 1975 when the declaration of a national emergency severely restricted democratic freedoms and political parties. More recently, in the face of the 1992 confrontation of state and society in Ayodhya, the ability of a democratic India to sustain a civil society came in for national and international scrutiny once again.[3] Has India of the 1990s, a more prosperous and powerful country than at Independence, also become a less secure and less agreeable place for its religious and ethnic minorities? Have democratic freedoms and civic rights been lost to aggressive cultural nationalism, itself paradoxically a consequence of the blossoming of majoritarian democracy?

These questions, asked in the specific context of India, are part of a larger debate on civil society and the politics of transition in post-colonial and post-revolutionary societies. In the ideal type form, at the start of the process of transition, the state in these societies represents an alien presence sustained by a colonial power, or an elite that originates from within the society but espouses values alien to local culture. The quantitative question to ask here is as to what extent conditions that bridge the ideological gap between the state and society are present at a given point of time. Along with social movements and the market, a competitive party system, singled out here for analysis, constitutes three major distinct but complementary agencies through which post-colonial and post-revolutionary societies move in the direction of a civil society.[4]

Though the problematic relationship of multi-party democracy and civil society[5] is posed in the specific context of India, its ubiquitous presence can be seen in rich, Western, industrialised, stable democracies as well as in non-Western societies with fledgling democracies, where a largely agrarian population is making its uncertain way with the help of institutions that are often alien to the local political culture. The party system, which provides the crucial link between the social process and the policy makers, is usually the first to register the emergence of issues affecting the interests of large social groups, or questioning the values that underpin the political system. The rise of extreme right movements in the recent politics of stable Western democracies, suffering from recession, rising unemployment and violent crime, and the growth of political parties which are committed to restricting the public sphere (at least for sections of the population which are different in colour or religion), are examples of the problematic relationship of multi-party democracy and civil society from the contemporary West.[6] In non-Western societies where longstanding commitments to the public sphere on the part of citizens, a history of popular struggle for those values, and the legal and material basis of protest are not available, the emergence of issues threatening the public sphere can quickly take a fatal turn, leading to the collapse of the constitution altogether, with ominous implications for the threatened social groups, the political system and multi-party democracy.[7]

India offers an interesting case study for the problematic relationship of multi-party democracy and civil society. Its rather unusual combination of constitutional commitment to multi-party democracy and social and economic conditions of poor, post-colonial, non-Western societies provides a broad and diverse backdrop. The challenges to the integrative ability of the party system, emerging from rapid political mobilisation of a diverse population living in vastly different worlds, further divided by language, religion, caste and region, have been enormous. In response, the party system has transformed itself radically, and democracy, with the minimum civil liberties that make it meaningful, despite one near-collapse, has survived. The following sections analyse the reasons for this resilience, and its implications for the functioning of multi-party democracy and social change in post-colonial India.

The Empirical Context

The ambiguity that characterises India's democratic record has already been indicated in the introductory chapter. The objective indicators, such as the regularity, frequency and relative fairness of elections, their efficacy in bringing about political change and popular participation in elections have also been already mentioned.[8] Regular, properly organised elections and other similar achievements should normally place India among the stable multi-party democracies of the world.[9] But doubts persist because India's record as a stable, multi-party democracy is not positive in its entirety.[10]

Ethnic conflict and communal violence, which place informal but effective restrictions on free political participation and dialogue, are routinely reported in the media in India and abroad. A rough calculation would put the number of Indians living under informal army rule at 40 million people.[11] Even at the national level, democracy all but collapsed in 1975 when Indira Gandhi imposed Emergency Rule.[12] Democracy did bounce back at the central level in 1977, but then the resort to the curtailment of democracy through the declaration of direct central rule at the regional level has continued unabated. Even in normal times, a number of preventive detention laws, created over the past years to check terrorism, have restricted civil liberties.[13]

To the extent that multi-party democracy and civil society are effectively present, India, along with a few other poor, non-Western societies, such as Barbados, Botswana, Costa Rica, Jamaica, Malta, Mauritius and Papua New Guinea, appears as a counter-example to widely-held beliefs that link stable democracies with high levels of social and economic development (Dahl 1989: 253). Ensconced within the first puzzle is a second one: how does a poor society with no democratic tradition of its own manage to maintain not only democratic institutions, but a competitive, *multi-party* democracy as well, successfully warding off the challenges of non-party, plebiscitary democracy, and strong executive leadership based on popular authoritarianism, deemed by many non-Western societies as a more appropriate form of government?

We need to dwell briefly on a methodological issue before embarking on empirical analysis. Even after five decades of Independence and democratic government in a federal set-up, politics in India still faces a methodological problem of cross-cultural comparability with modern, industrial, liberal, stable democracies.[14] In contrast to the political culture of Western democracies, India comes across either as organic or as morally anomic. Whether it is seen in a well-meaning way or with fear and distrust,[15] the Indian mind is seen as incapable of the individual rationality, deemed indispensable for sustaining the complex political institutions of democracy. Even when political behaviour in India is seen in terms of individual calculations of interest, the very perceptions and preferences of individuals are seen as reflections of the interests of the family, caste and tribe.[16] Since the particulation and aggregation of *individual* interests are the crucial determinants of the existence and effectiveness of competing parties and elections, these presuppositions about India's political culture explain the unreality and unreliability attributed to elections and multi-party democracy in India. Western audiences sometimes find it difficult to think of Indians as skillful political actors, with goals and strategies, and enough information about their political opponents as they manoeuvre their way through the murky world of politics.

The main assumptions that underpin the behaviour of parties and electors in India are not any different from those typically made about voters in stable democracies.[17] They suggest that the peasant, like the businessman, is also an expected utility maximiser, and responds to changes in the institutional context which underpins their daily lives. Electoral information, just like political participation, is a political resource. The leaders of political parties as well as electors are engaged in purposive action, and the sum of their choices constitutes the primary explanation both for the evolution of multi-party democracy in India as well as its occasional collapse.

Competitive Elections and the Evolution of the Party System in India

The party system and elections in India are based on single-member constituencies, first-past-the-post system of plurality voting and a bicameral legislature at the centre. The leader of the majority party or coalition in the lower house forms the government. The President of the Republic normally plays the ceremonial role of a formal head of state. With minor differences, these rules resemble the British system of parliamentary democracy. However, the British party system is the product of the great economic and social changes that rocked society and state in nineteenth-century Europe and produced the political basis for the extension of franchise.[18] India did not go through a similar historical experience. The familiar sequence of the early stirring of the Industrial Revolution, the radical changes in agriculture, migration and the evolution of the working class movement for the extension of suffrage, did not occur in India prior to the institutionalisation of universal adult franchise and a competitive party system. Hence the puzzle: why did multi-party democracy appear in India and how do its people cope with Western-style political parties and elections?

Part of the explanation of this puzzle lies in the history of political developments in India during the last six decades prior to Independence in 1947. A brief perusal of the interaction of the British Raj and Indian resistance to it during this crucial period reveals that conditions for the emergence of political parties were improving steadily. Partly under the impact of utilitarianism, but mostly as a matter of expediency, the British had started experimenting with limited self-rule in issues of minor importance, such as municipal administration, by the 1880s. This formed part of the British strategy of ruling India with the help of Indian intermediaries, in this case selected by a very restricted electorate of urban, rich and loyal subjects. The Indian National Congress was set up in 1885 by Sir Alan Octavian Hume, a retired British civil servant, in order to present Indian interests to the British Crown in a systematic and organised manner. It soon became the leading voice of the Indian middle classes, constantly clamouring for more jobs under the colonial government and for greater political participation. The successive Acts of the British Parliament in

1909, 1919 and 1935 extended the franchise and brought an increasingly greater number of Indians into the scope of party politics based on restricted franchise.

The process was not as effortlessly incremental or linear as it may sound. Periods of extension of franchise and cooperation between colonial rulers and elected representatives were interspersed with ruthless suppression and imprisonment of Indian leaders. The Congress party itself was often divided in its opinion between collaboration with colonial rule, and radical resistance to it on the agenda of Independence. Gandhi brought these two strands together in his strategy of non-violent non-cooperation, and built a powerful mass movement that brought the peasantry and the national bourgeoisie together under the banner of the Congress party. By the 1930s however, the national movement was split once again, this time on the issue of religion. The majority of Muslims, under the banner of the Muslim League, had started agitating for an independent homeland for the Muslims of the subcontinent. As a result, when Independence finally arrived in 1947, British India was partitioned into India and Pakistan. The Congress party under Nehru inherited power in a smaller but politically and religiously more homogeneous country, with its links to the constituents intact. This was not the case in Pakistan, where the Muslim League, victorious at last, took power, but only at the cost of abandoning its political hinterland in northern India, which blighted the growth of a competitive party system in Pakistan.

This brief historical background partly explains the relative ease with which India developed electoral democracy and a competitive party system in contrast to Pakistan. Universal adult franchise was introduced in 1952, and both the non-democratic left and non-democratic right were authorised to compete equally with the centre and moderate left and right for political power through elections. At Independence, the electorate consisted of large numbers of voters who had not experienced direct British rule, and were stepping out of feudalism straight into popular democracy. Hindus, still recovering from the trauma of Partition, became citizens of a secular state which did not recognise any religion as its official religion. Millions of poor, marginal, land-hungry peasantry radicalised through communist agitations, and unorganised manual labourers and unionised industrial workers were expected to repose their faith in multi-party democracy as the most effective method of social change. What should have followed is described by several specialists. One of the most cited is Harrison (1960), whose *India: The Most Dangerous Decades* spelt out a future of communal conflict, disharmony and Balkanisation.[19] Huntington's (1968)

Political Order in Changing Societies predicted structural discontinuity in the face of popular mobilisation.[20] State theorists like Myrdal (1968) in his *Asian Drama* described India as a 'soft state', based on popular consent, which would necessarily be lacking in the authority with which to tackle problems of structural change. Weaving all these strands into a unified and comparative theory, Moore (1966), in his *Social Origins of Dictatorship and Democracy*, predicted a state of peaceful paralysis for India in the years following Independence.

But, as the record shows, elections have been held regularly (Table 1.1). Major policy initiatives have been taken by governments, and parties have alternated in power as a result of elections. On all aggregate indicators of participation, as discussed earlier, India has kept up steady progress. The level of electoral participation has gone up steadily, reaching the levels of continental European voting in some parts of the country. Participation in elections has been widespread across all social strata, and in urban areas as well as villages. The level of electoral participation of women, former untouchables and tribals does not lag far behind that of the national average.

The literature on civic culture informs us that the presence of substantial numbers of citizens opposed to parochialism is necessary in order to sustain the kind of electoral and party competition depicted above.[21] Elections and party competition in India, in view of its politically active castes, tribes and ethnic and religious conflict, appears problematic. The answer to this apparent contradiction lies in the fact that elections and party competition in India have played a double role. Rather than inhibiting the growth of party competition, social conflict (which has got interwoven with political conflict) helps deepen political partisanship. As beneficiaries of the process of political reform introduced by the British towards the end of colonial rule, elections with limited franchise facilitated political transition by acting as the institutional context in which power was transferred by the British rulers to elected Indian leaders. After Independence, the same process accelerated the pace of social change, leading to a second phase of political change when the social class and generation that was identified with the freedom movement was replaced by younger leaders, many of whom came from upwardly mobile, newly enfranchised, lower social classes.[22]

This transition from social hierarchy to egalitarianism has neither been uniform all over India, nor has the progression been linear. But, seen overall, and in comparison with the situation in the period immediately after Independence, it is possible to discern a radical difference in the level of political consciousness of the electorate.[23] A move in this direction had already started under colonial rule through two basic processes, namely, partial enfranchisement of the electorate, and the identification of specific groups for special representation, such as the Scheduled Castes and Scheduled Tribes, and 'minorities' under communal award. Towards the last years of the British Raj, as the competition between the Indian National Congress and the Muslim League was transforming the political geography of north India, the potential to generate power through group formation gave rise to new groups and political parties, such as the Justice Party in south India.[24] These processes set an important precedent for the acceleration of the pace of political mobilisation after Independence.

The introduction of universal adult franchise, and extension of the right to vote to social groups devoid of any prior political influence gave them a new political resource. The right to vote by secret ballot, exercised at a polling booth conveniently located in the village, created an environment which was helpful for political participation. The right to vote in secrecy, and without coercion, thanks to the presence of specially recruited election officers, acted as a direct challenge to social dominance. Since the literature of modernisation warns against the disorder that follows rapid expansion of participation in traditional societies,[25] the question (as it has been formulated in the introductory chapter of this book) is, why did the social pyramid not break chaotically?

The Indian experience shows, while the pace of social change has been accelerated through social reform legislation, recruitment of new social elites into the political arena and political mobilisation through electoral participation, their overall impact on the stability of the political system has been moderated by the existence of political intermediaries and parties at the regional and local levels. The process has been described by Lloyd and Susanne Rudolph as the transformation of social relations based on dominance of lower social castes by those at the upper levels of the social hierarchy into *differential* and *horizontal* mobilisation.[26] Typically, as the marginal social groups discovered the negotiable value of the vote during the early years after Independence, they became avid players in the political arena at the local and regional levels. Established *jajmani* systems—reciprocal social bonds based on the exchange of service and occupational specialisation—broke down to create new groupings. Finally, caste associations, based on horizontal social and economic interests, emerged as links between parties and society.[27] These processes that facilitate social and political mobility and multi-party competition have taken the form of federalism, consociationalism and elite policy initiatives.[28] This has created useful room to manoeuvre in the middle in the hands of national, regional and local elites.[29]

These innovations have been possible in India because of three factors. The first of these is the Gandhian legacy, which gave the first formal shape to the two-track strategy combining institutional politics such as voting, lobbying, and other forms of participation based on party politics and protest movements, undertaken as a rational device of this development.[30] The second factor is the ability of the national and regional elites to transfer knowledge from one arena to another.[31] The third was the availability of the 'Congress System' and the elite consensus that defined it during the formative years after Independence, helping India to build up a valuable stock of institutional capital.[32]

The Evolution of the Party System since Independence

A competitive party system provides the crucial backdrop to the political articulation of competing interests. As such, it is an important indicator of a functioning civil society. Party competition creates the political spaces in which social groups come together in order to engage in competition for the allocation of scarce public resources, and for the assertion of their collective identity and values on the public space. A non-competitive party system denotes the existence of social closure, a restricted public sphere, and of elite values and interests that are hegemonic in nature, in the sense that they are treated as if they were above politics. The absence of a party system altogether denotes the absence of an effective and enduring basis of a dialogue and transaction between social interests and the state.

The party system of contemporary India, as discussed earlier, is the result of the six decades of growth under British rule prior to Independence, which has been considerably reinforced with the political mobilisation of all sections of society.[33] It is a complex system which specialists of comparative party systems find hard to characterise because of the continuous and influential presence of the Congress party in the national political arena, the emergence of a powerful Hindu nationalist movement, the world's longest elected communist government at the regional level, and the occasional lapse into authoritarian rule. The picture becomes much clearer if we divide the post-Independence period into one of the 'one-dominant-party system' period (1952–77) presented in Table 4.1, and transformation into a multi-party system (1977–98), presented in Table 4.2.

The First Phase: 1952–77

The Indian National Congress, successor to the anti-colonial freedom movement, was the ruling party during this period both at the Centre and in India's States, except Kerala which was briefly ruled by the communists in the 1950s. Though parties of the left and right routinely took part in elections which were by and large both free and fair, the fragmented character of the Opposition and the combination of the first-past-the-post

Table 4.1
Summary of Lok Sabha Elections, 1952–71 (Seats and per cent of Vote)

Party	1952	1957	1962	1967	1971
INC (1)	364	371	361	283	352
	(45.0)	(47.8)	(44.7)	(40.8)	(43.7)
BJS/BJP	3	4	14	35	22
	(3.1)	(5.9)	(6.4)	(9.4)	(7.4)
JP/JD	—	—	—	—	—
CPM	—	—	—	19	25
				(4.4)	(5.1)
CPI	26	29	29	23	23
	(3.3)	(8.9)	(9.9)	(5.0)	(4.7)
BKD/LD/SJP	—	—	—	—	1
					(1.8)
INC (2)	—	—	—	—	16
					(10.4)
Socialists	21	19	18	36	5
	(16.4)	(10.4)	(9.5)	(8.0)	(3.4)
Swatantra	—	—	18	44	8
			(7.9)	(8.7)	(3.1)
Regional parties	14	20	20	32	41
	(14.1)	(6.2)	(8.9)	(9.1)	(8.4)
Independents	38	42	20	35	14
	(15.9)	(19.4)	(11.1)	(13.7)	(8.4)
Others	23	9	14	13	11
	(2.2)	(1.4)	(1.6)	(1.1)	(3.6)
Total	489	494	494	520	518

Abbrs: BJS—Bharatiya Jana Sangh; BJP—Bharatiya Janata Party; BKD—Bharatiya Kranti Dal; CPI—Communist Party of India; CPM—Communist Party of India (Marxist); INC (1)—Indian National Congress(-1967); Congress (Requisionist) (1971); Congress (Indira) (1980); INC (2)—Congress (Organisation); Congress (Urs) (1980); Congress (Socialist) (1984-); JD—Janata Dal; JP—Janata Party; LD—Lok Dal; SJP—Samajwadi Janata Party.

Note: The 'Socialist' category includes the Socialist Party, the Kisan Mazdoor Party, the Praja Socialist Party, and the Samyukta Socialist Party.

system of voting in single-member constituencies systematically resulted in a Congress majority in the legislature. This hegemonic position of the Congress has caused this period to be described as the period of one-party dominance.[34] The main ideological doctrines of the Congress party, such as secularism, democratic socialism and non-alignment, constituted the main parameters of the policy process during this period. The Opposition parties were present as active players in the parliament and in national politics, but their role was confined to influencing policy from the sidelines of the institutional process rather than making policy and alternating with the Congress in the wielding of ministerial office.

Figure 4.1
Percentage of Votes of the Congress Relative to the Largest Non-Congress Party or Coalition

* Largest Non-INC Parties or coalition (%)

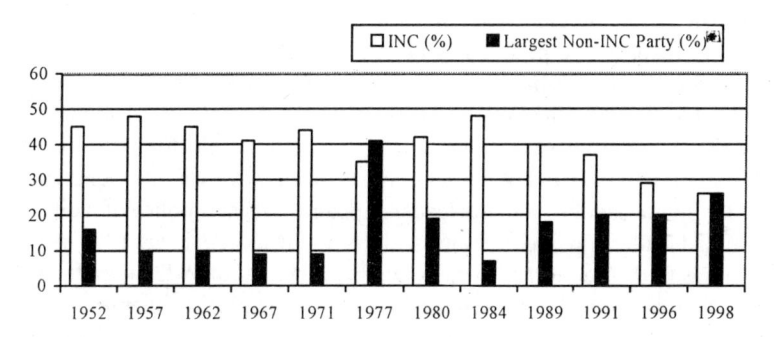

1952	Soc	16.4
1957	Soc	10.4
1962	CPI	9.9
1967	BJS	9.4
1971	INC (2)	10.4
1977	JP/JD	41.3
1980	JP/JD	19.0
1984	BJP	7.4
1989	JP/JD	17.7
1991	BJP	20.0
1996	BJP	20.3
1998	BJP	26.0

The challenge to the dominance of the Congress party had already become clear in the fourth General Election of 1967, when the first coalitions of the left and right took place at the regional level, leading to the breakdown of the dominance of the Congress party in several states. These opposition coalitions were successful in some states like Kerala and West Bengal and became the basis of the beginning of a multi-party system, with the Congress alternating with other political parties and coalitions very much like any other political party. At the national level, however, the Congress party continued to rule, albeit with a reduced majority. The situation changed radically after the split of the Congress party in 1969 into the Congress (Requisionist) and the Congress (Organisation). The faction led by Indira Gandhi, referred to as Congress (R), brought about radical changes in the programme of the centrist Congress party. A number of new, left-leaning policies like the nationalisation of banks, abolition of the special privileges of Indian princes and closer ties with Communists were reinforced with a more forceful populist leadership style. These policies brought the party great electoral success in 1971, but led to the corrosion of its organisational links with the electorate.

In retrospect, the period 1967–77 can be thought of as a period of transition from one-party dominance to multi-party democracy. The setback suffered by the Congress party in the election of 1967 demonstrated the vulnerability of the centrist Congress to broad electoral coalitions of the left and the right. After its initial setback, however, the Congress, under Indira Gandhi's forceful leadership, turned its new policy of radical, populist leadership into its main asset. Its initial success in the 1971 election was further reinforced in the Assembly Elections of 1972, when Indira Gandhi transformed India's successful intervention in the Liberation War in East Pakistan leading to the birth of Bangladesh into the electoral platform of the Congress party. However, the radical rhetoric rebounded on the party when a number of interest groups, including industrial workers, railway employees and students started political agitations. The culmination of this period of unrest was the authoritarian interlude of 1975–77.

The period of national Emergency was imposed by the President on the advice of the Prime Minister under Article 352 of the Constitution in June 1975 as a temporary measure against rising lawlessness. The conditions that facilitate the functioning of party competition, such as free assembly, participation, freedom of information and movement, were drastically curtailed. General elections were postponed and the term of the parliament was extended. Though the regime of Indira Gandhi claimed that the Emergency was brought about to ward off grave threats to the unity and integrity of India, it was more likely a response to the challenges to her rule. Elections were announced in 1977, when the regime got the impression that because of a significant improvement in law and order, food supply and general prosperity, the election would lead to a victory for the Congress party. However, as Table 4.2 shows, that was far from the case: the party was punished by the electorate for the authoritarian excesses of the Emergency in terms of a net fall in the percentage vote for the Congress from 43.7 to 34.5. But even more important was the drastic decline in the number of seats, from 352 to 154, reducing it to a minority in the Lok Sabha for the first time in the history of post-Independence India.

The Second Phase: 1977–98

The General Elections of 1977 ushered in a new period in Indian politics. Since then, Indian politics has entered a period of broad-based coalitions forming part of an unstable multi-party system. Table 4.2 presents the evolution of the second phase of the party system. During this period, India witnessed a situation where relatively stable multi-party systems at

Table 4.2
Summary of Lok Sabha Elections, 1977–98 (Seats and per cent of Vote)

Party	1977	1980	1984	1989	1991	1996	1998
INC (1)	154	353	415	197	244	140	141
	(34.5)	(42.7)	(48.0)	(39.5)	(36.6)	(28.8)	(26.4)
BJS/BJP	—	—	2	86	120	161	179
			(7.4)	(11.5)	(20.0)	(20.3)	(26.0)
JP/JD	295	31	10	142	59	46	6
	(41.3)	(19.0)	(6.7)	(17.7)	(10.8)	(8.1)	(3.3)
CPM	22	36	22	33	35	32	32
	(4.3)	(6.1)	(5.7)	(6.5)	(6.1)	(6.1)	(5.3)
CPI	7	11	6	12	14	12	9
	(2.8)	(2.6)	(2.7)	(2.6)	(2.5)	(2.0)	(1.8)
BKD/LD/SJP	—	41	3	—	*5	17	1
		(9.4)	(5.7)		(3.3)	(2.9)	(0.3)
INC (2)	3	13	5	1	1	4	—
	(1.7)	(5.3)	(1.6)	(0.3)	(0.4)	(1.5)	
Regional parties	49	34	73	27	51	118	100
	(8.8)	(7.7)	(13.3)	(10.5)	(13.3)	(20.6)	(19.2)
Independents	9	9	5	12	1	9	6
	(5.5)	(6.4)	(8.1)	(5.3)	(3.9)	(6.3)	(2.4)
Others	3	1	1	19	4	4	65
	(1.0)	(0.8)	(0.8)	(6.1)	(2.1)	(3.3)	(15.3)
Total	542	529	542	529	534	543	539

the regional level found themselves within an unstable multi-party system at the national level. The gap between the Congress and the vote share of the largest non-Congress party or coalition has steadily narrowed following the election of 1984, which, in view of the sympathy wave in favour of the Congress, led by Rajiv Gandhi following the assassination of Indira Gandhi, has been thought of as a deviant election, temporarily obscuring the secular decline of the Congress (Figure 4.1).

Competitive Elections and Interest Articulation: Political Parties and Social Cleavages

So far we have seen how the Indian party system originated under British rule as part of a deliberate policy to rule India effectively, chiefly through native intermediaries, whose character gradually changed in keeping with the pace of rising political consciousness. This core was greatly reinforced after Independence, when social change and political conflict got interwoven with the fabric of a democratic state. The ultimate expression of the plural character of Indian society was a multi-party system. The issue that we need to address now is what keeps the party system socially anchored and reasonably stable.

A stable multi-party democracy is based on an effective linkage between social cleavages and political parties. The nature of the party system typically follows the complexity of social cleavages. Political systems with the first-past-the-post system, where social class constitutes the main cleavage, tend to develop two-party systems. Those with other cleavages, such as religion, language and region in addition to social class, produce more complex, multi-party systems. India's multi-party system, as we shall see in Table 4.3, exhibits the effects of multiple cleavages. The Congress party, occupying the ideological centre of Indian politics, still continues to be a catch-all party, cutting into all social cleavages.[35] Parties of the left, such as the Communists, and the social democratic left, such as the National Front, tend to get more support from the lower social classes, whereas parties of the right, such as the Bharatiya Janata Party, get more support from the upper social groups. However, religion, at the heart of the controversy about the secular credentials of the state in India, divides the electorate into those who are for a closer relationship between Hinduism and the state, and others, who wish to retain the wall of separation between religion and the state, that Jawaharlal Nehru at the head of the Congress party had drawn on as the basis of India's institutions during the first phase of the party system. On this issue, the Bharatiya Janata Party finds itself closely identified with a strong 'Hindu' position, as compared to the National Front and the Left Front, who have allied themselves on a 'secular' agenda. One faction of the Congress party would like to count itself as a member of the secular front, but, keeping to its centrist character, the party itself tends to be ambiguous on the issue. The survey method provides an invaluable insight into the internal processes of parties on the basis of the perceptions and issue positions of their supporters. Some of these observations would be illustrated below, with reference to particular political parties.

The elections of 1996 and 1998 to the Lok Sabha produced the best results for the Bharatiya Janata Party, considered to be the main symbol of Hindu nationalism, in recent electoral history. The data presented in Table 4.3 reveal the strong support it enjoys among the more educated, urban, affluent and younger voters. However, its vote remains confined to particular regions of India. Moreover, within these regions, the party is identified with particular sub-populations. Thus, while on one hand the BJP has the most efficient vote-to-seat ratio, as the recent Uttar Pradesh elections demonstrate, it might have already exploited the support among its 'natural' clientele to saturation.

Exit-poll data of the 1996 Vidhan Sabha elections in UP suggest that the BJP received *en bloc* support from upper castes (77.0 per cent), from the Lodh community (78.2 per cent) to which Kalyan Singh belongs, and majority support from the upper-income group (59.3 per cent) and highly educated, i.e., graduates and above (58.1 per cent). Similarly, about half of the Other Backward Classes communities, excluding Ahirs, 74:1 per cent of whom voted for Mulayam Singh Yadav's Samajwadi Party, people having education up to intermediate level, and, of course, people belonging to the middle-income group voted for the BJP. As against this, only 2.3 per cent of Muslims, 8.8 per cent of the Scheduled Castes and 19.6 per cent of the very poor admitted to have voted for it. Such a lopsided support for the party casts serious aspersions on it and shows the social limit of its base. Unless it changes its positioning radically, it would have great difficulty in making further progress.[36]

Similar trends are discernible from the data presented in Table 4.3. Against its national average of 24.9 per cent votes in 1996, the BJP along with its allies polled much less from the Scheduled Castes (14.4 per cent), Scheduled Tribes (19.0 per cent), the illiterates (21.1 per cent), unskilled workers (17.0 per cent), and from the very poor (16.0 per cent). The

Table 4.3
Social Bases of Political Parties (1996 and 1998) (in per cent)

Background Characteristic	1996 INC+	BJP+	NF	LF	BSP	1998 INC	BJP+	UF	BSP
All-India Average	27.5	24.9	10.1	7.5	3.4	27.3	32.9	19.2	2.9
Gender									
Female	27.6	23.0	9.4	7.6	3.1	28.0	29.5	19.6	2.8
Male	27.4	26.8	10.8	7.4	3.6	26.5	36.3	18.7	3.0
Locality									
Rural	28.1	22.6	10.6	8.8	3.8	27.0	31.8	19.6	3.1
Urban	25.6	32.2	8.7	3.4	2.0	28.2	36.3	17.7	2.4
Age									
Up to 25 years	25.7	27.0	10.2	6.9	3.8	24.4	35.0	17.8	4.3
26–35 years	27.1	25.5	9.9	7.7	3.5	27.5	33.9	18.6	2.6
36–45 years	28.8	25.1	9.7	8.1	2.9	27.4	32.4	20.5	2.6
46–55 years	27.0	23.6	10.2	8.4	3.5	28.2	32.0	21.5	2.2
56 years and above	30.0	21.3	10.9	6.4	2.9	29.7	29.9	18.2	2.6
Education									
Illiterate	28.6	21.1	12.3	6.6	5.0	29.1	28.9	18.3	4.0
Up to middle	28.4	23.8	9.2	8.9	2.8	26.9	34.3	20.8	2.4
College, without degree	25.8	31.3	8.0	7.7	1.6	25.7	36.5	19.1	1.8
Graduate and above	21.1	36.7	6.1	6.0	0.9	21.5	42.5	16.6	1.6
Occupation									
Unskilled worker	30.6	17.0	9.9	10.8	5.2	34.6	23.0	21.4	4.1
Agricultural and allied worker	28.4	17.8	11.5	8.9	5.2	26.2	26.2	24.5	4.5
Artisan and skilled worker	27.3	24.1	9.3	7.7	3.0	26.9	30.6	23.1	2.1
Cultivator (≤ 5 acres)	26.1	26.2	14.0	6.4	4.9	21.7	32.8	18.3	3.1
Cultivator (> 5 acres)	29.7	34.6	8.2	1.6	2.5	31.1	41.9	10.8	2.0
Business	23.3	33.0	10.1	7.6	0.7	26.2	37.9	21.5	1.5
White collar and professional	26.2	30.8	5.6	8.0	0.3	24.3	39.6	15.7	1.0
Caste									
Scheduled Caste	31.6	14.4	5.6	11.0	12.1	29.6	20.9	22.2	11.2
Scheduled Tribe	39.2	19.0	6.2	6.5	1.0	41.9	25.6	11.6	0.4
Other Backward Caste	21.7	23.6	16.3	5.9	2.3	22.5	34.6	21.0	1.6
Upper caste	28.4	33.6	7.1	7.3	0.4	28.1	38.5	17.4	1.1
Religion									
Hindu	26.2	28.9	8.4	7.4	3.7	25.6	37.4	17.4	3.0
Muslim	35.3	3.1	25.3	10.1	1.2	35.1	6.8	34.4	1.3
Christian	39.9	3.0	2.0	5.6	–	42.1	9.1	18.6	0.4
Sikh	18.3	14.3	16.7	2.4	5.6	21.9	39.8	18.0	10.2
Other	26.5	6.0	12.0	2.4	4.8	39.5	19.7	3.9	10.5

(Table 4.3 contd.)

Background Characteristic	1996 INC+	BJP+	NF	LF	BSP	1998 INC	BJP+	UF	BSP
Economic Class									
Very poor	29.6	16.0	10.7	11.3	4.4	27.3	27.1	23.7	2.7
Poor	28.3	23.1	10.5	6.7	4.7	27.4	31.8	19.0	3.3
Middle	26.1	31.1	10.9	5.6	2.2	26.9	37.3	16.6	2.7
Upper	22.4	40.1	7.9	3.4	0.4	28.3	38.9	14.3	1.9

Note: Parties here represent pre-poll alliances.
1996: INC+   INC + AIADMK
       BJP+   BJP + Samata + Shiv Sena + Haryana Vikas Party
       NF   JD + Samajwadi Party
       LF   CPM + CPI + RSP + FBL
1998 : BJP+   BJP + Samata + Shiv Sena + Haryana Vikas Party + AIADMK + Akali Dal + Trinamul Congress + Lok Shakti + Biju Janata Dal + TDP (NTR)
       UF   Janata Dal + SP (Mulayam) + TDP (N) + AGP + TMC + DMK + MGP + CPI + CPI (M) + RSP + FBL

same pattern of support continued in 1998. Notwithstanding an overall increase in the vote share of the BJP alliance in 1998, the gap between the national average and the votes polled from these groups remained more or less the same. Thus, the lesser share of votes from the lower segments of society clearly indicates an upper-class and caste image of the party. A close look at the same data, however, may provide some solace to the BJP and its sympathisers. That is, its above-average support among the younger age group, among the white collar and professional job-holders and among graduates and above, put the party at some advantage. As all of these belong to the group called 'opinion makers', this may help the party to expand its base in future.

In spite of a net fall in votes cast in its favour, the Congress party appears to have retained the broadly dispersed character of its social base in both elections. The image of the Congress as a 'coalition of minorities' lingers on. Its support among Muslims is about 8 percentage points above its national average. Roughly one-third of the Scheduled Castes, and slightly over one-third of Muslims, Christians and the Scheduled Tribes have lent their support to the Congress. It is a remarkable feat indeed. If there appears any desertion from the party, it is in fact of the OBCs, who have gone to various regional formations and to the National Front and to the BJP. From 39.4 per cent in 1971, the OBC support for the Congress fell down to 21.7 per cent in 1996 and remained at 22.5 per cent in 1998. Similarly, its support among the Scheduled Castes (from 47.8 to 29.6 per cent), Muslims (from 58.5 to 35.1 per cent) and among Scheduled Tribes (from 41.2 to 41.9 per cent) registered a heavy loss in 1998. However, seen either in terms of religion or caste, the Congress is still a broad-

Figure 4.2
Shift in OBC vote for Congress and BJP+ (1967-98)

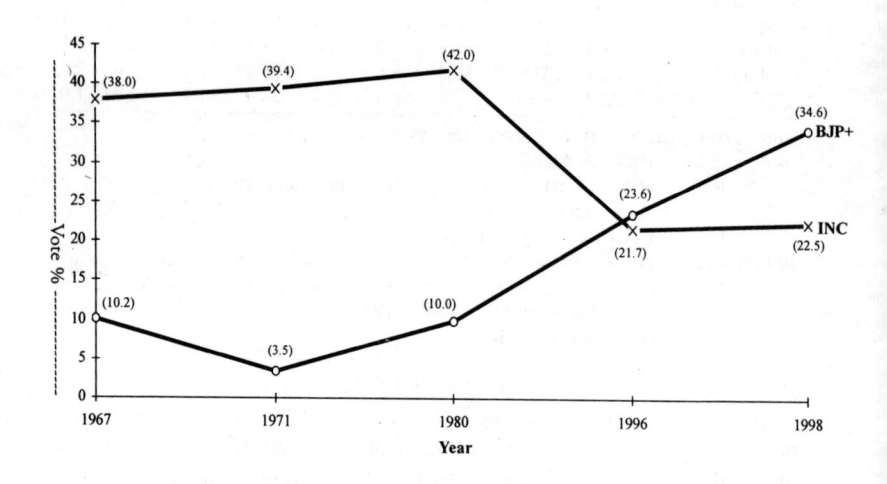

Figure 4.3
Shift in Upper Caste vote for Congress and BJP+ (1967-98)

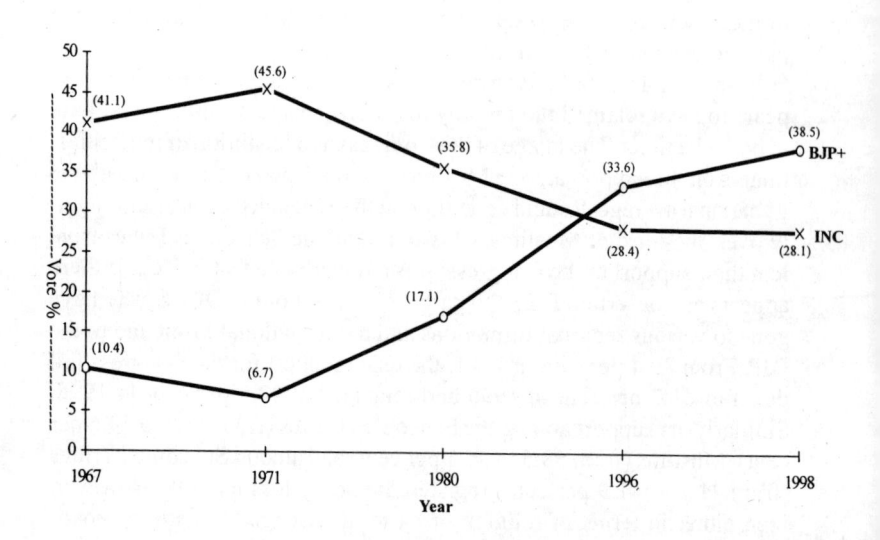

Figure 4.4
Shift in Dalit vote for Congress and BJP+ (1967-98)

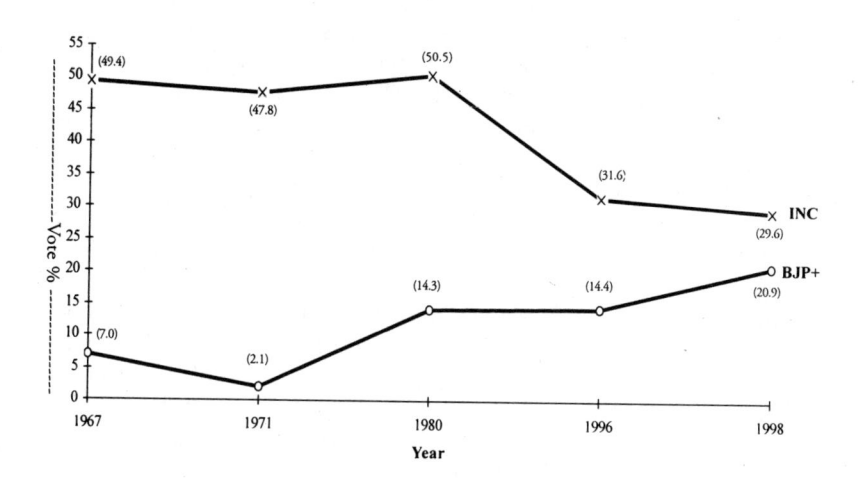

Figure 4.5
Shift in Tribal vote for Congress and BJP + (1967-98)

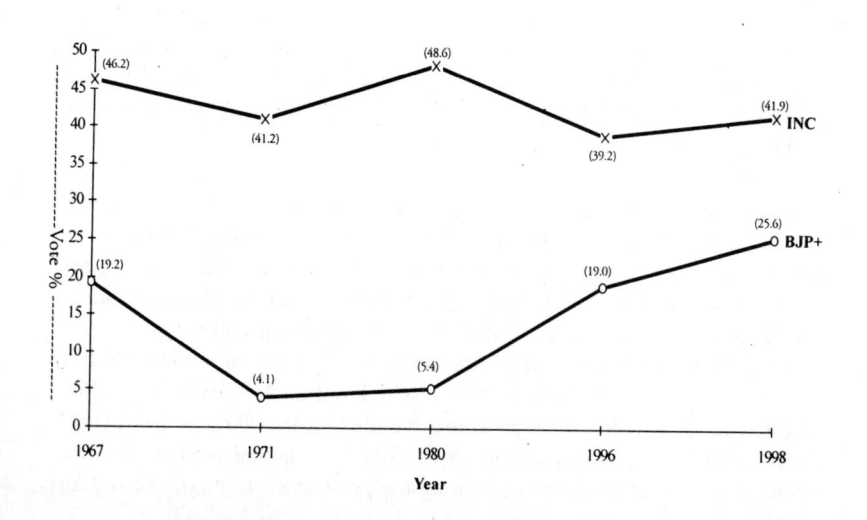

based party—much broader than any of its main competitors in the fray. Both the 1996 and the 1998 data confirm the heterogeneous social base of the Congress party, but also demonstrates, as we will see later, the presence of other contenders (the National Front for the Muslim vote and the BSP for the Scheduled Caste vote) for support from these groups, and their increasing ability to lure support away from the Congress. It should be noted that support for the Congress is proportionately low among the educated and the young, who represent the mirror image of the BJP.

The National Front, drawing on the legacy of the previous Lok Dals and still led by some of their leaders, gets more support in rural India than from urban voters. Its rural character is further reinforced by its strong showing among the Other Backward Classes, where its support is 6 per cent higher than its national average in 1996. At 25.3 per cent, its support among Muslims is outstanding by the standards of its national support of 10 per cent. The survey data also cast a shadow of doubt on the characterisation of the National Front as a party of peasant proprietors and the upwardly mobile and more affluent sections of the rural population. This is seen in the more than average support for the National Front among the illiterates. Significantly, its support among Scheduled Castes (5.6 per cent) and Scheduled Tribes (6.2 per cent) is much below its national average. There was not much change in 1998 except of SCs, where the United Front polled about 6 per cent more than the combined strength of the National and Left Fronts in 1996.

The Left Front appears as a 'rural' party, with its support confined to 3.4 per cent of the urban population, compared to 8.8 per cent among rural voters. This is explained by the regionally localised character of the Left movement, which, from its beginning in the urban electorate, has moved to the countryside, as the example of West Bengal shows. Its support is marginally higher at both extremes of the social scale, with more than average support among both the Scheduled Castes and the upper castes. The picture appears to resemble that of the Congress party. But unlike the Congress, the Left Front draws less support among the illiterates. Its main support comes from low/average-educated and middle-aged people. The 1998 elections also reflect the same, except that their combined vote appears to have improved slightly among urban voters.

The Bahujan Samaj Party—the joker in the pack of Indian politics today—is very much the party of the Scheduled Castes. Two-thirds of its voters belong to this group, whose members come largely from rural areas and are characterised mostly as illiterate, manual workers and the poor class. Its strong support among the poorest sections of the Indian population is further reinforced by the data on education, as the level of education is negatively related to support for the party. The picture resembles a mirror image to that of the profile of the Bharatiya Janata Party.

The relationship between voters' preferences and their social status as reflected by caste, education and occupational classification is amplified when we examine the same by one's ranking on economic class. The BJP's capacity to attract voters from the upper economic strata of society is very well demonstrated by the data presented at the bottom of Table 4.3. The higher the status one occupies on the class variable, the greater the possibility of her/his being a supporter of the BJP, the opposite being the case for non-BJP parties. In order to pinpoint the class effect on vote, we tabulated the data on vote choice by caste and class (data not presented here) and found that class-based support for the BJP is so significant that as the SC (a group which is quite hostile to the party) move up occupying higher rungs on the class ladder, their preference for the BJP also increases, from merely 10.7 per cent from the very poor, to 19.0 per cent among the poor, to 25.3 per cent among the middle class, to 40.8 per cent among the upper class. More or less similar trends have been noticed for the OBC and ST as well.

Considering the converse relationship between the Congress and the BJP in drawing their support from different social groups, we have tried to examine shifts in their vote in different elections. To do so, we have used data from three national election studies conducted earlier.[37] Figures 4.2, 4.3, 4.4 and 4.5 present the shares of votes polled by the two parties from among the four social groups. First, excepting the upper castes, there is an increase in the Congress vote from all other groups in the 1980 elections, and the BJP (with Chandra Shekhar's Janata Party in it) also registered a slight improvement over its 1971 figure which it contested in alliance with the Congress (O), Swatantra and the SSP. Second, the Congress suffered the sharpest decline among the OBCs. Between 1980 and 1998, it lost about 20 per cent, the bulk of which went to the BJP while the rest was cornered by the JD and its allies. Third, there has been steady decline in the Congress vote from among the upper castes. In fact, having taken the lead in deserting the Congress in 1977—we do not have survey data but other evidence suggests that in 1977 the Congress lost heavily among the upper castes and the OBCs—they never turned back to it. Obviously, the BJP was the sole gainer, as reflected in the figures presented here. Fourth, tribal support for the Congress party still appears to be quite strong. It has lost only 9 per cent, from 48.6 per cent in 1980 to 39.2 per cent in 1996, showing a minor recovery in 1998. On the other hand, the BJP improved its share of votes by 20 per cent, indicating thereby the party's organisational capacity to garner support from a largely committed social base in the upper social groups. And despite a sharp decline in the Congress support from among the *dalits*, there does not seem much improvement in the BJP support. With 14.4 per cent of the *dalit* vote in 1996, which went up to 21 per cent in 1998, it has yet to cross a threshold of minimum support of over 25 per cent. Like Muslims, the Scheduled Castes too are proving least receptive to the BJP appeal. Winning Scheduled Castes reserved seats with the common electorate (which is very widely claimed by the BJP) is one thing, and *attracting voters from amongst them* is totally different, but the fact that the BJP has been able to form alliances in different parts of the country may improve its position in future.

Broad-based Sense of Political Efficacy

Established patterns of party-cleavage linkages would be meaningful only if individuals who constitute those social cleavages perceive political parties as efficient instruments for the articulation of their interests. The survey data, as we can see from Table 4.4, provide adequate evidence that such a sense of efficacy is present in large sections of the Indian electorate.

The question, *Do you think your vote has an effect on how things are run in this country, or do you think your vote makes no difference?* was asked to measure voters' sense of efficacy in their vote. A majority of people believe that their vote has an effect on the political state of affairs in the country. The percentage of such people has gone up from 48.5 in 1971 to 58.6 in 1996. Interestingly, though it is very much a minority phenomenon, the number of those who do not believe that their vote has any effect has also gone up, from 16.2 per cent in 1971 to 21.3 per cent in 1996. Over the past 25 years, there has been a steady growth in consciousness of the efficacy of the vote as well as a sense of relative inefficacy. As a consequence, the percentage of those who could not answer this question one way or another has gone down from 35.3 in 1971 to 19.1 in 1996.

Like participation in different electoral activities, here too, we find that the lower social orders have lesser confidence in their votes. Women and older people also belong, more or less, to this group. The highly efficacious groups are the well-educated (79.6 per cent), Christians (66.4 per cent) and people from higher-income groups/classes (62.1 per cent). It is important to note here that even at its lowest, the sense of efficacy is still respectably high. Even among the illiterates, close to half hold their vote as efficacious. The Scheduled Castes and Muslims as groups are not too far behind, indicating thereby their above-average sense of political efficacy. The most important for us, among 'partisans', i.e., those who say that they have voted for one of the major parties, the figure for 'vote has effect' is higher than the national average.[38]

Table 4.4
Efficacy of Vote (in per cent)

	1971	1996
Has effect	48.5	58.6
Makes no difference	16.2	21.3
Don't know	35.3	19.1

Vote has effect	1996
Illiterate	47.0
Scheduled Tribe	47.8
Very poor	50.4
Female	50.8
Aged 56 years or above	51.9
Rural	56.9
OBC	58.0
Hindu	58.0
All India	58.6
Scheduled Caste	60.0
Muslim	60.3
Aged 25 years or less	60.8
Upper caste	61.5
Upper class	62.1
Urban	64.1
Male	66.2
Christian	66.4
College and above	79.6

Political Legitimacy

While the existence of a sense of efficacy at the micro-level is a necessary condition for the effectiveness of a multi-party system, the perception of the system of competing parties and elections as legitimate constitutes a sufficient condition. The larger implications for the relationship between efficacy and legitimacy should be clear by now: an efficacious electorate which does not hold the party system as legitimate would look for other institutions to articulate and aggregate its interests. Worldwide comparison makes it quickly obvious that candidates for selection as representatives of popular interest against the background of a failing party system are indeed many. Political parties are among the main agencies available to people to articulate and aggregate their demands, censor errant officials, and seek to influence public policy. But they are not the only ones. The same arguments have been made for the justification of military intervention, for the political role of the church, *mullahs, sadhus, bhikhus* (religious leaders active in politics), students and all manner of Left radicals.

The survey asked two main questions to measure the legitimacy of the system of parties and elections. The first question, *How much in your opinion do political parties help to make government pay attention to the people—a good deal, somewhat or not much?* provides an answer to the usefulness of parties (Table 4.5). In 1996 as well as in 1971, only a minority of the people was prepared to describe the instrumentality of political parties in positive terms. It is important, however, to make the point that the positive evaluation of parties has grown relatively, from 32.5 per cent to over 42 per cent. Opinion is more sharply polarised now, which is why the 'don't know' category has shrunk from 41.7 per cent to 30.3 per cent.

Table 4.5
Usefulness of Political Parties (in per cent)

Response	1971	1996
Good deal	10.9	9.5
Somewhat	21.6	33.0
Not much	25.7	27.2
Don't know	41.7	30.3

Usefulness of Parties	Somewhat and Good Deal
Illiterate	27.7
Female	32.5
Scheduled Tribe	33.0
Very poor	35.1
56 years or above	37.1
Rural	41.1
Scheduled Caste	41.4
OBC	41.4
Hindu	41.9
All India	42.5
25 years or less	44.8
Muslim	45.4
Upper caste	46.9
Urban	47.0
Upper class	47.8
Male	52.2
College and above	65.6

It is good to find that the highly educated with a great deal of ambivalence still belong to a group having maximum faith in political parties. As high as 65.6 per cent of graduate and above perceive the usefulness of parties. Similarly, people belonging to opinionated sections of the society, like urbanites, the younger age group, upper castes and upper classes have larger shares of people who feel that political parties play a useful role in drawing attention to peoples' problems. Interestingly, Muslims also belong to this group and the Scheduled Castes and OBCs are not far behind the more efficacious sections of society. However, the STs, along with women, represent the lowest shares of such people in them. This is largely because they constitute the maximum number of the 'don't know' types who lack awareness of and exposure to the political world.

The second question (a more direct measurement of system legitimacy) asked, *Suppose there were no parties or assemblies and elections were not held, do you think that the government in this country could be run better?* and the responses show how much significance people attach to the system which provides basis for their direct participation in it (Table 4.6).

When asked to conjecture on a situation where no elections are available (this question was deliberately asked in a manner that highlights the absence of elections rather than their presence), the general electorate overwhelmingly rejected a future without parties and elections. An impressively large 68.8 per cent of the sample disagrees with the proposition that the country could be run better without elections. Significantly, this percentage has gone up from the relative low of 43.4 in 1971 to 68.8 in 1996. In retrospect, the high voting for Indira Gandhi's Congress in the 1971 election did not have the backing of deep trust in the institution of elections which, perhaps, facilitated the imposition of authoritarian rule in a matter of years following the resounding electoral victory of her party. Perhaps as a lasting legacy, particularly in view of the high trust we see in the 1996 data, a repetition of the 1975–77 type of Emergency regime is less likely today. The confidence that the voter exudes in the process of voting is the consequence of the successful removal of Indira Gandhi's Congress from power in the Parliamentary election of 1977.

Younger people (71.3 per cent), the educated (74.1 per cent) and upper caste and class people constituting the group called 'opinion-makers' have come out overwhelmingly in favour of sustaining the present system. More important, they are also joined, at least on this indicator, by Muslims (72.1 per cent) and Christians (73.4 per cent), but interestingly, not by

Table 4.6
Better Government without Parties, Assemblies and Elections? *(in per cent)*

Response	1971	1996
Yes	14.2	11.4
No	43.4	68.8
Can't say or don't know	42.4	19.8

Not better government without parties	1996
Very poor	61.5
Illiterate	61.6
Sikh	62.7
56 years or above	63.2
Female	64.0
OBC	65.4
Scheduled Tribe	66.3
Scheduled Caste	67.3
Urban	68.1
Hindu	68.2
All India	68.8
Rural	69.0
25 years or less	71.3
Upper class	71.6
Muslim	72.1
Male	73.4
Christian	73.4
Upper caste	73.9
College and above	74.1

Sikhs, who, at 62.7 per cent, are 6 per cent lower than the national average. The positive evaluation of the political system based on parties and elections by the better informed and the minority Muslims reinforces the picture of steady empowerment of the electorate through participation in electoral politics. Against this background, below the average support that elections and parties receive from Sikhs can perhaps be understood in terms of the failure of the system based on parties and elections during the long years of political unrest in Punjab which led to one of the longest stretches of direct rule by the Centre. The most encouraging feature reflected by these data (Table 4.6) is that it cuts across all social boundaries, as there are very small gaps between different sections of the society, at least on this indicator. Informed or uninformed, rich or poor, male or female, etc., all of them feel, more less, alike.

Cross-cutting Value Conflict and Partisan Competition

The demolition of the Babri masjid at Ayodhya on 6 December 1992 was one of the most important landmarks in Indian politics after Independence. The world media and the Indian press have consistently focused on it as a key issue in Indian politics, and a key indicator of civil society in India. The interesting point to note here is that, contrary to speculations in the media, Indian opinion is neither as homogeneous nor as hostile to Muslims as one is led to believe. Of all those who express an opinion on it, 63 per cent do not believe that the demolition was justified.

The Babri mosque in Ayodhya has been used as a bone of contention by religious extremists on both sides for ages, but what happened in 1992 rocked the nation. The mosque was demolished by *kar sevaks* (voluntary workers), activists of the Vishwa Hindu Parishad and the Bajrang Dal, supposedly with the connivance of the BJP which headed the state government at that time. Many places in the country witnessed the worst communal riots of their kind; people got divided, albeit temporarily, and the BJP was isolated by almost all the political parties of the country.

Interest in the data on the attitudes towards the destruction of the Babri mosque arises from the fact that in view of the propagation in the media of the spectre of Hindu fundamentalism, one would expect an internally undifferentiated phalanx of Hindus (and Muslims) taking radically opposite stances. However, when the electorate was asked to pass a judgement whether it considered the demolition justified or unjustified, it largely condemned the act as unjustified. Only 22.7 per cent of the Indian electorate found the demolition justified. Against this, 38.1 per cent termed it as unjustified. A large section of 39.2 per cent had either not heard about this episode, or failed to take a definite position on it. If one decides to exclude 'non-opinion' cases, the share of those condemning the act goes up to 62.6 per cent, as compared to 37.4 per cent of those who justified the demolition. Considering the opinion holders only, while 97.8 per cent of Muslims found the act unjustified, a majority of Hindus (54.4 per cent) have also expressed the same opinion.

A closer look at Table 4.7 suggests that people with greater information and exposure constitute larger shares of those who have found the demolition unjustified. For example, people belonging to urban areas, the highly educated, the upper castes and upper classes, do not approve of the demolition. Similarly, party-wise analysis of justified and unjustified responses also does not show much polarisation on this line. Except the Left Front

(9.1 per cent) all other parties have significant shares of those who justified the demolition. For example, as against 40.7 per cent of the BJP voters, 16.5 per cent of the Congress, 24.1 per cent of the NF and 27.3 per cent of the BSP voters come from those who happened to have justified the act. More important, as many as one-fourth (25.7 per cent) of the BJP supporters have condemned the act of demolition. If the 'don't know' and 'not-heard' cases are excluded, all parties have sizeable proportions of support from both groups. While the larger share of the 'justified' category in the BJP support reflects its north Indian bias, sizeable support from amongst those condemning the act shows a limit beyond which the BJP can not go to capitalise on its *Hindutva* stand.

Table 4.7
Partisan Response to the Demolition of Babri Mosque (in per cent)

	INC	BJP+	NF	LF	BSP	Total
Unjustified	42.9	25.7	48.2	54.9	26.7	**38.1**
Don't know	8.0	11.4	7.6	9.2	19.9	**10.2**
Justified	16.5	40.7	24.1	9.1	27.3	**22.7**
Not heard about demolition	32.6	22.2	20.0	26.9	26.1	**29.0**

Demolition was not Justified	(%)
Scheduled Tribe	18.6
Illiterate	23.8
Very poor	29.3
Hindu	31.6
Female	32.0
Scheduled Caste	33.3
56 years or above	33.7
Rural	34.2
OBC	37.5
25 years or less	37.9
All India	38.1
Upper class	40.7
Male	44.0
Upper caste	46.6
Urban	50.3
College and above	59.6
Muslim	86.3

People's responses to an emotive issue like Kashmir also do not show any communal bias. Giving credence to their secular values, 33.4 per cent of Indian electors have rejected the option of suppressing the agitation by any means. Of the opinion holders, as many as 75.6 per cent have suggested that the problem of Kashmir cannot be solved by using suppressive measures, but by negotiations only.

The suggestion to resolve the Kashmir problem through negotiation receives support from almost all relevant segments of society. That is, roughly half of the urban population, the upper castes and upper classes are in favour of negotiation. Muslims have a slightly higher percentage of such people, but the maximum support it receives from the highly educated people (62.1 per cent) followed by urban dwellers, indicates thereby greater scope for a peaceful solution of the problem.

Responses to the question, *People's opinions are divided on the issue of the Kashmir problem—some people say that the government should suppress the agitation by any means, while others say that this problem should be resolved by negotiations. What would you say, should the agitation be suppressed or resolved by negotiations?* are presented in Table 4.8.

Table 4.8
Partisan Opinion on Resolution of Kashmir Problem (in per cent)

	INC	BJP+	NF	LF	BSP	**Total**
Negotiation	33.8	34.7	32.6	32.9	25.5	**33.4**
Can't say	32.8	26.4	30.7	28.7	28.9	**32.0**
Should be suppressed	9.7	17.5	11.0	4.9	14.3	**11.1**
Not heard of Kashmir	21.2	19.8	23.3	32.2	30.7	**21.6**

Kashmir Problem to be Solved by Negotiation	(%)
Illiterate	15.3
Very poor	18.3
Scheduled Tribe	20.5
Female	24.7
Scheduled Caste	25.4
Rural	28.7
56 years or above	29.6
Hindu	31.3
OBC	33.0
All India	33.4
25 years or less	37.5
Upper class	39.2
Upper caste	41.7
Male	41.9
Muslim	45.7
Urban	48.5
College and above	62.1

Like views on the demolition issue, except the Left Front all other parties have, more or less, equal shares in those who support the resolution of the Kashmir problem by force. Of course, the BJP accounts for slightly above the average, and the Congress falls slightly below it. But the fact that all parties have received one-third of their support from those advocating resolution through negotiations puts the problem in the right perspective. This finding is a dissuading factor indeed, for parties as well as their leaders, to take any unpopular stand on it.

The same positive attitude of religious and regional reconciliation within India is also reflected in attitudes towards Pakistan. Those who suggest that India should make more efforts to develop friendly relations with Pakistan outnumber those who suggest the opposite, or do not have an opinion on the issue. If we consider only those who are either for friendly relations or its opposite, the percentage of those in favour of friendly relations goes up to 72.

People's views on Indo-Pak relations are positively in favour of negotiation. The people of India, by and large, want that the government should make more efforts to develop friendly relations with Pakistan. Not only do 44.5 per cent of the total sample or 71.7 per cent of the opinion holders support the development of friendly relations, but the people who matter in building national opinion have come forward to lend more support than the non-opinionated sections of society. For example, against an all-India average of 44.5 per cent, urban dwellers (59.3 per cent), people pursuing high ranking occupations (61.8 per cent), the well-educated (68.2 per cent), the rich (49.8 per cent) and the upper caste (51.9 per cent) agreed to the proposition that India should make more efforts to develop friendly relations with Pakistan. Muslims, the worst sufferers from the hostility between the two governments, have supported this viewpoint overwhelmingly: 72.5 per cent of them want friendly relations with Pakistan, compared to 40.8 per cent of Hindus and 44.5 per cent for the population as a whole.

A certain congruence of opinion across parties, at least on national issues, is once again reflected by the data presented in Table 4.9. There are hardly any major variations in the proportions of votes different political parties have received from those advocating friendly relations with Pakistan or opposing it. The National Front and the BSP with 51.8 per cent and 50.0 per cent respectively have received most of their support from the pro-friendship group, but then it reflects their above-average appeal among Muslims. The Congress and the Left Front represent the national average, while the BJP accounts for slightly above the average from among those who disagree with this proposition.

Table 4.9
India should Develop Friendly Relations with Pakistan (in per cent)

Response	INC	BJP+	NF	LF	BSP	Total
Disagree	17.1	23.4	11.6	17.4	12.4	**17.6**
Don't know/No opinion	37.0	34.5	36.6	37.3	37.6	**37.9**
Agree	45.8	42.1	51.8	45.3	50.0	**44.5**

Develop Friendly Relations with Pakistan	
Illiterate	30.4
Scheduled Tribe	32.5
Very poor	33.0
Female	36.5
Scheduled Caste	39.4
Rural	39.8
Hindu	40.8
56 years or above	43.2
OBC	43.2
All India	44.5
25 years or less	46.8
Upper class	49.8
Upper caste	51.9
Male	52.2
Urban	59.3
College and above	68.2
Muslim	72.5

The issue of a common personal law for all Indians is one of the most important issues facing the country today. In this context, it is interesting to note here that a significant percentage of Indians are willing to concede to each community the right to retain its own personal law in the areas of marriage and property rights.

The issue reflects the tensions regarding the unresolved issue of identity and nationhood in India. Proponents of an exclusive definition of a nation in India plead for a uniform law on all aspects of life. This position, very strongly propagated by the BJP, gets far less support than the more inclusive view of nationalism in India. An impressive 44.4 per cent of the total sample, or 60 per cent of the opinion holders, say that every community should be allowed to have its own laws to govern marriage and property rights. Against this, only 30.4 per cent say the opposite and the rest, that is 25 per cent, fail to express any opinion on it. It is true that Muslims have lent greater support (67.1 per cent) to the idea of having or continuing with a separate Civil Code, but the fact that their stand is also supported by the majority community makes a strong case for continuing with the present law. However, this has a caveat to it, that is, like Muslim personal law, other communities would also like to enjoy autonomy, at least on governing their marriage and property rights.

In order to measure attitudes towards personal law, the survey asked: *Every community should be allowed to have its own laws to govern marriage and property rights. Do you agree or disagree?* The responses are presented in Table 4.10.

Table 4.10
Need for Separate Civil Code for Every Community by Party Support (in per cent)

Response	INC	BJP+	NF	LF	BSP	Total
Disagree	29.9	36.5	29.4	22.1	30.4	**30.4**
Don't know	23.8	22.9	28.5	18.2	24.8	**25.1**
Agree	46.3	40.6	42.2	59.6	44.7	**44.4**

Support for Separate Civil Code	
Hindu	41.5
All India	44.5
Christian	50.2
Sikh	51.6
Muslim	67.1

Judging the above, there is considerable support within the electorate for a civil society in India. Of course, there is greater sensitivity among Muslims for their own community to have the right to define the scope of their social institutions similar to other minority communities, also concerned about their personal law. However, this position is supported by a considerable section within the majority community, as well as across the broad spectrum of India's political parties, including the supporters of the Hindu nationalist Bharatiya Janata Party.

Conclusion

The analysis undertaken in this chapter has shown how well established political parties and elections have become as the preferred method of political and social change in India. However, while the legitimacy and efficacy of a political party as an institution is clearly borne out by the evidence presented here, the same cannot be said about the politicians who actually run these institutions. To that extent, the survey data closely reflect the sordid picture of scandals, corruption and illegal transactions on the part of politicians high and low that are routinely reported by the media.

This creates a paradoxical situation, where people routinely turn out for elections, participate enthusiastically in the voting, and witness the swearing in of elected governments. However, the low trust reposed in politicians leads to disenchantment at the first indication of wrong-doing. As any number of reports from the obsessive interest of the media in post-election revelations of corrupt regional and national ministers would indicate, the combination of high trust in elections but low trust in politicians leads to a situation where efforts to establish trust replace the real business of government, which is to govern through the enactment and implementation of public policy. The systemic implications of this phenomenon would be examined in detail later in the book. We shall next turn to another interesting characteristic of the politics of social change in India, namely, the juxtaposition of the assertion of regional identity in the context of the efforts to promote national unity.

Notes

1. North (1990: 3) defines the role of institutions in the political process as follows: 'Institutions are the rules of the game in a society or, more formally, are the humanly devised constraints that shape human interaction. In consequence they structure incentives in human exchange, whether political, social, or economic. Institutional change shapes the way societies evolve through time and hence is the way to understanding historical change.'
2. Rudolph and Rudolph (1987) refer to the leading role of the state as 'state dominated pluralism'.
3. Some of the values that constitute the basis of civil society in India, such as equal citizenship, rights of participation, occupation and association, freedom of worship and practice, movement and residence, are defined in the preamble and article 19 of the Constitution of India. The empirical research agenda on civil society in India consists of the measurement of these rights and their perception at the level of the masses.
4. Considering the fact that the concept of civil society originated from Western historical experience, its application to contexts with different historical trajectories and social characteristics can be problematic. It is important to conceptualise the formation of civil society in quantitative terms, so as to avoid the possible incursions into cultural relativism. Otherwise, the scientific question tends to get mired in a polemical debate on national values or in a vague search for the true meaning of

democracy. Such debates make sense in the context of a philosophical analysis of the formation of civil society. For further discussion of this point, see White, Howell and Xiaoyuan (1996: 1–6).

5. This can be seen as a collective goods problem. The problem arises from the fact that parties, locked in competition as they are for increasing their share of the vote, must cater to the political needs of the electorate. On the other hand, by individually committing themselves to political and racial intolerance, they might contribute to the demise of those political and civil liberties that make party competition possible in the first place.

6. The political crisis being faced by the centre-right government in France which intends to restrict immigration is an example of both the nature of the crisis as well as of the ability and willingness of citizen groups to engage in political protest in order to defend the threatened public sphere. The problem of political parties in general, and the left in particular, arises from the fact that public opinion is divided, with an articulate section of French intellectuals expressing their commitment to the Rights of Man which form part of the legacy of the French Revolution while two-thirds of the people saying that 'there are too many Arabs' in France (*The Economist*, p. 32, 1–7 March 1991). For a detailed case study of the rise of the extreme right in France, see Brechon and Mitra (1992).

7. The difficulty of providing the conditions for political dialogue hindered the functioning of multi-party democracy in Pakistan, eventually leading to the Liberation War and the creation of Bangladesh, and currently plagues the political process in Sri Lanka.

8. 'A deeply divided society with, supposedly, a mainly majoritarian type of democracy, India nevertheless has been able to maintain its democratic system' Lijphart (1996: 258). Lijphart describes the institutionalisation of a sophisticated system of power sharing as the main cause of success in maintaining democratic institutions.

9. Both inflation and explosive population growth have been tamed. And now, with the liberalisation of India's economy, international business confidence in India is higher than ever. For a detailed discussion of some of these indicators, see Mitra (1996).

10. Weiner (1989: 9) describes the existence of high levels of political violence and India's ability to maintain a democratic process as a 'puzzling contradiction'. The contradictory aspect of this phenomenon can be partly explained as a fallacy of aggregation, because political violence in India is not uniformly distributed across regions. Those that are most afflicted by political insurgency such as Punjab, Kashmir, Nagaland, Assam, Manipur and Mizoram, are also precisely the regions where multi-party democracy has been less successful. This is cushioned by the other regions which are both comparatively free of this form of extreme political violence and enjoy stable, multi-party democracy. Weiner's point will stand because even the regions afflicted by insurgency are not terminally lost to democracy. Following the successful Assembly Elections of 1996 and 1997, Kashmir and Punjab have gone back to popular multi-party rule.

11. For the specification of the concept of 'informal army rule' and the discussion of the reasons for the absence of an explicit role of the military in India's high politics, see Cohen (1988).

12. The Constitution of India provides for temporary suspension of popular rule at the Centre as well as in the states in extreme cases when lawful government is no longer

possible. On the basis of the authoritarian spell of 1975–77, Powell (1982: 169) classifies India, along with Sri Lanka, Jamaica and Turkey, under 'Major suspension of democracy'.
13. Draconian anti-terrorist laws such as TADA and other forms of preventive detention have become a source of restriction on civil liberties.
14. Outside the narrow circle of North American political scientists, India continues to be the subject of a *Methodenstreit*. Though Lijphart (1996) makes no mention of the difficulty of cross-cultural comparison, understanding India in terms of individual interests continues to be a problem for the Western mass public, where India remains the quintessential example of 'otherness'. Huntington (1996: 367), discussed, reviewed and translated around the world, is a recent example of the idiosyncratic description of India (and other non-Western societies) in terms of civilisations rather than political systems.
15. We can call it the 'Little Buddha' syndrome after the film of the same name. This attitude to India has a historical genealogy in European Orientalist constructions of India, vigorously questioned by Inden (1990).
16. For a succinct analysis of a political culture dominated by 'amoral familism', see Banfield's (1958) classic study of Southern Italy.
17. These assumptions are consistent with those made by Downs (1957). See Chapter 2, 'Party Motivation and the Function of Government in Society', for the basic models on electoral choice and partisan behaviour. For a discussion of the basic assumptions of individuals' expected utility maximisation, see Riker and Ordeshook (1973).
18. See Joseph La Palombara and Myron Weiner, 'The Origin and Development of Political Parties' in La Palombara and Weiner (1966).
19. Harrison (1960) was one of the earliest to warn of the dangers of disintegration in India.
20. Huntington (1968) reflects the strong commitment to orderly change, if need be at the cost of political coercion, characteristic of the modernisation approach.
21. See Gabriel Almond's 'The Intellectual History of the Civic Culture Concept' in Almond and Verba (1989). On issue dimensions and political parties, see Lijphart (1984: 130).
22. The issue has been debated by a number of authors. See in particular, Rudolph and Rudolph (1967), Frankel and Rao (1989/90), Kothari (1970). For detailed analysis of the electoral process, see Mitra and Chiriyankandath (1992). Sheth (1975) is an excellent source for the political sociology of the electoral process. Hardgrave and Kochanek (1993) is a very good source for manifestos and background information. See especially Chapter 6, 'Parties and Politics'.
23. This theme has given rise to a vast literature on the *jajmani* system and its steady transformation through the effect of economic change, social reform and political mobilisation. The traditional *jajmani* system describes a system of social relations in terms of the reciprocal bonds of obligation through which social groups owning land are tied to other social groups on the basis of status, occupation and power. Politically, the social bonds of *jajmani* lead to a 'pyramid' of dominance. Politically, the small group of social elite accumulate power, status and wealth, which makes it possible for them to dominate the many others devoid of these resources. Once again, since the bond that thus binds the elite and the non-elite is deeply ingrained, the social pyramid looks like a natural rather than a political construction. Empowered by the principle of universal adult franchise, the relatively powerless bottom of the

pyramid quickly learns how to pool its collective voting strength and use it as a political resource. See Frankel and Rao (1989/90) for regional variations on this main theme.
24. See Irschick (1969, 1994) for the contrast between northern and southern India in terms of politics and social change.
25. Huntington (1968: 55) warns about the potential for political decay when participation expands faster than institutionalisation.
26. *Vertical* mobilisation refers to political linkages that draw on and reinforce social and economic dominance. *Horizontal* mobilisation takes place when people situated at the same social and economic level get together to use their combined political strength to improve their situation. *Differential* mobilisation refers to coalitions that cut across social strata (Rudolph and Rudolph [1967]).
27. For the formulation of these ideas in terms of an analytical framework on elections and social change in India based on a model of electoral norms and organisational structure corresponding to them, see Mitra (1994b).
28. See Lijphart (1996) for a discussion of the efficacy of federalism and consociationalism in promoting democracy and social change.
29. For an application of this concept as a framework for the discussion of political participation in India, see Mitra (1991).
30. For a discussion of this point based on an analysis of local elite in India, see Mitra (1992).
31. *Panchayati raj*, a traditional political institution rejuvenated and recast as the basic foundation stone of democracy at the local level, first developed in western India and then transported with great success to the Communist-ruled state of West Bengal, is a good example. See the chapter on 'Institutional Innovation: The Politicized Panchayats' in Kohli (1987: 108–16) for a discussion of the efficacy of West Bengal's Communist regime in making use of the panchayati system in promoting order and welfare.
32. The concept is discussed at length below. The two most useful references to its functioning are Kothari (1964, 1974).
33. See Mitra (1999: Ch. 10) for a discussion of the findings reported in this chapter in the context of a general discussion of institutitonal change and civil society in India.
34. The literature on the Congress party is enormous. See Mitra (1994b), Shepperdson and Simmons (1988), Sisson and Wolpert (1988), Joshi and Hebsur (1987), and Jain (1991)
35. See Kirchheimer (1966).
36. V.B. Singh, *Naya Sangharsh* (Hindi), pp. 54–62, January–March 1997; also see, 'Hastakshep', *Rashtriya Sahara* (Hindi), 19 October 1996.
37. The 1967 and 1971 National Election studies were conducted by the Centre for the Study of Developing Societies (Delhi) while the 1980 study was done by the Indian Institute of Public Opinion, New Delhi. The Centre's faculty was closely associated in the preparation of research instruments and the sample design.
38. The figures are as follows: Left Front voters 67.9 per cent, National Front 62.2 per cent, BJP 61.4 per cent, Congress 59.4 per cent, and Bahujan Samaj Party 55.8 per cent. This shows both the close relationship between partisanship and efficacy, as well as the widely dispersed nature of the sense of efficacy across the whole ideological spectrum of political parties.

5

The Dialectics of Nation and Region in Indian Politics

While political parties provide the main institutional context within which electoral participation and articulation and aggregation of interests takes place, it is the national, regional and local arenas that provide the spatial context for the operation of institutions. The main reason as to why the spatial basis of politics is relevant to the discussion of social change is because conventional theory has always maintained that the current of social change normally runs from the specific to the general, and in spatial terms, from the locality to the nation. What conventional theory does not clearly indicate is whether these concepts are to be seen in dichotomous terms, or as concentric circles, where the outer rings encapsulate the inner. Under the latter formulation, social change adds successive layers to the multi-layered political persona of the society in change, rather than necessarily fragmenting it in line with spatial and primordial divisions. The political salience of this theoretical question can be seen from the apprehensions of Balkanisation, which always accompanied the discussion of modernisation and social change in the literature on nation-building from the 1950s. The objective of this chapter is to pursue these questions by mapping of locality, region and nation into the political space.

The presence of regional leaders at the apex of Indian politics, and the campaign rhetoric questioning the supremacy of the Centre, were the main features of the 11th General Election. The prominent role that many regional parties and leaders played in the formation of coalitions, in campaigning and in jockeying for power in the aftermath of the election have created an impression of the regionalisation of the national political arena. Many commentators suggest that the national electorate is actually a series of regional arenas, managed by regional and local leaders with their networks; that the calculations of politicians, and by inference, those of the voters are focused, on the regional government.[1] This assumption underpins much analysis, including that of the poll *pundits*, newspaper reports as well as the more academic observers.[2] Talk of regionalism is not new in Indian politics, but the primal fear of Balkanisation which always accompanied such observations in the years after Independence,[3] in testimony to the growing confidence in the resilience of the Indian state, is not there any more. The presence of the region on the national scene is seen by many as positive, as part of the process of community formation and empowerment, as 'the emergence of a more competitive and polarised party system and the increasing regionalisation of the party system'.[4] Some commentators even see the emergence of the region as a prime consideration in the electoral choice in a positive light. We learn from D.L. Sheth:

> Our representative democracy is indeed moving closer to the people. They now feel more involved and show greater concern for institutions of local and regional governance. They perceive governance from Delhi to be increasingly remote. Their loyalty and trust are stronger for the local and regional governments than for the Centre. More important, the rarefied field of 'national politics' which once pitted the 'nation' against the 'region' has opened up for the regional and 'vernacular' elites.[5]

Nevertheless, doubters persist. In spite of its regular appearance in discussions of the electoral process, the assertion of regionalisation often remains unspecific and empirically unsubstantiated, with dark hints of a monster that has not been entirely slayed. Regionalisation might infuse new blood into the political system[6] and hasten the decline of the Congress party,[7] but what are its systemic implications? With regionalism rampant, will there be a 'vacuum in the party system at the national level'?[8]

Drawing mainly on the opinions and attitudes of the national electorate, this section intends to enquire into some of the implications of regionalisation for the resilience and integrity of the nation in India. That the 'region' is much talked about is plain for everyone to see. But its theoretical implication can be seen in two different lights. Is the region merely a convenient location from which to report on a national phenomenon, or is the region an exclusive political arena in India's macro-politics—the most appropriate level of analysis for what is only putatively a national phenomenon? Should nation and region be conceptualised in dichotomous terms, or are they overlapping categories, distinctive and yet mutually enriching and reinforcing? The analysis presented in this section examines these conjectures on the basis of partisan voting in Lok Sabha elections from Independence onwards, and public opinion data, derived from the present survey of the Indian electorate.

Some Specific Research Questions and Conjectures

Placed in the electoral context, the potential voter has to choose whether to vote at all, and in case she/he decides to turn out for the poll, whom to vote for. Both decisions are influenced by a multiplicity of factors, including, in ascending order of abstraction, personal links to candidates, family connections, social networks, professional associations, political identification, party membership and ideological leanings.[9] Many of these factors are local in origin; others originate from higher levels of the system. The salience that voters attach to them, and the manner in which politicians manipulate them, are critical inputs for the process of nation-building in a post-colonial context. The candidate and his agents, standing at the interface of the constituency and the state, can strengthen the muscles and sinews of the nation by the manner in which they get the vote out, just as they can contribute to its decay by demonising the nation working out of a regional platform for their own electoral benefit.

A number of empirical instruments can be constructed in order to evaluate the significance of the regionalisation process. A parliamentary election provides an ideal opportunity to apply these measures in order to study the depth of penetration of the national political arena into the regional and the local levels of the system. The perception of the electorate, particularly the way it constructs the salience of the regional arena compared to the national, is the crucial bit of evidence we need for this purpose. But the mere presence of local and regional bigwigs in campaigns or national leaders donning colourful local costumes does not necessarily constitute any compelling evidence in favour of the regionalisation conjecture. A certain degree of identification with the locality and region almost always comes across as one of the factors influencing the vote anywhere in the world.[10] Nor does one need to look at the scenario where regional identity acts as an exclusive factor in leading the bulk of voters to the polling booth, as in East Pakistan's ill-fated Parliamentary Election of 1970, or to stay away from polls, as in the recent elections in Punjab (1992) and Kashmir (1996), in order to establish the importance of regional identity.[11] In such cases the voters have already decided the fate of the nation by not participating in the elections.

To test the regionalisation conjecture in the vast majority of cases that fall between the diametrically opposite situations of near-perfect integration, as in the United States, where, at least since the Civil War, regional identities exist but have not been a divisive issue in national politics, and East Pakistan on the eve of the War of Liberation, where the nation had been reduced to a mere abstraction without any serious bearing on reality, it is important at the outset to specify the empirical attributes of the regionalisation conjecture in explicit terms. Several empirical questions suggest themselves. Does the electorate recognise region as a phenomenon in its own right? Is it conceptualised in terms of an exclusive identity, pitted against the nation as its diametric opposite? Or, is the nation an inclusive category, a Matruska doll that contains layers of region and locality encapsulated within?

At the macro level, the regionalisation conjecture can be tested by considering the weight of the vote and seat shares of 'national' political parties in the parliamentary elections since Independence.[12] The empirical issue then is to see how the seat and vote shares of national parties in the Lok Sabha are distributed during the period after Independence. The findings on the basis of ecological data should be juxtaposed with those on the basis of survey data. How do individual electors—our ultimate unit of analysis—situate the region and the nation? At the level of the voter, the first question to ask is: How aware is the voter of the region in terms of the information she/he possesses? Next is the question of regional sentiments. Do voters consider their specific region—loyalty to and identification with it—as salient values? Finally, do these sentiments extend to parties and institutions? Do voters express greater trust in regional governments and parties than in national government and parties?

Vote and Seat Shares of National Parties in the Lok Sabha: The Macro-aggregate Context

As the data presented in Table 5.1 indicate, both in terms of votes and seats, national parties have collectively stayed at a reasonably high level.

The start of the decline of the dominant role of the Indian National Congress, conventionally pegged at 1967, does not appear to have marked a trend in the vote and seat shares of national parties (Figure 5.1). At least on the basis of aggregate data, one can assert that the nation and the Congress party have become independent of one another. Contrary to the assumptions of the one-dominant-party system model, national political debates do not necessarily have to be intermediated by the presence of an overarching Congress party.[13]

Table 5.1
National Parties in Lok Sabha Elections: Seats and Votes

Election Years	Seats (Total)	Seats (%)	Votes (%)
1952	489	82.6	67.8
1957	494	85.2	73.0
1962	494	89.0	78.4
1967	520	84.6	76.3
1971	518	85.1	77.8
1977	542	88.7	84.6
1980	529	91.7	85.1
1984	542	85.4	77.8
1989	529	89.0	79.3
1991	534	89.5	80.8
1996	543	76.6	69.6
1998	539	71.2	68.0

Source: Butler, Lahiri and Roy (1995); Election Commission of India (1996 and 1998).

Specification of National Parties in Lok Sabha Elections
1952:   INC, BJS, CPI, SOC, KMPP
1957:   INC, PSP, CPI, BJS
1962:   INC, SWA, BJS, CPI, PSP, SOC
1967:   INC, SWA, BJS, CPI, CPM, SSP, PSP
1971:   INC, INC (O), SWA, BJS, SSP, PSP, CPI, CPM
1977:   INC, BLD, CPI, CPM, INC (O)
1980:   INC (I), INC (U), JP, JP(S), CPI, CPM
1984:   INC, BJP, JP, LKD, CPI, CPM, ICS
1989:   INC, JD, BJP, JP, LKD (B), CPI, CPM, ICS
1991:   INC, JD, BJP, JP, LKD (B), CPI, CPM, ICS
1996:   INC, INC (I), BJP, CPI, CPM, JD, JP, SAP
1998   INC, BJP, BSP, CPI, CPM, JD, SAP

Note: Elections were not held in Assam in 1989. Elections were not held in 12 constituencies of Assam and one in Meghalaya in 1980. Elections were not held for six seats in Jammu & Kashmir and were countermanded for two seats in Bihar and one seat in Uttar Pradesh in 1991.

Figure 5.1
Votes and Seats Share of National Parties in Lok Sabha, 1952–98

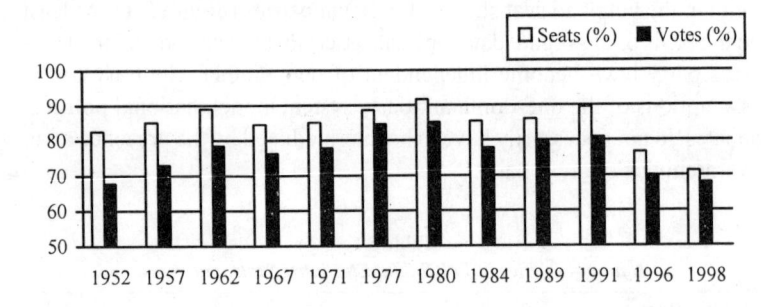

Opinions and Attitudes of the Electors: The Micro-political Considerations

The micro-perceptions of region and nation are the crucial building blocks that underpin macro-structures such as political parties and institutions like the Lok Sabha. Without the requisite degree of information and supportive attitudes from individuals, national institutions, like in the majority of post-colonial states, can atrophy and eventually pale into insignificance. Empirical analysis of these issues can be undertaken in terms of the electorate's concern for what the regional government does and information about the regional level of the political system; personal identification with the regional level; and, trust in the regional government.

Level of Concern and Information

Three sets of direct questions (where we have comparative data from 1971 and 1996) help us measure the concern for and information about the regional level on the part of the mass public. Responses to the question, *People are generally concerned about what governments do—some are more concerned about what the government in Delhi does, others are more concerned with what the State government does. How about you? Are you more concerned about what the Central government in Delhi does or the* [name of the State] *government does?* are presented in Table 5.2.

The main questions, *Who is the Prime Minister of our country?* and *Who is the Chief Minister of your State?* to test the level of information of the electorate have already been introduced (Tables 3.11 and 3.12).

Table 5.2
Concern about Central and State Government (in per cent)

	1971	1996
Neither	24.9	39.7
Central government	21.0	11.0
Both	14.5	20.9
State	18.9	23.0
D.K., N.A., Other	20.7	5.4

Compared to 1971, as we have learnt from the data presented in the general section above, more people are concerned about what the regional government rather than the Central government does, and, more people are able to identify the Chief Minister rather than the Prime Minister in 1996. Of course, the high figure of 56.5 per cent correct identification of the Prime Minister in 1971 should, to some extent, be attributed to the fact that the Prime Minister in office at that time was Indira Gandhi, probably (with the exception of Jawaharlal Nehru), the most discussed political leader of post-Independence India. At 53.6 per cent, the correct identification of Chief Ministers in 1996 does in fact come close to this figure. The almost 70 per cent *incorrect* identification of the Chief Ministers in 1971 bears testimony to Indira Gandhi's style of functioning, shifting the regional leadership of the Congress frequently to ensure greater and continued allegiance. The uncertainty of the tenure of the Chief Minister is reflected in the low recognition the office itself received from the public. During the span of 25 years, the trends, from the evidence we see above, suggest a higher awareness of the regional level of the government.

Loyalty to the Region

The survey sought to measure this by means of a direct question, *We should be loyal to our own region first and then to India. Do you agree with this, or disagree?* The results are presented in Table 5.3.

Table 5.3
Loyalty to Region First and Then to India (in per cent)

	1967	1996
Agree	67.1	53.4
Disagree	22.3	21.0
D.K./No opinion	8.4	25.6

The high level of loyalty to the region expressed in 1967—this question was not asked in 1971—needs to be seen in the context of the emergence of regional political forces to prominence for the first time since Independence in 1967. The Congress party lost control of about half the legislatures in the States. Its strength in the Lok Sabha was slashed down to a bare majority. The resurgent regional forces reflect the high expression of loyalty towards the region on the part of the electorate. Loyalty to the region was still expressed by a majority of the electorate in 1996, but a quarter of the respondents were not able to put their loyalties towards region and nation in the form of a strict dichotomy. Thus, while region is understood as a distinct category, its preferential position with regard to the nation is, at least for a substantial part of the respondents, not clear.

The same question, when repeated with regard to trust in the capacity of regional parties (*Compared to national parties, regional/local parties can provide better government in States. Do you agree or disagree with this?*) shows that one-third of the respondents prefer regional parties. But then, close to a majority of the people are unable or unwilling to decide between regional and national parties in exclusive and preferential terms (Table 5.4).

Table 5.4
Regional Parties Provide Better Government (in per cent)

	1996
Agree	34.0
Disagree	20.1
D.K./No opinion	45.9

However interesting or suggestive specific survey instruments might be, it is always desirable to seek corroboration of evidence from different sources, or other questions in the same survey with some comparable dimension built into it. In order to test the consistency of response, we have cross-tabulated the two measures of trust and loyalty towards the region. Not surprisingly, the two individual measures of regional attitude and support to regional parties are strongly correlated. We report below the results of the cross-tabulation of the two sets of measurements of attitudes towards the region and trust in the efficacy of regional parties.

The above results indicate a strong correlation between attitudes towards the region and trust in the abilities of regional parties. Once again, it is noticeable that there is a significant consistency in the two questions: those who are not sure that the regional parties could not provide better government (see the figures in the top left and bottom right columns of Table 5.5). We shall next consider the level of trust in the government at different levels of the system.

Table 5.5
Loyalty to Region by 'Regional Parties Provide Better Government' (in per cent)

Region comes before Nation	Regional Parties Provide Better Government		
	Agree	D.K./No opinion	Disagree
Agree	47.6	34.3	18.1
D.K./No opinion	10.7	86.0	3.3
Disagree	27.8	26.7	45.5

Table 5.6
Trust in Local/State/Central Government (in per cent)

	Great Deal	Somewhat	Not At All
Local government	39.0	37.8	23.2
State government	37.2	43.6	19.2
Central government	35.2	42.5	22.3

We can combine the results obtained so far in terms of a summary table.

Table 5.7
Loyalty to Region by Trust in Different Levels of Government (in per cent)

Regional Loyalty	Great Deal of Trust In		
	Central Government	Regional Government	Local Government
Loyalty to region before nation	38.3	40.9	42.4
Regional parties provide better government	38.5	45.2	44.8

Key: Cell entries in the above table are row percentages, i.e., of those who consider loyalty to the region more important than loyalty to the nation, 38.5% have a great deal of trust in the Central government, 41.2% in the regional government, 42.6% in the local government, etc.

It is important here to recall that the two groups of questions that have been cross-tabulated to produce the above table were asked at different points in the questionnaire. The measurement of sentiments towards region and attitudes towards regional parties appeared before the 'trust in government' series. In the latter, the three levels of government in India were measured one after another. As such, each cell entry measures an internally consistent variable that seeks to relate sentiments to measurement of trust in the government. In that light, we can suggest that there is a reasonable amount of consistency in the relation of sentiments to trust, i.e., a positive sentiment towards the region leads to a high level of trust in the efficacy of the regional government. In both cases, trust in the regional government is higher than the corresponding level for the national government.

What makes this inference problematic for a strong conclusion in favour of a strictly regional mindset—regional sentiment leading to trust in the regional government—is that the corresponding figure for the national government is not much different. A large number of those who have positive sentiments towards the regional government also trust the national as well as the local governments, suggesting the possibility that positive sentiments towards the regional level of the political system and towards regional parties do not necessarily preclude trust in the national government.

Regionalisation Conjecture Reformulated

Up to this point, we have operationalised the regionalisation conjecture, in the sense that regionalists are people for whom the regional political arena is not only important, it is so in preference to other political levels of the system. That largely answers the first question regarding the popular recognition of the regional level of governance in India. The appreciably high level of people who were unwilling or unable to come down on the side of or against regions suggests that perhaps the nation/region duality might have missed other potential and possible forms of the coexistence of the nation and region. In order to understand the perplexing anomaly of an astoundingly high 45.9 per cent of non-response in Table 5.4, we ought to look more deeply at the data on the social background of the regionalists.

In order to relate social background to attitudes, a new variable, 'regionalists', was created by combining loyalty to the region *before* the nation with the belief that regional parties provide better government than national parties. This is a 'strong' specification of the regionalisation conjecture, in the sense that only those who have indicated a strong response in favour of regional identity to both questions are put together in the category of 'regionalists'. That yielded a group of 2,433 people, which constitutes about 25 per cent of the sample. The rest are specified as 'others'. Consider the cross-tabulation of regionalists with a number of characteristics describing the people.

Social Profile of Regionalists

Subsequent tables present the social background of the regionalist. From Table 5.8, it should be possible to identify those sections of the Indian population that have greater trust in the regional government. The most important social group to be found among those who hold strongly positive attitudes towards the region are the Other Backward Classes.

Table 5.8
Regionalists by Caste (in per cent)

Caste	Regionalists	Others
SC	16.1	19.5
ST	8.8	9.7
OBC	41.3	35.6
Others*	33.8	35.1

*Refers to mostly the erstwhile 'elite' castes including the first three twice-born *jatis* (the upper three castes of the *varna* scheme) of Brahmin, Kshatriya and Vaisya.

These are social groups which did not have effective access to the civil services and professions under the British, nor were they in the forefront of the national anti-colonial movement which caused regional and national party organisations to be dominated by the twice-born castes. Nor could these groups, not being members of either the Scheduled Castes or the Scheduled Tribes, take advantage of the facilities made available under various reservation laws, at least in the central government services and legislatures. But these social groups did take advantage of the land reforms, particularly the zamindari abolition laws that the Congress governments introduced after Independence. With greater access to land, security of tenure, access to infrastructure and new agrarian technology, and equally important, thanks to family labour, the OBCs became the main beneficiaries of agricultural modernisation. Their next objective was to capture political power as a part of region-based peasant or Lok Dal parties. State politics of the 1960s is replete with such attempts. The political experience and linkages gained by them became valuable legacies, which even the return of the Congress party under Indira Gandhi in the Parliamentary election of 1971 could not destroy.

The survey data, which help us visualise the other facets of the social base of regionalists, also show the extent of political change and social mobilisation that has taken place since. The upwardly mobile peasant–OBC–regional forces coalitions of the 1960s have matured into broader political groupings, with other socially and economically marginal forces, bereft of political access that comes from high social status or constitutional guarantee as in the case of the Scheduled Castes and Scheduled Tribes, gravitating in the direction of the OBCs and aiming at drawing upon the regional level of the political system as a realistic chance for them to exercise real political power. Some of these conjectures are borne out by Table 5.8.

Table 5.9
Regionalists by Religion (in per cent)

Religion	Regionalists	Others
Hindu	81.6	84.8
Muslim	12.0	10.2
Christian	4.7	2.6
Sikh	1.1	1.4
Others	0.7	0.9

The relatively higher presence of Muslims and Christians and the lower presence of Hindus among regionalists (Table 5.9) gives us some insights into this coalition of minorities which has found the region an effective entry point into mainstream politics. Table 5.10 shows the higher level of education among regionalists, suggesting that these social groups also possess the educational resources with which to reinforce their intention to use the regional political system for the purposes of political leverage.

Table 5.10
Regionalists by Level of Education (in per cent)

Education	Regionalists	Others
Illiterate	28.3	46.5
Up to middle	35.7	30.6
College, no degree	28.5	17.3
College degree and above	7.3	5.3

The data on the social background of the section of respondents who have expressed a generally positive attitude towards the region rather than the nation as the more important level of India's political system (the regionalists). Regionalists are likely to be upwardly mobile educated males, the erstwhile 'bullock capitalists' who first entered politics in a major way in the 1960s. They have now graduated beyond exclusive reliance on agriculture to other avenues increasingly opening up in the countryside thanks to the plethora of new programmes being introduced by the government as well as non-governmental agencies. They are into agri-business, small-time contracts, acting as brokers for outsiders seeking access to ministers, officials, local markets. As we shall see below, the 1990s, which set the political and economic processes free from the dominance of the erstwhile political classes, the bureaucracy, the urban power brokers, and above all, the metropolitan 'High Commands', has brought a great sense of efficacy to the regionalists.

Sense of Efficacy

Several direct questions were asked to measure the sense of political and economic efficacy of the electorate. By cross-tabulating these questions with our two filter questions regarding loyalty to region and trust in regional parties, we are able to check to what extent regionalists see themselves as people who matter. Following the conventional measurements of efficacy, questions have been asked about political efficacy and financial success.

Political Efficacy

Considering the answers to the questions as presented in Table 5.11, regionalists have a far greater sense of efficacy in terms of being able to draw the attention of the government towards popular needs and grievances, particularly through the instrumentality of political parties. They

Table 5.11
Sense of Political Efficacy of Regionalists (in per cent)

Question:	Regionalists	Others
How much in your opinion do political parties help to make the government pay attention to the people? (A great deal, or somewhat)	68.4	57.6
Do you think your vote has an effect on how things are run in this country, or do you think your vote makes no difference? (Vote has effect)	71.1	74.2
Suppose there were no parties or assemblies and elections were not held, do you think that the government in this country could be run better? (No, elections are necessary)	82.8	86.9
The government generally takes care of the common people. (Agree)	59.4	47.0

are great believers in elections too, and their level of satisfaction with the general performance of the government is higher than that of non-regionalists.

Financial Efficacy

The greater sense of efficacy of regionalists compared to others is reinforced by their general sense of financial well-being (Table 5.12). But nowhere is this tendency as noticeable as it is in their boldly buoyant view of the shape of things to come. More than half of them expect things to get better.

Table 5.12
Sense of Financial Satisfaction of Regionalists (in per cent)

Question	Regionalists	Others
During the past few years, has your financial situation improved, worsened, or has it stayed the same? (Improved)	31.1	28.5
In whatever financial condition you are placed today, on the whole, are you satisfied with your present financial situation? (Satisfied)	31.9	27.2
Now looking ahead and thinking about the next few years, do you expect that your financial situation will stay about the way it is now, get better or get worse? (Will get better)	60.0	56.1

Construction of the Centre from the Periphery

From the distribution of regionalists over the States that are represented in our sample, people with loyalty and trust towards regions are only slightly more likely to be found in certain parts of India, such as Tamil Nadu, Andhra Pradesh and Assam (States with a record of regional movements), but also Karnataka, Gujarat, Haryana and Kerala, which have not experienced regional movements of comparative strength. It is best, thus, to characterise regionalism as an attitude, found in a certain section of the Indian population, with specific socio-demographic features. The question we now wish to raise is whether these people are also distinguished by a specific view of the nature of the state, state–society relations, and inter-communal relations in India. The relevant questions from the survey have been cross-tabulated with regionalists. The results are discussed here.

Communal Accommodation

As the responses presented in Table 5.13 indicate, regionalists have a coherent and distinct view on a range of issues that constitute the core of Indian politics today. At 85.2 per cent approval rate, they are firmly of the opinion that it is the responsibility of the government to protect the minorities. The supportive attitude towards minorities is more clearly spelled out in terms of similarly supportive attitudes towards the Muslim community in particular, towards the contentious issue of personal law and a significantly large rate of disapproval of the destruction of the Babri mosque. Presumably, the regionalists' perception of the state is that of a culturally plural, tolerant, inclusive political institution, committed to distributive justice and the accommodation of minorities. The latter is seen in its strong defence of the interests of the backward castes, whom the regionalists would like to come under the purview of the reservation laws.

Table 5.13
Regionalists and their Attitudes towards Communal Accommodation (in per cent)

	Regionalists	Others
It is the responsibility of the government to protect the interests of minorities.(Agree)	85.2	54.7
Some people say that the demolition (of the Babri masjid at Ayodhya) was justified while others say it was not justified. What would you say: was it justified or not justified? (Not justified)	49.3	54.3
The needs and problems of Muslims have been neglected in India. (Agree)	27.8	15.7
Every community should be allowed to have its own laws to govern marriage and property rights. (Agree)	54.0	41.3
Backward castes should have reservation in government jobs. (Agree)	79.2	68.6

Methods of State Integration

The other issue that polarises India's politics today is the nature of the state itself, particularly with regard to India's neighbours and the use of force to suppress those contesting the authority of the state rather than negotiate with them. From the responses to the question on Kashmir (*People's opinions are divided on the issue of the Kashmir problem—*

some people say that the government should suppress the agitation by any means while others say that this problem should be resolved by negotiations. What would you say: should the agitation be suppressed or resolved by negotiation?) regionalists are more keen on negotiation, both within as well as outside India. On the issue of Kashmir, regionalists are less likely to be indecisive than non-regionalists. Fewer of them plead ignorance of Kashmir: 9.5 per cent of regionalists have not heard of Kashmir as compared to 25.7 per cent among non-regionalists; 33.5 per cent of non-regionalists do not know the best line to take on Kashmir as compared to 27.7 per cent for regionalists. Regionalists are also somewhat more likely to invoke force against militancy but the most important difference is the attitude towards resolution of the conflict through negotiation. Close to half of the regionalists are for negotiation, compared to a little over a quarter of the non-regionalists who share this opinion.

Table 5.14
Regionalists' Attitudes towards Kashmir Issue and Friendship with Pakistan (in per cent)

	Regionalists	Others
Resolved through negotiation	49.0	28.0
Should be suppressed	12.5	10.8
Other	1.4	1.4
Respondent cannot say	27.5	33.7
Not heard of Kashmir	9.6	26.1
India should make more efforts to develop friendly relations with Pakistan. (Agree)	57.5	40.0

One point that comes across clearly from the analysis of attitudes towards Kashmir is that the average regionalist is unlikely to be the 'my region, right or wrong' variety. As we have seen, their attitudes towards centre/region issues are not specific only to *their region*, but to the general way in which they would like regional issues to be solved. It is this attitude of accommodation and negotiation which is also reflected in the answer to the question regarding Pakistan.

Partisan Preferences

Parliamentary Election

In terms of partisan preferences, regionalists have a general tendency to prefer regional parties and a corresponding tendency *not* to vote for national parties. Well-known regional parties like the TDP, AGP and DMK are beneficiaries of this tendency, whereas national parties like the Congress and the BJP are worse off in consequence.

Table 5.15
Regionalists and Partisan Preference (in per cent)

	Regionalists	Others
INC	24.9	27.9
BJP	16.5	22.2
Janata Dal	6.8	7.0
CPI	2.1	1.2
CPM	5.2	4.6
TMC (Tamil Maanila Congress)	3.7	1.4
DMK	4.4	1.8
TDP (Naidu)	3.6	1.3
AGP	2.1	0.6

Table 5.16
Regionalists and Partisan Preference: Assam (in per cent)

	Lok Sabha 1996		Assembly 1996	
Parties	Regionalists	Others	Regionalists	Others
INC	25.3	34.9	18.2	28.7
BJP	16.2	18.6	6.1	10.9
Asom Gana Parishad	50.5	31.8	59.6	44.2

This tendency of regionalists to favour regional parties gets much further intensified when we concentrate on specific regions with a history of regional movements. We have chosen the case of Assam to illustrate the point. Thus, from Table 5.16, the tendency to vote for the AGP is much higher for regionalists than non-regionalists, both in the Lok Sabha poll as well as in the Assembly poll which took place simultaneously with the Parliamentary Elections in 1996. The same tendency reproduces itself in the case of the two major national parties present in Assam, namely, the Congress and the BJP.

Effect of Regionalism: Vote Splitting in Assam

Once again, however, regionalists are able to conceptualise the voting process in strategic terms. If the main fight is against one national party and elections are taking place simultaneously to the Assembly and the Lok Sabha, the regionalist voter is able to split his support in a manner that maximises the chances of his party in the regional arena, while hurting the interests of the main nationalist competitor in the national arena. Thus, from Table 5.17, we can gather that 20.3 per cent of AGP voters in the Assembly voted for the BJP for the Lok Sabha, while 66.7 per cent of BJP voters in the Assembly voted for the AGP in the Lok Sabha. It is interesting to note that no vote splitting took place between the two national parties, namely the Congress and the BJP.

Table 5.17
Regionalists and Partisan Stability (in per cent)

Assembly	Lok Sabha 1996		
	Congress (25.3)	BJP (16.2)	AGP (50.5)
Congress	88.9	0.0	11.1
(18.2)	64.0	0.0	4.0
BJP	0.0	33.3	66.7
(6.1)	0.0	12.5	8.0
AGP	5.1	20.3	72.9
(59.6)	12.0	75.0	85.6

Key: The upper figure in each cell indicates the percentage of people who voted for the party named on the left in the Assembly poll, for the party named at the head of the column in the Lok Sabha poll. The lower figure corresponds to the percentage of voters for the party named at the head of the column in the Lok Sabha poll, for the party named on the left in the Assembly poll.

Ticket splitting, whether implicit or a result of short-term alliances between regional and national parties, helps moderate the electoral rhetoric and contains the more rabid separatist tendencies. The emergence of the AGP as a political party illustrates this process. Recent Akali politics is yet another example of the containment of regionalism. The point is borne out by the following statement of Prakash Singh Badal, made on the 75th birth anniversary of the Akali Dal.

> [The] Shiromani Akali Dal is a symbol of the aspirations and hopes of Punjab. The Dal has always struggled for human rights, Punjab, Punjabi and the rights of Sikhs. For this the Akali Dal has made innumerable sacrifices. [He went on to add] We are committed to peace and shall not allow it to be disturbed at any cost. We have full faith in constitutional methods. We shall curb corruption and shall strive to give a clean government...when today we are celebrating

our 75th anniversary we reaffirm our commitment to our goals. [He then confirmed the resolve of the Akali Dal to 'rejoin the national mainstream']...now regional parties and national parties who believe in internal autonomy for States are coming together. [The] Akali Dal is very keen to co-operate with them.[14]

To sum up, the data from the Lok Sabha electoral results and the survey findings strongly indicate the presence of a keen awareness of the region as an important level of the Indian political system. That the region is present in a distinctive way does not, of course, suggest that it is exclusive, or that regionalists necessarily pit the region and nation as diametric opposites, separated by a chasm of distrust and conflict of loyalties. While the survey data support the existence of the two as separate and distinct entities on the basis of popular perceptions, the relationship of the two emerges as much more complex than is commonly supposed. The bark of the regional chauvinist is louder than his bite: the political scientist measuring the depth of national integration can accept the separatist rhetoric of the regional leader as an indicator of the imminent dissolution of national unity only at his peril.

The regionalists who were identified in the course of the analysis presented here emerge as a significant section of the Indian electorate which has had the benefit of greater education, is upwardly mobile and confident in its ability to negotiate its way through the economy and the policy process. It has a tendency to back the best agent available to promote the regional interest in a given arena. Thus, when a credible regional party is available, the regionalists prefer it to its nationalist competitors. But they are unwilling to do so mechanically or uncritically. The annihilation of Jayalalitha's AIADMK bears this out. On the other hand, self-confessed regional parties are able to come to terms with national parties in a manner that promotes common interest. The vote trading of the AGP and BJP in Assam bears testimony to this.

The existence of regionalists in the mass electorate provides the popular base for the formation of regional parties. From the point of view of social forces concentrated in a specific part of the country, control of the regional government appears both as a desirable and achievable goal, and an effective method of reaching the objectives important to regional movements, such as use of the mother tongue as the official language, cultural hegemony, control over the practice of faith in everyday life, religious property, law and order, agricultural and developmental subsidies and various forms of state-administered welfare.

Having established themselves in their regions, regionalists have, in this new phase of Indian politics that we have now entered, set their sights on constructing the kind of nation that would be appropriate to the new scheme of things. Increasingly, rather than remaining content with their own region, they are stretching out their hands, and—using their alliances with similar forces from outside—beginning to define the nature of the national community in their own way. Recent experience has demonstrated in different parts of the country that the pursuit of these goals can not only coexist with similar aspirations elsewhere, regional movements can, in fact, reinforce one another by pooling their political resources. Hence, the unprecedented scenes of regional leaders from one part of India campaigning for regional parties in other parts of the country in local and regional elections, in addition to elections to the Lok Sabha.

Plus ça change? Those with memories of Congress rule during the period of its long hegemony would recall that something similar was also tried by the Congress high command during the period of Congress hegemony. It always sent 'observers' from the Centre to attempt reconciliation among warring factions in the States, and these observers were invariably people from other regions. Also, local and regional Congressmen—a Pant here, an Atulya Ghose there—were even allowed to take on local colours and rhetoric at variance with the central line. The big difference between now and then is that whereas earlier these expressions of local and regional interests were tolerated rather than encouraged, legitimacy of the regional idiom in the regional arena and the construction of different variants of the nation out of these multicoloured regional beads is now the norm. Before, the outside 'observer' (the term was one of those euphemisms from the period of Congress hegemony) came very much as a Central representative, a stern bearer of the message of party unity with little room to manoeuvre of his own, rather than as a fellow regional leader with similar problems. During the 1996 parliamentary election campaign, Jyoti Basu visiting Bihar, or Laloo Prasad Yadav visiting Bengal, could be seen both as insider and outsider to the regional way of looking at things. This atmosphere, which accommodates regional conflict resolution within a national framework, can also be seen in leaders of regional origin like Deve Gowda's successful intervention in river water disputes. The Congress System encapsulated the expressions of local and regional interests and symbols at lower levels of the system; the new element in Indian politics makes these processes of consultation a systematic way of bringing India's outlying areas and peoples, and what the nation is about and who has the legitimate right to speak in its name.

The politics of coalitions that has replaced Congress hegemony has greatly facilitated the process of the integration of the local and regional for the purpose of launching a new debate on the nature of the nation, and for identifying the variable boundaries of the nation and region. In consequence, looking for regional allies has now become an imperative for all national parties. The process, of course, got highly intensified as the prospect of a hung Parliament loomed large even before the election. The BJP, in addition to its formal coalition with the Shiv Sena in Maharashtra, looked for informal alliances far and wide.[15] Not that the BJP was alone in seeking alliances: every national party sought out partners with regional parties or factions.[16] The reverse was also true. A commentator observes: '...all the various regional sectarian parties in major States have allied with a more or less national party'.[17]

Having come to their own, the regional parties are increasingly self-confident in terms of working out deals with one another as well as with national parties.[18] The Congress is still suspect, but that may change once the afterglow of Congress hegemony has completely burnt out, leaving the Congress to behave much as any other political party. One sure sign of this is that the terms of political discourse are no longer mediated by the salient values that once defined the core of India's high politics. Regionalists—who as a group draw in people from India's periphery, in terms of religion, elite caste-status or geographic distance from the Centre—are able to generate a different construction of the nation-state that is in sync with the times in terms of being market-friendly, yet with a humane face. When speaking in the national mode, regionalists do not dismiss the need to be well-informed and decisive in defence of the security and integrity of the nation. But in terms of actual policies of the state, regionalists are much more willing, and in view of its social base, able to listen to the minorities, to regions with historical grievances, to sections of society that entered post-Independence politics with unsolved, pre-Independence (in some cases, pre-modern) grievances. It is thanks to these regionalists that the emerging multi-party democracy of India is not merely an anomic battle for power and short-term gain but the releasing of pent-up creativity and visions that provide a fertile and cohesive backdrop to the realignment of social forces. Far from being its antithesis, the region has actually emerged as the nursery of the nation.

The analysis of regionalisation on the basis of electoral surveys might invite a technical criticism that the data are likely to underestimate the true extent of regionalism in the country. Those fully committed to the autonomy and exclusive identity of a region are likely to stay away from the electoral process altogether.[19] Past practice indicates that parties and movements committed to an exclusive political identity for their region which would be satisfied with nothing short of full control over their political fortunes, stay off elections altogether (e.g., the Hurriyat in the Parliamentary elections of 1996 in Jammu and Kashmir), or participate in the electoral process to the extent of inciting voters against electoral participation (e.g., the Hurriyat leaders actively campaigned against participation in the Assembly polls in Jammu and Kashmir held shortly after the Parliamentary elections of 1996). A second situation is one where the party, fully committed to the regional ideal, takes part in the electoral process (such as the Awami League of East Pakistan in the election of 1970), and if successful in winning a majority, precipitates a political crisis subsequent to the election.

The use of the results of a post-poll survey as the main source of data, it might be argued, somehow stacks the scales in favour of the nation (in preference to the region) at the outset. This technical criticism indicates a lack of familiarity with the method of post-poll surveys. Unlike normal exit polls, which concentrate exclusively on voters, post-poll surveys of the kind on which our findings are based draw on the whole electorate, including people who did not take part in the election. The limits of its reach are thus more likely to be caused by the process of shifting and mobile sections of the population, rather than any implicit selection bias. A more important limitation of the data is that the regionalisation conjecture, to be fully tested, must also take into account the strategies and rhetoric of local and regional politicians as they negotiate their way through changing times. This lacuna can be filled by supplementing survey data with a tracking study that follows a selected grid of regional parties and political leaders over time in order to measure changes in their alignments, issue positions and campaign rhetoric.

The 1996 parliamentary and legislative elections would, in retrospect, have established one important point of reference in the unfolding of the Indian nation: it has surely established the fact that the Indian National Congress and the Indian nation have become firmly delinked. Different forms of construction and representation of national identity—in the east and the west, the south and the north, not ignoring the Hindu/Hindi-heartland—have become legitimate parts of the national political discourse.

By complementing the perception of the electorate with that of local and regional leaders, we would be able to specify the regionalisation conjecture in theoretical and comparative terms. The research on region and nation in India can then join similar projects elsewhere. We can thus unite the fragmented discourse on nation building, divided on the lines of Western and non-Western societies, a division imposed and legitimised by orientalist prejudices whose time is now past. One can now formulate the problematic in terms of a common research agenda: Is national identity in India (as in Germany or France) like a Matruska doll, such that, once we strip off the upper layers, one begins to discern a series of identities, carefully constructed by the political actor in a manner that optimises its chances of achieving a life of affluence and dignity, in a secure environment? Some of these themes would be explored further in Chapter 8 in terms of local and regional institutions that facilitate the interweaving of the different levels of the nation into a federal structure. The dynamic interaction is, in turn, made possible through the synergy created by the process of political competition and economic reform, which will be the theme of the next chapter.

Notes

1. One commentator suggested at the peak of the campaign: 'About 10,000 candidates are in the fray, waiting to win the hearts of the 590 million voters in 543 Lok Sabha constituencies. The number of parties? Well, not less than 3,000 of them registered with the Election Commission before the dates of the elections were announced. Between then and now, a score might have been added. Only a handful of them are what the Election Commission calls "national parties". The rest are regional. And it is some of them who may turn out to be decisive in the formation of the power balance in the Centre.' He goes on to suggest a period of growing 'regionalisation', that 'Indian politics is likely to be more dominated by regional interests, and the era of one national party ruling the Centre and many States is coming to an end.' Kumaresh Chakravarty, 'Rise of regional interests', in *The Tribune*, p. 9, 9 April 1996.
2. Though the media and TV are gaining in importance in India's electoral campaigns, their role is still nowhere as important as in the US or the UK. Nor do the parties dispose of the national bureaucratised apparatus and political worker whose movements could be centrally directed. *Faute de mieux*, the region appears as the most effective point from where to set up an ad hoc campaign organisation for Lok Sabha elections, mobilise resources and manpower and solicit the support of important social forces. The constituency segment rather than the parliamentary constituency is often the main unit in the conduct of campaign strategies. Press reports in the last Lok Sabha election were often done on a region by region basis. See, for example, 'Shifting Alignments', *India Today*, pp. 32–35, 15 May 1996. In commenting on the role of regional power brokers, G.C. Shekhar identifies Tamil Nadu's Jayalalitha, the 'three Lals' of Haryana, Andhra Pradesh's Lakshmi Parvati 'who will play a key role in the formation of the next government' in 'Jayalalita–Karunanidhi: Fight to the Finish', *India Today*, pp. 35–37, 15 May 1996.
3. Harrison (1960) is of course the best exemplar of this fear of disintegration.

4. Zoya Hasan, 'The Regionalisation of Politics', *The Hindu*, 23 April 1996.
5. D.L. Sheth, 'The Prospects and Pitfalls', *India Today*, p. 37, 31 August 1996.
6. See the report on the new faces in the 11th Lok Sabha. 'Different Strokes', *India Today*, pp. 32–36, 15 July 1996.
7. Zoya Hasan, ibid.
8. Yogendra Yadav, 'Elections 1996: Towards a Post-Congress Polity', *The Times of India*, 30 March 1996.
9. For a discussion of the modelling of these factors that contribute to both electoral participation and partisanship, see Riker and Ordeshook (1973).
10. A scrutiny of the presidential campaign in the United States as the national leaders press the flesh and seek to humour local worthies would prove the point.
11. The Pakistani national elections of 1970 in which the Awami League had a massive win in East Pakistan were fought on the basis of the salient issue of regional autonomy. The success of the Awami League precipitated a serious political crisis, eventually leading to the Liberation War of 1970–71 and the secession of East Pakistan. The Hurriyat in Jammu and Kashmir has been campaigning for a poll boycott in order to bring pressure on the Government of India to concede the autonomy of Kashmir.
12. Which party is a national party is not always a straightforward question. Is it enough for a party to present itself as one? We have opted for the standard definition of the Election Commission which is that a party is a national party if it is present in at least three regions.
13. In the one-dominant-party system, national political debates took place mostly between factions of the Congress party, and privately, between them and members of the opposition. Now, such debates take place publicly, between national parties, regional parties and local leaders.
14. B.K. Chum, 'Akali Dal goes for mainstream politics', *Deccan Herald*, 27 February 1996.
15. At various times during the campaign, the BJP sought to have deals with the Asom Gana Parishad, Shiromani Akali Dal, Maharashtra Gomantak Party and the Samajvadi Janata Party. In addition to the formal coalition with the Shiv Sena, however, these efforts succeeded only with the Samata party of Bihar and the Haryana Vikas Party of Haryana. See N.K. Singh, 'BJP: Confident by Default', *India Today*, pp. 6–27, 30 April 1996.
16. J.N. Dixit, 'Wisner's Assessment: Elections and Image', *The Indian Express*, 23 April 1996.
17. David Devdas, 'Left, right or centre?', *Business Standard*, 16 April 1996.
18. The growing assertiveness of the Shiv Sena in Maharashtra is a case in point. Not only has this regional party, in alliance with a national party, achieved control of the regional government, it has also managed to retain its specific identity and room to manoeuvre. Explaining an incident (where the activists of the Shiv Sena had blackened the face of a minister) in an interview, Bal Thackeray elaborated on the double strategy of his regional party in terms of combining effective governance with agitation when necessary. See Smruti Koppikar, 'Shiv Sena: Blowing hot and cold', *India Today*, pp. 40–41, 15 August 1996.
19. The entry and exit of regional forces from the electoral arena is a process of rational calculation that seeks to strike a balance between the need to assert their specific identity on the regional political space and the likelihood of achieving political power. The argument has been made at length in Mitra and Lewis (1996).

6

Poverty, Economic Policy and Social Opportunity in India

The triangular relationship of the economy, society and politics remains essentially problematic in the context of a post-colonial state. Political mobilisation in a symbiotically-related hierarchical social structure and an agricultural setting based on subsistence economy spreads the consciousness of inequality. This creates new groups of haves and have nots in the place of traditional social relations based on the system of reciprocal economic and social relations. Such relations, which under colonial rule or in the pre-colonial past might have been seen in some sense as natural, organic and necessary, appear contested, political and susceptible to change in the post-colonial context. The political consequences that emerge from this conflict of interests and wills are variable. In a society where the political process provides the room to manoeuvre to ordinary individuals, deprived social groups give vent to their resentment in a variety of ways.[1] If the elites in charge, through a combination of force, fraud and constitutional manipulation, deny the opportunity for articulation and aggregation of the demands of deprived groups, the result may be a temporary lull in the extent of manifest social conflict. But history warns of the long-term implications in terms of angry explosions, with disastrous consequences for political order.

Even after five decades of Independence, mass poverty continues to remain a salient fact of India's politics and a painful complement to its democratic credentials.[2] Right from the outset, a range of policies aimed at the eradication of mass poverty have been designed by the government and left to be implemented by a sprawling central, state and local bureaucracy. The main objective of this chapter is to examine the perception of the consequences of these efforts at development, and of the economic policies aimed at achieving structural change and poverty eradication of the public.

Power, Protest and Participation

In its broader sense, social change brings about a radical and comprehensive change in the economic world-view of individuals. The changes in the means of communication and exchange encourage the members of traditional societies to look beyond the insular and fragmented world of the village or guild, and view themselves as fellow citizens. These new, impersonal links connect them with their neighbours, the modern state and the world beyond the nation-state. In a comprehensive sense, thus, social and economic changes are closely related. The politics of postcolonial states leads to the creation of new social roles, aspirations for higher status, induction into the ranks of local and regional elites, and a myriad of other factors that accelerate the pace of social change. The process affects the material expectations of the newly mobilised citizenry and produces the tendency to compare their lot with those of others, and, consequently, creates a steep rise in the sense of relative deprivation. In authoritarian regimes, the sense of anger at being denied what one considers one's legitimate due may be suppressed for a while, only to surface in bouts of rioting, coups, peasant insurrections or violent uprisings led by workers and students. In democratic countries where deep class divisions exist, rapid social change and the resulting imbalance in the levels of popular economic aspirations and perceived achievements can lead to a spate of unstable governments, with a discontented citizenry 'throwing the rascals out', and getting rapidly disenchanted with the newly-elected politicians.

Under the leadership of Jawaharlal Nehru and an egalitarian consensus that prevailed within the Congress 'High Command', the state, right from the outset, committed itself to the norms of social democracy. Nehru's bold and visionary 'Freedom at Midnight' speech spelt out both the ultimate objectives of independence, and the political means of attaining them. 'The achievements we celebrate today', Nehru said, 'is but a step, an opening of opportunity, to the great triumphs and the achievements that await us.' The task included 'the ending of poverty and ignorance and disease and inequality of opportunity.'[3]

The political and administrative resources at the disposal of the government headed by Nehru were, however, the result of a compromise between many sets of contradictory values and interests.[4] The departure of the colonial rulers and the creation of the Republic removed princes and zamindars, arch-enemies of the Congress-sponsored vision of Independence, democracy and modernity, from a formal presence within the executive. However, many of them were brought back to power through the logic of the electoral process, which inevitably seeks out the wielders of social and economic power as peddlers of influence, and inducts them to the circle of the political elites. Thus, unlike revolutionary countries as China, or war-ravaged societies as South Korea, Independence and the transfer of power created no major dent in the structure of social power in India. Nor did it affect the form of its administration. The police and bureaucracy maintained structural continuity with the past. So strong was the sense of corporate identity and administrative autonomy of these vital organs of the state, that this continuity remained unaffected by the departure of large contingents of British civilians and police officers. Their places were rapidly filled by Indians deeply steeped in the culture of the Raj.

In the event, the burden of administrative implementation of Nehru's vision fell on those who neither necessarily shared the values, nor their political implications. Finally, the political process of economic decision-making was to be composed of a complex structure of a mixed economy. The state and private capital were to enter a partnership, with the state providing the long-term vision and investment in areas of the economy that were vital for the whole, but were unlikely to yield immediate profits, and the private sector providing the link between investments and the efficient production and distribution of goods and resources.

In theory, the Constitution committed the state in unambiguous terms to a concept of citizen entitlements. Drèze and Sen comment:

> Expansion of basic human capabilities, including such freedoms as the ability to live long, to read and write, to escape preventable illnesses, to work outside the family irrespective of gender, and to participate in collaborative as well as adversarial politics, not only influence the quality of life that the Indian people can enjoy, but also affect the real opportunities they have to participate in economic expansion (Drèze and Sen 1995: vii).

The process of democratic empowerment was meant to hold the key to both state-initiated reform and government-sponsored policies of redistribution. Drèze and Sen add:

> In a multi-party democracy, there is scope for influencing the agenda of the government through systematic opposition and the need to examine the priorities of public criticism is as strong as is the necessity that the government should scrutinise its own relative weights and concerns (Drèze and Sen 1995: vii–viii).

Thus, the constitutional structure bore the marks of the compromise in terms of sharp measures of control, holding enormous potential for bureaucratic power over the economy and society, and a series of exceptions. That provided a useful entry point to interest groups, operating through politicians, which could influence regulation and lower public accountability, slowing down the economy as a whole. The fundamental rights to property and occupation were thus hemmed in by a number of restrictions in favour of equalisation of chances and economic reform. The Congress governments at the Centre and in the States, immediately after the first General Election in 1952, set about giving legislative shape to these norms. Rather than letting the free play of the forces of the market (for it was argued that a fully developed market with consumers in a position to harness the potentials of the market to the greatest welfare of the society did not yet exist), the government took over the onerous task of bringing about an equitable distribution of material resources in the country.

As we have already seen in the introduction to the book, India's subsistence economy at the time of Independence and her resolve to eradicate mass poverty and maldistribution while operating from within the structure of parliamentary democracy was greeted with incredulity by the specialists of economic development. Among the major countries of the world, India was the only one to follow this path. Not surprisingly, over the years, in a cruel twist of irony, the poverty of India's economy has been matched by the plentifulness of scholarship on it. The relative transparency of India, availability of good and reliable data, legions of home-grown, skilled economists, post-War interest in democratic poverty alleviation through foreign aid, and, most of all, the tradition of building global models of political economy where India is present as the quintessential embodiment of underdevelopment, account for the ubiquitous presence of India in development literature. Both at home and abroad, India has often been made the exemplar of everything that was not right with economic policy and its implementation. The debate has got a new impetus following the resolve of the government of Narasimha Rao in 1992 to liberalise the economy.

This chapter does not intend to delve into actual poverty statistics as such. Instead, our objective is to concentrate on the perception of the relative deprivation by individuals, and, as such, indirectly, their evaluation of the general state of the economy, distributive justice and structural change. A battery of four questions has been asked to measure this sense of relative improvement of the life chances of the individual and his progeny. The issue of distributive justice is studied with the help of specific questions about economic and social reform. In view of the importance of policies of structural adjustment, popularly known as liberalisation, which formed a salient part of India's economic agenda when the survey was carried out, we would focus attention on its perception by the Indian electorate with the help of questions relating to integration with the international market economy and privatisation of public sector enterprises.

The relationship between economic change and governance within the context of a functioning democracy is the basic source of conjectures that underpin this chapter. This also forms the main basis of our explanation for India's 'half-hearted' liberalisation. The core issue here is the conflict between mobilised, empowered, and occasionally discontented groups of citizens and the state. As protest mounts, the ability of the state to impose rules that are fair, transparent, comprehensive, neutral and effective, declines. The decline of governmental effectiveness is a self-sustaining, downward-moving spiral, for the short-term success of a specific group in benefiting by breaking the rules only encourages similar demands by others, multiplying the state's inability to locate itself over and above the groups in conflict.[5] Once the state itself is the target, its neutral profile gets seriously compromised, generating what Kohli has succinctly described as the crisis of governability.

> Detailed investigation of local, regional, and national politics leads to the proposition that the roots of India's growing problems of governability are more political than socio-economic; that is, they are located mainly in India's political structure. A highly interventionist state dealing with a poor economy has become an object of intense political competition. The spread of egalitarian political values and the opportunities provided by democracy have, in turn, helped to transform what was once a heterogeneous social structure into many

groups of mobilised activists. Failure of leaders to make timely concessions has only intensified political demands and activity. And, finally, the growing weakness of fragmented political parties, which both reflects and exacerbates this process of over-politicisation has made it difficult for leaders to rule effectively (Kohli 1990: ix).

Why are post-colonial states typically afflicted with problems of governance? Part of the answer lies in what Gurr has described as *relative deprivation*. The problem is by no means specific to poor agrarian societies in the process of economic change. It is the weak and thin institutional structure that constitutes the interface between the state and society which enhances the intensity of the conflict generated by these developments in post-colonial societies. Rapid social and economic change combined with inadequate institutionalisation and parties with narrow social bases can lead to violent protest, crisis and decline of legitimacy. The theoretical linkage postulated by Huntington (1968) and Kohli (1990), both of which provide the sufficient conditions of mass political disorder, are thus reinforced with the conjectures of Gurr (1970), who provides the necessary conditions for the same to occur. These conjectures can be put together in the form of the following model, which suggests the hypothesis that for those who feel relatively deprived, and who have been politically mobilised, the authority of the state rapidly loses its legitimacy.

Figure 6.1
The Polarisation Model

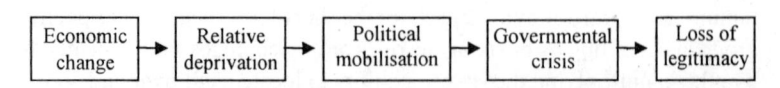

Economic change → Relative deprivation → Political mobilisation → Governmental crisis → Loss of legitimacy

The issue that emerges here concerns the fundamental problem of the relative autonomy of politics from that of the social and economic structures. The mainstream position of comparative politics, as summed up by Huntington, painted a picture of a quasi-automatic escalation of conflict. In a bold gesture, Huntington (1968: 55) gave it a law-like shape.

The impact of modernisation on traditional agrarian societies thus involves the following relationships.

1. $$\frac{\text{Social Mobilisation}}{\text{Economic Development}} = \text{Social Frustration}$$

2. $$\frac{\text{Social Frustration}}{\text{Mobility Opportunities}} = \text{Political Participation}$$

3. $$\frac{\text{Political Participation}}{\text{Political Institutionalisation}} = \text{Political Instability}$$

The insight implicit in the formulation of Huntington, seen in the context of Figure 6.1, establishes what we have called the polarisation model. The main break with traditional society comes with the spread of the notions of citizenship, individual rights, enfranchisement and entitlement. The whole process, referred to as modernisation in literature, can lead to tremendous frustration when economic growth and redistribution do not keep pace with the growth of aspirations, when the failure to achieve what one considers one's normal due for no fault of one's own, results in a sense of deprivation. The availability of radical leadership and its ability to make an issue out of the social closure, referred to in Figure 1.2 (Chapter 1) as the glass ceiling effect, can play a crucial role here. The political mobilisation of the angry masses, seething in rage against what they consider unjust deprivation, creates a radical demand for participation in the process of decision-making at the highest level of the system. In a political system that is not institutionalised, i.e., one where there exist few arenas at intermediate levels where some of this radical demand for participation can be actualised in the form of representation, all anger is aimed at the highest level, creating governmental crisis and political instability. The persistence of this condition can lead to an irreversible loss in legitimacy.

The socio-psychological approach, particularly the J-curve analysis of Gurr and Davis[6] provided further support to this conjecture, elevating this grim picture of class conflict to an inevitable side-effect of the process of modernisation of traditional societies. The role of the state in this context is crucial. A responsive state, operating under the democratic compulsion of being inclusive of social interests, rather than identifying itself exclusively with dominant groups, makes all the difference. India, as we have argued in this book, has not succumbed to this fate of intense, protracted and general social polarisation, expressing itself in the form of political unrest, cumulating in a fatal challenge to the legitimacy of the state. One reason could be the role of the political elite in putting the constitutional and institutional resources to their optimal use for the purpose of conflict resolution.

The Post-colonial State and the Room to Manoeuvre in the Middle

Following the turbulent 1960s, the assaults on constitutional norms and liberal institutions during the Emergency (1975–77) the governmental instability following the electoral victory of the Janata Party and the installation of the first non-Congress government in Delhi, many had started speculating about the final arrival of the long-predicted crisis of governance in India. Though the concerted pessimism about India's political future appears to have given way to cautious optimism, the issues of governmental crisis and deinstitutionalisation have continued to dominate academic debates on the relationship of democracy and economic change in India, first given general currency in Kohli (1990). Contrary to earlier predictions, the dire prospects of a rising crisis of governability engulfing the state have not been borne out by events. Instead, some institutions have been reinvigorated, and the state has found the necessary resources to bring other mutants into line—enough to continue the process of incremental social and economic change within a structure of democracy and legality.[7]

The ability of the state to acquire critical knowledge of the social process and to self-correct in consequence, is one of the main underlying themes of India's political economy. Some of these developments, expressing themselves in terms of effective reform and governance are beginning to trickle through, thanks to some recent writings such as Lewis (1995).[8] Other notable contributions to this theme are Drèze and Sen (1995) and Khilnani (1997).

What makes the new approach to India's political economy refreshingly different from the past attempts at theorisation is that, unlike the previous attempts at the application of models, whether derived from liberalism or Marxism, the new approaches are unorthodox and unconventional. Drèze and Sen, for example, talk about taking liberalisation seriously as a necessary reform, and plead for a radical reorientation of the social values of compassion and policy commitments to mass literacy, health and women's empowerment that should underpin economic models. The new economists have thus ventured into areas such as the political economy of social control that were previously, by default, left open for the less qualified to deliberate on. Even more reassuringly, some of this serious new political economy of India has started finding its way into the popular print media.[9]

Reform and governance are the two key ideas that provide a connecting thread to the specific themes that underpin Lewis' important contribution to the debate. Put simply, reform refers to changing the basic rules of transaction that underpin the economy. Governance refers to the conduct of social and economic transactions in an orderly fashion. The orthodoxy that has characterised scholarly understanding of development in India from Gunnar Myrdal's *Asian Drama* onwards, as we have already seen in the introductory section, suggests that reform is difficult to achieve in a peasant economy that attempts to follow the democratic path in order to achieve the transition from an agrarian to an industrial society. There are too many interests at stake. Those subaltern voices, empowered and enfranchised by democracy, are unlikely to go down as mere footnotes to history in the long and painful march to the modern world. The result is, therefore, either peaceful paralysis or chaotic political collapse and economic malfunctioning. This dictum, powerfully stated by Moore (1966) and reinforced by Bardhan's (1984: 78) stalemated conflict of social forces, has created a kind of conventional knowledge that depicts democratic change in the context of a peasant economy as an oxymoron. Rock the boat through reform: out goes governance.

Lewis' explanations confirm the assertions made in the introduction to this book. He shows how India has broken through the democracy-poverty-policy ineffectiveness trap. There is steady average per capita growth in income over five decades in the place of zero net growth during the preceding century-and-a-half. The percentage of people living below the poverty line has dropped significantly from about half of the population at Independence to much less, though some States like Bihar contain a disproportionate share of the poor. Though Lewis sagely refrains from scoring a point here, he could have drawn attention to the fact that the major battles on income distribution in India today are being fought on the minute differences in various estimates of the percentage of people below the poverty line, but not on the causality behind the robust trend away from the image of the stagnant pool of a majority poor that popular images in the West still associate with India. A vast middle class today enjoys access to infrastructural facilities and commodities of the kind that were not available previously. India has not yet tamed nature through technology, but the effects of drought, flood, pestilence and international price fluctuations have been brought under firm economic and administrative management.

The suggestion we get from Lewis helps us reformulate the Gurr–Huntington polarisation thesis discussed earlier by bringing in the theme of 'room to manoeuvre in the middle', and state in an explicit fashion some conjectures implicit in Kohli. Thus, when a reform-minded 'responsive' state provides the institutional space for marginal and deprived individuals to exercise their rights to economic democracy within the political space of the system, it injects much-needed governance into the system. In order to test the conjecture that this might explain the relative success of India in retaining both incremental change and democracy, the crucial evidence we need here is on the attitudes and perceptions of individuals aware of their own marginality and their heightened aspirations of life.

The chapter will next discuss the responses of the sample to a series of specific issues dealing with the redistribution of resources and perception of the measures of liberalisation. Among others, we shall next examine the implications of cumulative deprivation with regard to participation and the sense of efficacy, mainly to be able to see what the deprived actually do, and how they evaluate the institutions of state. The final section of this chapter will examine the extent to which India's political elites provide a linkage between institutions and the people, over and above the linkage provided by the party system.

'Objective' and 'Subjective' Measurement of Deprivation

The standard measurement of participation in the economy and enjoyment of the fruits of economic growth concentrates on data relating to consumption and the possession of enduring goods. The former constitute the base for the calculation of poverty-line statistics. Indian data relating to people living below the poverty line typically take into account the average calorie consumption by the individual. The possession of assets is the second technique favoured by statisticians. Both these indicators are considered objective measurements in the sense that the data do not depend upon the individual's attitude as much as his precise information with regard to his ownership of certain goods which, with regard to the society in question, are supposed to endow the beneficiary with an appropriate point on the scale of economic welfare. The 1996 survey formulated these indicators in terms of occupation, ownership of assets, type of house and an assessment of 'required income' as a proxy for the economic standard of living of the interviewee. A class variable was constructed by combining the responses to these questions. The class variable thus produced was cross-tabulated with other background variables in order to establish the social profile of the poor and the well-to-do.

The table clearly demonstrates the relationship between class and caste in Indian society. The Scheduled Castes and Tribes are more highly repre-

Table 6.1
Cross-tabulation of Class with Caste

Class (%)	Scheduled Castes	Scheduled Tribes	OBCs	Others
Very poor (30.6)	30.1	14.7	39.9	15.3
Poor (31.0)	19.5	11.1	42.4	27.0
Middle (25.2)	11.6	5.1	23.4	46.4
Upper (13.2)	5.0	2.1	23.4	69.4
Total	18.8	9.5	37.7	33.9

Note: 797 missing values not included.

sented at the lower end of the class scale. Respectively 30.1 per cent and 14.7 per cent of the very poor are Scheduled Castes or Scheduled Tribes, whereas the comparable proportions in the population as a whole for the SC and ST are 18.8 per cent and 9.5 per cent. The upper castes are present more at the higher levels of the class variable: respectively 46.4 per cent and 69.4 per cent of the middle and upper categories of the class variable belong to the elite castes, whose proportion in the population as a whole is 33.6 per cent. Among the poor and the very poor, the proportion of elite castes is respectively 27 per cent and 15.3 per cent—a far cry from their proportion in the population as a whole.

A similar pattern is sustained by the cross-tabulation of class and education (Table 6.2), which shows a clear correlation of the economic class with education. The poor and the very poor are much more likely to be illiterate than the middle or the upper classes (63.2 per cent illiteracy among the very poor compared to 32.2 per cent among the upper classes). At the upper level of the educational scale, the upper and middle classes are much more likely to be educated at the secondary level (24.7 per cent and 30.5 per cent) as compared to the poor or the very poor (16.8 per cent or 7.7 per cent). The comparable figures are even more pronounced in this direction for college education or above, namely, 13 per cent and 10.2 per cent for the upper and middle classes, as compared to 2.4 per cent and 0.1 per cent for the poor and the very poor respectively. The level of education is obviously a strong correlate of class in India.

So far, we have dealt with indicators that are objective in the sense that they are invariant with persons and apply uniformly to all people within specific measurable social and economic categories. Class in that sense is a social phenomenon, and the indicators that measure it are socially 'constructed'. At a different level, however, the individual's sense of his or her own welfare is essentially *personal*. People have a tendency to evaluate their personal situations in terms of their own life experience,

Table 6.2
Cross-tabulation of Class with Education (in per cent)

	Illiterate	Up to Primary	Middle School	Higher Secondary	College and above
Very poor	63.2	20.8	8.2	7.7	0.1
Poor	44.4	21.1	15.3	16.8	2.4
Middle	27.0	17.2	15.2	30.5	10.2
Upper	32.2	15.7	14.3	24.7	13.0
Total	41.9	18.9	13.1	20.2	5.9

and their personal expectations of life. As such, one's past affluence or poverty, own situation in comparison to the reference group, future expectations or, for that matter, the life chances that one expects one's children to have, are important determinants of the subjective evaluation of one's state of welfare. These are, what one may call, the actor's categories of welfare as compared to the objective measures which, in this sense, are the observer's categories. We present four sets of objective assessments of the financial situation by our respondents, presented in terms of the usual socio-economic categories, as well as by the 'constructed' category of class.

The findings reported in Table 6.3 show two interesting trends. The first and the most striking aspect of these findings is that they do not sustain the image of a strongly polarised society where the conventional cleavage of class, status and generation would represent diametrically opposed levels of personal experience with regard to the perception of the financial situation. The levels of satisfaction reported by different sub-groups are invariably within a few percentage points of the sample average for the population as a whole. In this sense, these findings lend a certain credibility to the image of incremental growth and redistribution presented by Lewis. This is true particularly with regard to the robust optimism about the future, the past and the satisfaction with the present as compared to the future one envisages for oneself, and for one's children.

Some of the facts reported here provide empirical support to the conjectures by Lewis. They suggest a revisionist view that questions the earlier image of immiserisation and class conflict. The specific contribution of Lewis to this debate which is salient for the purposes of this book is that Lewis puts the economic statistics in the context of national politics, in order to show that India's achievements in this area, possibly unknown to the leading commentators on India's political economy, draw on knowledge and expertise that have been 'quietly' accumulating in India's policy community now for over two decades. India's top policy makers, imple-

Table 6.3
Perception of Financial Satisfaction by Socio-demographic Groups (in per cent)

Groups	Financial Situation has Improved	Satisfied with Present Financial Situation	Financial Situation will Get Better	Children have Better Opportunities
All Groups	29.2	28.4	47.9	54.5
Gender				
Men	31.6	31.0	50.5	55.8
Women	26.7	25.7	45.3	53.2
Locality				
Rural	26.6	25.8	45.1	51.4
Urban	37.3	36.6	56.9	64.4
Age				
< 25 years	32.9	29.9	52.5	49.3
26–35 years	31.2	28.0	50.1	58.1
36–45 years	27.4	27.5	45.7	56.5
46–55 years	25.9	29.1	46.9	55.5
56 years or more	24.3	27.4	40.1	53.0
Education				
Illiterate	22.3	22.0	39.5	44.7
Up to middle	27.8	27.1	47.5	58.4
College, no degree	39.9	38.7	60.0	64.5
College+	49.0	47.4	69.4	69.9
Religion				
Hindu	29.1	28.6	47.9	54.1
Muslim	26.6	25.9	45.2	52.9
Christian	34.6	31.2	59.1	72.4
Sikh	48.4	34.1	52.4	61.1
Caste				
Scheduled Caste	24.5	21.2	42.3	50.8
Scheduled Tribe	25.3	23.5	50.5	50.9
OBC	25.7	27.3	45.7	53.4
Upper caste	36.4	34.9	52.6	58.8
Class				
Very poor	18.1	17.7	37.5	46.3
Poor	27.5	25.8	46.7	52.8
Middle	34.6	43.0	54.3	60.3
Upper class	51.2	50.2	68.7	72.9

menters of public policy in the national and regional bureaucracies and the generations of middle managers whom they have trained, have taken charge of policy and have created a culture where things happen, perhaps slowly, but registering nevertheless incremental, linear growth.

The second important aspect of these findings is that the difference in the levels of satisfaction of the different sub-groups present a striking linearity along the conventional lines of social conflict. In spite of the generally optimistic picture created by the data, Table 6.3 indicates effects of gender, age and class on the opinions that respondents have about the financial situation and its implications for their welfare. Men tend to be more optimistic than women, reflecting the relative powerlessness of women which makes them more cautious and non-committal. Similarly, urban India is clearly more optimistic than rural India. The upwardly mobile tend to migrate to urban areas, which perhaps reflects their more robust attitude. It may also be the case that the new economic *mantra* of liberalisation, initiative and the visible material consequences of integration with the world economy through the ownership of household appliances is more pronounced in urban India than in rural areas.

The attitudes of the young as opposed to the elderly are generally more optimistic. This may reflect the effect of education, which closely parallels the same trend. But either way, it shows that, *ceteris paribus*, the sheer generational change would increase the chances of the greater spread of the atmosphere of buoyant optimism and positive attitudes towards liberalisation.

With regard to the attitudes of religious groups, the findings reported here should be treated with caution and seen only as a first approximation of a complex reality. Thus, Muslim attitudes towards the four different measures of one's personal experience with the economy—generally lower than the national average—confirm the fact that there are perhaps some underlying factors responsible for the condition of that community. But more research is necessary to conclude whether the fact that they tend to be less optimistic about their financial situation is reflective of their community, class or level of education. The same argument holds for the Sikh community, which is placed above the national average on all counts. Once again, it is perhaps reflective of its class and education, rather than on the idiosyncratic factor of religious affiliation.

The caste variable operates on predictable lines, with the upper castes reporting higher scores on all four indicators compared to the lower castes. It is very interesting here, however, to note that the absolute differences between the scores reported by the two extremes of the caste status are not very sharp, as compared to the effects of education, or more significantly, class. Education and class are not, like caste, primordial factors of life. One invests time and effort to gain them, and in the process, becomes conscious of differential rewards in life. Caste identification without caste consciousness can actually dull the edges of anger and resentment at the inquitousness of life. Higher status in terms of education and higher class status are the main factors of political consciousness, and hence lead to a greater sense of relative deprivation. The latter two are the most discriminating in terms of their impact on subjective perception of welfare, with the college educated or the upper class being in some cases twice as well off as compared to the illiterate or the very poor.

Devising a Combined Measure of Deprivation

The perception of one's own welfare and that of one's children (Table 6.3) appear mutually inter-correlated, i.e., those who are better off on one indicator, appear to be better off on the others and vice versa. On the basis of the generally positive and linear relations of the perception of welfare along the lines of conventional social cleavages, it is possible to think of these specific indicators as parts of a general dimension of achievement-deprivation. The evidence we need for the construction of a general scale of this kind is to demonstrate the propensity of these four measures in some sense to 'hang together'. As such, the responses to the four single dimensions were transformed, putting the 'no responses' at the mid-point in each case, thus producing, in each case, a scale measuring a specific aspect of the achievements that one might look forward to. A general achievement-deprivation variable was constructed by adding up the four indicators. The multiple correlations of these five variables are reported in Table 6.4.

It should be noted that the four indicators are indeed quite strongly correlated to one another as well as to a new variable, namely, achievement-deprivation, generated by adding up the responses to the four indicators of satisfaction with the personal benefit from the economy. Thanks to the two measures of satisfaction, the objective measure being economic class and achievement-deprivation being the subjective scale, we now have two different and complementary ways of measuring deprivation. A new variable, 'deprivation', with four levels, was created by combining the two.[10] The social profile of the new measure of deprivation is presented in Table 6.5.

The new 'deprivation' index divides the sample into four categories. In the first are the most deprived who perform the worst both in terms of class (where they appear among the very poor), and the general subjective satisfaction variable where they are among the lowest achievers. This group of 10 per cent thus represents the bottom of the pyramid in terms of the material and psychological achievers of India. Their symmetric

Table 6.4
Multiple Correlation of the Indicators of Relative Deprivation

	Financial Situation has Improved	Satisfaction with Present Financial Situation	Financial Situation will be Better	Children have Better Opportunities	Level of General Achievement
Financial situation has improved	1	—	—	—	—
Satisfaction with present situation	0.49	1	—	—	—
Financial situation will be better	0.34	0.33	1	—	—
Children have better opportunities	0.19	0.21	0.27	1	—
Level of general achievement	0.71	0.74	0.67	0.64	1

Note: All the correlations reported above are significant at 0.000 level.

opposite are the top 12.5 per cent, the 'high achievers' who perform the best on both the general indicators. Interspersed in between the two categories are the 'moderately deprived' group of 28.8 per cent, which performs relatively well on the class variable but not on psychological satisfaction with their achievement, and the 40.8 per cent of the 'moderate achievers', who perform well on the psychological dimension of achievement but not on the material side.

The findings in Table 6.5 help define the social profiles of achievement and deprivation in India. The most deprived are more likely to be women rather than men, and the achievers, both moderate and high, more likely to be men than women. Similarly, people living in rural areas are more likely to be among the low achievers of India.

The performance of urban dwellers is actually quite striking among high achievers. A quarter of urban dwellers count themselves among the highest achievers compared to just over a tenth of rural dwellers, a phenomenon that indicates the double effect of the larger concentration of opportunities in urban India on one hand, and the effect of self-selection, for it is the more highly motivated and resourceful who migrate to towns, and

Table 6.5
Social Profile of the Most and Least Deprived (in per cent)

Groups	Most Deprived	Moderately Deprived	Moderate Achievers	High Achievers
All	10.0	28.8	40.8	12.5
Gender				
Men	8.8	28.6	43.2	13.9
Women	11.3	29.0	38.3	11.2
Locality				
Rural	12.0	30.5	41.8	8.5
Urban	4.0	23.7	37.8	25.1
Education				
Illiterate	15.8	33.6	39.0	4.5
Primary	9.4	30.6	42.9	9.6
Middle school	6.3	26.3	45.4	14.6
Higher Secondary	3.7	22.7	41.9	23.1
College and above	2.1	16.2	33.5	38.5
Age				
Up to 45 years	9.6	28.2	41.8	13.1
46 or more	11.1	30.3	38.1	11.1
Religion				
Hindu	10.2	28.9	40.8	12.5
Muslim	11.1	30.8	39.9	10.4
Christian	4.8	21.8	50.3	12.5
Sikh	0.8	25.4	30.2	33.3
Caste				
Scheduled Caste	15.7	30.4	42.1	4.5
Scheduled Tribe	11.8	29.7	45.8	4.6
OBC	11.0	30.0	42.7	9.9
Upper caste	5.6	26.4	37.0	21.6

Note: Excluding missing values from the deprivation scale; see Appendix 2 on scale construction.

once there, these tendencies are further reinforced through the peer group pressure of other aspiring high achievers.

The effect of education on achievement is the most important among the socio-demographic features reported in Table 6.5. The illiterate, as compared to those with higher secondary or above level of education, are quite unlikely to be among the high achievers of India, for only 4.5 per cent of the illiterate make it to this select group, compared to 38.5 per cent of those with college education or above. At the other end of the scale, only 2.1 per cent of the college educated and 3.7 per cent of those with education up to the higher secondary level are among the most deprived, compared to 15.8 per cent among the illiterate. Closely related to the educational dimension is age, grouped together into those who are 45 or less, and those older than 45. The generation of Midnight's Children, i.e., those who are 45 years or less in age, are among the higher achievers of India compared to older people.

As before, the performances of religious groups should be treated with caution, lest we confuse religious affiliation as the cause of under-achievement. Muslims appear to be among the lower achievers compared to other religions. Christians perform better than Hindus, whose achievements are higher than those of Muslims. But the best performers are Sikhs, with more than twice the likelihood of being among the highest achievers of India compared to the sample average. But religion, at the first approximation, represents only a grouping of individuals; much more detailed statistical analysis is required to establish the role of religion in the causal path towards high achievement. There are complex historical factors at work here, indicating the long-term effect of migration of the Muslim middle class to Pakistan after Partition, and the role of missionaries and colonial rule on the material and psychological situation of India's Christians. That the Sikhs of India are generally high achievers is widely acknowledged; how much of this can be attributed to the propensity of the Sikh community to reinforce these high-achieving tendencies, and how much can be attributed to the fortuitous combination of factors essential to high growth and sociological factors inimical to large concentrations of wealth (Punjab's *ryotwari* land relations compared to the zamindari systems of land tenure in Bihar and Orissa under colonial rule, for example) appear as pointers to further investigation.

Finally, the relationship between caste and achievement is on predictable lines. Scheduled Castes and Tribes are more likely to be among the most deprived of India as compared to the upper castes, and the upper castes are more likely to be among the highest achievers as compared to members of the Scheduled Castes and Tribes.

Deprivation and the Politics of Redistribution

How one construes the path from low to high achievement depends on a number of factors. At one extreme is the passive acceptance of one's individual situation. For some, the main responsibility for misery or the good fortune of a high standard of living lies mainly with one's *karma*. At the other extreme are those who believe in *purusakara*, the symmetric opposite of passive fatality. For them, a combination of individual initiative and the optimal use of all one's resources is what makes the difference. Most people evince a combination of attitudes, with elements of belief in individual initiative judiciously added to a passive resignation to fate. The role of the state and the effect of government policies, however, increasingly appear as important factors responsible for what happens to the material and moral life of individuals. The government can make a difference in a number of ways. It can try to bring about policies of major structural change, such as redistribution of property, changing laws of land-ownership, or for that matter, it can roll back the unfettered control of the bureaucracy on the free flow of goods and services. Similarly, even without necessarily changing the structure of property relations, the government can bring about measures of egalitarianism by giving handouts to the less advantaged. A democratic society assumes that such legislative and administrative measures are undertaken as a result of popular pressure or in anticipation of popular approval. Our objective in this section is to see to what extent the people are aware of some of the crucial measures taken by the Government of India from the outset, and to the extent that people are aware of them, and how their opinions are distributed across these key issues.

In order to examine the attitudes of the different sections of the population towards the policies of economic and social reform, the following question was asked with specific reference to land ceilings: *Some people say that the government should pass legislation so that people are not allowed to own and possess a large amount of land and property. Others say that people should be allowed to own as much land and property as they can make/acquire. What would you say?*

The findings reported in Table 6.6 show first of all how strong the belief is in limiting ownership at all levels of society. Roughly 70 per cent of Indian society believes that there should be some form of limit on ownership of land and property in India. Failure to have an opinion on this issue is also an interesting finding. Predictably, the illiterate are more likely not to have an answer compared to the educated: 19.2 per cent of the illiterate do not know if the government should limit the extent of land and property by legislation, compared to 1.4 per cent of those with college education or above who do not pronounce an opinion on this. Equally interesting is the variation around the position opposed to legislative upper limits to land and property: Christians, Sikhs, upper castes, upper classes and high achievers are more likely to want to have no such upper limits than the Indian population as a whole.

Table 6.6
Limit of Ownership by Social Background (in per cent)

Groups	Limit Ownership	Qualified Answer	No Ceiling on Property	Don't Know
All Groups	69.4	2.0	17.8	10.9
Men	72.6	1.4	18.5	7.6
Women	65.2	3.2	17.0	14.5
Rural	68.8	2.6	17.3	11.3
Urban	69.5	1.4	19.2	9.9
< 25 years	68.7	2.2	18.2	10.9
26–35 years	69.6	2.2	18.2	10.0
36–45 years	70.3	1.6	16.9	11.3
46–55 years	67.7	2.5	17.2	12.6
56 years or more	67.3	3.5	17.8	11.3
Illiterate	64.1	3.0	13.6	19.2
Up to primary	71.9	2.4	17.4	8.2
Middle school	73.3	1.6	20.4	4.7
Higher secondary	73.4	1.4	21.8	3.3
College+	68.4	1.8	28.3	1.4
Hindu	68.5	2.5	17.4	11.6
Muslim	72.9	1.5	16.1	9.5
Christian	65.7	2.2	30.1	1.9
Sikh	61.9	0.0	25.4	12.7
Scheduled Caste	71.4	2.3	14.0	12.3
Scheduled Tribe	71.9	4.0	11.8	12.4
OBC	68.1	2.0	18.1	11.8
Upper caste	67.6	2.2	21.1	9.0
Very poor	71.2	3.0	13.9	12.0
Poor	71.3	1.5	15.5	11.7
Middle	67.8	1.9	19.6	10.7
Upper class	64.0	0.9	28.5	6.6
Most deprived	70.3	3.8	9.7	16.1
Moderately deprived	70.8	2.4	14.7	12.1
Moderate achievers	68.8	1.5	19.7	10.0
High achievers	67.6	1.0	24.9	6.6

The relationship of deprivation and policy preference as reported in Table 6.6 goes in the 'right' direction. Taking the preference for 'no ceiling on property' as an indicator, we see that about 14 per cent of the very poor pronounce themselves for this option, whereas the proportion of the upper class taking this position (at 28.5 per cent) is twice as large. The remarkable point that emerges from this Table is the high consensus in

India for some form of social control over property. Not only is the level of support for limiting ownership is high at all levels of achievement; the difference between the most desired and the high achievers is only about 2 per cent.

Democracy and the Politics of Liberalisation

The overwhelming support for limits to land and property within the populace describes the core of the post-Independence political culture of India. It grew as a consequence of the socialistic ideals that underpinned the struggle for Independence. Subsequently, it was further reinforced with the structure of planning that the Congress party, under the leadership of Nehru, adopted as the basis of the model of a mixed economy. However, the control of the economy steadily passed into the hands of those who did not have any immediate stake in it. The lack of competition from within or from outside had produced no incentives to *innovate*, but merely to *replicate*. When the government of Narasimha Rao took advantage of the desperate financial crisis of 1991 in order to open India's economy to the operations of market processes, the country started making basic changes in the structure of the economy without much debate within the public. Liberalisation had not figured prominently in the election campaign. At the best of times, the austerity and the sharp turns of the economy, at least in the short term, hurt many powerful interests. The policies of liberalisation are rarely the best method to win elections. The government, nevertheless, kept the momentum for further liberalisation on a steady course, and, urged on by the World Bank and a section of the Indian elites, soon reached a point of no return as far as the two key components of the policy of liberalisation, namely, access to the multinationals to the Indian market, and the privatisation of public sector undertakings are concerned. Popular responses to the two questions are analysed below.

The structure of planned development and the mixed economy assumed tariff barriers and other mechanisms through which India was intended to achieve import substitution. Naturally, there was little room for foreign multinational companies in this scheme of things. Now that the main policy has changed, the survey posed the following question in order to test the extent of public knowledge and sympathy or antipathy towards this policy: *Foreign companies should not be allowed free trade in India. Do you agree or disagree with this?*

Table 6.7
No Free Trade for Foreign Companies (in per cent)

Groups	Disagree	Don't Know/ No Opinion	Agree
All	21.4	40.9	37.3
Men	25.9	28.6	45.2
Women	16.7	53.5	29.3
Rural	21.4	45.0	33.3
Urban	21.3	28.0	50.1
< 25 years	24.0	36.8	38.9
26–35 years	21.4	38.1	40.1
36–45 years	21.0	42.2	36.6
46–55 years	19.4	45.4	34.7
56 years or more	19.0	47.4	33.0
Illiterate	15.8	60.6	23.1
Up to primary	19.5	40.1	40.0
Middle school	24.8	30.1	44.6
Higher Secondary	29.4	18.0	52.4
College +	32.5	5.0	62.3
Hindu	21.5	40.8	37.2
Muslim	21.6	40.6	37.7
Christian	21.2	35.9	42.5
Sikh	17.3	53.5	29.1
Scheduled Caste	19.6	44.7	35.5
Scheduled Tribe	17.5	55.7	26.5
OBC	21.4	42.6	35.4
Upper caste	24.6	31.3	43.8
Very poor	16.7	53.8	29.5
Poor	21.3	41.8	36.9
Middle	25.4	33.1	41.6
Upper class	29.0	20.9	50.0
Most deprived	15.7	53.5	30.7
Moderately deprived	19.8	45.7	34.5
Moderate achiever	23.1	39.2	37.7
High achiever	28.0	22.3	49.7

Liberalisation was possibly an elite-initiated policy with little popular support or knowledge at the time of its original inception: it certainly was so after a full term in office by the Rao government which made it the cornerstone of its politics. Only about a fifth of the population approved of the policy of integration with the international market economy, particularly with regard to the open access to multinationals, and 37.3 per cent were opposed to this policy. Roughly two-fifths of the population was not aware of this policy initiative, or considered it so far removed from everyday life that it had no opinion on the issue. But Table 6.7 makes it clear that strong support for this form of liberalisation did exist within some vocal and articulate sections of the population, namely, the higher secondary and college educated, urban, upper-class people, and the high achievers.

The issue of integration with the world market certainly divided the electorate into those keen on the protection of India's own business and industry, essentially a *swadeshi* view of the policy towards liberalisation. Taking education as a characteristic, we can see that non-response falls from a high of 61 per cent among the illiterate, to 5 per cent among the degree educated and above. But as we go up the educational ladder, both the level of support and opposition go up, respectively, from about 16 per cent to 32.5 per cent for support, and 23 per cent to 63 per cent of opposition. This appears to be the trend when we take age (the younger are less likely to be without opinion), or class or deprivation, where the better provided for are both more opinionated (i. e., less likely to say 'don't know') as well as fragmented.

The second question, *Government companies should be given to private hands. Do you agree or disagree with this?* was asked to test popular opinion on the other important aspect of liberalisation, namely, privatisation. Table 6.8 reports on this.

The picture we get here is a replica of the previous image: over two-fifths of the population without any specific knowledge of the policy (to the extent they do not have an opinion on the issue); meagre overall support (23.5 per cent); and rather substantial opposition (34 per cent). Like before, people without an opinion on the issue are more likely to be women, rural, illiterate, old, Scheduled Castes and Scheduled Tribes, very poor, and those who have not had much direct participation in the fruits of economic development. Support, on the other hand, comes from the symmetrically opposite groups: men, urban, higher secondary and college educated, middle and upper castes, but quite strongly from the high achievers and the upper class. But the pattern of opposition also grows, indicating a polarisation of opinion towards liberalisation within the population as a whole.

Table 6.8
Privatise Government Companies (in per cent)

Groups	Disagree	Don't Know/ No Opinion	Agree
All	34.0	42.0	23.5
Men	41.0	29.7	28.9
Women	26.9	54.7	17.9
Rural	33.2	45.6	20.9
Urban	36.6	30.7	32.0
< 25 years	36.3	38.6	24.7
26–35 years	35.3	40.6	23.6
36–45 years	35.2	40.8	23.7
46–55 years	32.8	44.8	22.1
56 years or more	27.5	50.0	21.9
Illiterate	24.9	61.1	13.7
Up to primary	33.4	41.0	25.3
Middle school	42.9	31.6	25.0
Higher Secondary	45.0	19.9	34.8
College +	44.8	9.2	45.6
Hindu	33.9	41.9	23.7
Muslim	34.4	43.0	22.4
Christian	42.1	36.3	21.2
Sikh	21.3	52.0	26.8
Scheduled Caste	36.4	43.7	19.6
Scheduled Tribe	31.0	51.5	17.0
OBC	31.1	44.9	23.5
Upper caste	37.1	34.0	28.5
Very poor	28.8	55.1	16.1
Poor	35.3	41.9	22.8
Middle	39.9	34.2	25.9
Upper class	38.2	24.7	37.1
Most deprived	26.1	56.3	17.6
Moderately deprived	32.3	46.5	21.1
Moderate achiever	37.4	39.7	23.0
High achiever	39.5	25.7	34.8

Does Democracy Promote Social Opportunity and Economic Security?

India's liberalisation policy is probably an extreme example of surreptitious attempts to bring about structural change in a democracy where political participation and transparency, thanks to a vigilant press, zealous judiciary and contentious parliament, take a watchful interest in economic policy and its implementation. The circumstances under which this initiative towards liberalisation was taken are well known and have already been mentioned in the text. The fact remains, however, that even after five years of application and propagation, as we have seen above, liberalisation is not an overwhelmingly popular policy. What implications does this have for the functioning of democracy in India, particularly with regard to the initiation and implementation of economic policy?

The question acquires a specific meaning when we put the issue in comparative perspective. A case in point is China, where specific economic policies, considered rational and necessary by the leadership, have been implemented with exceptional brutality in the past. Commenting on the terrible costs of Maoist policies meant for revolutionary economic growth, Waldron writes,

> ... in China between 1959 and 1961, cannibalism was perhaps more widely practised than at any other time or place in human history. It was the consequence of probably the greatest famine of all time, which was directly caused by Communist policy and cost somewhere between 30 and 60 million dead.[11]

It is a smug and therefore dangerous idea to suggest that such things could not take place in India which has a culture and tradition that is more respectful of life. One need only recall the terrible costs of the 'man-made' 1943 Bengal famine where, by one calculation, between two and three million people died of starvation.[12] The question that arises here is: To what extent is there a potential for the elite 'hijacking' of economic policy from popular control, and to the extent we have some evidence (which is plainly the case with regard to liberalisation), why does Indian democracy thus hold its political elites under careful observation? In order to explore this issue further, several questions with some bearing on economic policy and leadership were cross-tabulated with the main deprivation-achievement variable (Table 6.9).

The survey shows that the relatively more deprived among the people are aware of the fact that development has not benefited all sections of society equally. Nor are they all cared for in the same manner: the government stands guilty of this asymmetry as much as the political representatives. But even among the most deprived, over 60 per cent believe in strong leadership, and would presumably concede the government the authority to take initiative in matters of high policy of the state. The percentage goes up among the high achievers.

Table 6.9
Deprivation and Attitudes Social towards Social Policy (in per cent)

Questions about Policy	All	Most Deprived	Moderately Deprived	Moderate Achievers	High Achievers
What this country needs more than all the laws and talk is a few determined and strong leaders. (Agree)	72.6	63.4	69.8	73.8	84.2
Government policies are not responsible for the poverty of the people. (Agree)	26.4	20.7	22.7	29.8	31.6
The government generally takes care of the interests of the common people. (Agree)	39.0	30.2	33.1	44.8	44.1
Would you say that persons we elect by voting generally care about what people like you think, or that they don't care? (Care)	22.7	13.3	18.8	25.9	30.3
The poor and deprived enjoy better social status now than before. (Agree)	48.4	29.8	40.0	54.6	64.1
Have the benefits of development gone only to the well-to-do or have the poor and the needy also benefited?[13] (Poor and needy also benefited)	28.6	17.5	23.1	31.6	41.7
The government has initiated several schemes and programmes for the benefit of the people, such as housing schemes, employment schemes, old-age pension, loans/subsidies, etc. Have you or your family ever availed of such benefits? (Yes)	16.0	14.5	15.6	17.8	13.1

The high achievers (12.5 per cent of the sample as we learn from Table 6.5) present the paternalist image that one often ascribes to India's elite. They are, as we find in Table 6.9, overwhelmingly in favour of strong leadership (84 per cent as compared to 63 per cent for the most deprived). They are more likely to absolve the government of its responsibility for poverty and are more likely to believe than the most deprived (44 per cent as compared to 30 per cent) that the government generally takes care of the interest of common people. They are more than twice likely to repose their faith in elected representatives as compared to the most deprived (30 per cent as against 13 per cent). They also have relatively greater faith in the redistributive capacity of the Indian political system. Of the high achievers, 64 per cent believe that the poor and needy enjoy better status now than before, compared to 30 per cent for the most deprived. The corresponding figure, when it comes to the belief that the benefits of development have gone to the poor and needy as well as the well-to-do, is at about 42 per cent, more than twice as high for the most deprived, only 17.5 per cent of whom share that opinion. The only area where the high achievers are behind the most deprived, is in the confirmation that they have actually availed of some government welfare scheme, such as housing, employment, old age pension, loans or subsidies. Interestingly, when we look at the moderate achievers of India, who, at 40.8 per cent (Table 6.5) are the largest group, their attitudes run parallel in every respect to the high achievers except this one.

Conclusion

Though this chapter concerns itself with popular perceptions of the political economy of development, its scope does not permit a detailed examination of the economic and social indicators of growth and redistribution in India. The main emphasis has been on people's perception of the larger structures of the economy, and the political process which helps ordinary men and women express their opinions on the larger shape of things. Structural change in the economy, particularly policies intended to produce a market-friendly environment at home and making it accessible to the international economic system, are no longer completely foreign to the strategic thinking regarding the Indian economy today, though the specific nuance varies from one government to another. But in a democratic set-up, such plans cannot go very far without popular acceptance. The chapter, therefore, made a special attempt to study popular information, perception and evaluation of the economic process.

What one learns from the statistical indicators, however, shows a trend towards incremental progress in the perception of growth and redistribution. The economy has gained momentum. The extent of mass poverty has been reduced in comparison to the situation at Independence. This raises two questions in terms of our study. How did a poor country which takes democracy and reform seriously break out of the low-level equilibrium trap? Even more important, why does the discourse of poverty and justice in India remain overwhelmingly democratic?

Some of the findings reported in this chapter give credibility to the claim that some of the progress made by the Indian economy has indeed trickled down, to the point where even the bottom of the social pyramid has some participation in the economy to report. Comparable findings have also been studied by Lewis (1995), who finds support in the new writing on India's economy. Citing the work of Ranade, Lewis shows how 'leakage' of developmental resources through corruption and inefficient utilisation has not been as extensive or damaging as previously believed.[14] The Integrated Rural Development Programme (IRDP) is credited with having reached the poor, including the very poor, and increasing their productivity. The policy implication in this respect is to identify the most opportune point in the social matrix where a developmental intervention would be most effective.

Those familiar with the American prognosis of the Indian situation in the 1960s will find a contrast in the findings reported in this chapter. As a matter of fact, this revisionist view of India, which is in stark contrast to the basket case image of before, is already appearing in mainstream literature. There is a remarkable turnaround in Lewis' own line of thinking itself. In his *India: A Quiet Crisis*, Lewis (1962) had foreseen an impending crisis, born out of the Indian inability to sustain policy formulation and implementation. Fears of an impending political and economic crisis were also voiced by the other main political commentary of the period, Harrison (1960). Three decades later, with the halcyon days of Jawaharlal Nehru and the hegemonic role of the Congress party only a fading memory, Lewis has set the record straight in *India's Political Economy*. The findings belie some of the prognoses of *Redistribution with Growth*[15] a classic landmark from the seventies as well, ironically through the application of precisely some of the policies, such as irreversible transfer of resources and reformist political coalitions which were not thought of in the 1960s scholarship as likely to take place in India.

So what actually happened in India, and to what extent do our findings help us understand this? One of our main contentions is to draw attention to the disjunction of political prominence and articulate policy makers on one hand, and entrepreneurship and real economic power on the other. Relatively unknown, and uncelebrated, the latter—many of them our moderate and high achievers—have done more than make do over the years. With allies in unlikely places, these agents of the new economic policy of the 1990s have pressed ahead over the past decades. This interface of the town and the village where the new political elites operate lies beyond the scope of conventional analysis of the Indian economy, which concentrates on either the 'commanding heights' of the economy located in metropolitan capitals, or in the hopeless misery of the most deprived villages. But this is where an opinion survey can be most helpful. The 'room to manoeuvre in the middle' that democratic politics has brought to this politics of the meso level, has also given a new lease of life to the village economy, besides generating a sustained basis for agrarian productivity, at least in those parts of India where the new agricultural technology has been matched with adequate infrastructure.

New policies of liberalisation and the older structure of redistribution have combined to blunt the edges of radical politics, and brought an added measure of legitimacy to the political system. The interaction of protest movements and new economic processes has opened up greater room to manoeuvre for marginal social groups. This, in turn, has produced new challenges, sometimes stretching the resilience of the system to the limits. The further implications of this issue are the main themes of the next chapter.

Notes

1. There is, as a matter of fact, room to manoeuvre in every society, for it is difficult to imagine a situation where the writ of one person might run so effectively that no consultation or participation is needed. As Scott (1985) shows, in most situations the formally powerless have a range of techniques through which to bring pressure to bear on the decision makers. But the real scope of participation might vary radically from one political system to another, depending on the constitutional structure that underpins it, the values and norms of the society, the nature of group consciousness and organisation of the groups in society.
2. The challenging combination of poverty and democracy was the main thrust of Moore's (1966) pessimistic reading of the Indian situation. In comparison, a more optimistic case for the effectiveness of democratic intervention for the removal of mass poverty has been made by Drèze and Sen (1995) and Lewis (1995).
3. Jawaharlal Nehru's speech in the Constituent Assembly, New Delhi, on 14 August 1947. See Drèze and Sen (1995: 1).
4. Austin (1966) gives an excellent introduction to the process of constitution making as a result of compromise, the elusive search of consensus and the necessary accommodation of contradictions.

5. Rudolph and Rudolph (1987) refer to the phenomenon as demand groups. The room to manoeuvre of the Indian state consists in its ability of transforming dyadic conflicts between capital and labour, landowners and agricultural workers, neighbouring regions and localities, students and teachers, teachers and universities, and so on, into triadic transactions where the state becomes the arbitrator and the initiator of negotiations.
6. See the volume edited by Graham and Gurr (1969).
7. Thus, some of the main institutions of the Emergency have survived. The Research and Analysis Wing (RAW), an innovation of the Emergency regime of 1975–77 was not disbanded by the subsequent governments but integrated into the normal institutional set-up.
8. The book brings together 12 essays that Professor Lewis has written over a period of 35 years. The essays, seen in the historical contexts in which they were originally written, reflect many of the concerns and preconceptions of India's economic policy and their recent reorientation.
9. Thus, Kaushik Basu, 'View point: Left and Trite', *India Today*, p. 52, 19 January 1998, argues that by 'reducing "market" to a dirty word, you can't check economic inequality'.
10. See Appendix 2 for the details of the construction of this scale.
11. Arthur Waldron, '"Eat people"—a Chinese reckoning', *Current*, 396: 17, October 1997.
12. See Sen (1981).
13. The full question was asked in the following way: *Some people say that whatever progress was made over the last few years through development schemes and programmes of the government has benefited only the well-to-do. Others say no, the poor and needy have also benefited from them. What would you say? Have the benefits of development gone only to the well-to-do or have the poor and needy also benefited?*
14. Citing the work of Ranade (1991), Lewis (1995: 361n) provides an account of incremental progress. On the basis of a study of the rate of growth of real consumption expenditure of the bottom four deciles of India's rural population, Ranade shows that their average consumption has increased from 0.46 per cent annually during 1970–77 to 1.85 per cent annually during 1977–83.
15. Chenery, Hallis et al. 1974, Oxford: Oxford University Press.

7

Community, Conflict and Local Democracy: Patterns of Regional Variation

This chapter has two main objectives. The first objective is to explain why Indian democracy simultaneously brings out potential conflict in the most explicit (and sometimes disorderly) way, and simultaneously generates a cohesive substance in which differences of religion, language, caste, class, tribe, generation and gender find accommodation. Previous chapters of this book have already explored some aspects of community and conflict. We have already seen from the survey data that region and nation are not strictly exclusive categories. The regionalist is not necessarily 'anti-nationalist': 'region' is also a source of a redefinition of 'nation'. Our attempt in this chapter would be to explore how the dynamic process of local democracy provides a fusion of the duality of community and conflict, and contributes to the evolution of a robust national identity of a unique kind.

Our second objective is to pursue the theme of community and conflict at the level of regions. Popular usage of these categories draws on the putative existence of greatly diverging trends across regions. It is assumed that the gaps between regions are widening, from which one deduces that the threats to the unity and integrity of the nation are serious. To verify such assertions, we have undertaken a preliminary analysis of the pattern of regional variation in India across the main indicators developed in the survey.

After five decades of Independence, 'community' remains the elusive goal of India's nation and state. Despite the frequent reference to *Bharat Mata* ('Mother India') and other cultural symbols of Indian nationhood, the cultural depiction of the community was a muted theme during the long years of the struggle for Independence. 'Divide and rule' became the dictum of British rule during the last decades prior to Independence. And just as the British took every possible advantage of the cultural, linguistic and religious divisions of India, the Congress party, under the leadership of Gandhi and Nehru, found its effective counter-strategy in its resolve to unite and oppose. But if unity brought strength to the top leadership, some of the costs of unity had to be borne by the cultural and religious minorities at the lower levels. The political need for unity made it imperative to play down differences. Where such differences were the results of resentment against past oppression or exploitation, or against social and moral marginalisation, the support of the aggrieved party for the cause of a national community could be at best lukewarm, or absent altogether.

As we learn from the tragic history of India's partition, even a deliberately contrived 'thin' definition of the Indian nation was not effective in retaining the loyalty of the majority of India's Muslims, who preferred the more categorical and exclusive definition of an Islamic nation state and followed Jinnah and the Muslim League to Pakistan. The retention of the loyalties of other non-Hindus—Christians, Sikhs, Buddhists, Jains, Parsis was relatively less problematic and could be accommodated within a fuzzy definition of a twin identity—India, and Bharat.[1] At Independence, therefore, the nebulous 'nation' of Nehru, which, after centuries of oppression and denial had found 'utterance', actually started its career as an ambiguous construct, with community and conflict written on its two faces. This tenuous unity, kept under wraps as the Congress system institutionalised this duality in many formal and informal ways, has gradually come unstuck as the inexorable logic of majoritarian democracy has relentlessly driven home the connected realities of communal cohesion and conflict.

The analysis undertaken in this section seeks to juxtapose the survey data with aggregate statistical data at the regional level by drawing on the issues of community and conflict. Six regions were chosen for the preliminary analysis of regional diversity. We need to say a few words on why we selected six regions to depict Indian diversity. This was done deliberately on the assumption that the diversity of the underlying variables was a function of such factors as: poverty and affluence; geographic location; ideological leaning; social structure of the elites; institutionalisation of conflict (as compared to stalemated class conflict); perceived orderliness and political disorder; and criminalisation of politics and a reputation for clean and efficient administration. The six regions, namely, Bihar, Gujarat, Maharashtra, Punjab, Tamil Nadu and West Bengal, were chosen to reflect the extremes of these variables. These select States, which represent the 'four corners' of India, regions at the highest, lowest and middle levels of affluence, regions which have satisfactorily solved the problem of regional identity and those still struggling with it, and, finally, regions representing political ideologies of the left, right and centre, were chosen for the study of variation in trust in local, regional and national government. Out of these six, three—Maharashtra, West Bengal and Bihar—were chosen for more detailed and in-depth analysis of the process of local democracy.

Building Civil Society from Below

The focus on region and locality makes it possible to analyse the functioning of Indian democracy from an unusual angle in comparison with stable Western democracies. The role of local government and politics in the making of modern nation states and industrial societies remains an unresolved issue. Whether it is seen in terms of their spatial location at the lowest level of the political system, or in class terms as the voices of the *petits gens*, politics from below has been seen as that of hapless victims (Moore 1966), of supplication (Huntington 1968), of the angry rebel fighting for what he considers justly his (Gurr 1970), or of effete resistance to the relentless march of the central power (Scott 1991). But the debate is far from closed. The publication of Putnam (1993) has revived a debate about local community and civil society as the basic building blocks of modern, democratic nation states.

The roles of local government and politics assume special significance in the context of India—a desperately poor, post-colonial, agrarian society that chose the democratic path towards the building of a modern nation state and an industrial economy at the outset of its career as a Republic, and has kept to it with relative success over the five decades since Independence. Formal democracy and universal adult franchise, right from the outset, brought the legal right to participate to all existing social groups, sectional interests and spatial levels. This not only guaranteed their juridical existence, the functioning of competitive elections ensured a certain degree of power to them as well. Tragically, the very path of economic change and nation building that India was about to follow held rather dire consequences for certain social groups and spatial units that would become unsustainable in a world where large industry, efficient administrative units and one large nationhood were seen as ideals. However, once empowered, one could not expect the vulnerable and marginal groups to go under without a fight, unlike their hapless counterparts during the transformation from agrarian, feudal societies to modern states and economies in Europe. The marginal social groups of the contemporary stable democracies had neither the legal status nor the political power to resist a fate they did not approve of. The social history of eighteenth-century Europe is replete with accounts of their suffering and resistance. This was no accident of history. The causal relationship between this massive destruction of the lifestyles and habitats of these people, and the building of new state and economic forms is now reasonably well settled.

Out of moral and political considerations, many within India's struggle for Independence sought to avert a replication of the tragic history of European state building and economic transformation. Others were equally keen to follow what they considered the natural course of history on the path towards the great transformation from tradition to modernity. Not surprisingly, there was considerable difference of opinion on the role of the local and marginal social groups, suggesting deeper differences at the highest level about the form of the future state and nation in India. Just as Gandhi held on to the role of the village republic as the necessary building block of nation, state and society in India, Nehru famously held the opposite view.[2] This duality—the conflict between two opposite ways of characterising the nature of state and nation in India, variously referred to as the modern and the traditional, the scientific-rational as opposed to the endogenous-vernacular, the macro view of Delhi as opposed to the meso- and micro-perspectives from India's regions, districts and villages—has characterised the value conflict that underpinned political discourse in India from Independence onwards, surfacing in India's high politics at regular intervals. These views have been articulated by individuals, political movements and established political formations. They have been formulated respectively in terms of the modern-secular programme of development long associated with the founding fathers of the Republic and the Congress party as the keeper of the flame, as opposed to other formulations of the same objectives, but drawing on different ideological and cultural resources, identified with names of pre-Independence icons like Savarkar and Bose and post-Independence celebrity dissidents like Lohia and Jai Prakash, and electorally formulated by the Janata Party in the 1970s and two ideologically distinct versions of this opposition from the 1980s onwards.

The main argument of this chapter is that the judicious use of the local—the lowest spatial unit in its literal sense, but more broadly, the subaltern and minority social groups and their ideas—has infused new political resources into the political system of India, enhanced the legitimacy of the state, and has given resilience to the Indian nation. This has come about through a number of national legal and political initiatives, and has been more successful in those parts of India where a competitive party system in combination with regional policy has created a successful integration of the local with the national. By extension of the same argument, the experimentation in local democracy has been the least successful in those regions where no autonomous empowerment of subaltern social groups has taken place, and no persistent attempt has been made by the regional government to integrate the local in their legal and public policy framework. The survey data relating to popular attitudes towards the role of the regional and local governments as compared to the Central, and the analysis of case study and interview data from secondary sources are helpful to examine the theoretical implications of the twin processes of modernisation and democratisation. The chapter concludes with an analysis of the implications of the survey and the case study material for India as a whole.

Region: A Crucial Link between Nation and Locality

Though they vary in the extent of autonomy they are willing to concede the room to manoeuvre at the disposal of the state to meet challenges from social groups (to one another or to the state itself), mainstream theories of the state in India have recognised the ability of the state to accommodate regional, local and communal interests as the crucial building blocks of legitimacy in India. The basic commitment on the part of the state to negotiated solutions to conflicts over distribution of resources and allocation of values is the essence of stateness in India. The most substantial statement of this commitment on the part of the state, and within reasonable measures, its ability to deliver, comes from Rudolph and Rudolph.

Like Hindu conceptions of the divine, the state in India is polymorphous, a creature of manifold forms and orientations. One is the third actor whose scale and power contribute to the marginality of class politics. Another is a liberal or citizens' state, a juridical body whose legislative reach is limited by a written constitution, judicial review, and fundamental rights. Still another is a capitalist state that guards the boundaries of the mixed economy by protecting the rights and promoting the interests of property in agriculture, commerce, and industry. Finally, a socialist state is concerned to use public power to eradicate poverty and privilege and tame private power. Which combination prevails in a particular historical setting is a matter for inquiry (Rudolph and Rudolph 1987: 400–401).

The mainstream view, which has drawn some criticism from the Left,[3] has been further refined in subsequent research. On the basis of the analysis of a broad spectrum of India's regions, Kohli (1987) has shown that the state is at its most effective when it is reinforced by a regime at the regional level also committed to the same objectives as the national state, and has the political support of a well-organised political party with its own links to the peasantry. The negotiating stance of the state could be a crucial variable on its own. When the state sends mixed signals, such as its readiness to negotiate on transactional issues like redistribution, but resistant to such transcendental considerations as the territorial integrity of the state, or the secular basis of the nation, its legitimacy is considerably enhanced.[4] Many of these considerations have been recently brought together by Lijphart (1996) in a general interpretation of Indian democracy drawing on consociational theory.

Some recent developments in India show how, set free from the formal control of the National Planning Commission and the informal control by the Congress party, India's regions have increasingly appeared as the focus of political initiative in the direction of economic development and community formation. Commenting on this new face of regional governments, James Manor shows how, in Andhra Pradesh, the government of Chandrababu Naidu has come up with a programme of political accountability, intended to promote good governance. Commenting on Naidu's programme, Manor says:

> His main emphasis is on information technology, which he thinks can provide not just new jobs and wealth but also what he calls SMART governance. The capital letters stand for Simple, Moral, Accountable,

Responsive and Transparent government. He couples this with promises of greater popular participation and visionary leadership.[5] [Manor asserts that Naidu's statement is not mere rhetoric but is grounded on real achievements at the level of administration.] What Mr Naidu has done is to provide a more disciplined, effective administration. He has begun building information infrastructure that disperses and collects ideas through electronic kiosks across the State, which has a population of 72 million. Citizens will soon be able to register their views in 'social audit' on the performance of government programs.[6]

On the basis of the mainstream position on the state in India, empirical research, in search of explanations for the variations in the effectiveness of the state in time and space, has branched off into the nature of political institutions, political parties and movements, interventions in the economy in terms of public policy and other specific points. The role of the local political arena in the spread and deepening of democracy in India, the puzzle specific to this chapter, provides an important insight into the functioning of all these subsystems because local institutions, political processes and their leadership are the ultimate interface between the state and the people. The contrast with the stable Western democracies could not be more striking, for in India, democratisation has taken place in a society where, unlike in the stable democracies, as we learn from the history of nation and state formation (Tilly 1985, Gilmour 1987, Rudolph 1987) the obstacles to this form of governance were violently cleansed prior to the introduction of liberal democratic institutions. India at Independence faced a different, and from the point of view of the modern state, difficult scenario. Juxtaposed with the macro-political structure based on the assumption of a rational-legal authority structure were half a million rural political systems, sustained by an opposite set of values. Nehru would have seen in them bastions of caste dominance, religious bigotry, feudal social and economic relations and gender oppression. The democratic constitution and universal adult franchise ensured that the project of modernisation and nation and state formation would not be in a position to jettison the weight of traditional society. Marginalised by the process of economic change and urbanisation, the vulnerable social groups, drawing on the full range of democratic participation and radical protest, using their international visibility thanks to the electronic media, would be in a position to hit back, unlike their hapless counterparts in Europe during the period of enclosures, the Industrial Revolution and crushing of religious and ethnic minorities. Looking five decades back, comparing India's multi-party democracy and incremental economic growth to the dire predictions,[7] one is entitled to ask: How could these 'undemocratic roots' ensconced within the traditional world of local politics sustain a democratic system, based on radically different values?

The chapter attempts to formulate answers to these questions by drawing on politics at the regional and local levels, and particularly the institutionalisation of the latter within the structure of panchayati raj, and their contribution to the stability of the state and deepening of democracy in India. A brief discussion of existing theory is followed by an analysis of trust in local government, as compared to the regional and the national on the basis of survey findings from 1996 and a detailed examination of the social and regional contexts of groups that repose their trust in local government. Analysis of the perception of the political universe by political actors, the institutional context in which they are ensconced, and the strategies in which they are engaged in order to achieve their political objectives will be undertaken in the next section. These further steps call for an analysis of the experiences of India's political actors (whom we have stratified in terms of rural elites and non-elites, and urban elites and non-elites) with the state machinery, their evaluation of the legitimacy and effectiveness of India's great political institutions, the structure of local governance, of national issues as well as of social harmony, poverty and injustice in the local arena. Further empirical analysis would be confined to the case of West Bengal.

The main conjecture that underpins the analysis undertaken here suggests that local democracy is at its most effective when local institutions enjoy the trust and confidence of local elites, and are politically accountable to the local electorate. Frequent and competitive political participation of the local electorate is crucial to the viability and efficacy of local governance and the legitimacy of the state. The rich associational life, interpersonal trust and networks depicted by Putnam as necessary to local democracy are in fact the consequence of the existence of political competition and not its cause. To suggest otherwise, such as the fond hope that divisive party politics should be kept out of the local arena, is indeed to abandon hard political realities in favour of a neo-communitarian utopia.[8] At issue are: Why is it that within the context of a roughly comparable constitutional-legal structure instituting local government and democracy, there is such regional variation in the breadth and depth of local governance; and, what broad implications can we draw from the successes and failures of local democracy for the resilience of the state in India?

The Context of Regional Variation

In order to give an idea of the tremendous variation of the factors critical to the functioning of democracy, we have undertaken below a brief survey of some aggregate indicators at the regional level in India.

Whether in terms of average income or level of participation, as Table 7.1 makes abundantly clear, there is tremendous variance at the regional level in India. The States, organised in decreasing order in terms of population, give an indication of the extent of variation in levels of development. Bihar, with the lowest literacy rate and lowest per capita income, defines the lower level of the range, whereas States like Maharashtra, with literacy at about 65 per cent and the 1992–93 average per capita income well above Rs 9,000 per annum, is at the other extreme. The data with regard to the level of participation in the earlier elections, particularly if we compare Maharashtra (high on literacy and income) with Bihar, also indicate the correlation that is typical of low achievement with low aspiration, which, in a perverse way, gives tradition its stable character. But the spread of the message of modernisation and democracy has little respect for political frontiers or cultural barriers. Taking the election of 1977 as the great equaliser of Indian politics, one can see how participation in Bihar has caught up with Maharashtra, and on occasion, has even surpassed it.

We present some other features of the democratic culture and process in the selected States in Table 7.2.

The differential development of India's regions comes across quite clearly in Table 7.2. For example, Bihar (with its low income and literacy), when compared to Maharashtra, displays a lower level of political information (36.6 per cent compared to 43.3 per cent) and a lower level of organisational membership (10.5 per cent compared to 15.4 per cent). But once again, the equalising effects of democracy and political competition are obviously at work, for when it comes to other indicators, more sensitive to the diffusion of the norms of egalitarianism, the gap between highly developed and backward regions is bridged. On campaign exposure, Bihar and Maharashtra, respectively at 9.2 and 9.8 per cent, are practically drawing level, whereas with respect to the sense of political efficacy, Bihar at 21.7 per cent is actually ahead of Maharashtra with 19.4 per cent. The level of financial satisfaction, however, continues to remain lower in Bihar (11.6 per cent) compared to 24.3 per cent in Maharashtra. The result, as we can see from the lower level of institutional trust, 23.2 per cent in Bihar as compared to 25.4 per cent in Maharashtra,

Table 7.1
Population, Literacy, Urbanisation, Turnout and per capita Net Domestic Product by States

States (Ranked as per 1991 Population)	Pop. (%)	Lit. (%)	Urban (%)	1957	1967	1977	1984	1996	Mean 1957–85	Per Capita Net Domestic Product 1992–93 (Rupees)
Uttar Pradesh	16.6	41.6	19.8	47.8	54.5	56.4	55.8	46.5	50	4,345
Bihar	10.3	38.5	13.1	42.9	51.5	60.8	58.8	59.5	55	3,053
Maharashtra	9.4	64.9	38.7	55.7	64.8	60.3	61.7	52.5	57	9,795
West Bengal	8.1	57.7	27.5	48.6	66.0	60.2	78.6	82.7	69	5,633
Andhra Pradesh	7.9	44.1	26.9	43.9	68.7	62.5	69.0	63.0	71	5,718
Madhya Pradesh	7.9	44.2	23.2	38.0	53.5	54.9	57.5	54.1	51	4,558
Tamil Nadu	6.7	62.7	34.2	49.1	76.6	67.1	73.0	66.9	66	6,809
Karnataka	5.4	56.0	30.9	52.8	63.0	63.2	65.7	60.2	60	6,331
Rajasthan	5.3	38.6	22.9	40.6	58.3	56.9	57.0	43.4	51	5,086
Gujarat	4.9	61.3	34.5	—	63.8	59.2	57.9	35.9	51	8,045
Orissa	3.8	49.1	13.4	36.1	43.7	44.3	56.3	59.2	48	4,114
Kerala	3.5	89.8	26.4	66.6	75.6	79.2	77.1	71.1	72	5,768
Assam	2.7	52.9	11.1	46.6	59.3	54.9	79.7	78.5	65	4,973
Punjab	2.4	58.5	29.6	55.0	71.1	70.1	67.6	62.3	58	11,217
Haryana	2.0	55.9	24.6	—	72.6	73.3	66.8	70.5	68	9,037
India	96.9*	52.2	26.1	47.7	61.3	60.5	64.1	57.9	58	6,261

* Excluding minor states and all Union Territories.

Table 7.2
Performance of Select States on Various Indices

Indices	National Average	Bihar	Gujarat	Maha- rashtra	Punjab	Tamil Nadu	West Bengal
Campaign exposure: high exposure	14.8	9.2	5.0	9.8	9.7	20.4	19.4
Political efficacy: high efficacy	23.7	21.7	9.1	19.4	14.9	26.6	29.8
Political legitimacy: high legitimacy	11.0	10.8	7.7	9.1	4.1	12.1	11.6
Trust in institutions: high trust	29.6	23.2	24.0	25.4	14.9	28.1	30.0
Political information: high information	40.0	36.6	27.0	43.3	35.4	49.6	46.4
Financial satisfaction: high satisfaction	23.3	11.6	24.6	24.3	27.2	26.8	9.8
Economic liberalisation: high liberalisation	14.7	14.8	32.3	10.3	9.7	15.2	13.4
Law and order: high sense of order	31.3	20.9	29.8	32.3	48.7	22.1	36.3
Social harmony: high sense of harmony	17.4	14.1	18.6	19.9	8.2	16.0	16.9
Organisational membership: members	14.5	10.5	6.0	15.4	3.1	18.5	22.4

and more seriously, with regard to social harmony where Bihar registers 14.1 per cent compared to 19.9 per cent in Maharashtra.

It is important to remember that the data presented above are organised around the region as the unit of analysis, whereas the logic of our analysis is at the level of the individual. This would normally not pose great problems of lack of congruence between data and theory, except in regions which are extremely heterogeneous where the level of extreme differences between subregions, or among social groups can be somewhat flattened because of aggregation. There is little that can be done methodologically against subregional variations, because that does not form part of the sample design. However, our prior knowledge of extreme regional variation has been drawn upon in the selection of the States. Thus, instead of taking Uttar Pradesh as an exemplar of the category of the less developed we have selected Bihar, precisely in order to avoid the problem of subregional variation. On the issue of variations at the level of groups, however, we have the possibility of using the potential of survey research to direct the analysis in the direction of groups based on social class and other indicators of deprivation. The other point that needs to be taken into account is the fact that the broad comparisons we have made using Bihar and Maharashtra as exemplars of the categories should not take our attention away from the fact of regional specificities. The specific historical and political itinerary that a region has traversed (militancy and its aftermath in Punjab, or the long spell of Communist rule in West Bengal for example), continue to play a role and in that sense, affect the data in directions not predicted by our model.

Looking at the differential patterns across the states, one finds Tamil Nadu and West Bengal at a high level of political interest and campaign exposure. At 20 per cent it is 6 percentage points above the national average and far ahead of Gujarat, which has an astoundingly low level of interest in politics. These figures reflect the underlying trends in participation at the level of voting as well. The Gujarat situation, as a matter of fact, reflects a certain disillusionment with the electoral process which has deep roots in the emergence of the KHAM (Kshatriya, Harijan, Adivasi, Muslim) strategy which successfully challenged the political dominance of the upper castes in the 1980s. Subsequently, as the upper strata started finding a new political home in the BJP, the emergence of deep fissures within the party, part of which walked out and formed a new party, once again brought in a certain amount of disenchantment. Exposure in Punjab, interestingly enough, while still lower than the national average, is actually not so far below as in the case of Gujarat. Closely related to political exposure is political efficacy, where West Bengal, thanks to the 22-year-long unbroken rule of the Left Front, has reached a very high level. The low participation in Gujarat is certainly an underlying factor of the low efficacy.

The high financial satisfaction in Punjab, Tamil Nadu, Gujarat and Maharashtra reflects the underlying material progress that these States have achieved. We shall, of course, have to look closely at the composition of the respective populations in order to see if this is a reflection of class factors, or if the State itself is a significant source of variation. Or, in other words, *ceteris paribus*, the Scheduled Castes in Gujarat have a more buoyant view of their financial situation (present and future) than that of the comparable population in Bihar. The very low statistics in West Bengal are probably reflective of the fact that Communist political propaganda homes in on the issue of immiserisation, and the data might reflect some effect of this political rhetoric.

West Bengal, in spite of the poor record on financial satisfaction, nevertheless scores very highly on trust in institutions and political information. The Left Front government, which has successfully institutionalised its support base, completely dominates the scene when it comes to the press, the educational system in the State, command over the political, bureaucratic and legislative machinery in the panchayat, region as well as the West Bengal component of the national arena. The diametric opposite is the case of Punjab—lagging behind in the means of spreading political information, trust in institutions, and perhaps consequently, in legitimacy. A long spell of Central rule and the imposing government of the late Beant Singh acted as delegitimising factors in the State. With the highest financial satisfaction, it scores the lowest on both political legitimacy and trust in institutions. Gujarat and Bihar are both placed on the lower side of these scales.

Closely related to financial satisfaction is liberalisation, where Gujarat is not only on the higher side of this indicator, but scores more than double the national average. Maharashtra's low score probably reflects the fallout of the Enron controversy given prominent coverage in the election campaign. Punjab's low score is a puzzle—due probably to a combination of 'don't knows' and the largely agrarian character of its economy—which is not immediately affected by liberalisation except in terms of the increase of prices of agricultural inputs.

The high level of law and order in Punjab reflects the vastly changed political conditions. We would, however, be making a mistake to take it as an indicator of a stable or resilient political situation. On two elements which contribute to an enduring sense of political order—social harmony and organisational membership—Punjab is way below the national average. Here, Maharashtra provides an interesting diametric opposite. Its performance on all three indicators is more than the national average, indicating steady progress in social change and political institutionalisation over the years. West Bengal's low score on harmony is once again reflective of the use of the rhetoric of class war by the regime, but the sterling achievement of the Left Front in transforming the decade of chaos into a high sense of order is certainly borne out by the data.

The data presented in Table 7.2 support the arguments put forth earlier. That is, urbanisation, economic development and literacy are all positively related to political participation. Thus, for example, in terms of the voter turnout figures in this Table, States with higher per capita net domestic product and having higher proportions of urban and literate population show higher turnout figures as well. Regional disparities on indicators of economic development, urbanisation and literacy have contributed to regional variations in political participation. These figures, read with the performances of different States on various indicators of socio-political views and attitudes of the people, help understand the problem of regional variations better.

222 ■ Democracy and Social Change in India

The data presented in Table 7.3 takes the differences we have already noticed between the different regions even further. Once again, the working

Table 7.3
Perception of Conflict and Social Change by State (in per cent)

	All India	Bihar	Gujarat	Maharashtra	Punjab	Tamil Nadu	West Bengal
Would you say that compared to five years ago, the relationship between various groups of people has become more harmonious, remained the same, or tension among them has increased? (More harmonious)	26.8	23.2	34.0	20.2	29.2	34.8	23.7
Has the relationship between different castes become more harmonious? (Harmonious)	61.6	50.0	67.3	63.2	53.3	54.3	46.0
Has tension between tribals and non-tribals increased? (Not increased)	25.3	15.6	25.9	31.5	11.3	28.5	26.7
Has tension between different religious communities decreased? (Decreased)	43.2	40.9	50.5	45.5	41.0	40.2	37.6
Has tension between *dalits* and non-*dalits* increased? (Not increased)	35.8	35.0	25.7	39.8	22.1	33.9	25.6
Now, is there more tension between the rich and the poor? (Not more)	38.4	32.5	36.6	37.7	25.1	34.2	39.8
Compared to five years ago, are life and property less safe now than before? (Not less safe)	30.0	23.3	27.5	29.0	24.6	22.2	38.1
Is struggle leading to violence a proper or not a proper method of fulfilling peoples' demands? (Proper)	12.6	21.6	17.6	17.2	7.7	21.8	9.2
Would you say that the government should limit ownership of property, or people should be allowed to own as much as they can? (Limit ownership)	68.9	66.1	77.2	79.4	81.0	62.5	72.8
Have the benefits of development gone only to the well-to-do, or have the poor and the needy also benefited? (Poor also benefited)	53.2	25.3	23.4	46.6	68.7	52.7	39.0

model we have here suggests that economic differences, when added to radical mobilisation, lead to opinions and attitudes that indicate the existence of a state of low legitimacy and governmental crisis. Taking Bihar and Maharashtra as the two exemplars, we can see in Table 7.3 that in Maharashtra, the level of perception of harmonious relations between castes is higher (63.2 per cent as compared to 50 per cent) for Bihar. The same goes for the perception of conflict between tribals and non-tribals, and different religious communities, perceived to be higher in Bihar than in Maharashtra. The rich and poor are perceived to have more of an adversarial relation in Bihar than in Maharashtra. Life and property are perceived to be less safe in Bihar than in Maharashtra. Finally, part of the reason Bihar is perceived as less orderly is because of relative deprivation, higher in Bihar as compared to Maharashtra—46.6 per cent of the people interviewed in Maharashtra believe that the benefits of development have gone to the poor and needy as well as the well-to-do, compared to only 25.3 per cent who feel that way in Bihar. This is further reinforced by a greater approval of struggle leading to violence as a proper way of fulfilling people's demands (21.6 per cent in Bihar compared to 17.2 per cent in Maharashtra).

Many of these observations would surely need to be further examined, reinforced, and in some cases, amended on deeper analysis. It is interesting, nevertheless, to notice that the findings already bear out some of the established images—Bihar's low interest and exposure and low perception of the law and order situation, and Tamil Nadu's high interest and exposure and high efficacy. But then, there are surprises too. There is no clear pattern of political decay or deinstitutionalisation indicating how, in the context of democracy and social change, a number of factors cross-cut; how, or, individual regions are drawn back to a national mean through a process of political dispersion.

Local Democracy in the Context of State Formation in India

The state in India is the result of an incremental evolution rather than a revolutionary creation. A perusal of the history of the relations between the Central government of India and administration at the local level over the past centuries shows how the two have kept in step with one another. Looking back at the past five decades, one can see that with regard to local government and its relationship with the local political system and beyond, India's politicians have gone through radical changes of policy from time to time. Local government, which had already acquired a rudimentary presence under British rule in the 1880s, made a formal appearance after Independence in terms of legislative enactment by provincial governments. This was formally enshrined in the Constitution (Art. 40). Following the Balwant Rai Mehta Committee report of 1957, and its incorporation into the recommendations of the Planning Commission, a three-tier structure was expected to become the institutional basis for local self-government for the whole of India.[9] Maharashtra took a lead with the V.P. Naik Committee report, which recommended the devolution of the power of taxation and disbursement of development funds to the zila parishad, the majority of whose members were to be elected directly. However, a period of decline set in soon, which lasted from Nehru's death up to the revival of the idea of panchayats as the basic units of the political system by Rajiv Gandhi in 1985. Khanna (1994) lists a number of factors as responsible for this decline, among them, the foodgrain crisis of the early sixties, followed by the introduction of the cluster of policies known as the Green Revolution, which transferred the initiative for production and distribution of vital agrarian resources to the State government departments.

The subsequent programmes of poverty alleviation and agrarian reform, such as Small and Marginal Farmers, Food for Work, Drought Prone Areas, and Minimum Needs programmes, were often conceived, financed and administered by central agencies. Besides, under the dominant Central government of Indira Gandhi, many State governments turned on local democracy with the same authoritarian measures as the Centre, namely, postponement of elections, and the supersession of local political institutions by the administration, which cut off the periodic infusion of new blood into these institutions. The Janata Party, upon taking office in 1977, set up the Asoka Mehta Committee in order to revive local autonomy and participation. However, in spite of its recommendations, which are of great theoretical implication for understanding local politics in India, very little changed in terms of ground reality.[10] Internal conflict greatly paralysed central initiative during the brief Janata rule of 1977–80. Except in West Bengal, where the Left Front government seized the initiative,[11] the central administration and coordination of all development activity in the district under the auspices of the District Rural Development Agency (DRDA) became the rule. The next radical change in policy came from Rajiv Gandhi, who initiated the move to institutionalise panchayati raj in terms of a distinct tier of the federal system with constitutionally guaranteed power.[12] Though the initiative failed to get through the parliament, leading to an amendment of the Constitution, the idea was not entirely lost. It resurfaced in 1992 in the form of the 73rd Amendment of the Constitution, which gives constitutional recognition to panchayati raj as a tier of the federation. Elections to panchayats have been mandatory, to be supervised by an independent State Election Commission. Similarly, the panchayati raj bodies are to be endowed with independent taxation powers, and Central funds whose disbursement is to be supervised by a State finance commission.[13] The panchayats today have far more potential power than before, and in some parts of India, they have become viable political units in their own right, playing a crucial, catalytic role in bringing about largely peaceful and incremental political change.[14] Why and how it came about, what makes it effective, and how it varies from one region to another, are issues which will be taken up below.

The literature on local politics in general, but panchayati raj in particular, tends to be mostly normative in character. A combination of factors, among others, a certain Gandhian nostalgia, the emphasis on local autonomy in the contemporary discourse on civil society, the putative authenticity of panchayati raj because of its endogenous origin, are pointed out by some commentators as reasons why India *ought* to have panchayats. The empirical accounts then concentrate on the extent to which the project of reviving the past has been successful. Not much effort is invested in treating panchayati raj as a specific form of rule, one among many, as a matter of fact, so that its spread can be analysed in terms of its political choice, and the empirical conditions that were responsible for the divergent picture of the spread of panchayati raj that has emerged over the years since its formal introduction.

As a form of governance, panchayati raj has two main elements: (*a*) local autonomy, i.e., the extent of real power in the hands of local representatives, and (*b*) local democracy, i.e., the sharing of this power by local people through participation in free and fair elections. The 73rd Amendment of the Constitution (1992) gives an institutional shape to both conditions.

Faced with the challenge of implementation, the Congress leadership and the experts who formed part of the 'critical decision-making elite during the crucial, formative years of 1947–51, found themselves contemplating a number of options. The Congress Socialists (and fellow travellers) advocated 'structural change' as the only way forward. Gandhians came up with a variety of communitarian ideas. The Congress right wing under the leadership of Patel held out for a vision of state-dominated capitalism. The policy struggle of the 1947–51 period resolved the conflict in favour of a grand compromise, built into the two industrial policy resolutions of 1948 and 1956. Nehru, the embodiment of this compromise, was assisted by both fate and guile, thanks to the departure of the Socialists through the voluntary withdrawal of some and the expulsion of others. The feasibility of the compromise measure was helped in no small measure by the removal of the other two challengers—Gandhi through assassination in 1948, and Patel through death in 1951. The micro-instrument of this macro-compromise was to be the village panchayat.

Panchayati raj was installed because it offered several attractive features to the post-Independence policy community, namely:

1. non-violent and incremental structural change,[15]
2. communal mobilisation of resources in a decentralised context,[16]
3. a micro-basis for local initiative crucial for the structure of a mixed economy,[17] and
4. a potential source of unlimited patronage to service the needs of the Congress 'system'.[18]

Not surprisingly, panchayati raj drew a lot of criticism from those committed to structural change as a precondition of democracy and development in India. One of the most ruthless criticisms came from Barrington Moore. Writing in the 1960s, shortly after the implementation of the Balwant Rai Mehta committee's recommendations for the introduction of three-tier local self-government at the village, block and district levels, Moore wrote:

> ...if democracy means the opportunity to play a meaningful part as a rational human being in determining one's fate in life, *democracy does not yet exist in the Indian countryside* [emphasis added]. The Indian peasant has not yet acquired the material and intellectual prerequisites for democratic society. The panchayat 'revival'...is mainly romantic rhetoric (Moore 1966: 408).

Trust in Government: Local, Regional and National

We do not have any independent survey evidence to determine the extent to which Moore's rather dismissive comments about the viability of local governments as units of development were true for his time. However, assuming they offer a reasonable benchmark, survey data from 1996 give a picture of the considerable gains that local political arenas have made in the intervening three decades. The results of the question *How much trust/confidence do you have in the Central government—a great deal, somewhat or no trust at all?* and repeated for the 'State government' and 'local government/panchayat/municipality', are reported in Table 7.4.

Table 7.4
Regional Variation in Trust in Central, State and Local Government (in per cent)

High Trust in Different Levels of Government	Central	State	Local
All India	35.3	37.5	39.9
Bihar	29.9	30.0	29.9
Gujarat	22.7	22.1	39.7
Maharashtra	30.8	34.0	40.7
Punjab	14.9	16.0	13.9
Tamil Nadu	28.6	36.5	40.3
West Bengal	35.9	40.8	50.6

Considering India as a whole, the level of trust in the local government is actually higher than for either the regional or the Central government. The effectiveness of panchayati raj in terms of the trust that people have in it varies widely across India. At the lower end are Punjab and Bihar, where trust in all three levels of government tends to be low. At the upper end are West Bengal and Maharashtra, where trust in government is higher.

Since trust in government is affected by the visibility and effectiveness of the governmental structure, we need to examine the brief history of implementation of panchayati raj in India in order to explain the variation in the levels of legitimacy accorded to local government. Until the passing of the 73rd Amendment of the Constitution, which radically altered the picture and brought about a certain measure of uniformity in the institutional structure of panchayati raj all over the country, the States of India had very different practices. They can be divided in roughly three different types: States like Maharashtra where panchayati raj became a reality before other regions of India; West Bengal, which entered the race for successful panchayati raj later, but a combination of circumstances made panchayats the focus of State activity, leading to spectacular success; and those like Bihar where a mobilised, politicised and rural population divided on the lines of class and caste has found in panchayats their main arena of the battle for supremacy, reducing the institution to low levels of efficacy and trust. In order to examine the variation in terms of regions, and within each region, across social classes, we need first to look at the history of implementation of panchayati raj in these regions.

Implementation is seen as the classic Achilles' heel of developing countries. The bureaucracy and its hangers on, who, in view of the inadequate development of intermediary groups often find themselves as the main link between society and the political system, manage to skim off vital resources, besides diluting the norms of rational management and contributing to the misperception of development resources as consumption goods by their recipients.[19] Successful implementation of panchayati raj requires a balance between retaining the support of the local rich and professional classes, while increasing their legitimacy through the participation of the local poor. The division of the trajectory of implementation into three different types is based on their temporality, the type of political linkages, and their perception by the rural elites in the States.

Elite Mobilisation from Above: Maharashtra

This is a category of States where panchayati raj was introduced in the first wave.[20] The panchayats became the bastion of the local elites, then dominated by the landowning, relatively high-status regional castes. Subsequently, as political mobilisation brought in the lower social classes into the local political arena, the richer, erstwhile social elites fled the panchayat arena to higher-level political arenas, to more lucrative markets abroad, or to take refuge in such non-egalitarian arenas as cooperatives, where membership is not by democratic franchise but undemocratic ownership of the means of production. In Maharashtra, the panchayat is an administrative outlet of the largesse of the welfare state, the more important political decisions and their implementation being more under the control of the regional government and cooperatives, and coalitions of agribusiness, NGOs and caste associations. Panchayat elections have become less regular than during the heyday of their early prominence. Even 'the important subjects pertaining to "co-operation and industries" which were initially entrusted to the zilla parishads have been [subsequently] withdrawn' (Khanna 1994: 213).

Popular Mobilisation from Below: West Bengal

West Bengal represents the category of regions where gram panchayats became the chosen political and legal instruments for the implementation of State policy with regard to land reform, distribution of surplus land, registration of land records, rights of sharecroppers, tenancy rights, distribution of state subsidies, welfare and loans. Politics from above (in this case, the CPM-led state government) favoured these changes; politics from below (the political machinery of the CPM and its allies) was in a position to take advantage of these new political resources and harness them for its own political purposes, leading to the creation of *red* panchayats. Panchayats in this case emerged as the focus of both implementation and legitimisation. Though the normative and legislative basis of panchayati raj were already present on an all-India scale by the 1970s, a fortuitous set of circumstances led to panchayati raj being adopted as the main focus of the State government. The explanation in this case goes beyond the politics of the State to the partisan preferences of the CPM, for reasons that we shall see below. Towards the late 1970s, the CPM was locked in a battle on two fronts in the Bengal countryside. On one hand, the party felt that without the countervailing institutional power of the State, the Left Front would not be able to break the dominance of the *jotdar* (local rich peasants), nor implement its agrarian programme because of the apathy of the lower bureaucracy towards land reform and redistribution, and in some cases, its active collusion with the *jotdar*, who largely constituted the support base of the Congress. On the other hand, taking recourse to peasant activism held the potential of getting out of hand and developing into insurrectionary violence, both politically damaging to the electoral prospects of the CPM, and a likely harbinger of direct central rule on the grounds of the deterioration of law and order. Out of this double bind was born a consensus that saw the panchayat as the optimal strategy to promote the political goals of the party and empowerment of the poor in the most effective way.

Stalemated Conflict: Fragmentation and Anomic Violence (Bihar)

This is a situation where the mobilised poor, taking advantage of their numbers, have often succeeded in capturing panchayats. But the local social and economic elites, who see power ebbing away from their control, have not found any alternative arena. As a result, panchayats and local politics have become the scene of sporadic violence and caste conflict. Reports on panchayati raj in Bihar suggest that the institution has made its appearance as early as 1949 though the 'upper two tiers, the panchayat samiti and zila parishad functioned only in some parts of the State continuously from 1964 onwards and all over the State from 1979 onwards till their supersession in 1986' (Khanna 1994: 84). Khanna rates the contribution of panchayati raj in Bihar to the 'politico-administrative system, democratisation and development' as limited. Two government-appointed committees, the Bage Subcommittee of 1973 on gram panchayats and the Tyagi Subcommittee on panchayat samitis and zila parishads, recognised the malaise and made specific recommendations. Little action was taken towards the implementation of these recommendations. Khanna, drawing on the observations of a number of 'social scientists', sums up the state of affairs in local politics and local institutions in Bihar.

Traditional local leadership has been dominating the panchayat raj, by and large. However, recently this domination is beginning to weaken at several places. Factionalism, casteism and use of violent means continues to afflict [the] working of a large number of panchayati raj institutions. Decentralisation of administrative power and financial resources of panchayati raj institutions is very inadequate so far, thereby restricting their role. Neither the panchayati raj leadership nor its bureaucracy has appropriately a clear understanding of the concept and practice of democratic decentralisation. They have, therefore, shown 'little committment to development and democratic processes' (Khanna 1994: 87–88).

Khanna quotes from another report of 1985 that 'caste domination of Panchayati Raj is apparently visible and that the majority caste uses all sorts of means and practices to capture positions within panchayati raj institutions. Factionalism based upon caste and personality has affected working of panchayati raj institutions at many places.' The same report points towards some of the reasons of the poor performance of panchayati raj, among which the more important ones are irregular elections and supersession of local democracy by the state government on 'extraneous considerations'. Yet another report from 1988–89 suggests that panchayat institutions in Bihar were malfunctioning due to

...inadequate finance, insufficient staff and self-seeking leadership. Vested interests were grabbing, by and large, benefits of panchayat managed programmes and services. Corruption was widely rampant. [In consequence] Recently the rural proletariat and poor peasantry started mobilising themselves for waging struggles for their rights and benefits. There were increasing conflicts, both violent and non-violent between those in power in panchayati raj and the mobilised poor people.

Finally, a team of social scientists from the Indian Institute of Public Administration summed up the situation as follows after a study visit to Bihar in 1989–90:

Inordinate delays in holding elections to Panchayati Raj institutions contribute to their emasculation. Supersession of the zila parishad has temporarily crippled the panchayati raj system. Financial position of the panchayati raj institutions is very bad and this is hampering meaningful development activities by them. Neither these institutions nor the government are taking any effective measures to improve it substantially. Jawahar Rojgar Yojna funds provided by the union government to panchayats are being misused by them. Gram Sabha is a defunct body, thereby people's participation in panchayat activities is being adversely affected. Women's participation in panchayati raj institutions is 'far from satisfactory'.

Political and Social Dynamics of Panchayat Elite in West Bengal

The survey data reported in Table 7.4 and the anecdotal accounts in the section above provide between them some insights into the combination of circumstances that produce success stories of panchayati raj. We shall probe deeper into those conditions in this section by concentrating on the case of West Bengal. By all accounts, West Bengal is undoubtedly one of the most successful cases of the implementation of panchayati raj in India today. As we have noticed from the survey data, the success of Bengal's panchayati raj in terms of regularity of elections, auditing of accounts, the volume of political transactions and local legislation, is matched by the perception of the Bengal interviewees of the efficacy of their local government and their trust in it. Some of these observations would be further illustrated in this section on the basis of terms of interviews with office holders at various levels of Bengal's panchayats. One of the main achievements of the Left Front government has been success in persuading the *jotdars* that their best chance of achieving moderate affluence and security was by conceding legitimacy to panchayats as the intermediary between them and agricultural workers, their class enemies. Once in place, effective links between rural society and the state were established, panchayati raj democracy became an optimal instrument of 'parliamentary communism'.[21] The instruments through which this has been achieved include the recording of sharecroppers, distributing land deeds to poor peasants, and causing a more accessible and transparent bureaucratic process, as among some of the main achievements. Thanks to these initiatives, the panchayat assumed a significant role. From arranging credits to the supply of seeds and fertilisers, from rationalisation of the available employment opportunities in the village to the determination of a uniform wage rate, everything is channelled through the panchayat.

> As a political institution the panchayat became the most immediate structure of democratic representation; the villagers turned into its functionaries and the courtyards of their houses were now used as venues for its meetings. Suddenly the esoteric rule of the state got partly de-mystified and the villagers themselves became witness to, if not actual participants in, the planning and prioritisation of administrative works. In addition to this, and this is important, the panchayat eventually gave the village a common identity by formally unifying the entire village into a single unit and liquidating the divisions based on caste based localities.... As an arbitrator between individuals and families in disputes, the panchayat and the entire population of the village involved and delivered a process of adjudication which is quicker, cheaper and more transparent (Bhattacharya 1996: 22–23).[22]

The functioning of West Bengal's panchayats takes place in the context of a panchayat-friendly legal environment. The Left Front government has ruthlessly implemented the ceiling laws regarding ownership of agricultural land. It secured legal right of share for about its 200,000 sharecroppers and stopped for good their coercive eviction from land by the landlords. Finally, it has instituted a three-tier panchayat system (at village, block and district levels) on competitive party lines, and held four successive elections to these bodies since 1978, the last (1993) of which had sent more than 91,000 elected representatives (a third of them women).

> Together, these three vigorous steps by the Left Front have gone a long way in diluting the concentration of economic and political power in rural West Bengal. The panchayat now implements plans worth 50 per cent of the outlay of the state budget. The exercise of political power, therefore, is more diffused and participatory in the state today than it was, say, twenty years ago (Bhattacharya 1996: 23).

So far, drawing on survey data, we have been able to analyse the variations in the perception of the efficacy of local government and trust in local government across the three types of regions. The rural elites are the crucial links between local government and the local people. Further questions, such as the actual role of the rural elites, particularly those directly involved with panchayats, their social origins, the dynamics of the social process in which they are ensconced, require us to look beyond survey data and into an in-depth case study of West Bengal's panchayats.[23] Roughly, three sets of factors are identified by Bhattacharyya as explanations for the environment in which panchayats in Bengal function, and the role played by the rural elites.

The Effectiveness of Other Complementary Organisations such as Cooperatives

Panchayats in West Bengal are part of a grid of organisations that are engaged in giving loans, supervising the welfare, making lists of minor developmental works that should be taken up, and making lists of beneficiaries who would be entitled to different forms of resources once they are available. There is considerable awareness at the level of the ordinary citizen of the existence of such organisations, their functioning, their lapses and the difference they have made in their welfare. Bhattacharyya's interview data are rich with examples, viz., of a 'literate agricultural labourer, aged 40, landless, belonging to the Scheduled Castes who has been receiving loans for quite some time and that too, without the help of any middleman'.

> He takes the help of a co-operative leader who arranges loan quite easily for him. Attached to DYFI and the Agricultural Workers' Union since 1980 and his life condition has not improved much. Nonetheless, he believes the co-operatives as the most important instrument for improvement in life and is quite optimistic about the same (Bhattacharyya 1997: 34).[24]

Bhattacharyya gives other examples of a 'poor peasant' who 'directly goes to the [co-operative] society to receive loan[s]', [is] 'attached to the Kisan Sabha and DYFI', '[who] believes the co-operatives are the only instrument for improving life situation[s], although sadly he often has to take loan[s] from "*mahajans*" (money-lenders) to repay co-operative loan[s]' and a 'rich peasant' who is 'confident about the role of co-operatives' (Bhattacharyya 1997: 35).[25] Bhattacharyya concludes from these interviews that

> ...there was a very striking similarity of the effects of co-operatives on the [panchayat] members' lives and hence their views of and confidence in co-operatives. True, co-operatives have not been able to produce the same effects on each member because its members are differently located in the socio-economic scales. But they have helped each member to make a difference to their life-situation. Even the very poorer classes who as members have not been able to improve their lot much thanks to lower levels of loans, still have a fairer impression of and a good measure of confidence in the co-operative. We have not come across any member we interviewed who has held a negative view of and is pessimistic about the role of co-operatives (Bhattacharyya 1997: 36).

Combination of Communist Pradhans and Non-party Ordinary Members of Panchayats

The political leadership that the Bengal panchayats have developed shows the combination of the organisational resources of the CPM at the level of the higher leadership, and an openness to induct a wide cross-section of local society as ordinary members. The pradhan (known as the sarpanch in other parts of India) is the veritable fulcrum of the panchayat organisation. Usually, the pradhan is a partyman.[26] The average profile of the Bengal pradhan shows a veritable workhorse, involved in a number of subcommittees specialising with the problems of particular segments of society, such as agricultural labour, women, literacy and culture both at the level of the village as well as at higher levels of the panchayat system. Middle-aged men coming from the middle castes predominate, but there are appreciable numbers of pradhans who are Muslim, or come from the Scheduled Castes and Scheduled Tribes. But these semi-professional organisation men are ensconced within a more politically open milieu with substantial representations of non-party men and women. These are housewives, wage workers, rich or poor peasants, and so on, who are engaged in myriad committees (neighbourhood committees, roads and beneficiary committees). There is little money involved. What stands out from the descriptions of their role-perception is an impression of efficacy and the satisfaction of being engaged in public works.[27]

The Symbiotic Relations of Party and Panchayat

The West Bengal CPM has developed an effective policy with regard to the functioning of panchayat institutions. The CPM has developed a specialised party organ, the PPN or *Panchayat Parichalona Nirdeshika* ('Directives on Running Panchayats') in the form of a newsletter issued directly by the West Bengal State Committee of the CPM and sent to every panchayat and municipality through the district committee in order to coordinate its ideological and political work with that of the panchayat institutions. The panchayati raj institution is part of the public manifesto of the CPM, and the party is keen on defending its record on this score. In an interview, a party spokesman explained the founding of the party's panchayat newsletter as part of its efforts to '*strengthen democratic method[s]* in running the panchayats, and to encourage *more active popular participation in panchayats.*'[28] The less visible private face of the party is more keen on the political and ideological dividends that this bourgeois democratic initiative might bring.[29] This constant struggle between the public and the private—in an environment that has increasingly become more conscious of democratic rights and the need for transparency—has become the hallmark of CPM politics in contemporary West Bengal.

The top party brass are aware of the pernicious effect of power and patronage and of the Opposition parties lurking in the shadows. As a consequence, a self-denying ordinance is very much the rule at lower levels, though here, as elsewhere, exceptions to the rule are not unknown. Thus, the party is ever solicitous of the opinions of those panchayat members who are elected on the party symbol without being party members. There is an explicit party directive to the effect that

> elected members or their relatives should not be on the top of the list of beneficiaries so that the people must see that the panchayats are not meant for the elected members or their relatives. The directives also caution against basing the Beneficiary Committee on the extent of the Party's support in an area (Bhattacharyya 1997: 45).

While the main incentive for the CPM in supporting panchayat institutions is undoubtedly instrumental—for the panchayat is the new fountainhead of resources in the countryside and allegations of irregularities are not unknown[30]—the consequence of the partnership between party and panchayat has been the creation of a supportive political environment for the new institution to strike root in the interstices of rural Bengal society, to the point where the institution has become autonomous of continuous ideological and governmental sustenance. The range of committees such as the public health standing committee, the village education committee, ration committee, afforestation committee, night school committee, with their rules and formal procedures, their records, the watchful members creating an environment of transparency and self-policing, create a dynamic of their own. These organisational innovations have succeeded in inducting whole new groups of people into leadership roles, with tiny amounts of power and responsibility. These indicate long-term gains for Bengal society. Even organisations like the cooperatives which 'until very recently were taken with suspicion, are now quite easily recognised by members as their own' (Bhattacharyya 1997: 36). One implication arising out of this is a rather optimistic prospect for long-term institution building, independent of the rule by a specific political party, though the process still has a few obstacles to overcome.[31]

Trust in Local Government by Region and Class

The focus on West Bengal in the context of comparative regional analysis raises further issues: Is West Bengal unique? What implications, if any, can be drawn for India as a whole from the case study of Bengal? Now that the 73rd Amendment provides a national legislative context, what scope is there to achieve a transfer of knowledge from one region to another, so far as the know-how of local governance is concerned? The analysis to follow will take up some of these questions.

We shall go back once again to the survey finding on trust in government. Trust is a product of personal experience, affected by the life situation of the actor, the effectiveness of the institutions, and processes that constitute his political world. The variation in trust, thus, offers some insights to the performance of local government and its implications for people in different regions and in different social situations. Table 7.5 reports these findings. By comparing across columns and rows, one can make a comparison across regions and social classes.

Looking at the distribution across the urban and rural population in the three States, one can see the spectacularly low level of trust in local institutions in Bihar's urban residents. Exactly the opposite is the case with the urban population in West Bengal, a possible consequence of good performance of Bengal's panchayats and good communication of

Community, Conflict and Local Democracy ▪ 237

Table 7.5
Trust in Local Government Across Regions and Socio-economic Strata (in per cent)

	Bihar	Maharashtra	West Bengal	All India
All	29.9	40.7	50.6	39.3
Rural	31.2	45.3	50.0	42.5
Urban	18.2	30.0	59.3	29.3
Men	35.5	39.7	52.7	42.9
Women	24.0	41.6	48.2	35.6
Hindu + Jain	30.0	42.6	50.6	39.1
Muslim	29.2	33.0	51.5	43.8
Christian	—	—	—	34.8
Sikh	—	—	—	29.1
Other	—	34.3	—	32.1
Scheduled Caste	27.0	41.7	52.5	39.2
Scheduled Tribe	6.5	50.0	57.1	38.9
OBC	33.6	44.6	48.4	40.9
Upper caste	31.7	31.5	50.0	37.3
Illiterate	23.5	42.2	56.5	35.8
Up to primary	37.6	43.6	47.6	43.1
Middle school	38.6	38.3	39.4	40.6
Higher Secondary	43.9	38.8	51.5	42.4
College +	36.1	34.7	58.6	38.9
Up to 25 years	34.5	37.3	42.9	38.2
26–35 years	30.2	43.1	50.0	40.4
36–45 years	23.9	40.9	56.1	39.2
46–55 years	30.7	38.5	56.1	37.6
56 years or more	28.1	43.2	52.1	40.6

this performance by the State government. On the difference of perception across gender and religion, Bihar once again lives up to the image one has, and the reports one gets of violence against women and minorities. Once again, West Bengal represents the diametric opposite, with women and Muslims being either close to the same level as men (and Hindus) or better. The same scenario continues with caste status in Bihar, where members of the Scheduled Castes and Tribes are below the upper castes, unlike Bengal, where the Scheduled Tribes are actually far ahead of the rest of the population. On education, Bihar presents an almost linear relationship with the level of education and trust in local government, the level going down somewhat for those at the highest level of education (the small number of cases of $n = 13$ reduces the statistical significance of this observation somewhat), but not dipping to the level of the illiterate, and staying way above the average. Bengal presents an interesting curvi-linearity, the levels being high at the highest and lowest levels of education (possibly active adherents of the Left Front where party ideology compensates for the low trust, 'normal' in the illiterate caused by personal inefficacy, and lower trust in the most highly educated from an elitist disenchantment with mass politics). The true surprise of Bihar is the relatively high trust in local government among the youngest—at 34.5 per cent not far from the comparable level in the national sample, and way above other age groups in Bihar. Bengal, on the other hand, expects the youth possibly to serve their time before they can stand up and be counted, and be in a position to have a relationship based on trust with the local government. The CPM banks heavily on the trusted and loyal middle-aged cadre in key positions, and inducts those locally influential as candidates for local elections, who are allowed to compete under its symbol even if they do not belong to the party. Neither of the two tactics favours the rapid induction of the youth into playing an influential role in the panchayat structure, unlike in regions which are relatively less institutionalised and where the younger and the more educated have fewer organisational hurdles to cross. The Maharashtrian data confirm the image one gets from the literature of moderately performing panchayat institutions which have lost some of their earlier prominence—and trust from the upper and more educated strata—but continue to be strong, welfare-administering institutions, inspiring more trust in women than men (unlike the national average and unlike our two other regions), but not from Muslims, who are significantly below Hindus when it comes to trusting local government.

Elites, Non-elites and Local Government

Local government, like other institutions of society, is affected by how elites—the locally influential and politically connected people—perceive them, and the use they make of them in their own strategies to gain power and influence in society. One can start with a baseline situation where the local elites are not aware of the existence of certain institutions, or simply do not consider them worthwhile enough to take an interest in them. In that case, the institutions exist merely nominally, devoid of any legitimacy or effectiveness. Next in order are two different scenarios: one where the elites are aware of institutions and the opportunities they represent, and have managed to capture leading positions within them, cornering the resources for their own use, and successfully fending off the non-elites from entering the charmed circle of beneficiaries of local institutions. In a situation like this, local institutions may be partly effective but not enjoy a lot of legitimacy.

The obverse situation is one where the non-elites—poor but empowered—manage to take over local institutions, to the extent where the elites withdraw from them altogether, leading to a situation where local institutions may enjoy some legitimacy, but, devoid of seasoned managers and contacts at higher levels due to non-cooperation of the elites, are not very effective. The fourth (ideal-type) situation is one where the local elites are in control of local institutions, but are seen by the non-elites as accountable and self-denying (or not excessively self-aggrandising), running institutions in a manner that is relatively transparent, and holding open the possibility of recruitment of non-elites into positions of influence. In this case, local government would be both effective and legitimate.

The above typology helps understand the variation in the effectiveness and legitimacy of local governance in India. Which type a specific local government belongs to depends upon a number of factors. But a crucial component is the perception of local government by the local elites and non-elites. In order to analyse the variation of local governance in terms of the above typology, the survey sample was stratified into four categories, namely, rural elites, rural non-elites, urban elites and urban non-elites, using membership of parties (present or past), personal sense of efficacy ('vote has effect') and place of residence (urban or rural) as the constituent variables.[32] The urban elites are normally resident in an area classed by the Indian census as urban, they are or have been members of a political party and believe that their vote 'has effect'. The rural elites, like their urban counterparts, are people with a high sense of personal efficacy and party membership, except that they reside in areas classified as rural. The national sample, thus stratified, produced four categories: rural non-elites (66.7 per cent), rural elites (9.4 per cent), urban non-elites (20.3 per cent) and urban elites (3.7 per cent).

Before we can use the statistical variable of elite status as an empirical surrogate for the conceptual variable, we need to perform a further test to establish its validity. It should be noticed here that elite status is the product of at least two different attributes. On one hand, those described as the elite of the rural universe must think of themselves as the movers and shakers of their world—an aspect that has already been incorporated into the construction of the variable in terms of their sense of personal efficacy, or membership of a political party. But one needs a second attribute, namely, social perception of these people as elites, i.e., those who are better informed, more active in mobilising opinion, and important enough to be sought out by parties and candidates looking for entry points into the world of mass politics. Some of these data are analysed in Table 7.6.

Table 7.6
Social Construction of Elite Status (in per cent)

	Rural Non-elites	Rural Elites	Urban Non-elites	Urban Elites	All
Correct naming of local MP	47.6	76.0	63.6	82.9	**54.8**
Great deal of interest in campaign	7.6	30.5	7.4	29.3	**10.5**
Campaign meeting attended	11.8	44.7	12.9	42.4	**16.2**
Participation in campaign	5.1	35.3	6.3	35.3	**9.2**
Canvasser came home	37.4	64.4	44.6	65.0	**42.4**

We learn from Table 7.6 that our elites are indeed people who matter, not only in terms of their self-perception, but also in terms of more than average political information, in this case, the name of the member of Parliament from their constituency, a level of interest in the campaign about three times that of the national average, a similarly high level of participation in the electoral campaign, and finally, a higher than average probability of being contacted by election canvassers. The second important message we get from looking at the data in Table 7.6 is that there is practically no difference any more between rural and urban elites in terms of these indicators. Democracy, in this respect, has been a great leveller.

Having thus tested the measurement of elite status in terms of the new variable created for this purpose, we can now compare their perceptions of the three levels of government in India. The data, presented in Table 7.7, show first of all how high the level of trust rural elites have in local government compared to the national average, as well as compared to their trust in the national government. In this, they are well above the urban elites. Interestingly, even rural non-elites have a level of trust in local government at a level higher than the urban elites, and a level of trust in the Central government which is comparable to that of the urban elites.

Table 7.7
Great Deal of Trust in Different Levels of Government (in per cent)

Great Deal of Trust in...	Rural Non-elites	Rural Elites	Urban Non-elites	Urban Elites	All
Central government	35.6	47.6	28.8	35.3	**35.3**
State government	36.6	50.1	32.9	47.3	**37.5**
Local government	41.4	49.4	27.3	40.5	**39.3**

Finally, we shall turn to the variation in 'great deal of trust in local government' across our three regions, analysed in terms of the perception by different types of respondents according to their status on the elite typology in Table 7.8.

Table 7.8
Great Deal of Trust in Local Government by Region (in per cent)

Great Deal of Trust in Local Government	Rural Non-elites	Rural Elites	Urban Non-elites	Urban Elites	All
Bihar	29.0 (82.2)	53.6 (7.8)	17.9 (8.9)	20.0 (1.1)	29.9
Maharashtra	45.2 (63.3)	46.4 (6.5)	26.1 (24.1)	45.3 (6.2)	40.7
West Bengal	49.7 (74.4)	51.0 (18.6)	58.5 (5.3)	61.5 (1.7)	50.6

Key: Figures in parentheses indicate the percentage of the sample in each state who belong to a given category, i.e., rural non-elites, rural elites, urban non-elites and urban elites.

One of the most important features of the findings reported in Table 7.8 is the narrowing of the gap between the rural elites and rural non-elites in West Bengal and Maharashtra, in both of which the rural elites are above the non-elites in terms of the great deal of trust in local government, but only barely. In comparison, Bihar stands out dramatically, with the majority (even higher than in Maharashtra and West Bengal) expressing its trust in local government, leaving the rural non-elites a good 20 percentage points below. The survey findings confirm the anecdotal and interview data we have about the venality, corruption and nepotism that characterise panchayats in Bihar, as compared to the relatively more transparency and propriety one hears about West Bengal and Maharashtra. The other feature of West Bengal is the generally high level of trust in local government across all four categories, showing perhaps the combination of secular gains through two decades of good administration, but perhaps also the result of sustained propaganda. The opposite is the case in Bihar, where all except the rural elites show low trust, the rural elites being obviously in the know about where the new fountainhead of resources lies and making good use of this knowledge. But this is not an entirely negative finding from the point of view of local government, for the rural elites are the link between the Indian state and the rural world of Bihar. Table 7.8 certainly shows us where to focus state policy if one wishes to reach the panchayats of Bihar.

Conclusion

India's achievement in the realms of government, state and nation formation provides a striking contrast to the record of the majority of post-colonial states. A governmental system based on multi-party democracy and free, fair and regular general elections has gradually emerged from the hegemonic rule of the Congress party and the Congress system of the first decades after Independence. A federal state that has been able to retain the bulk of the territory with which it started its life as a Republic in 1950 through periodic redrawing of internal boundaries and radical constitutional innovations to give juridical shape to subnational identities has helped contain separatist tendencies. Finally, though perhaps not with the same degree of success, it is becoming a multinational society where the constitutionally stipulated ideal of communal accommodation is in the process of being continuously negotiated within the boundaries of the political process.

By the early years of the 1980s, India had already lived through two inconclusive experiments in governmental forms. The short-lived authoritarian rule of Indira Gandhi's Emergency, shrouded in dubious legitimacy and mild by the standards of the South Asian subcontinent, left few enduring achievements and fewer public defenders. The successor Janata government, of a broad-based coalition of national and regional parties whose authority simply ebbed away because of its internal political, ideological and temperamental differences could not, as a result, claim to have been a conspicuously better or more appropriate form of rule either. An unrepentant Indira Gandhi was back in power through popular acclaim, but it was becoming abundantly clear that governance in the regions was falling apart, and that the Centre could not hold, except through the use of force.

It was against this background that 'deinstitutionalisation' became the main theme of academic discourse on Indian politics. Manor spoke of anomie, Morris-Jones of a state of civil war, Kohli of the crisis of governability. Paul Brass, describing extant Indian politics as an alternation between centrally coordinated patronage and the dramatic rhetoric of crisis management typical of Indira Gandhi, gave voice to these misgivings.

> The system, therefore, shifts back and forth between jobbery and demagoguery and fails to confront effectively major issues concerning the economic future of India and the spread of lawlessness and violence in the countryside (Brass 1997: 335).

In view of such heady speculations about deinstitutionalisation and disintegration, the remarkable turnaround that came for Indian politics starting with the aftermath of the destruction of the Babri mosque in 1992 in the course of which the back of hardcore terrorism in Punjab was broken, insurgency in Kashmir was contained, Hindu nationalism came to be seen as a legitimate partner in the governance of India, and major policy initiatives with regard to India's economy and its South Asian neighbours attained a certain degree of stability in spite of governmental instability, appears quite puzzling.

To this broader theme of decline and resurgence of the system which is being debated at length elsewhere, the empirical evidence from India's local politics is expected to add one specific conjecture. Perhaps partly as a consequence of the transactional politics of the first decades of Independence that produced some conspicuous corruption in high quarters and led to the slow decline of the Congress system, also created a political environment of systematic recruitment of local and regional leaders. These local and regional leaders, often functioning on their own without the benefit of Central direction, drew on whatever resources they could, and in the process, produced an integration of the national-secular and the vernacular-traditional themes. These processes, taking place on the fringes of the national mainstream, both challenged and enriched it, and in the process, in evident testimony to the robustness of India's federal process,[33] got stretched and transformed to the extent where they could enter into negotiations with national and international political leaders. Some of these resources constituted a national pool of leadership, which, in spite of its dismal failure in the first Janata experiment at the national level in the 1970s, succeeded in reinforcing multi-party democracy in the States, and finally at the Centre.

The chapter, drawing on evidence from the survey and archival, documentary and interview sources and anecdotal narratives shows that democratic participation has become the 'normal' form of politics for a very wide range of people. However, there are tremendous variations across regions in the depth and breadth of involvement with local government. The main thrust of our findings is to show that since political power in the Indian political system emerges from coalition formation at the lower levels, everyone engaged in the game has a vested interest in keeping the 'democratic' game going, though, once again, the stakes are not the same for everyone. Democratic participation can very well coexist with legal and political irregularities, unfair and unequal distribution, corruption and venality. True, general elections often succeed in throwing rascals out, but they also induct other rascals, and the political process turns some into rascals once they are within the government. In the final analysis, the resilience of Indian democracy is the outcome of the 'million mutinies' against historical and current injustice and the successful political management of the 'crisis of governance' that the radical articulation of injustice often leads to. This is how the three levels of Indian democracy are intertwined—with the Election Commission and the Supreme Court providing relatively fixed points of reference at the macro level, the numerous local arenas introducing new social elite into the political process, and the regional leadership striking a dynamic balance between the desirable and the possible.

Instead of thinking of India's regions in idiosyncratic terms, this chapter has concentrated on understanding their experience with regard to local governance as the consequence of a cluster of factors, most of which are general to all regions, and in some sense collectively describe the nature of the state and the political process in India. While it takes a capable and imaginative leadership at the regional level to put many of the legislative, political and material resources to work in order to produce the required results in local governance, those resources are generally available. West Bengal, in this sense, is not unique and other States of India could profitably transfer some of the knowledge gained from the West Bengal experiment with great profit. Important among this moveable feast of good practices are cooperatives, proper use of local bureaucracy, effective implementation of land reform and minimum wage legislation. The CPM's presence happens to provide the sufficient political condition at the local level to bring all these resources to their optimal use, but it is not a necessary condition. The crucial test case are regions with non-CPM governments. Karnataka could be one such State.

General trust in government as a measure of legitimacy could be only a starting point of analysis because one encounters difficulties almost immediately. Do the local elites trust local government precisely because they do not fulfil norms of rational public management? Since surveys are typically used to measure behaviour and attitudes rather than causal motives, we need to look at the partial evidence that we have from in-depth interviews to develop further conjectures on this score. On the face of it, Bihar's rural elites trust 'their' local government, for reasons that one associates with warlord regimes rather than democratic governance. On the other hand, we have enough evidence to assert that while corruption and nepotism are not entirely unknown in West Bengal panchayats, they are ruthlessly exposed and punished not only by the Left government itself, but also by local political and bureaucratic figures. These make general trust in government an inadequate measure of legitimacy. Perhaps non-elites trust in government is a better measure, one where West Bengal performs better than Maharashtra (a close second so far as the rural non-elites are concerned but not the urban non-elites) and Bihar, which performs abysmally both among the rural as well as urban non-elites.

In terms of public policy, the analysis undertaken here shows that it is possible to bring government closer to people through state initiatives taken at the local level, decentralisation, and local popular involvement, without necessarily diluting the norms of rational public management. The local elites and their linkage to the regional government play a crucial role in the process of the creation and legitimisation of these norms of governance. The cluster of factors that make this optimal combination possible is often the production of a unique history. Yet, through the imaginative 73rd Amendment of the Constitution, the Indian political system has once again demonstrated its capacity to transfer good practices across cultural and ideological frontiers. Its effective implementation would keep Indian democracy on its steady path for the next decades.[34] Finally, it can be argued that local politics plays a crucial role in sustaining the conservative dynamism of the Indian state.[35] Local institutions (and the *neta*s [leaders] that populate them, many of whom are in fact the second-generation beneficiaries already of local self-government of the sixties) connect the modern state and traditional society. By creating new opportunities for popular participation, providing information and creating interest, setting up horizontal and vertical networks, local institutions open up greater 'room to manoeuvre in the middle'.[36] In consequence, in those parts of India where local government and local democracy have been successful, the state seems to 'work' better. That this result has been achieved both by governments of the left and the right in Indian States goes to show to what extent statecraft can be independent of rival ideologies of state.[37]

The emphasis on the local, also suggested by the new communitarianism of Putnam (1993) and others has an important implication for post-colonial societies. It suggests that one should accord legitimacy and the status of full actors to pre-modern social structures and groups as these countries start their long march towards statehood and nationhood. This sits uncomfortably with the more conventional theories of social and political change, born out of the historical and political context of European nation states. The incorporation of variables such as social networks, interpersonal trust and shared norms into conventional theories of social and economic change create a dilemma for the development planner and the builders of states and nations. How is one to reconcile the twin tasks of accumulation, extraction, transformation and rationalisation on one hand, and the legitimisation of these measures within the framework of representative democracy on the other? Caught in this double bind of contemporary norms of political correctness, which require Central governments to be responsive to the interests of marginal social groups and deprived regions, and the norms of rational management whose criteria of efficiency often dictate otherwise, politicians—in Yeltsin's Russia, Mandela's South Africa or Laloo Yadav's Bihar—prefer to fudge the issues and muddle through, with the usual combination of rhetoric and inaction. Broadly speaking, India has been generally successful in negotiating its way through a combination of leaders with vision and administrative talent, and the historical good fortune of institutional capital at the time of Independence. As the analysis undertaken here shows, in spite of stubborn problems of regional separation and residual discontent in some sections of the population, the state and nation can be said to be firmly set on a steady course. Presenting these occasionally contradictory challenges within the broader context of Indian politics would be the main theme of the concluding chapter.

Notes

1. Note the ambiguity deliberately built into the Indian Constitution: 'India, that is Bharat, shall be a Union of States' (Art. 1). The grouping together of several different religions in Art. 25 and opening up Hindu religious institutions to all sections of Hindus can also be seen in this light, as part of the attempt to create an inclusive nation in India.
2. 'I do not understand why a village should necessarily embody truth and non-violence. A village, normally speaking, is backward intellectually and culturally and no progress can be made from a backward environment. Narrow-minded people are much more likely to be untruthful and violent' (Nehru 1960: 508). Equally dismissive of the current reality and future potential of the village as a political unit for the building of the new India was Ambedkar: 'That they (the villages) have survived through all vicissitudes may be a fact. But mere survival has no value. The question is on what plane they have survived. Surely, on a low, selfish level. I hold that these village republics have been the ruination of India. I am therefore surprised that those who condemn provincialism and communalism should come forward as champions of the village. What is the village but a stink of localism, a den of ignorance, narrow-mindedness and communalism? I am glad that the Draf. Constitution has discarded

the village and adopted the individual as its unit', (Debates of the Constituent Assembly, VII[1]: 39).
3. Such as Byres (1988).
4. For further discussion of these arguments, see Mitra (1990a).
5. James, Manor. 1998. 'A Coming Asian Tiger in India?', *The International Herald Tribune*, 7 January.
6. Ibid.
7. See Harrison (1960). The point is made more fully in Mitra (1986).
8. Keeping political parties out of panchayats was advocated by the Congress party in the first years following the introduction of local self-government. There was no doubt a grain of Gandhian communitarianism about it. But the less noble intention of keeping competition out and using panchayats as their personal fief could not have been far from the strategic calculations of national political parties. See Weiner (1962a).
9. See Khanna (1994) for a detailed account of the growth of local self-government in Indian States.
10. See Government of India (1978).
11. See Bhattacharyya (1998: Ch. 4).
12. The initiative lost bipartisan support in Parliament when it appeared that Rajiv Gandhi might have been motivated by the prospects of having a more pliable instrument of government in a nationally constituted prefecture of local governments, as compared to the more assertive regional Chief Ministers.
13. For details of the 73rd Amendment, see Khanna (1994: 34–35).
14. Bhattacharya (1993) suggests that as much as 50 per cent of public funds in West Bengal pass through the hands of the gram panchayats.
15. This seems to have described the thin consensus that held the Nehru coalition of 1947–51 together. Panchayats were used as a contemporary mantra, rather like one of those periodic slogans like 'Green Revolution', *'garibi hatao'*, or 'liberalisation' in the 1990s that afflicts Indian politics every so often, which are supposed to achieve important political results without entailing too much politics—at any rate, without causing violence.
16. The influence of Gandhian thinking is clearly discernible with regard to a future polity whose 'structure [was] composed of innumerable villages, [with]...ever widening never ascending circles. Life will not be a pyramid with the apex sustained by the bottom. But it will be an oceanic circle whose centre will be the individual always ready to perish for the village, the latter ready to perish for the circle of villages' (Gandhi, *Harijan*, 28 July 1946).
17. Local participation was seen as a crucial instrument of capital mobilisation. The Balwant Rai Mehta Committee argued: 'So long as we do not discover or create a representative and democratic institution which will supply the local interest, supervision and care necessary to ensure that expenditure of money upon local objects conforms with the needs and wishes of the locality, invest it with adequate power, and assign it appropriate finances, we will never be able to evoke local initiative in the field of development' (Government of India, 1956, vol. 1: 5).
18. For the Congress 'vote banks', to be more precise. See Kothari (1970).
19. The phenomenon has been described as 'bureaucratic rent' by Krueger (1974), *'pyraveekar'* by Reddy and Hargopal (1985).
20. See Khanna (1994: 210–44); also Sirsikar (1995).

248 ■ Democracy and Social Change in India

21. See Kohli (1983) for a detailed discussion of this point.
22. Both the non-partisan character of Bengal's panchayats and the extent of their efficacy in creating a village community might have been somewhat overstated. See Bhattacharya's account for a critical analysis of the role of the CPM in the running of Bengal's panchayats.
23. Except for newspaper reports, the bulk of the field data on which this section is based are drawn from an unpublished study, Bhattacharyya (1997). The permission to quote is gratefully acknowledged.
24. Interview conducted on 7 April 1996.
25. In the words of the rich peasant, 'Due to the cooperative, I am able to cultivate land twice, and to produce sufficient quantity of potato. I did not know before that such an organisation can be so helpful' (Interview, 7 April 1996).
26. 'The party has seen to it that such strategic posts do not go out to non-party men/women. This shows, among others, that the party lays emphasis on this post. In many cases, the Prodhan is the sole party man in the Panchayat' (Bhattacharyya 1997: 81).
27. The following self-portrayal of a middle-class, middle-caste, middle-aged housewife, member of the panchayat and the road committee, provides some insights into the construction of the office by ordinary members of the rural society: 'I attend to all the problems of the villagers, from the construction of roads to family problems, often I tend to defy the party's strictures. I cater to Panchayat needs after looking after my family. The Scheduled Castes predominate in my area and have got me elected as I stand by their problems. The Panchayat should always obey rules though that is not always done' (Bhattacharyya 1997: 90).
28. Interview, Bhattacharyya (1997: 41), emphasis in original.
29. Bhattacharyya (1997: 42) quotes from an inner party document (Hoogly District Committee) to suggest as much: 'That the activities of the panchayat will be performed by elected members of Panchayats alone is the outlook which is opposed to the long term political objective of the Party. In order to transform Panchayats into the weapons for struggle, what is necessary is strong party control over panchayat units, collective decision and leadership and regular check up of Panchayat activities in party committee meetings.'
30. Under a news item entitled 'Panchayats told to account for funds', *The Panchayati Raj Update* (Delhi: Institute of Social Sciences, July 1997), no. 43 reports: 'The government [of West Bengal] has directed all panchayats in the state to account for the money that had been sanctioned to them in fiscal years 1995–96 and 1996–97. District magistrates have been told to personally check the accounts and ensure that no part of the money is misused. In a circular, the Chief Secretary warned panchayats of penal action if, despite repeated notices, they defaulted in furnishing detailed accounts of the money they had spent. According to a state government official, the panchayats were granted over Rs 500 crore during the past year and a half for various rural development programmes. This fund was jointly provided by the union and state governments. Many panchayats have not furnished audited reports for the money they have spent' (p. 5). Two further reports also deserve our attention. In the first, 'Task Force to check Panchayat Irregularities', Surjya Kanta Mishra, the panchayat minister, had set up a task force consisting of officials from panchayats and rural development departments to check confirmed reports against several panchayat units and to check their accounts; and, in the second, 'CAG flays municipal bodies', the

Comptroller and Auditor General of West Bengal had made recommendations for investigations into various irregularities, including 'idle investments'. It is noteworthy that the initiative for these inquiries came from people who are either party men, or had the approval of the party.

31. This view is shared by those who have examined panchayati raj in West Bengal from close quarters. Thus, Mukherjee and Bandopadhyay, in a report submitted to the government of West Bengal, observe that 'In the decade and a half of their existence, the Panchayats have achieved much that is tangible, especially in land reform but also in rural development. More than this, they have also brought about a churning of the submerged humanity in the rural areas and created a high degree of social and political awareness among all sections'.

'These are encouraging developments, indicating that the panchayats have helped in strengthening the roots of democracy. The intangible achievement this represents is of inestimable value. [However, on the negative side, they note that] the leaders among the elected functionaries are not clear about the objectives of the panchayats.... The concept of the panchayats being institutions of self-government is either missing or only dimly perceived' (cited in Khanna 1994).

32. See Appendix 2 for statistical details regarding the construction of the scale.
33. See Harish Khare, 'The union endures, the federation flourishes', in the special issue of *The Hindu* (Delhi), p. 39, 15 August 1997 to mark the 50th anniversary of India's Independence. Several articles in this collection point in the direction of this main theme.
34. Pai (1996: 79) suggests: ' ...the new panchayat institutions mooted in the late 1980s by the Rajiv Gandhi government, and created by the 73rd Constitutional Amendment Act, 1992 are an important experiment. The twin governmental policies of liberalisation and decentralisation in the 1990s provide the new panchayats space to function by both reducing the role of bureaucracy and increasing grassroots participation, while at the same time maintaining the support of the state. A third factor supporting the new role of panchayats "from below" is the rising level of political consciousness of the hitherto underprivileged groups in north India since the mid-1980s, due to large-scale mobilisation by political parties. These changes can collectively lead to greater mass democratisation of the Indian polity, a process in which panchayat institutions at the local level play a crucial role.'
35. The regions discussed in this chapter represent specific clusters of factors critical to the functioning of local democracy. These clusters, in a historical sense, appear unique, but, as argued here, are capable of general analysis. The state in India in this sense is the interface of the regions.
36. As indeed is argued in Mitra (1991).
37. Rudolph and Rudolph (1987: 19–59) have a comparable formulation in their convergence hypothesis, especially the chapter entitled 'Centrist Politics, Class Politics and the Indian State'.

8

Conclusion: Social Change and the Resilience of Democracy in India

As India works its uncertain way towards the next century, struggling to build on the heritage of democratic rule while questioning some of the main assumptions behind the Nehruvian nation and state, the issues of legitimacy, governance, integration with the world market and probity in public life have emerged at the forefront of the political agenda. The electoral process, for the reasons of its complex dynamics, does not always give full voice to all the issues that those a few steps removed from the cross-pressures of everyday politics might elect as the most salient of the day. Both sets of agenda—that of the concerned and the committed specialist and that generated from the summation of the *vox populi*—constitute the two main strands of this book.

The concluding chapter brings us back to the central issue of Indian politics. How comfortably do *jati, varna* and *dharma,* the core concepts of Indian tradition, sit on the corpus of a modern, liberal, secular nation-state, as envisioned by the Constitution? How do we reconcile the empirical evidence of the robust vitality of Indian democracy and the periodic occurence of communal carnage? In attempting to answer these questions the book has drawn primarily on survey data and contextual information. This approach to empirical analysis may pose methodological problems for some students of society and state in India. For, survey research, even by the permissive standards of the social sciences, cannot claim to be a 'scientific' discipline, much less provide a comprehensive *explanation* of social phenomena. Social and attitudinal measurements in the context of a complex, multicultural society is a relatively new innovation. Even in its role as a technique of precise description of a complex social situation, the survey researcher often finds himself playing second fiddle to the shrewd observer, working alone, equipped with nothing more ostentatious than the day's newspaper and a few well-placed phone calls. Finally, even under the most rigorously controlled conditions, a survey is at best only a still picture of a dynamic reality, so much so that even the use of survey data for the simplest description of reality would require a montage, inviting charges of trickery from the uninitiated.

A satisfactory account of the reality 'out there' calls for the empirical verification of hypotheses about the phenomena in question, derived from analytical models of general social and political behaviour that underpin the literature. This has been the method followed in this book, which begins with an introduction to the concept of a pyramidal society, bound together in reciprocal and hierarchical social relations, imploding as a consequence of the introduction of universal franchise and competitive, sometimes acrimonious elections. It then goes on to discuss the specific themes of continuity and change over successive generations, elections and the party system, the nation and the region, economic and social policies in India, always focusing on the perception of the institutions and processes by the electorate of India.

The book generally suggests that insofar as mass political and social behaviour are concerned, a well-executed survey offers the only possibility of going beyond what the 'naked' eye. For, only in the context of a survey is it possible to look for patterns of relationships within and across large social groups that a good narrative or a revealing anecdote can only suggest but cannot establish with a precise degree of reliability. The ideal method is thus to combine the insights gained from different techniques of description of reality into a composite picture, for the carefully done micro-study can immeasurably enhance the value of a survey by providing missing links, deep insights into the motives and strategic thinking of actors, and contextualise the findings by providing it with the necessary space-time coordinates.

Those who have followed Indian politics in the media over the past years would readily concede that the survey culture has now come to stay. Much as in the rich, stable democracies of the West, the Indian newspaper reader today is an avid consumer of opinion polls. The private and academic agencies engaged in surveys have taken the method to great professional heights. Their ability to forecast, or to provide data on very small but specific sub-groups of the public certainly rivals that of their counterparts in Western countries. These developments have deep implications for the academic study of political and social change in India. The student of Indian politics today has far greater access to data, and thanks to television and the Internet, to political rhetoric, than the previous generation. The specialist has a responsibility to take advantage of the greater base of information, and to draw on it as he engages in a debate about the basic principles of the political structure and its gradual amendment through the democratic political process.

To bring the rich source of data that survey research makes possible to the attention of the students and teachers of Indian politics and society has thus been one of the main challenges of this book. With the limitations and potential resources that survey research presents, the 1996 study, the largest scientific social survey held in India so far study, helps us chart the spread of the norms of citizenship across the various strata of the Indian population. This book has made an attempt to present the major findings in an accessible manner. The data will surely be analysed more comprehensively by political scientists and sociologists in the years to come. Our presentation of the first reading of the data is meant to provide the incentive for further analysis, and to spread awareness among the research community engaged in understanding contemporary India about moving from political observation to political analysis, and from there to policy analysis based on concrete data about the attitudes and expectations of social groups.

By its very nature, in addition to precise information on enduring issues of politics and society, every survey also produces a lot of ephemera—'noise' and 'fluff' in the jargon of the data analyst. Such information can, however, be put to use in the most effective manner when placed in the historical context that frames the study. The second main intention of this book has been to look at the still picture of India in the aftermath of the Parliamentary election of 1996 in the context of the 50-year record of the post-colonial state in India. The opinions and attitudes discussed here have thus become what might be termed a debate between the state and society, both poised for change as a result of a mutually fructifying, democratic interpenetration.

In that sense, some of our findings provide a contrasting picture of India to that reported in the media, both in Europe as well as in India itself. In the place of murderous fundamentalism, its poisonous fumes wafting over the gullible masses and vicious fires stoked by the passions of an election, one certainly finds the muted musings of a mature electorate. There is also a sense of celebration about the powers of democracy. It is useful to recapitulate that message and give it greater shelf life, for though the celebration of 50 years of Independence has brought out an avalanche of good news regarding Indian democracy, now that the brief euphoria is over, one is back to the standard image, which is quite pessimistic.

In sum, this book primarily aims at being an intelligent newspaper reader's guide to the travails and triumphs of Indian democracy. The printed media in India set the tone in listing the ills that afflict society, state and norms. Freewheeling politicians, venality, freebooting civil servants and ministers, ethnic conflict and violence, political fragmentation, are the order of the day. In the place of the sacrifice that characterised the generation of Gandhi and Nehru, we have short-term calculations of personal and narrow sectarian interests of the most blatant kind. Whereas the early years after Independence were marked by great governmental stability, minority regimes and unstable coalitions now appear to be the rule. In the place of the dignified and good party men running the regions—a Gobind Ballabh Pant here and a Kamaraj Nadar there—we have the tainted figures of politicians of all ideological hues.

Those familiar with the campaign speeches of leaders in the early years of the Republic would notice many radical changes when compared to the themes that constitute the main thrust of political rhetoric today. Whereas one would have heard mainly the themes of nation building, the glory of eternal India and the exploits of the leaders of the freedom movement, the main themes of leaders like Laloo Prasad Yadav of Bihar or Mayawati in Uttar Pradesh are more closely based on sectional interest, more directly pitched against the class enemy at the doorstep, and necessarily more personal because they address themselves to a world of here and now, with known culprits and concrete rewards, to be reaped by those immediately connected with the campaign should victory be theirs. Is there another side to it? Might one view politics as strategy, detach oneself from specific individuals and look at the mass in motion and deduce the nature and pace of structural change that underpins it? Could analysis become the panacea against rising cynicism, born out of repugnance against the populist antics of particularly rapacious and corrupt politicians?

Steady and Incremental Growth of Democracy

A short answer to the questions that have been raised above is to look at the entire data in terms of the inter-correlation of the main indicators of democracy and social change in India (Table 8.1). The findings presented in Table 8.1 give a synoptic view of the main correlates of the legitimacy of the democratic political system in India. They also alert us to its downside, and to the potential for deeper, structural problems that lie unresolved. In the main, three observations should be noted from the above matrix. The first refers to the overall positive correlation of political legitimacy, constituted mainly of process variables, such as the accountability of government and how people view the efficacy of political parties and elections in communicating the popular will to the commanding heights of the government, with all the other indicators of the interaction of state and society in India. Thus, those with a greater exposure to campaigns and political meetings hold the legitimacy of the political system to be high. Similarly, those who perceive the financial situation to be generally positive, both the present and compared to the past and in the perspective of future outcomes for themselves and their children, have a positive evaluation of system legitimacy. Institutional trust, a structural variable that measures trust in the local, regional, national governments and the other major arms of lawful and legitimate governance in India, namely the judiciary and the election commissions, also correlate positively with the process-based measure of legitimacy. Those better informed about politics, scoring positively in our stringent measure of the recall of the names of the Chief Minister, Prime Minister and the member of Parliament from the constituency of the interviewee correlate positively with legitimacy. The correlations with policy variables are, however, weaker, with liberalisation at 0.03 performing better than the performance of the government in areas pertaining to social harmony, such as the conflicts based on caste, class, land-ownership or atrocities with reference to *dalits* and minority religious communities coming in with a weaker correlation (though still positive) at 0.02. Interestingly, there is no significant correlation between the perception of the legitimacy of the government and the state of law and order in the country.

The second major observation to be made here is on the set of positive correlations with other aspects of the institutional aspects of state and

Table 8.1
Multiple Correlation of the Components of Democracy and Social Change

	Political Legitimacy	Political Exposure	Political Efficacy	Financial Efficacy	Institutional Trust	Political Information	Economic Liberalisation	Law and Order	Social Harmony
Political legitimacy	1.00	—	—	—	—	—	—	—	—
Political exposure	0.12	1.00	—	—	—	—	—	—	—
Political efficacy	0.15	0.16	1.00	—	—	—	—	—	—
Financial efficacy	0.06	0.12	0.08	1.00	—	—	—	—	—
Institutional trust	0.06	0.21	0.15	0.19	1.00	—	—	—	—
Political information	0.05	0.38	0.09	0.21	0.24	1.00	—	—	—
Liberalisation	0.03	0.00	-0.05	-0.02	0.00	-0.01	1.00	—	—
Law and order	0.00	-0.01	0.06	0.06	0.05	-0.07	0.02	1.00	—
Social harmony	0.02	-0.03	0.06	0.10	0.09	-0.03	0.01	0.18	1.00

Key: All correlations are significant at the 0.000 level. $N \geq 9{,}000$.

society in India that reinforce the picture of overall legitimacy. Thus political efficacy (a measure based on the individual's assessment of the value of his vote and the accountability of those elected to the bodies wielding power and influence), which correlates positively with legitimacy, also has a positive correlation with exposure to campaigns and political meetings. For that matter, those who are closer to the political process but are themselves not necessarily holders of office, have a positive correlation with institutional trust and political information. Political efficacy correlates positively with financial efficacy, institutional trust and political information. Financial efficacy correlates positively with political information, and institutional trust with the state of law and order.

While the positive correlations indicate an overall positive assessment of the political system and the democratic political process, the evaluation of specific policies is, however, uneven and in some crucial areas, negative. The third major observation points to the negative assessment of the policies of liberalisation by those who consider themselves to be politically efficacious, who have financially benefited from the political process, and have more political information. Liberalisation does not correlate significantly with political exposure, nor with institutional trust. Similarly, law and order is seen negatively by those with more political information and political exposure, the same groups whose perceptions also tend to correlate negatively with social harmony.

Our data, which suggest a picture of the progress over the past five decades in terms of empowerment, enfranchisement and emancipation, provide a firm basis for a conclusion regarding the gains in the deepening and quickening of the pace of democracy in India. Of course, there are still grey areas in terms of trust in institutions, but not in those actually in charge of them. However, India's political system has shown the institutional capacity to tackle these problems, and the people have rewarded precisely those institutions—the Election Commission and the Supreme Court in particular—in terms of high trust in them. The rejuvenation of India's political institutions comes as a timely correction to the picture of political decay and deinstitutionalisation to which many specialists had drawn our attention, particularly in the wake of violent ethnic conflict in Punjab, separatist movements in Assam and Kashmir and the demolition of the Babri masjid.

Those with long memories of Indian politics, particularly of the politics of poverty alleviation of the 1960s, might wish to note a radical change in the tenor of politics when compared to what one finds in the survey and in the general political rhetoric. Indian politics has moved away from *garibi* (poverty) to *kursi* (the 'chair', or power). The regional and local leaders today do not aim at state handouts; they want to wield power in their own right. The Janata victory of 1977 was the big dividing line. Indira Gandhi's authoritarian interlude of 1975–77 taught people that politics was all and power was its focus. The timid experiments of the 1960s gave way to the bold ventures of the 1970s in terms of the politics of coalitions. The intensive experimentation with coalitions and alliances and the culture of negotiation and accommodation that it has given rise to are the legacies on which India's multi-party democracy is based today.

In the main, three consequences have followed. In the first place, knowledge of and direct access to power of the previous subaltern classes is no longer an aspiration but a reality. Today's regional figures like Bihar's Laloo Yadav, dalit leaders like Mayawati or Kanshi Ram from Uttar Pradesh, or Chief Minister Chandrababu Naidu from Andhra Pradesh, are full-fledged leaders in their own right aspiring to national prominence on the strength of their regional power. In the second place, there is a general understanding of these changes on the part of politically conscious groups in all levels of society. There is, surprisingly, no Indian equivalent of the great 'white flight' in the United States, of the spectre of the affluent middle classes bolting representative politics altogether and escaping to the leafy suburbs searching for non-democratic alternatives. Our data show that the upper castes have accepted the legitimacy of the new parameters of politics in India; hence the support for reservation for the SC/ST, backwards, and women across all social classes. Those socially and economically better off, as we learn from regional comparisons[1] and our findings from this survey, make it abundantly clear how the upper crust of society has learnt to make do with new rules.

The form in which upper caste angst and frustration at the democratic rise of the masses is expressed is the third important aspect of contemporary Indian politics that emerges from the study. Shut out from social privilege automatically generating access to power, the upper echelons of Indian society have adopted a two-pronged strategy, consisting of support for parties of the right, a category where we can place the tendencies for social conservatism, religious and cultural nationalism and the increasing adoption of the market as an alternative to politics as a career. Integration with the world market comes as yet another way in which they can escape popular democracy's inexorable march, nibbling away at social privilege. Not surprisingly, the upwardly mobile sections of

Indian society are enthusiastic supporters of globalisation, staunch defenders of meritocracy, remaining all the while firm believers in the Indian model of accommodation.

These three main aspects of contemporary Indian politics manifest themselves in many forms and combinations. Under their impact, the regions have become social laboratories, of the cumulation of skills of administration, transfer of the knowledge of governance from one region to another, of the transformation of the local to the regional elites, of the regional elites to participants in the high politics of Delhi. That is the other side of the picture of the invasion by the vernacular elite of the hallowed halls of power in Patna and Lucknow. This questioning of norms and institutions indicate a quickening and deepening of Indian politics. That alone can keep democracy going, rather like Gandhi's intervention in the 1920s, ridiculed at first by the elites of his time, which dramatically changed the nature of Indian politics and put the freedom movement on a firm footing among workers and peasants.

The findings from survey data are supported by larger developments that one can pursue at the level of aggregate data and institutional changes in Indian politics. Thus, hung parliaments and coalition governments create a spectre of governmental instability in India; a perusal of regional politics, firmly ensconced stable party systems and party cleavage linkage at once question this image. As new research shows, India is experimenting with a combination of federalism and consociationalism.[2] Similarly, in the face of the earlier apprehensions of Balkanisation, one finds today a robust confidence about the stability and resilience of the state, and as such, an acceptance of the inclusive character of the national and regional identities.[3] Hence, the nation and regions appear as 'layers' of identity. The picture of social harmony is moderated with the implicit presence of class conflict, so the support for liberalisation is moderated with a reminder of the interests of the less advantaged. There is great support for institutions but less for actors. Hence the need to be watchful of institutional norms, and to move from *political* analysis to *policy* analysis.

Finally, for pragmatic reasons, one already discerns a greater tolerance of communal accommodation.[4] Will these strategic manoeuvres born out of pragmatic grounds give rise to a larger public space conducive to communal accommodation and tolerant pluralism? It is perhaps too early to say. But then, such scepticism did also characterise the description of coalitions in the 1960s as *khichri* (a hotch potch mixture) governments, a denigrating epithet one hardly comes across any more in national political discourse. Perhaps the political coalescence of cultural opposites would become the common basis of Indian politics of the next century, not quite in homage to the spirit of humanitarian rationalism that underpinned Nehru's bold vision, but as a by-product of political rationality, inculcated and sustained by the institutions that the post-colonial state is based on.

However strange this might sound at a time when the rhetoric of intolerance has entered politics in a big way, democracy in India is no longer seen as an imported and exotic concept, nor as the creation of an enlightened, determined minority. It is a style of governance that has neatly fitted the lifestyle of a majority of Indians, even if the fit is partly by default. The 1996 Parliamentary elections, in many ways, mark the beginning of a new phase in Indian politics. This beginning, however, also portends changes that may prove to be counter-productive for Indian democracy. The challenge, in short, is to create a new basis for the legitimacy of the Centre's political authority. For, there is the danger that political responsibility of the leadership and accountability of the central institutions of governance may be subverted by the 'newspeak'—that is, the elected leaders 'represent' and are 'accountable' primarily to their 'constituencies' which they increasingly perceive in caste-communal rather than in national-secular terms. The challenge crystallised by the change of 1996 is, thus, to rearrange the national political space in a synergic but rooted way, rather than reverting to the Nehruvian model of deracinated 'national' politics fabricated for the benefit of the 'national' elites.

The 'Grey Area' of Multi-party Democracy in India

So far, we have concentrated on the hypotheses that explore the basis of the functioning of multi-party democracy in India, and found reasonable evidence for its acceptance by the main actors in Indian politics. Is this, however, an act of faith, an unconditional commitment, or a limited commitment, conditional on performance? The question arises from the fact that Indira Gandhi, the unrepentant author of the 1975 Emergency, was actually brought back with popular acclaim in 1980 when the Janata Party, which was the hero of the anti-Emergency movement, failed to deliver stable and efficient governance. In this section we shall explore the reasons for the residual doubts about the stability of multi-party democracy in India. Once again, India is not alone. In historical and comparative perspective. The collapse of an established party system is known to occur when it fails to accommodate the interests of an emerging social group, or fails to aggregate the interests of groups which are articulate and assertive about their demands.[5] How does India fare on this score?

High Trust in Institutions but Distrust in Actors

The presumed collapse of India's institutions has been the staple of academic[6] and journalistic discourse on Indian politics[7] since the early 1980s. The deinstitutionalisation prognosis was greatly reinforced by the destruction of the Babri mosque in 1992, and gets prominent mention at every outbreak of communal violence. As such, it is important to examine the level of trust and confidence that the people of India have in its major institutions and in the people responsible for running them. When asked *How much trust/confidence do you have in different institutions of India?* the results are highly positive for institutions, but negative for those who are responsible for running those institutions (Table 8.2).

Table 8.2
Evaluation of Different Institutions and Actors (in per cent)

	Great Deal	Somewhat	Not at all
Election Commission	45.9	31.1	23.0
Judiciary	41.6	34.2	24.2
Local government	39.0	37.8	23.2
State government	37.2	43.6	19.2
Central government	35.2	42.5	22.3
Elected representatives	19.9	40.4	39.7
Political parties	17.4	43.6	39.0
Government officials	17.2	40.4	42.3
Police	13.0	29.9	57.1

In order of positive evaluation, the Election Commission, which, under the high-profile leadership of T.N. Seshan made elections much more orderly than before, gets the best score of 45.9 per cent of 'great deal of confidence' and 31.1 per cent of 'somewhat confident'. The judiciary, again the beneficiary of high-profile public interest litigation and prosecutions leading to the exposure of financial misdemeanour of politicians at the highest level, comes next in the order of positive evaluation. Local government, which, since the democratic decentralisation under the initiative of the Balwant Rai Mehta Committee of 1957 has steadily spread all over India, gets a positive evaluation from three-quarters of the population. Next in order come the State and Central governments of India. There is a precipitous fall, however, when it comes to elected representatives and political parties, for both of which the negative evaluation exceeds the positive score. Government officials do no better, and the police do the worst.

Trust in local government, next to the Election Commission and judiciary, followed by the State and then the Central government, tells us two things. First, that the performance of lower-level governments appears to be better judged than that of the Central government, and second, that people seem to be more concerned about lower units of governance than the higher ones. It may be matched with the identification of the Chief Minister vis-à-vis the Prime Minister, and also with interests in state or national governments. While the issue of nation-region will be discussed later, it may be noted that 23.0 per cent of people admit to have more concern with the State government as against only 11.0 per cent in the Central government, while 20.9 per cent in both and 39.0 per cent in none.

High Efficacy in the Context of Low Institutional Legitimacy

A situation where individual voters articulate their identity and interests but do not have a great deal of confidence in elected representatives and civil servants responsible for the implementation of policy does not augur well for the effectiveness and stability of multi-party democracy. To recall the theoretical insights of the civic culture and participation research of earlier years, a stable democracy would require reasonably high performance on both dimensions, whereas in a situation where low efficacy and low legitimacy is the rule, one can have little reason to expect a functioning multi-party democracy. In a context of high legitimacy and low efficacy, one can expect an authoritarian regime with limited participation. The fourth case, where personal efficacy overtakes system legitimacy, opens up the field for intervention from outside the party system from potential challengers to multi-party democracy, such as protest movements, the church, students, the army—in fact any organised group with the means to convince the masses that it can deliver better results.

The negative evaluation of government officials and the police on one hand and the plethora of corruption and other scandals involving political leaders on the other explain the uncertain feeling many Indians have about their own political system. While more research is necessary to pinpoint the causes for limited opposition to Indira Gandhi's Emergency at its height, and the triumphant return of Indira Gandhi's popular authoritarianism in 1980 shortly after the electoral humiliation of 1977 under the slogan 'vote for the government that works', indicates the scope that forceful and undemocratic leaders have in order to play a role in India's electoral politics. In order to test the strength of association of efficacy and legitimacy, these two variables were cross-tabulated. The results are presented in Table 8.3.

Table 8.3
Cross-tabulation of Efficacy and Legitimacy (in per cent)

Efficacy	Legitimacy			Total
	Low	Medium	High	
Low	36.8	56.0	7.2	100.0
	21.9	12.9	9.5	14.7
	5.4	8.3	1.1	
Medium	24.7	67.4	7.9	100.0
	61.5	64.6	43.5	61.5
	15.2	41.5	4.8	
High	17.2	60.8	22.0	100.0
	16.5	22.5	47.0	23.7
	4.1	14.4	5.2	
Total	100.0	100.0	100.0	
	24.7	64.2	11.1	

Key: The first entry in each cell refers to the row percentage, the second, to the column percentage, and the third to the percentage of cases in each cell.
Kendall's tau $b = 0.17$.

We learn from the cross-tabulation of efficacy and legitimacy that the overall relationship between the two is positive, though the strength of association is rather low. This helps provide the necessary and sufficient conditions for the existence of a multi-party democracy in India. The 'centre' is occupied by a large group of people, constituting 41.5 per cent of the population who are moderately efficacious and hold the system to be moderately legitimate. The main sources of challenge to the stability of the system come from those at the bottom left corner of the matrix, namely, the 4.1 per cent who are highly efficacious but for whom system legitimacy is at its lowest, 15.2 per cent who are moderately efficacious but hold system legitimacy to be low, and 14.4 per cent who are highly efficacious but hold system legitimacy to be only moderate. But balancing this substantial group of about 34.0 per cent is 14.2 per cent of the Indian population occupying the top right corner of the matrix where legitimacy overtakes efficacy. Once again, while greater research is needed to identify the various social groups in terms of their location in the matrix, we have some interesting evidence here which provides new insights into both the stability of multi-party democracy in India as well as to the sources of its vulnerability.

To sum up the discussion, the growth of a competitive party system and the existence of inter-party consensus on key issues affecting civil liberties are crucial facilitating conditions for civil society. The party system, in turn, is effective and seen as legitimate only insofar as it succeeds in getting itself accepted by social groups as an effective means for the articulation and aggregation of demands, failing which a politically mobilised people have every incentive to turn to other agencies like the army, the clergy, radical groups of the left or the right, and last but not least, to mob violence, none of which has a proven record of an abiding commitment to civil society.

From the data and results of the present survey, multi-party democracy appears to have struck root in India. This is seen particularly from the linkage of partisanship and social cleavages, a broad-based sense of political efficacy and legitimacy, and cross-cutting value conflicts and partisanship. And yet, some doubts about the stability of multi-party democracy linger on, reinforced by such events as the national Emergency of 1975–77, the destruction of the Babri mosque in 1992, continuing communal conflict and tension and the sub-national movement in Kashmir. The danger to multi-party democracy from these issues is muted because, as we have seen in the data, opinions within India's political parties as well as social groups on these crucial issues are divided, with a substantial percentage of supporters within each major political party, as well as across major social groups in general, coming up with responses that provide a commitment to civil society in India.

The data also provide useful insights into a possible solution to the essential tension between majoritarian democracy and civil society in multi-ethnic societies. Parekh formulates these challenges as

...the range of permissible diversity, how to accommodate differences without losing [its] social cohesion, how to reconcile the apparently conflicting demands of equality of treatment and recognition of cultural differences, and how to create a spirit of common citizenship among [its] culturally diverse members (Parekh 1994: 199).

By opting for an inter-party consensus on tolerant pluralism, Indian voters have shown themselves capable of avoiding the extremes of both a naive advocacy of national values as well as a mechanical insistence on essentialised, universal human rights as the basis of civil society in India. This pragmatic pluralism, the policy of live and let live, and above all, the ability of different social groups to put themselves in the position of other communities, and to devise the rules of communal accommodation as the basis of the creation of a public space for a common citizenship, provides a contrasting picture to the 'Clash of Civilisations' and to the gladiatorial positions that Huntington attributes to members of different religions in divided societies.

Local and regional breakdowns of democracy are not unusual in many post-colonial and post-revolutionary countries. The issue is, why do they not become cumulative or terminal in India? As we have already seen from the survey data, the fact that there is a significant number of individuals who feel themselves to be efficacious, but do not accord a great measure of legitimacy to the institutions of the state, nor to political parties as the most effective instrument for the implementation of the popular will, provides some insights into these grey areas of Indian democracy. Pending further investigation, it can be suggested that the breakdown of democracy is a manifestation of attempts by political actors to bring pressure on the system. As long as the system responds, either through policy change or by a change in the rules of the game, the process of democratic politics bounces back. Research on the potential for a responsive political system to gain strength from protest movements and the ability of the Indian political process to accommodate 'rational protest' as a complement to institutional participation provides an additional explanation to the resilience of multi-party democracy and civil society in India.[8]

Speculation about the future of democracy and civil society in India is further complicated by the continued presence of the Congress party at centre stage, though not in the form of the dominant party that it used to be. The existence of a large, catch-all political party can be a source of some structural instability, because fragmentation of other parties is crucial to its own power and the formation of unstable multi-party coalitions is its preferred strategy. Though the Congress party, compared to its vote and seat share of the first-phase party system (1952–77) has experienced a net decline, it continues to be an important factor in Indian politics. The return of the Congress as a catch-all party (at least in some parts of India) on one hand and the emergence of the Bharatiya Janata Party in other areas on the other, and the present experiment of coalition governments at the Centre are sending signals in different directions. We can look forward to a certain period of instability of the multi-party coalition, but not of a kind that affects the legitimacy of the system or the stability and effectiveness of policy making.[9]

Democratic Politics and the Ambiguities of Identity

The fact that under the compelling rationality of political choice, the Indian voter and those desperately soliciting his support have put all available resources into instrumental use, is a theme that has been implicitly present all throughout this book. Democracy flourishes only when the political market is seen as an integral part of public life. In that sense, the fact that the electoral process draws on all possible sources of social influence is by no means unique to India. Where the issue becomes complex and controversial is the limit that one can legitimately place on the reach of politics, either because it is against the law or because the indiscriminate use of certain political resources have dire implications for the very stability of the nation and state in India. It is in this context that the political use of caste, religion and region gain considerable salience.

The role of primordial identities in societies caught in the process of transition from the agricultural to the industrial has received much scholarly attention.[10] Today, the linear view of modernisation which once defined the leading opinion among specialists is questioned by radical divergences from the predicted path. Looking back, the Indian Constitution, one of the first acts of self-definition among newly decolonised societies, appears to have been prescient, for its first article itself gave voice to India's double identity: 'India, that is Bharat, shall be a Union of States.'[11] 'India' represented the legal structure based on the individual, fundamental rights and participation, exuding the 'scientific spirit' of which Nehru was the main inspiration, while 'Bharat' was evocative of links with India's pre-colonial past. The competitive political process that the Constitution had foreseen has brought this duality into its most explicit statement, simultaneously drawing upon the primordial identities in order to mobilise members of those traditional groups for the purposes of political support, but also making it possible for groups of very different social origins to work together as members of larger political coalitions or as parties to the formal institutions of the state and thus, to inculcate the values of equal citizenship. Thus, caste, religion and region are much talked about, but the concepts as used in politics are far from what they might indicate in their social context.

Clearly, the textbook definition of caste as an endogamous status group, traditionally based on occupational specialisation and shared rituals, no longer applies to the sphere of politics.[12] The current debate on the nature and function of caste in India's society and politics[13] has given an explicit form to the duality implicit in the very conceptualisation of the role of tradition in the Indian Constitution. Nothing gives voice to the duality as effectively as the very flowering of Indian democracy: caste is simultaneously essence and instrument, symbolic commitments to Bharat and India, organic identities and individual interests, social networks and the location of a given individual in a social matrix. The issue that puzzles many observers of Indian society is: Why does caste survive in India and among Indians abroad, in spite of long and sustained attempts at modernisation?

When Jawaharlal Nehru inaugurated the new Republic of India with the famous speech on Freedom at Midnight, he gave voice to a section of the Indian elites that wished to see India transformed into a modern, secular state. Its aspirations were enshrined in the constitutional norms of equal citizenship, fundamental rights to equality and liberty, irrespective of caste, creed, religion or place of birth, and the judicial and bureaucratic apparatus of a modern state with which to implement these lofty ideals. Four decades after Independence, some of these hopes lie shattered in the ruins of the Babri mosque of Ayodhya and in the killing fields of Bihar and other places routinely afflicted with caste wars. The emergence of the politics of identity, where groups based on caste, religion, tribe and region appear as the main actors, once again raises an issue that gave rise to the original orientalist discourse: Are the institutions of liberal democracy appropriate to India? Nehru, intensely aware of the dangers of communal violence, was familiar with the problem. Reproachful as it was, the modernist leadership of the Congress had watched with helpless fascination as the Muslim League, wielding religion as a vehicle of mass mobilisation, had fought for and won the right to have a separate homeland for Muslims. The stigma of the failure to resist the demand for the partition of India on the basis of religion, and the communal carnage that marked the birth of the new Republic had convinced Nehru that the evils of caste and religion had to be firmly kept out of the public arena. In Nehru's view, shared by the ruling elites, drawn from a largely urban, professional and Western-educated background, scientific spirit, technology, planning, social legislation and a rational bureaucracy were the answer.

Why does caste, after four decades of social legislation, modern education and liberal democratic politics, continue to be a significant factor in India's public life? The question, posed to oriental circles at the turn of the century, would have raised few eyebrows, because Indian society was meant to be like that, and the thin modern veneer added to it by British rule notwithstanding, could not behave in any other way. Today, an active electorate of 500 million people questions some of the premises of the orientalist approach which considered Indian society incapable of self-definition or self-regulation. Nevertheless, as the spectre of 'caste war' and communal violence live up to a scenario all too familiar to the orientalists, there is the occasional throwback to the heady days of orientalism among 'essentialists', who present caste as the immutable essence of Indian society. Opposed to this is the instrumentalist approach, which presents caste as merely a politically convenient self-classification for the purpose of material benefits. All through this book, tangential references have been made to the issue of the resilience of caste with reference to essence and agency, two views of caste that compete and occasionally conflate in the context of India's vibrant political process.

In view of the aspirations of India's modernising elites, the ability of castes to survive large-scale social and economic change and to mutate into modern forms like caste associations continues to be a puzzle. That caste 'survives' is clear from several diachronic studies based on fieldwork, the campaign rhetoric of practically all political parties including those explicitly committed to 'secularism', electoral alliances and evidence from various surveys. What remains unclear is exactly which attributes of caste survive and why. Its protagonists constantly slip in and out of the two faces of caste—the traditional endogamous status groups organised around specific occupations—and caste associations where people come together using social ties for the purpose of promoting collective interest. Thanks to its liminality, caste appears as the quintessential Janus of Indian politics, with a *jati* face, turned towards the *varna* scheme and through it, to Indian tradition and identity, capable of moving people in ways and areas beyond the reach of modern institutions; and, an associational face which links it with the institutional fabric of the modern state. The political actor deftly manipulates both faces in order to generate power through this complex repertoire.

Interpreting caste therefore leads to the larger issue of how to relate the ontology of *jati* and *varna* (of which caste and the caste system are but inadequate representations) to the moral basis of society and state in India. Here, the battle lines are clearly drawn. Essentialists and orientalists have a similar understanding of Indian tradition. Both views hold that castes, ensconced in the *varna* scheme, are the bedrock of Indian tradition.

The secular modernists of India, on the other hand, view caste as synonymous with underdevelopment, hierarchy and prejudice. They wish to jettison it altogether. Essentialists, whose instinctive and political sympathies are for preserving the pure spirit of Indian civilisation in amber, ridicule such attempts as derivative, and ultimately self-defeating. The fact, however, that in reality caste survives, and mutates, serves only to raise empirical doubts about both the rival schools.

India's political discourse with regard to caste today is full of references to the various conceptual *avatars* of the concept itself. Thus, Dumont's theory of caste with references to *homo hierarchicus* and purity and pollution, complete with a theory of the natural subordination of the inferior to the superior, is interspersed with that of caste as a grid of identities, the local *jati*, regional *varna* schemes and the all-India Hindu *varna* system and caste as *jajmani*, exchange of economic needs, status and reinforced by power, caste as the essence of a traditional society and the traditional caste system as the institutionalisation of this essence as well as a mode of resistance to all of the above. That the traditional view of caste survives in spite of the efforts of the modern state and democracy as challenges to the ideology of the caste system and its institutions and the various legislative efforts after Independence such as the Untouchability Offences Act 1955, various forms of reservations, electoral and political mobilisation, and the long-term effects of urbanisation, continues to puzzle. The empirical evidence discussed in this book, seen in the larger political context, provides some insights into the resilience of caste and its mutations. While these issues would surely form the subject of more detailed and theoretical explorations in future research, some indications of the kind of questions that can be raised can be given through the suggestion of two analytical categories.

Primordial Identities and Competitive Politics

The introduction of limited franchise under British rule had already created a stir among the Indian electorate. The ensuing competition, and the differential mobilisation by untouchables had led to a strong reaction among the Congress leadership which saw the communal electorate as an attempt by the British to divide and rule. One of the legacies of the Poona Pact (1936), which symbolised a historic rapprochement between the leaders of the untouchables and the Congress leadership was to set aside a quota for the representatives of the untouchables. The second legacy was the knowledge that local hierarchy could be renegotiated at the level of high politics through competitive electoral mobilisation. The lesson was not lost on the electorate, particularly among the less privileged sections after Independence, when universal adult suffrage was introduced in one fell swoop. After an initial interlude, the locally dominant castes transformed the *jajmani* relations into a veritable vote bank through what the Rudolphs have called vertical mobilisation. However, intra-elite conflict and land reforms which helped further loosen the dependent relations between the locally dominant caste and those who worked for it, quickly led to a situation of factional conflict and short-term political alliances, called differential mobilisation. By the 1960s, electoral mobilisation had led to a new phenomenon called horizontal mobilisation, whereby people situated at comparable levels within the local caste hierarchy came together in caste associations. One consequence of horizontal mobilisation was the formation of new parties like the Republican Party, the Bahujan Samaj Party primarily supported by former untouchables or the various *kisan* (farmers') parties, and movements like the Lok Dal which draw their support mainly from the backward classes, which aggressively promoted sectional interests through the electoral arena.

One of the main consequences of four decades of competitive electoral politics on the local caste hierarchy has been to render all inherited relations of power necessarily contestable. The congruence of status, power and wealth, tenuous even at a period when little recourse for status negotiation was available outside the local arena has been further contested. As Washbrook reminds us, '...the merest sight or smell of privilege in any area of society instantly provokes antipathetic response among those who see or smell it. No privilege is inherently legitimate and no authority exists uncontested' (Washbrook 1989/90: 227).

For ease of presentation, we can conceptualise the role of caste as a factor in political behaviour in terms of an analytical scheme (Table 8.4). Membership of a caste, ensconced within the local caste hierarchy, can be perceived by some of its members as an obligation to support their social superiors. As the logic of political participation has spread through the Indian electorate, and the percentage of people taking part in elections has grown, vote banks which functioned on the basis of vertical obligation have become progressively rare. As things stand now, it is common to find factions—short-term political alliances—where one can find voters following their own interest and utilising all political resources at their command, including the membership of a caste.

Table 8.4
Caste and Political Competition

	Caste Competition	Political Competition
Value	Primordial (essence)	Rational (agency)
Norm	Obligation	Interest
Modality	*Jajmani*	Political organisation
Structure	Vote bank	Multi-caste association
Form of mobilisation	Vertical	Differential horizontal

The scenario of contestation that Washbrook describes from the case of Tamil Nadu is repeated daily in all parts of India.[14] Underneath the violence and atrocities perpetrated in its name, caste is actively present as a factor in electoral mobilisation. Does caste consciousness perpetuate inherited caste-related inequalities? What might sound counter-intuitive is in fact one of the enigmas of caste, for caste consciousness in fact destroys precisely those attributes of the caste system, such as traditional social obligations, hierarchy and dominance, which the essentialist view presented as necessarily fixed in time and space. The point will be discussed at greater length below.

Caste, Community and Modern Politics

Formation of communities is the predictable outcome of the new atmosphere of competitive, modern politics, where the logic of numbers and scarce resources is increasingly clear to social groups trying to acquire new privileges or to hold on to what once appeared securely theirs, but is now coveted by other groups. The politics of community formation can be presented in terms of an analytical schema (Table 8.5). Unlike 'modern' or 'traditional' organisations, a community is a necessarily liminal structure, with a vernacular face turned towards local society to which it appeals in terms recognisable to the local arena, and a universal associational face turned towards the modern state and the market. The caste association is the most frequent (but not the only) type of community one is likely to come across in contemporary Indian politics.

Table 8.5
The Politics of Community Formation

Social Base	Identity	Territorial Boundary	Political Strategy
Localised caste (*jati*)	Thick	Insular	Close
Community (*sampradaya*)	Thin	Broad	Open

Seen as communities, castes are uniquely Indian in form but universal in content. Under the impact of four decades of electoral competition and social legislation, new economic opportunities and new political linkages have developed. Caste, as its correlations with political attitudes and social visions discussed in this book shows, is far from the rigid, timeless essence of an unchanging India. The use of caste as a form of identification is primarily strategic.[15] The introduction of competitive politics and democratic institutions have quickened the pace of change in the social and political organisation of castes, increasingly perceived as communities in which people come together to promote collective interest. Castes are now perceived not as rigid but as flexible by their members, who treat them more as vehicles of self-promotion rather than as structures of domination by the powerful and self-censorship by the powerless. 'Scholars', as Inden argues, kept India 'eternally ancient' by attributing to it various 'essences', most notably that of caste. A new perspective which can depict India's institutions and political discourse as instruments through which its people seek to influence the course of their history therefore should start with a re-evaluation of caste.

The use of caste for electoral purposes is an example of similar use of other primordial identities such as region, language, religion and tribe. This is done quite deliberately as a collective political strategy. The emphasis here is on the fact of collective deliberation and optimisation of all political resources. Therefore, to depict the electoral process as a mechanical manifestation of caste arithmetic, based on the fact that primordial identities are salient in the campaign, would be an inadequate representation of reality. The second important point to infer from the manner in which primordial identities are used for political purposes is the concept of delinking one from the other when it suits the actor. We find an excellent example of how religion, once its salience was regionally established, receded into the background and the localised *jati* resurfaced as the anchor of political mobilisation in a case study from an Assembly Election in Uttar Pradesh. Reporting a 'conversation that took place between an old woman (possibly an *ahir* by caste) and a BJP canvasser', Singh shows how the political actor is able to put religion 'in its place' once the religion-based political movement has made its point, so that the everyday politics of caste-community-interest can take over.

Canvasser: O mother! Are you Hindu?
Woman: Yes.
Canvasser: Do you believe in Rama?

Woman:	Yes. He is our god.
Canvasser:	Do you not want a grand Sri Ram temple built in Ayodhya?
Woman:	Sure. It must be built. I too have contributed for this purpose during '*shila pujan*'.
Canvasser:	Then you should vote for the BJP because it is the only party which will get the Sri Ram temple built at Ayodhya.
Woman:	Yes, yes. I shall vote for it. (A small pause.) But will you tell me the caste of the candidate who is fighting on the BJP ticket?
Canvasser:	Yes. He is a *rajput*.
Woman:	No, my son. I cannot do that. When everybody is voting for his caste, how can I go against that? I will also vote for my caste men.[16]

The above exchange brings out the strategic character of the electoral discourse, in which people from all levels of society take part and where, depending upon the occasion, all political resources are put into effective use. When traditional networks and primordial identities are drawn upon, the intention is clearly political, and not exclusively social. But this complex repertoire draws on the 'modern' identities of class as well. If the electoral process continues to sharpen the 'binary opposites of caste and class', the exigencies of practical politics continue to fuse them in the organisational mode of the political caste, which is neither purely interest nor identity, but intersects both in a manner that the actors concerned consider optimal.[17] In the process, the politics of primordial identities has called into question their traditional roles as the building blocks of society. Commenting on caste in particular, Sheth says, 'The singular impact of the competitive democratic politics on the caste system thus was that it delegitimised the old hierarchical relations among caste, facilitating new, horizontal power relations among them.'[18] The process has come full circle, with the voter choosing the type of primordial identity he or she would allow a given party to use effectively at a given point of time. The use of religion in particular, in a multi-religious society where the largest religion itself is deeply fragmented on caste, sect, regional and linguistic lines, clearly has self-imposed limitations.

Finally, while the democratic character of the Indian political system has probably acquired the requisite resilience to withstand challenges from non-democratic ideologies of the left and the right, and has actually transformed these anti-system movements into legitimate partners in government, the future of political parties as the preferred mode of democratic government is not so secure. There is the impatience of the newly enfranchised electors who do not think highly of elected party politicians, visible evidence of corruption in high quarters within the political parties and the Gandhian nostalgia for a non-party, decentralised, direct democracy, based on village panchayats. Some of these ideas that were written into the Constitution have gradually found their way into law, political institutions and practice. These potential conflicts between the principles of partyless direct democracy and party-based parliamentary democracy did not matter very much during the early years after Independence when the first 'independent' generation presided over by Jawaharlal Nehru was in charge. India could have its consensus-based, accommodating Congress system which linked it to the tradition of united struggle against the British and the Gandhian legacy of non-partisan character of the village community, and the Nehruvian commitment to party-based parliamentary democracy. As if in recognition of the British and the implicit faith in British constitutional practice, the Indian Constitution provided for no guaranteed role or dedicated state finance for political parties.[19] As we have seen from the record of India's short-lived Emergency at the Centre and countless replications of it at the regional level, Nehru's successors have taken greater liberties with the internal restraints on authoritarianism that are built into the informal, customary basis of British parliamentary practice.

It follows from the above that India's multi-party democracy will continue to have a grey area surrounding it, not so much on its democratic institutions and practices, as on the stability of the party system on which it is based. If the present regime, based on multi-party democracy, fails to deliver the goods, it is certainly possible for an authoritarian populist to seize the opportunity and raise the banner of non-party democracy as the most effective instrument of the popular will, and cultural nationalism as the legitimising device of its power. In order to improve the odds against this possibility, it will probably not be a bad thing for India to take a leaf out of the German rule book and add a suitable amendment to the Indian Representation of the People Act, reinforcing the political necessity and constitutional status of political parties.

Crowding the Middle: The Central Tendency of Indian Politics

To the distant observer, the frequent outbreaks of political violence in India might come across as a sure sign of an imminent implosion. There is animated talk of majority rights and minority obligations, of revolutionary seizure of all assets and their just redistribution, and, equally, of the market principle substituting all else, of jettisoning the slow-moving democracy in favour of more effective leadership. But somehow, in the end, reason appears to prevail, heated debate gives in to moderation, adversaries become partners—all of which leaves the world more confused than ever about the mystical working of the Hindu (and increasingly, Indian) mind. How does one account for this?

One possible answer to this question lies in the underlying distribution of public opinion on the composite measure of the contents of the nation—soft, accommodationist, multicultural or hard, exclusivist, unicultural. Our data show a convergence to the mode for practically all sub-populations (Table 8.6).

The most outstanding aspect of Indian politics that is revealed by Table 8.6 is the general tendency to be close to the sample mean of 7.29. On a scale based on 10 items with a maximum value of max = 20, where the lower figures indicate proximity to the accommodationist and inclusivist view of the nation in India, the sub-groups indicate rather small variations. The data, from this point of view, appear to support what the Rudolphs have called the tendency towards 'centrist politics' in India.

> Parties representing the scheduled castes (e.g. the factionalized Republican Party of India), the scheduled tribes (a large variety of local parties) and the Muslims (various Muslim leagues and several Uttar Pradesh parties of short duration) have proved notably unsuccessful in mobilizing and holding the support of the minority status groups they hoped to lead and represent (Rudolph and Rudolph 1987: 424).

But the Muslim attitude towards the state and nation in India, particularly in view of their position on the overall inclusion-exclusion scale, calls for a more detailed analysis. Their sub-sample average of 4.81 with a standard deviation lower than that of Hindus indicates both a major difference with the view of the nation, and significant homogeneity within the community on this issue. The Muslim view of the nation is one of the leading political questions of India, deliberately made into a non-issue during the long years of Congress rule. The Partition provided only a semi-solution to the question in the sense that those Muslims who stayed behind did not thereby automatically disown the two-nation theory. The fuzzy position on the issue of the role of religion within the structure of the state, suspended between that of the wall of separation and equidis-

Table 8.6
Mean and Standard Deviation on the Accommodation Scale

Sample	Mean	Standard Deviation
Total	**7.29**	**3.00**
Education		
Up to primary	6.95	3.01
Middle school	6.70	3.32
Illiterate	7.28	2.52
Higher Secondary	7.37	3.34
College and above	8.78	3.60
Locality		
Rural	7.21	2.85
Urban	7.53	3.40
Caste		
SC	6.99	2.69
OBC	7.00	2.82
ST	7.10	2.59
Other	7.83	3.40
Gender		
Female	7.16	2.84
Male	7.41	3.15
Religion		
Muslim	4.81	2.57
Christian	6.08	2.61
Other	6.16	2.47
Sikh	7.54	2.83
Hindu and Jain	7.64	2.90
Elite Status		
Non-elites	7.27	2.95
Elites	7.36	3.29
Party voted for		
Left Front	6.32	2.78
National Front	6.90	2.97
BSP	7.00	2.59
Congress	7.01	2.96
BJP	8.40	3.06
Regionalists		
Regionalist	6.37	2.99
Non-regionalist	7.60	2.94
Age		
Up to 45 years	7.24	3.05
46 years or more	7.43	2.91

Note: See Appendix 2 for the construction of the 'Accommodation Scale'.

tance, opening up the possibility of opportunistic manipulation, did not give many choices to the religious communities either. The dangerous potential of a sullen 'majority' community and distrustful 'minorities' has powerfully manifested itself in the context of the tragic incident of the Babri mosque. Its distant echo can still be perceived in our data, where the supporters of the BJP, along with those with college education and above, constitute the groups most inclined to an exclusivist definition of the nation in India.[20]

As India copes with yet another round of electoral consultation in the search for effective and representative government, and the media get saturated with campaign rhetoric from politicians whose venality and corruptibility is often beyond any doubt, one may be forgiven the moments of weakness when one questions the fit between Indian society and the political institutions of the post-colonial state, and look somewhat wistfully at the exacting standards by which Western democracies, the original source of many of these institutions, judge their leaders. This book should help the hard-pressed democrat in those moments of doubt from becoming cynical. For the evidence analysed here gives some insights into where and how Indian democracy is at its most effective. It also gives some food for thought about how the state in search of a nation is the beneficiary of the efforts from below to discover a common basis of civility, of tolerance and accommodation, of quiet pride in the nation and a reinforcement of its inclusive character. Indian democracy, in that sense, has definitely 'thickened' the nation, necessarily thinned by the needs for centrally prescribed communal amnesia as the price of unity against the masters of divide and rule, and the long years of the one-dominant-party system when the same spurious basis of communal unity remained frozen, the fear of another partition and guaranteed vote banks being the political fuel that nurtured it. By working together for 50 years, the people of India have discovered the political basis of accommodation. So, they converge to the mean on the 10-point scale of exclusion and accommodation. Political competition has thus produced the basis of the dynamic consensus which underpins social change in India.

The attitudinal data on legitimacy and nation formation presented in this book should provide further insights into the process that provides a bridge between the post-colonial state and the people. The mission, as Partha Chatterjee observes, might be impossible, for 'Nationalism sets out to assert its freedom from European domination. But in the very conception of its project, it remains a prisoner of the prevalent European intellectual fashion' (Chatterjee 1986: 10). Later in the same text, Chatterjee spells out why this might be a stillborn project. Chatterjee argues that the post-colonial state arrogates to itself the right to define the contents of the nation, and uses this legitimising device to use state power to promote the interests of capital.

Nowhere in the world has nationalism qua nationalism challenged the legitimacy of the marriage between Reason and capital. Nationalist thought, as we have tried to show above, does not possess the ideological means to make this challenge. The conflict between metropolitan capital and the people-nation it resolves by absorbing the political life of the nation into the body of the state. Conservatory of the passive revolution, the national state now proceeds to find for 'the nation' a place in the global order of capital, while striving to keep the contradictions between capital and the people in perpetual suspension. All politics is now sought to be subsumed under the overwhelming requirement of the state-representing-the-nation. The state now acts as the rational allocator and arbitrator for the nation. Any movement which questions this presumed identity between the people-nation and the state-representing-the-nation is denied the status of legitimate politics. Protected by the cultural-ideological sway of this identity between the nation and the state, capital continues its passive revolution by assiduously exploring the possibilities of marginal development, using the state as the principal mobiliser, planner, guarantor and legitimator of productive investment (Chatterjee 1986: 168–69).

From these premises, which see the role of the state as necessarily limited insofar as the creation of genuine nationalism is concerned, Chatterjee turns towards the 'people' as the ultimate agent of the creation of the state and nation in its own image.

Thus, much that has been suppressed in the historical creation of post-colonial nation-states, much that has been erased or glossed over when nationalist discourse has set down its own life history, bear the marks of the people-nation struggling in an inchoate, undirected and wholly unequal battle against forces that have sought to dominate it. The critique of nationalist discourse must find for itself the ideological means to connect the popular strength of those struggles with the consciousness of a new universality, to subvert the ideological sway of a state which falsely claims to speak on behalf of the nation and to challenge the presumed sovereignty of a science which puts itself at the service of capital, to replace, in other words, the old problematic and thematic with new ones (Chatterjee 1986: 170).

Some supportive evidence for the process Chatterjee envisages can be found in the institution of representative democracy which provide multiple points of entry for the people. The Indian state, through the deepening and broadening of federalism, extension of representation in effective ways to groups historically excluded from participation, through the judicious use of affirmative action, and through strategic tolerance and covert encouragement to rational protest movements, has opened up myriad ways in which to be active in promoting one's own welfare. The Indian experiment has established an important point of reference for state formation and nation building in post-colonial states.[21]

While there is little doubt that democracy in India 'works', for the very sake of democracy it is important to remember that the dazzle of Indian democracy can blind both Indians and the foreign observer to its shortcomings. Democratic rhetoric can get trapped in the fashionable duality of secularism engaged in a noisy battle against Hindutva, or liberalisation as compared to socialism, whereas the real issue is, as Drèze and Sen point out, not between being for or against the market, but of deciding what the socially acceptable and politically feasible basis of integration with the world market is. Similarly, the issue with regard to cultural nationalism is not whether religious and cultural values have a role in politics, but in what form the traditional values of India should explicitly and publicly constitute the basis of the nation and state in India.

Since the issues of high politics are made by the elites, some concerns of great importance to the non-elites do not make it to the national electoral agenda in an effective manner. The obsession with secularism (and now liberalisation) has tended to take attention away from the fundamental issues of poverty and illiteracy, both of which have become non-issues in India's high politics. One can also forget that the price of populism—the product of democracy in the context of weak and unstable political parties—is unaccountable power of which India has had a national experience during the Emergency. The antics of the worst kind of populism that continue to haunt regional politics are reason enough to believe that not all the demons that stand in the way of the deepening and quickening of the pace of democracy have been slain yet. That is the point where one needs to look in the direction of the judiciary and the bureaucracy, the tired but vigilant workhorses of the state, and the press—India's great asset—to come to the aid of politics.

Notes

1. Gujarat's social elites in the study village, at the time of the study still dominated by the landholding *patels*, had learnt the democratic game enough to extend running water and electricity to the tribal parts of the village at the expense of the panchayat. 'Even if we do not give it to them, they will take it from us anyway. This way we shall have the pleasure of giving, and keep the village unity intact' was the answer of an elderly *patel*, member of the panchayat, when asked why the panchayat spent the money for the electrification of the tribal parts of the village and to extend the pipelines to their houses, whereas the original water and electric facilities for the upper-caste parts of the village were borne by their residents themselves. The Orissa upper-caste elites were a study in contrast. There was little communication or commonality between them and their Scheduled Caste and Tribe fellow villagers. The results of this comparative study were published in Mitra (1992).
2. This is the main thrust of Lijphart (1996).
3. Contrast, for example, the tones of Harrison (1960) and Mitra and Lewis (1996).
4. For the new tendency of culturally exclusive parties like the DMK, AIADMK, BJP and Akali Dal to coalesce with other 'secular' as well as 'communal' parties, see A.G. Noorani, 'The BJP today', *The Statesman Weekly*, pp. 10–11, 24 January 1998; and Saba Naqvi Bhaumik, 'BJP: Surviving Friends', *India Today*, pp. 26–28, 19 January 1998.
5. The main question asked to measure this phenomenon in the survey was: *Would you say that persons we elect by voting generally care about what people like you think, or that they don't care?* An alarmingly high percentage (63.1) say that the elected representatives do not care. The larger implications of this would be discussed below at length.
6. See in particular Kohli (1990) and Sen Gupta (1996).
7. See Akbar (1988).
8. See Marsh (1977), Kaase (1972) and Mitra (1992) for applications of these theoretical conjectures.
9. The Fourth Republic of France, contemporary Italy, Israel and Japan, provide interesting points of comparison.
10. In the euphoria over the post-war decade of development when decolonisation was sweeping the face of the globe, a natural and necessary dissolution of primordial identities into modern forms of citizenship was considered the norm. It was also the main moving spirit behind mainstream development literature, which suggested a linear and incremental course of modernisation of traditional societies as the likely shape of things to come. History has proved to be rather different from such predictions. One of the early warnings of a different possibility, informed by a different theoretical construction of the nature of interaction between tradition and modernity, was provided by Rudolph and Rudolph (1967).
11. Art. 1, the Constitution of India. Curiously, the Hindi version of the Constitution reverses the order, where 'Bharat' precedes 'India'.
12. For succinct definitions and operationalisation of the traditional view of caste, see Gerald Berreman, 'The Concept of Caste', in *The International Encyclopedia of the Social Sciences*, p. 334, New York 1968. Most of the textbook definitions of caste are derived from or based on Dumont (1966). A sociological mapping of the

traditional view of the context of rural India can be found in Gould (1990) and Mitra (1982). The grid that connects local *jatis* and the all-India *varna* scheme is described in Fox (1969).

13. The questioning the 'master' is done most trenchantly by Quigley (1994). On this theme, also see Mitra (1994a) and Quigley (1993). The theoretical inspiration for some of this questioning is derived from Said (1978).

14. For theoretical and empirical discussions of resistance from within the Indian social system and the various forms it takes, see Robinson (1988). Also on the theme of resistance from below by marginal social groups, see Scott (1985). For an insight into the long process of caste consciousness as a form of resistance to the caste system, partly instigated by missionaries and the new value system introduced into Indian society by British rule, see Hardgrave (1982) and Washbrook (1989/90). Haynes and Prakash (1991) provide several historical and contemporary examples of resistance against social dominance.

15. Electoral campaigns are replete with anecdotes of the strategic use of caste identities and solidarities. Vijay Bahadur Singh explains the role of caste as follows. 'In order to consolidate his position further, Balaram [the candidate] attempted to create a fear psychosis among Muslims and to warn the backward castes against the malign attitude of the forward castes, particularly the *rajputs*.' Singh cites the comments of a speaker at a meeting organised by Mulayam Singh Yadav, describing how *rajputs* use them for political purposes: 'They are clever in exploitation, cruel in oppression and, above all, they unleash atrocities on the poor, especially the *dalits*. They use us as a driver uses a stone or a brick as a stopper to his vehicle on the road. After we have been used, we are kicked in the same fashion as the driver kicks the stopper which he must have very earnestly searched for all around the place.' V.B. Singh, 'Grass Roots Political Process: Atraulia Constituency', *Economic and Political Weekly*, p. 27, 13–20 January 1996.

16. Singh reports: 'This conversation I overheard on the outskirts of a village in the constituency, 16 November 1993', ibid., p. 127.

17. D.L. Sheth, 'Caste: The Challenge of Stratification', in *The Hindu* (special 50th anniversary of Independence supplement), p. 87, 15 August 1997.

18. Sheth, ibid.

19. There is a Representation of the People Act, but no equivalent of the German *Parteienrecht*. The Indian Election Commission has recently moved in this direction by directly requiring parties to be accountable for campaign expenses, and more important, to hold internal elections.

20. It should be added here that four out of the 10 items that have gone into the construction of the scale of inclusion-exclusion (see Appendix 2) relate to issues of great significance for Muslims. As such, the overall position on the scale might be weighted in favour of the confessional component of nation building in India, not taking into account the other areas of social, economic and political integration. Conversely, the finding also points us in the direction of the unsolved issue of the role of religion in Indian politics, long (thanks to the equivocations of the politics of accommodation) a non-issue in Indian politics.

21. The findings reported here provide supportive evidence for the assertions with regard to the role of the state in India made by Rudolph and Rudolph (1987: 400–401).

Appendices

Appendix 1

Note on Methodology

Drawing a random sample of the Indian population is made problematic by its sheer diversity. With 846 million people spread across 26 States and six Union Territories, India represents a very diverse society. Apart from numerous geographical divisions, it is a multicultural society. People are distributed in 16 major language groups. The minor languages and local dialects are about 1,000. Thousands of castes and sub-castes distinguishing themselves in terms of pursuit of occupations, ritual practices, lifestyle, food habits, etc., make the country still more complex. Though Hindus constitute the vast majority (82 per cent), India is populated by almost all the major religions of the world. With 100 million comprising 11.9 per cent Muslims, India ranks at the top as far as the total number of Muslims living in a country is concerned. In addition to Muslims, there is a sizeable population of Christians (2.3 per cent), Sikhs (1.9 per cent), Buddhists (0.8 per cent) and others (0.5 per cent) who do not only enjoy equality, but minority safeguards are also granted to them.

These are, at best, glimpses of social diversities Indian democracy is coping with. But more than these social diversities, economic inequality and its resultant effects are a greater cause of concern for the system. Regional imbalances, poor means of transport and communication, lack of literacy (as high as 47.8 per cent illiterate), over one-third of its population living below the poverty line, are all on the negative side of the democratic experiment. However, belying all popular myths about conditions hindering or helping a democratic experiment, India has not only ventured to defy these notions but has also succeeded, to a great extent, to integrate and unify them all through its democratic processes.

Since the answer to the questions posed here can be sought through ascertaining views from a wide variety of the country's population, only a survey method was found suitable for the purpose. The 1996 Lok Sabha elections provided the occasion, and the entire Indian electorate, as it existed in this election, became the universe of this study. For reasons of an abnormal law and order situation, it was decided to exclude the State of Jammu and Kashmir. That is, excluding the six Lok Sabha constituencies of Jammu and Kashmir, the remaining 537 constituencies falling in 25 States and six Union Territories of India constituted the universe. In other words, any person who figured on the electoral roll of these 537 constituencies was a potential subject of this study.

For a population of 846 million a sample of 4,000–5,000 persons chosen randomly might be considered an appropriate size to derive generalisations at the national level. However, the concerns of the present study aimed at analysing the data not only at State levels (at least for some of the States) but also by social groups, and their comparison across as well as within groups necessitated a larger sample. It became all the more important because any stratification at the social group level was not possible at all.

Thus, we decided for a larger sample and aimed at a sample size of 9,000-plus completed interviews. In order to meet this target without any substitution, we had no option but to inflate the sample size to meet the shortfall caused by non-completion. The experience of previous surveys shows that the rate of completion in similar surveys has varied between 55 and 70 per cent in different States. Considering the proportional contribution of each State, the national average works out to about 60 per cent. Given this rate of completion, if one has to meet the given target, the sample needs to be inflated by 66.67 per cent. Thus the original sample size of 9,000 was inflated to 15,015 (9,000 × 0.6667 + 9,000 = 15,015) so that a completion rate of 60 per cent could give us 9,000 completed interviews, which was our target exactly.

Sample Units and Distribution of Respondents

Individual electors being the ultimate source of our information, a method had to be evolved to identify them in a manner that would make them representative of the universe. Since we had decided to examine our concerns through the prism of elections, each elector had to be located and traced through the following different levels of electoral boundaries, viz., State, Lok Sabha constituency (PC), Vidhan Sabha constituency (AC), Polling Booth (PS), individual elector (i.e., respondent). Following this track and to give adequate coverage to each state or group of States and Union Territories, a quota of one-fifth of constituencies from each State was fixed to be selected. Accordingly, excluding Jammu and Kashmir, a total of 108 out of 537 Lok Sabha constituencies had to be chosen first. Since Lok Sabha constituencies are constituted by different Vidhan Sabha segments in them, it was decided to select two ACs from each PC falling in the sample. That is, 216 Vidhan Sabha constituencies (108 × 2 = 216) were selected in the second step. Similarly, two polling booths from each of the chosen ACs, which makes 432 polling booths (216 × 2 = 432), were selected in the third step. Finally, in the fourth step, a fixed number of respondents from all the selected booths sharing equally the quota proportionately allocated to each state was selected from the most recent electoral roll of the sampled booth (see Table A1.1).

Table A1.1
State-wise Distribution of Sampled Units and Respondents

States and Union Territories	No. of PCs	No. of Sampled PCs	No. of Sampled ACs	No. of Sampled Booths	Proportion of National Electorate	No. of Respondents Selected
Andhra Pradesh	42	8	16	32	0.084	1,264
Assam	14	3	6	12	0.023	345
Bihar	54	11	22	44	0.102	1,529
Delhi	7	1	2	4	0.014	210
Goa	2	1	2	4	0.002	30
Gujarat	26	5	10	20	0.051	765
Haryana	10	2	4	8	0.019	286
Himachal Pradesh	4	1	2	4	0.007	105
Karnataka	28	6	12	24	0.054	810
Kerala	20	4	8	16	0.035	524
Madhya Pradesh	40	8	16	32	0.075	1,128
Maharashtra	48	10	20	40	0.092	1,380
Orissa	21	4	8	16	0.038	572
Punjab	13	3	6	12	0.024	360
Rajasthan	25	5	10	20	0.052	780
Tamil Nadu	39	8	16	32	0.073	1,096
Uttar Pradesh	85	17	34	68	0.167	2,499
West Bengal	42	8	16	32	0.077	1,152
North-East:	11				0.010	
Meghalaya		1	2	4		75
Tripura		1	2	4		75
Union Territory	6				0.002	
Pondicherry		1	2	4		30
All India	537	108	216	432	1.001	15,015

Note: Calculations based on electorate figures for 1995 available with the Election Commission.

Sampling Procedure

In order to draw a representative sample of the Indian electorate, a multi-stage stratified random sampling procedure has been used, wherein we decided to select 20 per cent Lok Sabha constituencies from the list of all the constituencies in a State. The number of PCs thus selected from all the States and Union Territories of India (excluding Jammu and Kashmir) is 108. Selection of different sample units was done in different stages.

Stage One: Selection of Lok Sabha Constituencies

1. First of all, all PCs with their electorate in a State were serialised as per the Election Commission of India's Delimitation Order of 1976.
2. The cumulative total of electorate was assigned against each constituency in an ascending order.
3. In order to avoid selection of contiguous constituencies, the total electorate in the State was divided by the number of constituencies to be selected from that State. It helped to create as many geographical zones as the number of sampled constituencies in the State. The figure thus obtained represents one zone, and is called hereafter a 'constant'.
4. Since the intentions were to give zonal representation too, we decided to select one PC from each such zone.

And, finally, to select individual PCs a random number (using a Random Number table) was chosen from within the constant and compared with the cumulative total of the electorate listed against each PC. In whichever cumulative total it fell, the PC listed against that was chosen as the first sampled Lok Sabha constituency of that State. Subsequent constituencies were selected by adding the constant to the random number. That is, one addition of the constant would give a second PC, an addition of two would give the third, and so on and so forth.

While this procedure provided adequate (geographical) coverage of the State, it also ensured a proportional chance to every constituency. That is, constituencies with a larger electorate enjoyed a greater chance of selection in the sample and fulfilled the requirements of the PPS (Probability Proportionate to Size) sampling procedure.

Table A1.2
Comparable Figures for the Sample and the Universe

Characteristics	Sampled Constituencies	Universe
Per cent turnout	57.8	55.8
Votes polled by		
INC	36.3	36.7
BJP	20.1	20.1
JD	12.1	11.8
CPI	2.2	2.5
CPM	6.0	6.1
Share of reserved constituencies for:		
Scheduled Caste	16.0	79.0
Scheduled Tribe	8.0	41.0
Share of population (per cent):		
Scheduled Caste	14.1	14.4
Scheduled Tribe	6.4	6.5

These steps and the sampling procedure were repeated in each state to select a set of 108 Lok Sabha constituencies, and then repeated twice over to obtain two more such sets. Validation tests of representativeness were then carried out by matching the mean score of these sample sets with the national average in terms of some key variables, such as voter turnout and vote share of different political parties in the previous elections, proportion of reserved constituencies for Scheduled Castes (SC) and Scheduled Tribes (ST), share of SC and ST population and degree of urbanisation. The set which provided the best fit was thus selected. Table A1.2 presents comparable figures for the sample (the set which was finally selected) as well as of the universe, and validates the representative character of our sample to a great extent.

Stage Two: Selection of Vidhan Sabha Constituencies

1. All ACs with their electorate were serialised for every sampled PC in a State.
2. The cumulative total of the electorate was worked out and listed against each AC in ascending order.
3. The total electorate in a PC was divided by two (in the manner stated earlier) to obtain a constant.
4. Drawing a random number from within the constant, the first AC was selected and the constant was added to the random number to select the second AC.

Like stage one, this procedure was repeated in each sampled PC to select the given number of ACs (No. of PCs × 2) in a State. Similarly, like the PCs, two more such sets were drawn to choose the best fit by following the same validation tests for Vidhan Sabha elections.

These steps were repeated for each State to select a final set of 216 Vidhan Sabha constituencies. Table A1.3 presents the list of sampled Lok Sabha and Vidhan Sabha constituencies.

Table A1.3
List of Sampled Constituencies: Lok Sabha and Vidhan Sabha

Parliamentary Constituency		Assembly Constituencies	
Andhra Pradesh			
5	Bhadrachalam (ST)	38	Yellavaram (ST)
		274	Bhadrachalam (ST)
11	Eluru	67	Tadepalligudem
		70	Eluru
16	Bapatla	97	Ponnur
		113	Martur

(Table A1.3 contd.)

(Table A1.3 contd.)

Parliamentary Constituency			Assembly Constituencies	
	21	Chittoor	140	Chittoor
			143	Punganur
	26	Kurnool	177	Yemmiganur
			180	Pattikonda
	31	Secunderabad	208	Sanathnagar
			213	Asafnagar
	36	Peddapalli (SC)	248	Manthani
			251	Huzurabad
	42	Miryalguda	283	Tungaturthi
			286	Miryalguda
Assam				
	4	Dhubri	25	Golakganj
			39	Jaleswar
	8	Mangaldoi	56	Kamalpur
			66	Sipajhar
	13	Dibrugarh	117	Lahowal
			122	Tinsukia
Bihar				
	1	Bagaha (SC)	2	Bagha (SC)
			6	Lauria
	6	Maharajganj	33	Maharajganj
			37	Masrakh
	11	Sitamarhi	67	Sitamarhi
			72	Pupri
	16	Rosera (SC)	87	Baheri
			101	Singhia (SC)
	21	Madhepura	116	Singheshwar
			122	Kishanganj
	26	Rajmahal (ST)	148	Borio (ST)
			151	Pakaur
	31	Khagaria	169	Gopalpur
			182	Chautham
	36	Arrah	213	Paliganj
			216	Arrah
	40	Aurangabad	236	Nabinagar
			239	Rafiganj
	45	Kodarma	270	Barkatha
			273	Jamua (SC)
	49	Ranchi	305	Khijri (ST)
			308	Kanke (SC)
Delhi				
	4	East Delhi	37	Trilokpuri (SC)
			47	Rohtas Nagar
Goa				
	2	Marmugao	25	Vasco Da Gama
			34	Cuncolam

(Table A1.3 contd.)

Parliamentary Constituency		Assembly Constituencies	
Gujarat			
6	Junagadh	38	Somnath
		42	Junagadh
11	Gandhinagar	67	Sabarmati
		79	Gandhinagar
16	Kapadvanj	107	Prantij
		128	Kathlal
22	Baroda	147	Baroda City
		150	Vaghodia
26	Bulsar (ST)	178	Bulsar
		182	Umbergaon (ST)
Haryana			
3	Karnal	11	Indri
		16	Assandh (SC)
8	Bhiwani	66	Bhiwani
		72	Hansi
Himachal Pradesh			
3	Mandi	59	Karsog (SC)
		67	Darang
Karnataka			
2	Gulbarga	11	Shahabad
		15	Jewargi
7	Chitradurga	46	Molakalmuru
		51	Pavagada (SC)
11	Kanakapura	89	Uttarahalli
		100	Anekal (SC)
15	Chamarajnagar (SC)	112	Bannur
		120	Chamarajnagar
20	Chikmagalur	153	Mudigere (SC)
		157	Tarikere
25	Belgaum	194	Bailhongal
		200	Gokak (ST)
Kerala			
5	Manjeri	31	Wanchoor (SC)
		35	Kondotty
9	Trichur	58	Trichur
		65	Guruvayoor
15	Alleppey	98	Sherthalai
		102	Kuttanad
20	Trivandrum	136	Trivandrum East
		140	Parassala
Madhya Pradesh			
3	Gwalior	16	Lashkar East
		21	Bhander (SC)
8	Satna	62	Chitrakoot
		204	Vijairaghogarh

(Table A1.3 contd.)

Parliamentary Constituency		Assembly Constituencies	
13	Raigarh (ST)	98	Jashpur (ST)
		102	Lailunga (ST)
18	Mahasamund	139	Khallari
		144	Kurud
23	Balaghat	179	Kirnapur
		183	Balaghat
29	Hoshangabad	206	Bohani
		224	Itarsi
34	Khandwa	281	Harsud (ST)
		285	Nepa Nagar
39	Jhabua (ST)	306	Jhabua (ST)
		310	Ratlam Rural
Maharashtra			
3	Kolaba	14	Mangaon
		17	Panvel
9	Bombay North	43	Malad
		45	Borivili
11	Dahanu (ST)	60	Bhiwandi
		65	Shahapur (ST)
16	Erandal	91	Parola
		96	Pachora
21	Amravati	120	Achalpur
		125	Badnera
26	Chandrapur	154	Rajpura
		159	Bhadrawati
31	Parbhani	177	Singnapur
		183	Pathri
36	Osmanabad (SC)	208	Paranda
		221	Barshi
41	Khed	242	Khed Alandi
		244	Mulshi
46	Sangli	271	Sangli
		275	Kavathe-Mahankal
Meghalaya			
1	Meghalaya	6	Nongbahi Wahiajer
		24	Sohryugkham
Orissa			
5	Kendrapara	32	Rajnagar
		40	Mahanga
10	Aska	67	Suruda
		70	Kodala
15	Phulbani (SC)	102	Balliguda (ST)
		112	Sonepur (SC)
20	Sundargarh (ST)	137	Rajgangpur (ST)
		140	Raghunathpali (ST)

(Table A1.3 contd.)

Parliamentary Constituency			Assembly Constituencies	
Pondicherry				
	1	Pondicherry	14	Thirubuvanai (SC)
			27	Neduncadu (SC)
Punjab				
	4	Jullundur	30	Jullundur North
			35	Nakodar
	8	Patiala	72	Ghanaur
			76	Patiala Town
	13	Ferozepur	92	Fazilka
			97	Zira
Rajasthan				
	3	Churu	18	Ratangarh
			22	Sadulpur
	7	Dausa	49	Lalsot (ST)
			54	Jamwa Ramgarh
	13	Tonk (SC)	46	Dudu (SC)
			93	Malpura
	18	Udaipur	139	Mavli
			143	Udaipur Rural (ST)
	23	Barmer	177	Barmer
			181	Jaisalmer
Tamil Nadu				
	3	Madras South	12	Triplicane
			19	Alandur
	7	Vellore	36	Katpadi
			48	Vellore
	12	Chidambaram (SC)	66	Bhuvanagiri
			70	Mangalore (SC)
	17	Tiruchengode	98	Tiruchengode
			120	Erode
	22	Palani	117	Kangayam
			147	Natham
	27	Tiruchirapalli	159	Lalgudi
			168	Thiruverambur
	32	Pudukkottai	190	Kolathr (SC)
			193	Arantangi
	37	Tenkasi (SC)	214	Vasudevanallur (SC)
			217	Alangulam
Tripura				
	2	Tripura East (ST)	38	Hrishyamukh
			52	Chandipur
Uttar Pradesh				
	2	Garhwal	5	Pauri
			424	Dehra Dun

(Table A1.3 contd.)

Parliamentary Constituency		Assembly Constituencies	
7	Moradabad	31	Kunderki
		33	Moradabad
13	Pilibhit	57	Pilibhit
		60	Puranpur
18	Misrikh (SC)	77	Sidhauli (SC)
		83	Beniganj (SC)
23	Rai Bareli	109	Rae Bareli
		112	Dalmau
28	Faizabad	134	Ayodhya
		137	Sohawal (SC)
33	Gonda	159	Mankapur (SC)
		162	Katra Bazar
38	Gorakhpur	185	Gorakhpur
		193	Shyam Deurwa
42	Salempur	204	Bhatpar Rani
		222	Siar
48	Jaunpur	251	Mariahu
		255	Rari
52	Varanasi	241	Varanasi Cantt
		246	Gangapur
57	Chail (SC)	278	Chail (SC)
		281	Khaga
62	Jalaun (SC)	332	Kanchi (SC)
		335	Madhogarh
67	Kannauj	307	Bidhuna
		310	Chhibramau
72	Firozabad (SC)	351	Firozabad
		360	Kheragarh
77	Khurja (SC)	379	Khurja
		387	Dadri
82	Muzaffarnagar	406	Jansath (SC)
		408	Muzaffarnagar
West Bengal			
5	Raiganj	30	Karandighi
		42	Harish Chandrapur
10	Berhampore	64	Beldanga
		68	Bharatpur
15	Joynagar (SC)	100	Gosaba (SC)
		105	Canning West (SC)
20	Dum Dum	134	Khardah
		138	Dum Dum
25	Uluberia	171	Uluberia South
		174	Kalyanpur
31	Contai	209	Khajuri (SC)
		213	Egra

(Table A1.3 contd.)

Parliamentary Constituency		Assembly Constituencies	
36	Vishnupur (SC)	245	Raipur (ST)
		254	Kotulpur
41	Bolpur	281	Mangalkot
		286	Dubrajpur

Stage Three: Selection of Polling Booths

Two polling booths were to be selected from each of the 216 ACs in our sample. These were selected by simple random procedure. That is, the PPS method was not followed in the selection of polling booths. However, care was taken to avoid selection of contiguous units. To do so:

1. The total number of polling booths in an AC was divided by two to make two groups and to obtain a number (constant) that would determine the distance between the two sampled booths;
2. The first PS was selected by picking a random number from the first half; and,
3. The second PS was selected by adding the constant to the serial number of the first booth.

Stage Four: Selection of Respondents

As stated earlier, the number of respondents to be interviewed in each State was determined by the State's share in India's total population (excluding Jammu and Kashmir). That is, the target of 15,000 respondents was proportionately (according to the 1991 Census) distributed to each State. The number thus obtained was divided by the total number of polling booths to be selected from that State to fix a quota for each sampled booth in the state (see Table A1.1).

To select individual respondents from the sampled booth, the following steps were followed:

1. The most recent electoral roll of the sampled booth was obtained from the local election office.
2. If required, the electoral roll was serialised for any deletion, addition, and of course, inclusion of list(s) from other electoral units in case the booth covered more than one area.
3. The total number of electors in the booth was divided by the fixed quota of interviews to obtain a constant to divide the lowest sample unit (PS) into as many subunits as the number of respondents allocated to a booth.
4. A random number was chosen from within the constant to select the first respondent from that locality. The constant was added to the random

number to select the next respondent, and this exercise was repeated till the last respondent from that booth was selected.

This procedure was repeated for all the selected polling booths in each State and a list of 15,015 respondents was prepared to form a national representative sample for this study.

Research Instruments

A detailed interview schedule was prepared, involving scholars with considerable experience in survey research. Questions were tested in different socio-political milieus and were accordingly revised. The final version of the questionnaire was prepared in English (Appendix 3) and was translated into the local languages, which again was pre-tested for accuracy and standardisation across languages.

In addition to the main questionnaire, two more data collection schedules were prepared:

1. *Village/Town Data Schedule.* This was prepared to collect information about the locality from which our respondents were selected. Information like social composition and infrastructural facilities of the area were thought to be of great use in enhancing our understanding of the data.
2. *Summary Background Data Schedule.* This was prepared for those respondents whose interviews were not possible for one reason or the other. The information thus generated would help us to explain some methodological questions, e.g., over-reporting in turnouts and distortion in the representative character of our sample, if any.

Training of Field Staff

The success of large survey research lies in the quality of data collection. Since such surveys are conceived and designed by one person or a group of persons and carried out by different persons in the field, the investigators and other personnel associated with the fieldwork need to be adequately trained. They need to be trained to the extent that they are able to appreciate the basic concerns of the study, its relevance, and of course, why they have to follow the method, procedure and techniques they are told to. Accordingly, workshops were organised to train the trainers first, and they were equipped with the following:

1. Objective and focus of the study.
2. Objective of each question.
3. Sampling details.
4. Canvassing the questionnaire, editing and checking the recorded responses.
5. Coding.
6. Field logistics.

Training for field supervisors and field investigators was organised at different regional centres in which a group of trainers associated with the study participated. While the training covered all the aspects listed above, special attention was given on rapport building and skills in canvassing the interview schedule, recording of answers, using probes and coding the responses in the columns provided for them.

A detailed manual for interviewers was prepared in advance and was extensively used during the course of in-depth training.

Finally, to carry out the survey efficiently, the country was divided into 16 operational zones and as many 'State Coordinators' drawn from the nationwide network of senior social scientists associated with the programme were entrusted with responsibility of coordinating the fieldwork and data collection in their respective areas.

Appendix 2

Construction of Scales and Variables

Campaign Exposure

Campaign Exposure presents the sum score of three variables, viz., interest in campaigns, meetings attended, and direct participation in campaign activities. Values of 2 or 1 showing positive and negative responses respectively were assigned to each variable to obtain a sum score for each respondent. Finally the scores ranging between the lowest of 3 and the highest of 6 were divided into three groups: *No exposure*, *Low exposure*, and *High exposure*.

Political Information

Political Information presents the sum score of four variables measuring respondents' ability to name correctly the present and previous MPs from the area, the Prime Minister, and the Chief Minister of the State. Accordingly, values of 2 and 1 were assigned to correct and incorrect responses respectively, to obtain a sum score for each respondent. Finally the scores ranging between lowest of 4 and the highest of 8 were divided to make three levels: *No information*, *Low*, and *High level* of political information.

Financial Satisfaction

Financial Satisfaction presents the sum score of four variables, viz., perception of improvement during the last few years, satisfaction with the present situation, future prospects and better opportunities for children. Values of 3 and 1, showing positive and negative responses respectively, while a middle value of 2 to those perceiving no change in their situations, were assigned to obtain a sum score for each respondent. Finally the scores ranging between the lowest of 4 and the highest of 8 were divided into three to make three levels: *Low, Medium,* and *High Satisfaction.*

Economic Class

Economic Class is computed by summing the scores assigned to each respondent on four indicators, viz., expected monthly income of the household, occupational status of the respondent, asset holding status, and type of residential accommodation. First of all, values of 1, 2, 3, 4 or 5 (low to high) respectively were assigned to each indicator for every respondent. A sum of the values ranging between the lowest of 4 and the highest of 20 was obtained in the second step. Finally, considering the frequency distribution, the mean score and standard deviation of the summed score, four class intervals were created to make four *Economic Classes* labelled One (Very Poor), Two (Poor), Three (Middle), and Four (Rich).

Elite Status

The questions used for the creation of a scaled variable on *Elite Status*, with four values (rural non-elites, rural elites, urban non-elites and urban elites) are as follows:

Table A2.1
Do you think your vote has effect on how things are run in this country, or do you think your vote makes no difference?

Has effect	58.8
Other	0.6
Makes no difference	21.4
DK	18.9

Table A2.2
Are you a member of a political party?

Yes	6.3
No	93.7

Table A2.3
(If not a member of a party at the moment)
Were you ever a member of a political party?

Yes	1.4
No	98.6

Table A2.4
Place of Residence

Urban	24.7
Rural	75.3

The elite are defined as those who are both members of a political party or have been once, and who believe that their vote is effective.

Deprivation

The *Deprivation Scale* combines *objective deprivation* measured in terms of the class variable with the *perception of deprivation* measured in terms of the 'financial satisfaction' scale. This variable is constructed on the basis of the cross-tabulation matrix reported below, where the columns describe the categories of class, and the rows the levels of the subjective perception of deprivation. The members in the Table are individuals who belong to that particular category.

Table A2.5
Construction of Deprivation Scale

		Class			
		1 Very Poor	2 Poor	3 Middle	4 Rich
Financial efficacy	4	92	32	24	3
	5	154 **1**	91	63	8
	6	346	251	117 **2**	26
	7	451	371	226	69
	8	464	509	329	111
	9	520	514	441	169
	10	346 **3**	388	396	234
	11	196	349	368 **4**	276
	12	137	234	276	285

This leads to the following distribution:

Table A2.6
Frequencies of Deprivation Scale

	Level of Deprivation	(%)
1	Most deprived	10.0
2	Moderately deprived	28.8
3	Moderate achievers	40.8
4	High achievers	12.5
	Missing values	7.8
	All	100.0

Accommodation

The objective of this scale called *Accommodation* is to measure along an inclusiveness-exclusiveness dimension the willingness of the Indian electorate to accommodate minority and related interests. At one extreme of the scale are those who want a strong, nationalistic-culture, elitist and patriarchal state, and at the other extreme are those who prefer a multicultural, gender-sensitive and non-elitist society.

The following variables (attitudinal data) have been selected to form the index of accommodation. The 'no responses' and missing values have been regrouped in the middle (value = 1) and recoding has been done in order to adjust the direction of answers (inclusive = 0; exclusive = 2).

Table A2.7
Questions for Accommodation Scale

Number	Question
28d	*Only educated people should have the right to vote. Do you agree or disagree?*
28e	*Those who are not well-educated should not be allowed to contest elections.*
28k	*It is the responsibility of the government to protect the interests of the minority communities. Do you agree or disagree?*
29a	*Some people say that the destruction (of the disputed building [Babri Masjid]) was justified while others say it was not justified. What would you say? Was it justified or not justified?*
34a	*Backward castes should have reservation in government jobs. Do you agree or disagree?*
34b	*There is no need for India to make the atomic bomb. Do you agree or disagree?*
34d	*Like gram panchayats, there should be reservation for women in assemblies and parliament. Do you agree or disagree?*
34f	*India should make more efforts to develop friendly relations with Pakistan. Do you agree or disagree?*
34g	*The needs and problems of Muslims have been neglected in India. Do you agree or disagree?*
34h	*Every community should be allowed to have its own laws to govern marriage and property rights. Do you agree or disagree?*

The scale has been generated on the basis of the following correlations:

Accordingly, the values of these 10 variables have been added up, so that one gets a scale from min = 0 (inclusive) to max = 20 (exclusive). Graphically, one can see the distribution of the whole sample and two sub-populations, namely, the age cohorts as developed in Chapter 2 and the voters of the Left Front and the BJP.

Table A2.8
Multiple Correlation of Questions for Accommodation Scale

Spearman-Rho

	28d	28e	28k	29a	34a	34b	34d	34f	34g	34h
28d	1.000	—	—	—	—	—	—	—	—	—
28e	0.028**	1.000	—	—	—	—	—	—	—	—
28k	0.144**	−0.001	1.000	—	—	—	—	—	—	—
29a	0.045**	0.003	0.196**	1.000	—	—	—	—	—	—
34a	0.057**	0.079**	0.144**	0.066**	1.000	—	—	—	—	—
34b	−0.054**	0.000	0.001	0.092**	0.025*	1.000	—	—	—	—
34d	0.074**	0.017	0.137**	0.036**	0.185**	−0.025*	1.000	—	—	—
34f	0.058**	−0.013	0.197**	0.197**	0.080**	0.027**	0.087**	1.000	—	—
34g	0.060**	0.036**	−0.051**	0.120**	0.078**	0.121**	−0.061**	0.037**	1.000	—
34h	0.007	−0.006	0.095**	0.107**	0.105**	0.114**	0.005	0.101**	0.195**	1.00

** Correlation significant at 0.01 level.
* Correlation significant at 0.05 level.

Figure A2.1
Distribution of Accommodation Variable by Age

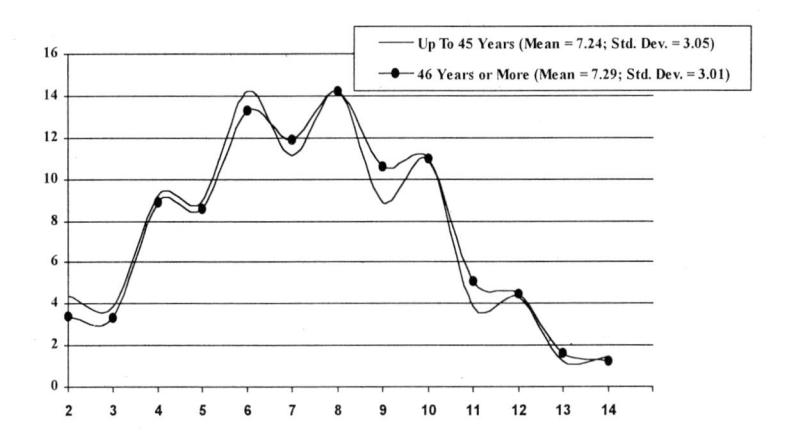

Figure A2.2
Distribution of Accommodation Variable by Party Voted For

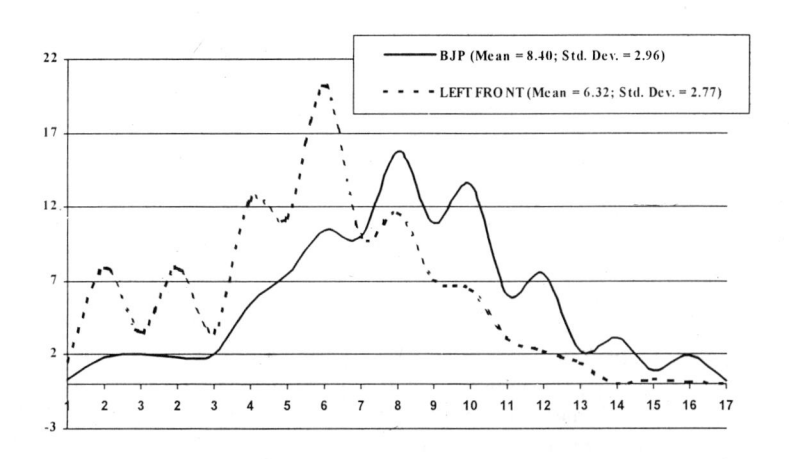

Appendix 3

Questionnaire

State ☐☐ PC ☐☐ PS ☐ Res. ☐☐

Centre for the Study of Developing Societies
29 Rajpur Road, Delhi-110054

**NATIONAL ELECTION STUDY, 1996
POST-POLL SURVEY**

Interview's Introduction

I come from Delhi—from the Centre for the Study of Developing Societies. We are studying the Lok Sabha elections and interviewing thousands of ordinary voters from different parts of the country. The findings of these interviews will be used to write in books and newspapers without giving any respondent's name. It has no connection with any political party or government. I need your cooperation to ensure the success of our study. Kindly spare some time to answer my questions.

Interview Begins

1. Let us first talk about this village/town you live in. How long have you lived here? (*If not entire life, probe for number of years lived here.*)

   8 ☐   1 Less than 10 yrs.   2 10 yrs. or more   3 Entire life

   IF NOT ENTIRE LIFE

   > 1a. From which village/town have you come?
   >
   > Name of village/town _____
   >
   > Name of district _____ state _____
   >
   > 1b. Where have you lived most of your life—in a village or a town?
   >
   > 9 ☐   1 Village   2 Town   3 Both   9 Inapplicable

2. In talking to people about the recent elections to the Lok Sabha, we find that some people were able to vote and some were not able to vote. How about you? Were you able to vote or not?

   10 ☐   2 Yes   1 No   8 Not sure

   2a. (*If yes*) Whom did you vote for? Please mark your preference on this slip and put in this box. (*Supply the dummy ballot and explain the procedure.*)

   11 ☐   **Ballot No.** ☐☐☐

   FOR ASSAM, HARYANA, KERALA, TAMIL NADU, WEST BENGAL AND PONDICHERRY ONLY

   > 2b. And what about the assembly elections—whom did you vote for? Please mark your preference on this slip and put in this box. (*Supply the dummy ballot and explain the procedure.*)
   >
   > 13 ☐   **Ballot No.** ☐☐☐

2c. (*If voted*) When did you finally make up your mind about whom to vote for ?

15 ☐

　1 On the polling day　　　　4 Before the campaign

　2 A few days before polling　8 Can't say

　3 As soon as the candidates　9 Not Applicable
　　were announced

2d. (*If not voted*) What was the main reason you could not vote in this election?

16 ☐

　1 Did not know I was a voter
　2 Out of station
　3 Not well
　4 Have no interest/did not feel like voting
　5 Prevented by some people from voting
　6 Somebody had already voted before I went to vote
　7 Fear of violence at polling station
　8 Any other (*specify*) _____
　9 Not Applicable (*Yes in Q. 2*)

3. Keeping in view the election results, who do you think deserved to form the government at the Centre?

17 ☐

　1 Congress/Congress-led　　4 Others (*specify*) _____
　2 BJP/BJP-led　　　　　　　5 No one
　3 NF-LF/Third Front　　　　8 D.K.

4. No single party has got a clear majority in the Lok Sabha in this election. There are now two opinions about the formation of government. Some say that different parties should come together to form a coalition government. Others say that elections should be held again. What would you prefer: a coalition government or fresh elections?

18 ☐

　1 Coalition government　　　　2 Fresh elections
　3 Others (*specify*) _____　8 Can't say/D.K.

5. In today's situation, who do you think can make the best Prime Minister of the country?

    1 P.V. Narasimha Rao   2 L.K. Advani
    3 Atal Bihari Vajpayee   4 V.P. Singh
    8 H.D. Deve Gowda   99 Can't say/D.K.
    13 Others (*specify*) _____

6. Who won from this parliamentary constituency in this election?

    2 Correct   1 Incorrect/D.K.

7. Now let us talk about the campaign during this election: How interested were you in the election campaign this year—a great deal, somewhat or not at all?

    3 Great deal   2 Somewhat   1 Not at all

8. How many of the election meetings that parties and candidates organised during the campaign did you attend?

    0 None   1 Some (one–two)   2 Many (more than two)

9. During the election people do various things like organising election meetings, joining processions, participating in canvassing, contributing money, etc., to help a party or candidate. Did you do any such thing yourself during the recent election campaign?

    2 Yes   1 No

9a. (*If yes*) For which party or candidate? _____

9b. (*If yes in Q. 9*) And what did you do? (*multiple response possible.*)

    1 Helped organise election meetings   8 Distributed publicity material
    2 Joined processions   16 Contributed money
    4 Participated in canvassing   32 Other (*specify*) _____

10. Did any candidate, party worker or canvasser come to your house during the campaign to ask for your votes?

    2 Yes   1 No

10a. (*If yes*) From which parties or candidates did they come? (*Record the first three in the order mentioned.*)

1. _____ (***Probe for 2nd, 3rd party.***)

2. _____

3. _____

11. In deciding whom to vote for, were you guided by anyone?

    2 Yes   1 No

11a. (*If yes*) Whose advice did you value most?

1 Spouse	4 Friends/co-workers
2 Other family members	7 Other (*specify*) _____
3 Caste/community leaders	9 Inapplicable (*'No' in Q. 11.*)

12. Now let us talk about the relationship among the people in your village/town/city. Would you say that compared to five years ago, the relationship between various groups of people has become more harmonious, remained the same or tension among these groups has increased?

1 More harmonious	3 Tension has increased
2 Same as before	8 D.K.

12a. (*If tension*) In your view, who among the following is best suited to resolve these tensions among various groups:

1 Village panchayat	5 Caste/community leaders
2 Government officials	7 Any others (*specify*) _____
3 Police	8 D.K.
4 Judiciary	9 N.A.

13. Now I would like to read some statements about the relationships between different groups. Please tell me about each one whether you agree or disagree with it.

	Statements	Agree	D.K./No opinion	Disagree
a.	Relationships between different castes have become more harmonious. *Do you agree with this or disagree?*	3	2	1
b.	Tension between tribals and non-tribals has increased. *Do you...?*	3	2	1
c.	Tension between different religious communities has decreased. *Do you...?*	3	2	1
d.	Tension between dalits and non-dalits (Harijans and non-Harijans) has increased. *Do you ...?*	3	2	1
e.	Tension between landowners and landless has decreased. *Do you...?*	3	2	1
f.	The relationship between people and the government officials has become more cordial. *Do you...?*	3	2	1
g.	Now there is more tension between the rich and the poor. *Do you...?*	3	2	1
h.	Police attitude towards common people has become more humane. *Do you...?*	3	2	1
i.	Compared to five years ago, life and property are less safe now than before. *Do you...?*	3	2	1
j.	The poor and deprived enjoy better social status now than before. *Do you...?*	3	2	1
k	The condition of the poor has improved during the last five years. *Do you...?*	3	2	1

40 ☐
41 ☐
42 ☐
43 ☐
44 ☐
45 ☐
46 ☐
47 ☐
48 ☐
49 ☐
50 ☐

14. People hold different opinions about struggle. Some people say that struggle, even when it leads to violence, is a proper method for the people to fulfil their demands, while others say that a struggle is not a proper method if it leads to violence. How do you feel—is struggle leading to violence a proper or not a proper method for fulfilling people's demands?

51 ☐

    3 **Proper**   2 **Other** (*specify*) _____

    1 **Not proper**   8 **D.K.**

15. Generally speaking, did most members of your caste group/community vote for one party or for different parties?

52 ☐

    2 **Different parties**   1 **One party**   8 **D.K.**

16. Do you think it is important or not important for you to vote the same way your caste group/community votes?

53 ☐

    2 **Important**   1 **Not important**   8 **D.K.**

17. Some political parties specially care for the interest of a particular caste group or community, while others don't. How about your caste group/community? Is there any political party that looks after the interest of your caste group/community?

54 ☐

    2 **Yes**   1 **No**   8 **D.K.**

55 ☐

17a. (*If yes*) Which party? _____

18. Now let us talk about the problems facing this country. What in your opinion are some of the major problems facing our country? (*Record exactly and in the order mentioned.*)

57 ☐   *   1 _____ (*Probe for 2nd & 3rd.*)

59 ☐   *   2 _____

61 ☐   *   3 _____

19. Which political party do you think can solve these problems better than others?

63 ☐   _____

20. Leaving aside the period of elections, how much interest would you say you have in politics and public affairs: a great deal of interest, some interest, or no interest at all?

3 Great deal   2 Some interest   1 No interest at all

21. How much, in your opinion, do political parties help to make government pay attention to the people: a good deal, somewhat or not much?

3 Good deal   2 Somewhat   1 Not much   8 D.K.

22. Is there any political party you feel close to?

2 Yes   1 No

22a. *(If yes)* Which is that party? _____

22b. *(If yes)* What are the things about *(name the party)* which you like most? *(Record exactly.)*

*   _____

23. Is there any political party for which you will never vote?

2 Yes   1 No

23a. *(If yes)* Which is that party? _____

*   23b. *(If yes)* What is it that you do not like about *(name the party)*?

    (Record exactly) _____

24. Now I would like to ask you about the things that were done by Narasimha Rao's government in Delhi during the last five years, that you may have liked or disliked. Was there anything that Rao's government did during the last five years that you particularly liked?

2 Yes   1 No

8 Does not know about any work done by the government

310 ■ Democracy and Social Change in India

78 ☐   * 24a. (*If yes*) What was it? 1st _____

                                          2nd _____

24b. Was there anything in particular that you did not like?

80 ☐   **2 Yes   1 No   8 Does not know about any work**

81 ☐   * 24c. (*If yes*) What was it? 1st _____

                                          2nd _____

25. Do you think your vote has effect on how things are run in this country, or you think your vote makes no difference?

   3 Has effect

83 ☐ **2 Others (*specify*)** _____

   1 Makes no difference

   8 D.K.

26. Talking about the elections just completed, what do you think was the main issue around which the election was fought this time? (*Record exact answer.*)

84 ☐ * 1 _____ (*Probe for 2nd and 3rd issue.*)

86 ☐ * 2 _____

88 ☐ * 3 _____

27. Suppose there were no parties or assemblies and elections were not held. Do you think that the government in this country can be run better?

90 ☐   **2 Yes   1 No   8 Can't say/D.K.**

28. I would like to read some statements we often hear. Would you tell me about each one, whether you agree or disagree with it?

		Statement	Agree	D.K./No opinion	Disagree
91	a.	What this country needs more than all the laws and talk is a few determined and strong leaders. *Do you agree with this or disagree?*	3	2	1
92	b.	It is not desirable to have political parties struggling with each other for power. *Do you...?*	3	2	1
93	c.	Government policies are not responsible for the poverty of the people. *Do you...?*	3	2	1
94	d.	Only educated people should have the right to vote. *Do you...?*	3	2	1
95	e.	Those who are not well educated should not be allowed to contest elections. *Do you...?*	3	2	1
96	f.	What people get in this life is the result of their *karma* in the previous life. *Do you...?*	3	2	1
97	g.	The government generally takes care of the interests of the common people. *Do you...?*	3	2	1
98	h.	Women should take active part in politics. *Do you...?*	3	2	1
99	i.	We should be loyal to our own region first and then to India. *Do you...?*	3	2	1
100	j.	Compared to national parties, regional/local parties can provide better government in states. *Do you...?*	3	2	1
101	k.	It is the responsibility of the government to protect the interests of the minority communities. *Do you...?*	3	2	1

29. Have you heard of the disputed building (Babri masjid) at Ayodhya?

102☐ **2 Yes**　　　　　　　　　**1 No**

29a. (*If yes*) Some people say that the demolition was justified while others say it was not justified. What would you say: was it justified or not justified?

103☐　　**3 Justified**　　　　　　**1 Unjustified**

　　　2 Can't say/D.K.　　　**9 Inapplicable**

29b. (*If heard about demolition*) What would you suggest should be built on that site now?

1 Neither mosque nor temple

2 Mosque should be built

104☐　　**3 Temple should be built**

4 Both mosque and temple should be built

5 Any other (*specify*) _____

30. Would you say that persons we elect by voting generally care about what people like you think, or that they don't care?

105☐　　**2 Care**　　**1 Don't care**　　**8 D.K.**

31. How much does having elections from time to time make the government pay attention to the people—a good deal, somewhat or not much?

106☐　　**3 Good deal**　　**2 Somewhat**　　**1 Not much**　　**8 D.K.**

32. Peoples' opinions are divided on the issue of the Kashmir problem. Some people say that the government should suppress the agitation by any means, while others say that this problem should be resolved by negotiation. What would you say: should the agitation be suppressed or resolved by negotiation?

　　　3 Should be suppressed　　　**2 Cannot say**

107☐　　**1 Resolved through negotiation**　　**7 Other (*specify*)** _____

Appendix 3 ■ 313

33. During the last five years the Central government has made many changes in our economy. Have you heard about them?

108

2 Yes   **1 No**

33a *(If yes)* What are these changes?

109   *

1._____

2._____

33b. *(If yes in Q. 33)* On the whole, do you approve or disapprove of these changes?

111

2 Approve   **8 D.K.**

1 Disapprove   **9 Inapplicable**

34. Let us now talk about some specific issues on which different people seem to have different opinions. I would read out some statements with which you may agree or disagree. Please tell me about each one, whether you agree or disagree.

	Statements	Agree	D.K./No opinion	Disagree
a.	Backward castes should have reservation in government jobs. ***Do you agree or disagree with this?***	3	2	1
b.	There is no need for India to make an atomic bomb. ***Do you...?***	3	2	1
c.	Foreign companies should not be allowed free trade in India. ***Do you...?***	3	2	1
d.	Like gram panchayats, there should be reservation for women in assemblies and parliament. ***Do you...?***	3	2	1
e.	Government companies should be given into private hands. ***Do you...?***	3	2	1

112
113
114
115
116

	Statements	Agree	D.K./No opinion	Disagree
117	f. India should make more efforts to develop friendly relations with Pakistan. *Do you...?*	3	2	1
118	g. The needs and problems of Muslims have been neglected in India. *Do you ..?*	3	2	1
119	h. Every community should be allowed to have its own laws to govern marriage and property rights. *Do you...?*	3	2	1
120	i Prohibition should be imposed all over the country. *Do you...?*	3	2	1

35. Some people say that the government should pass legislation so that people are not allowed to own and possess a large amount of land and property. Others say that people should be allowed to own as much land and property as they can make/acquire. What would you say?

121   **3 Limit ownership**   **2 Other** (*specify*) _____

   1 Should not limit ownership

36. Some people say that whatever progress was made in the last few years through development schemes and programmes of the government has benefited only the well-to-do. Others say no, the poor and needy have also benefited from them. What would you say? Have the benefits of development gone only to the well-to-do, or have the poor and the needy also benefited?

   1 Benefits gone to well-to-do

   3 Poor and needy also benefited

122   (If 'all', do not probe, encircle 3)

   8 D.K.

   2 Other (*specify*) _____

37. People are generally concerned about what governments do: some are more concerned about what the government in Delhi does, others are more concerned with what the state government does. How about you? Are you more concerned about what the government in Delhi does or about what the (*name the state government*) does?

   123

   1 Interested in neither   2 State government   3 Both

   4 Government in Delhi   7 Other (*specify*) _____

38. The government has initiated several schemes and programmes for the benefit of the people, such as housing schemes, employment schemes, old-age pension, loans/subsidies, etc. Have you or your family ever availed of such benefits?

   124

   2 Yes   1 No   8 D.K.

   38a. (*If yes*) What type of benefits?

   125

   1 Housing scheme

   2 Rojgar Yojna

   4 Land allotment   (Multiple answers possible)

   8 Old-age pension

   16 Loan/subsidies

   32 Other (*specify*) _____

39. Thinking about the last 10 years, would you say that the law and order situation in your area has improved, deteriorated or remained the same?

   127

   3 Improved   1 Deteriorated

   2 Remained the same   8 D.K.

   39a. (*If deteriorated*) Why has it deteriorated?

   128   *   _____

40. I would like to seek your opinion about different institutions of India in which you may have good deal of trust, some trust or no trust at all.

Institutions	Great deal	Somewhat	Not at all
a. How much trust/confidence do you have in the Central government: a great deal, somewhat or no trust at all?	3	2	1
b. How much trust/confidence do you have in the state government: ...?	3	2	1
c. How much trust do you have in the local government/ panchayat/municipality: ...?	3	2	1
d. How much trust do you have in the judiciary: ...?	3	2	1
e. How much trust do you have in the Election Commission: ...?	3	2	1
f. How much trust do you have in political parties: ...?	3	2	1
g. How much trust do you have in government officials: ...?	3	2	1
h. How much trust do you have in elected representatives: ...?	3	2	1
i. How much trust do you have in the police: ...?	3	2	1

41. Are you a member of any political party?

    2 Yes   **1 No**

    41a. *(If yes)* Which party? _____

    41b. *(If no)* Were you ever a member of any political party?

    2 Yes   **1 No**

    41c. *(If yes)* Which party? _____

42. Let us talk about associations and organisations other than political parties: are you a member of any religious or caste organisation?

144

2 Yes   **1 No**

145   *   42a. (*If yes*) What are these?   1 _____

147   *   2 _____

43. Aside from caste and religious organisations, do you belong to any other associations and organisations, like the cooperatives, farmers' association, trade unions, welfare organisations, cultural and sports organisations, etc.? (*Give two/three relevant examples of the locality*)

149

2 Yes   **1 No**

150   *   43a. (*If yes*) What are these   1 _____

152   *   2 _____

(*Probe: Any other*) _____

44. There is quite a bit of talk these days about different social classes. Some people say they belong to the middle class, others say they belong to the working class, yet others say they do not belong to either of these classes but to some other class. Now thinking of people like you, to which class would you say you belong?

154

1 Middle class   2 Working class   7 Other (*specify*) _____

44a. Do you think that the people of some other classes come in the way of progress and welfare of the people of your class, or do you think this is not the case?

155

1 Come in way   **2 Do not come in way**

44b. (*If come in way*) People of which class? (*Record exactly*)

156   *   _____

_____

45. During the last few years, has your financial situation improved, worsened, or has it stayed the same?

    3 Improved   2 Same   1 Worsened

46. In whatever financial condition you are placed today, on the whole, are you satisfied with your present financial situation, somewhat satisfied, or not satisfied?

    3 Satisfied   2 Somewhat satisfied   1 Not satisfied

47. Now looking ahead and thinking about the next few years, do you expect that your financial situation will stay about the way it is now, get better, or get worse?

    3 Better   2 Same   1 Worse

48. Looking to your needs and the needs of your household, how much income per month do you think you must have to meet your needs? (***Record exact answer***)

49. Do you think your children have better opportunities in life than you had?

    2 Yes   1 No   8 D.K.

50. Have you ever contacted any government official for any need or problem?

    2 Yes   1 No

51. Have you ever contacted any political leader for any need or problem?

    2 Yes   1 No

52. Do you personally know any party leaders or any of the candidates in this constituency?

    2 Yes   1 No

53. Who was your previous MP from this constituency?

    2 Correct   1 Incorrect/D.K.

54. Who is the Prime Minister of our country?

   171☐   2 Correct   1 Incorrect

55. And who is the Chief Minister of your state?

   172☐   2 Correct   1 Incorrect

56. Do you read a newspaper?

   173☐   2 Yes   1 No

57. (*If yes*) How often: regularly, sometimes or rarely?

   174☐
      3 Regularly   1 Rarely
      2 Sometimes   9 Inapplicable

58. Do you listen to the radio?

   175☐   2 Yes   1 No

   58a. (*If yes*) How often: regularly, sometimes or rarely?

   176☐
      3 Regularly   1 Rarely
      2 Sometimes   9 Inapplicable

59. Do you watch TV?

   177☐   2 Yes   1 No

   59a. (*If yes*) How often: regularly, sometimes or rarely?

   178☐
      3 Regularly   1 Rarely
      2 Sometimes   9 Inapplicable

60. Of these, on which source did you depend most for getting information about elections, parties and candidates?

   179☐
      0 None   4 Newspaper and radio
      1 Newspaper   5 Newspaper and TV
      2 Radio   6 Radio and TV
      3 TV   7 All three (newspaper, radio and TV)

61. This time the newspapers and magazines carried several surveys and forecasts about who would win the elections. Did you read it or hear about it?

180 ☐

    1 Read   2 Heard   3 Neither read nor heard   8 D.K.

    61a. (*If read or heard*) Do you think your voting decision was influenced by it?

181 ☐

    2 Yes   1 No   8 D.K.   9 Inapplicable

182 ☐ * 61b. (*If yes*) In what way? _____

BACKGROUND DATA

200 ☐ 1. Age *(in completed years)* _____

202 ☐ 2. Sex: **1 Male   2 Female**

203 ☐ 3. Marital status: **1 Unmarried   2 Married   1 Divorced, etc.**

4. Level of education: Write appropriate category in relevant columns

204 ☐

Level	Respondent	Spouse	Father	Mother
1. Illiterate				
2. Literate: no formal education				
3. Primary				
4. Middle school				
5. High school				
6. College: no degree				
7. College: degree				
8. Post-graduate/ professional				
9. N.A.				

208 ☐☐ 5. What is/has been your main occupation? _____

210 ☐☐ 6. What is/has been the main occupation of your husband/wife?
             _____

212 ☐☐ 7. What is/has been the main occupation of your father?
             _____

214 ☐☐ 8. What is/has been the main occupation of your mother?
             _____

         9. Total land owned by the respondent and his/her family:

216 ☐☐   Total land _____ acres   Irrigated land _____ acres
219 ☐☐   (*Coding format xx.x*)

         10. Do you or your family own any non-agricultural land for housing, etc.?

222 ☐   **2 Yes**   **1 No**

         11. Religion: **1 Hindu**   **2 Muslim**   **3 Christian**
223 ☐☐   **4 Sikh**   **5 Buddhist**   **6 Jain**
                        7 Parsi   **8 Other (*specify*)** _____

         12. Caste/Tribe: _____ (***Write exact caste irrespective
224 ☐☐   of religion.***)

             12a. Also ascertain the caste group:
227 ☐   **1 SC**   **2 ST**   **3 OBC**   **4 Others**

         13. Do you or your family own the following:
228 ☐   a. House/flat   **2 Yes**   **1 No**
229 ☐   b. Car/jeep/tractor   **2 Yes**   **1 No**
230 ☐   c. Pumping set/tube-well   **2 Yes**   **1 No**
231 ☐   d. Scooter/motorcycle   **2 Yes**   **1 No**

232	e.	Bicycle		2 Yes	1 No
233	f.	Television		2 Yes	1 No
234	g.	Radio/transistor		2 Yes	1 No
235	h.	Bullock–cart		2 Yes	1 No
236	i	Buffalo/cow	No. _____		
238	j	Bullocks	No. _____		
240	k.	Goat/sheep	No. _____		

14. Source of drinking water: (*Multiple source expected.*)

1 Tap water   2 Handpump   4 Well   8 River/tank

242

16 Other (*specify*) _____

15. Type of residential accommodation:

1 Pucca   **2 Pucca–kutcha mixed**

244

3 Kutcha   **4 Hut (thatched house)**

16. Ascertain sanitary condition of the living surroundings:

245   **1 Clean   2 Average   3 Unclean   4 Very unclean**

246   17. Locality: **1 Rural   2 Urban**

Not to be asked

Date of interview _____ Time of interview _____ Time taken _____

Place of Interview: **1 R's home   2 R's place of work**

247   **3 Public place   4 Other (*specify*)** _____

Was anyone else present at the time of interview?

248

    1 No one present (or only children under 14 present)

    2 Others present but they took no part

    3 Others took part

Was the respondent cooperative?

249

    1 Very cooperative

    2 Cooperative but did not seem actively interested

    3 Uncooperative

Address

Name of Respondent _____ S. No. on Electoral Roll ____

House No. and Street _____

R's village/town _____

District _____ State _____

PC name _____ AC name _____

PS name _____ Official no. _____

Interviewer's name _____ Signature _____

Checked by: Superviser's name _____ Signature _____

Bibliography

Ahmed, Bashiruddin. 1971. 'Political Stratification and the Indian Electorate', *Economic and Political Weekly*, VI (3–5): 251–58.
Ahmed, Bashiruddin and Samuel J. Eldersveld. 1978. *Citizens and Politics: Mass Political Behavior in India* (Chicago: University of Chicago Press).
Ahmed, Bashiruddin and V.B. Singh. 1975. 'Dimensions of Party System Change: The Case of Madhya Pradesh', in Sheth (1975, *Citizens and Parties: Aspects of Competitive Politics in India*, pp. 165–205, New Delhi: Allied).
Akbar, M.J. 1988. *Riot after Riot: Reports on Caste and Communal Violence in India* (Delhi: Penguin).
Almond, Gabriel. 1989. 'The Intellectual History of the Civic Culture Concept', in Gabriel/Verba (1989, *The Civic Culture Revisited*, pp. 1–36, London: Sage).
Almond, Gabriel and G. Bingham Powell. 1986. *Comparative Politics Today* (New York: Harper Collins).
Almond, Gabriel and Sidney Verba (eds.). 1989. *The Civic Culture Revisited* (London: Sage).
Anderson, Benedict. 1991. *Imagined Communities: Reflections on the Origin and Spread of Nationalism*, 2nd edn. (London: Verso).
Apter, David E. (ed.). 1964. *Ideology and Discontent* (New York: The Free Press of Glencoe).
——————. 1965. *The Politics of Modernisation* (Chicago: University of Chicago Press).
——————. 1971. *Choice and the Politics of Allocation: A Development Theory* (New Haven: Yale University Press).
——————. 1987. *Rethinking Development: Modernization, Dependency and Postmodern Politics* (Beverley Hills: Sage).
Austin, Granville. 1966. *The Indian Constitution* (Oxford: Oxford University Press).
Bachrach, Peter. 1962. 'Elite Consensus and Democracy', *Journal of Politics*, XXIV: 155–63, August.
Bailey, Frederic G. 1957. *Caste and the Economic Frontier: A Village in Highland Orissa* (Manchester: Manchester University Press).
——————. 1970. *Politics and Social Change: Orissa in 1959* (Berkeley: University of California Press).
Banfield, Edward. 1958. *The Moral Basis of a Backward Society* (New York: The Free Press of Glencoe).
Bardhan, Pranab. 1984. *The Political Economy of Development in India* (New York: Basil Blackwell).
Barth, Hans. 1960. *The Idea of Order: Contributions to a Philosophy of Politics* (Holland: D. Reidel).

Bibliography ■ 325

Basu, Sajal. 1982. *Politics of Violence: A Case Study of West Bengal* (Calcutta: Minerva Associates).
Bayley, David H. 1969. *The Police and Political Development in India* (Princeton, New Jersey: Princeton University Press).
─────────. 1983. 'The Police and Political Order in India', *Asian Survey*, 23 (4): 486–96, April.
Beetham, David (ed.). 1994. *Defining and Measuring Democracy* (London: Sage).
Bendix, Reinhard. 1964. *Nation-building and Citizenship: Studies of Our Changing Social Order* (New York: John Wiley & Sons).
Bernstorff, Dagmar. 1981. 'India's 7th General Elections: The Forgiving Electorate', *Asien. Deutsche Zeitschrift für Politik, Wirtschaft und Kultur*, 1: 7–30, Oktober.
Beteille, A. 1969. *Castes Old and New: Essays in Social Structure and Social Stratification* (Bombay: Asia Publishing House).
Bettelheim, Charles. 1968. *India Independent* (London: McGibbon & Kee).
Bhatt, Anil. 1973. 'Caste and Political Mobilization in Gujarat District', in Kothari (1974, 'The Congress System Revisited. A Decennial Review', *Asian Survey*, 14 [12]: 299–339).
Bhattacharya, Dwaipayan. 1993. 'Agrarian Reforms and the Politics of the Left'. Unpublished Ph.D. dissertation, Cambridge.
─────────. 1996. 'Social Capital, Redistributive Reforms, Panchayati Democracy and Norms of Justice in West Bengal', in Blomquist (1996, 'Agora Project: Democracy and Social Capital in Segmented Societies—Working Papers from the Conference on Social Capital and Democracy' at Toshali Sands, Orissa, India. Unpublished paper, Uppsala, March).
Bhattacharyya, Harihar. 1997. 'Post-colonial Context of Social Capital and Democratic Governance: The Case of West Bengal in India'. Unpublished manuscript, Burdwan.
─────────. 1998. *Micro Foundations of Bengal Communism* (Delhi: Ajanta).
Bjorkman, James (ed.). 1988. *Fundamentalism, Revivalists and Violence in South Asia* (Riverside, Md.: Riverdale).
Blomquist, Hans. 1996. 'Agora Project: Democracy and Social Capital in Segmented Societies—Working Papers from the Conference on Social Capital and Democracy' at Toshali Sands, Orissa, India. Unpublished paper, Uppsala, March.
Bondurant, Joan V. 1958. *Conquest of Violence: The Gandhian Philosophy of Conflict* (Princeton, New Jersey: Princeton University Press).
─────────. 1958. *Regionalism v. Provincialism: A Study in Problems of Indian National Unity* (Berkeley: University of California Press).
Brass, Paul R. 1984. 'National Power and Local Politics in India: A Twenty-year Perspective', *Modern Asian Studies*, 18 (1): 89–118.
─────────. 1997. 'National Power and Local Politics in India: A Twenty-year Perspective', in Chatterjee (1997, *State and Politics in India*, pp. 303–35, Delhi: Oxford University Press).
Brass, Paul R. and Francis Robinson. 1987. *The Indian National Congress and Indian Society, 1885–1985: Ideology, Social Structure and Political Dominance* (Delhi: Chanakya Publications).
Brechon, Pierre and Subrata Mitra. 1992. 'The National Front in France: The Emergence of an Extreme Right Protest Movement', *Comparative Politics*, 25 (1): 63–82, October.
Burns, James MacGregor and Jack Walter Peltason. 1963. *Government by the People: The Dynamics of American National, State, and Local Government* (New Jersey: Prentice-Hall).

Butler, David, Ashok Lahiri and Prannoy Roy. 1995. *India Decides: Elections 1952–1995* (Delhi: Books & Things).

Byres, Terrence J. 1988. 'A Chicago View of the Indian State: An Oriental Grin without an Oriental Cat and Political Economy without Classes', *The Journal of Commonwealth and Comparative Politics*, 26 (3): 246–69.

Chatterjee, Partha. 1986. *Nationalist Thought and the Colonial World: A Derivative Discourse* (London: Zed Books).

——— (ed.). 1997. *State and Politics in India* (Delhi: Oxford University Press).

Chiriyankandath, James. 1992. 'Democracy under the *Raj*: Elections and Separate Representation in British India', *The Journal of Commonwealth and Comparative Politics*, 30 (1): 39–63.

Cohen, Jean and Andrew Arato. 1992. *Civil Society and Political Theory* (Cambridge: Massachusetts Institute of Technology Press).

Cohen, Stephen. 1988. 'India's Military', in Kohli (1988, *India's Democracy: An Analysis of Changing State-society Relations*, pp. 99–144, Princeton, New Jersey: Princeton University Press).

Comte, Fernand. 1991. *The Wordsworth Dictionary of Mythology* (Ware, Hertfordshire: Wordsworth Editions).

Dahl, Robert. 1989. *Democracy and its Critics* (New Haven: Yale University Press).

Das Gupta, J. 1970. *Language Conflict and National Development: Group Politics and National Language Policy in India* (Bombay: Oxford University Press).

Deutsch, Karl W. 1961. 'Social Mobilization and Political Development', *American Political Science Review*, LIII: 218–20, September.

Downs, Anthony. 1957. *An Economic Theory of Democracy* (New York: Harper and Row).

Drèze, Jean and Amartya K. Sen. 1995. *Economic Development and Social Opportunities* (Oxford: Oxford University Press).

Dumont, Louis. 1966. *Homo Hierarchicus: The Caste System and its Implications* (Chicago: University of Chicago Press).

———. 1985. *Homo Aequalis: Genèse et Epanouissement de l'Ideologie Economique* (Paris: Gallimard).

Dutt, Rajani Palme. 1940. *India Today* (London: Gollancz).

Easton, David. 1957. 'An Approach to the Analysis of Political Systems', *World Politics*, IX: 383–400, April.

Eisenstadt, Shmuel Noah. 1965. 'Transformation of Social, Political and Cultural Orders in Modernization', *American Sociological Review*, XXX: 659–70, October.

Eldersveld, Samuel J. and Bashiruddin Ahmed. 1978. *Citizens and Politics: Mass Political Behavior in India* (Chicago: University of Chicago Press).

Election Commission of India. 1996. *Elections: Statistical Report on General Election 1996*, Vol. I (New Delhi: Government of India Press).

———. 1998. *Report of the Twelfth General Elections of the House of People in India 1998 (Statistical)* (New Delhi: Government of India Press).

Field, John O. 1980. *Consolidating Democracy: Politicization and Partisanship in India* (New Delhi: Manohar).

Fox, Richard G. 1969. 'Varna Schemes and Ideological Integration in Indian Society', *Comparative Studies in Society and History*, 11: 27–44.

———. 1970. '*Avatars* of Indian Research', *Comparative Studies in Society and History*, 12 (1): 59–72.

Frankel, Francine. 1978. *India's Political Economy, 1947–77: The Gradual Revolution.* (Princeton, New Jersey: Princeton University Press).
——————— 1989/90. 'Caste, Land and Dominance in Bihar', in Frankel and Rao (1989/90, *Dominance and State Power in Modern India: Decline of a Social Order*, pp. 46–132, two vols., Delhi: Oxford University Press).
Frankel, Francine and **M.S.A. Rao** (eds.). 1989/90. *Dominance and State Power in Modern India: Decline of a Social Order*, two vols. (Delhi: Oxford University Press).
Geertz, Clifford. 1964. 'Ideology as a Cultural System', in Apter (1964, *Ideology and Discontent*, pp. 47–67, New York: The Free Press of Glencoe).
Gilmour, Ian. 1992. *Riots, Risings and Revolution: Governance and Violence in Eighteenth-Century England* (London: Hutchinson).
Gould, Harold. 1990. *The Hindu Caste System* (Delhi: Chanakya).
Government of India. 1956. *Balawant Rai Mehta Committee Report.*
———————. 1965. *Report of the Committee on Panchayati Elections 1965* (New Delhi: Ministry of Community Development and Cooperation).
———————. 1978. *Report of the Committee on Panchayati Raj Institutions* (New Delhi: Ministry of Agriculture and Irrigation, Department of Rural Development).
Graff, Violette. 1965. 'The Muslim Vote in Indian Lok Sabha Elections of December 1984', in Brass/Robinson (1987, *The Indian National Congress and Indian Society, 1885–1985: Ideology, Social Structure and Political Dominance*, pp. 427–69, Delhi: Chanakya Publications).
Graham, Hugh Davis and **Ted Robert Gurr** (eds.). 1969. *The History of Violence in America: Historical and Comparative Perspectives. A Report to the National Commission on the Causes and Prevention of Violence* (New York: Bantam Books).
Guha, Ranajit. 1983. *Elementary Aspects of Peasant Insurgency in Colonial India* (Delhi: Oxford University Press).
Gurr, Ted Robert. 1970. *Why Men Rebel* (Princeton, New Jersey: Princeton University Press).
———————. 1982. 'The Breast Cloth Controversy', *Indian Economic History Review*, 5: 171–89.
Hardgrave, Robert. 1969. *The Nadars of Tamilnadu: The Political Culture of a Community in Change* (Berkeley: University of California Press).
Hardgrave, Robert and **Stanley Kochanek.** 1993. *India: Government and Politics in a Developing Nation* (Fort Worth: Harcourt).
Hardiman, David. 1987. *The Coming of the Devi: Adivasi Assertion in Western India* (Delhi: Oxford University Press).
Harrison, Selig. 1960. *India: The Most Dangerous Decades* (Delhi: Oxford University Press).
Harriss, John. 1982. *Capitalism and Peasant Farming, Agrarian Structure and Ideology in Northern Tamilnadu* (Delhi: Oxford University Press).
Hause, E.M. 1961. 'India Under the Impact of Western Political Ideas and Institutions', *Western Political Quarterly*, XIV: 879–95, December.
Haynes, Douglas and **Gyan Prakash** (eds.). 1991. *Contesting Power: Resistance and Everyday Social Relations in South Asia* (Berkeley: University of California Press).
Heimsath, Charles H. 1964. *Indian Nationalism and Hindu Social Reform* (Princeton, New Jersey: Princeton University Press).
Hobsbawm, Eric J. 1995. *Age of Extremes: The Short Twentieth Century, 1914–1981* (Delhi: Viking Penguin).

Hobsbawm, Eric J. and George Rudé. 1968. *Captain Swing: A Social History of the Great Agrarian Uprising of 1930* (New York: Pantheon).
Huntington, Samuel P. 1968. *Political Order in Changing Societies* (New Haven: Yale University Press).
——————. 1996. *The Clash of Civilisations and the Remaking of World Order* (New York: Simon and Schuster).
Inden, Ronald. 1990. *Imagining India* (Oxford: Blackwell).
Inkeles, Alex. 1969. 'Making Men Modern', *American Journal of Sociology*, LXXV: 208–25, September.
Irschick, Eugene. 1969. *Politics and Social Conflict in South India* (Berkeley: University of California Press).
——————. 1994. *Dialogue and History: Constructing South India, 1795–1895* (Delhi: Oxford University Press).
Jain, Meenakshi. 1991. *The Congress Party, 1967–1977: The Role of Caste in Indian Politics* (Delhi: Vikas).
Joshi, Ram and R.K. Hebsur (eds.). 1987. *Congress in Indian Politics: A Centenary Perspective* (Bombay: Popular).
Kaase, Max. 1972. *Political Ideology, Dissatisfaction and Protest* (Mannheim: Institut für Sozialwissenschaften).
Keane, John (ed.). 1988. *Civil Society and the State* (London: Verso).
Khanna, Bhim Sain. 1994. *Panchayati Raj: National Perspective and State Studies* (Delhi: Deep and Deep).
Khilnani, Sunil. 1997. *The Idea of India* (London: Hamish Hamilton).
Kirchheimer, Otto. 1972. 'The Transformation of the Western European Party Systems', in La Palombara and Weiner (1966, *Political Parties and Political Development*, pp. 177–200, Princeton, New Jersey: Princeton University Press).
Kogekar, S.V. and Richard L. Park (eds.). 1956. *Reports on the Indian General Elections 1951–52* (Bombay: Popular Book Depot).
Kohli, Atul. 1983. 'Parliamentary Communism and Agrarian Reform: The Evidence from India's Bengal', *Asian Survey*, 23 (7): 783–809, July.
——————. 1987. *The State and Poverty in India: The Politics of Reform* (Cambridge: Cambridge University Press).
——————. 1990. *Democracy and Discontent: India's Growing Crisis of Governability* (Cambridge: Cambridge University Press).
——————. (ed.). 1988. *India's Democracy: An Analysis of Changing State-Society Relations* (Princeton, New Jersey: Princeton University Press).
Kothari, Rajni. 1964. 'The Congress "System" in India', *Asian Survey*, 4 (12): 1161–63.
——————. 1970. *Politics in India* (Boston: Little Brown).
——————. 1974. 'The Congress System Revisited: A Decennial Review', *Asian Survey*, 14 (12): 1035–54.
——————. 1982. 'Towards Intervention', *Seminar*, 269: 22–27, January.
——————. (1983a). 'The Crisis of the Moderate State and the Decline of Democracy', in Lyon and Manor (1983, *Transfer and Transformation: Political Institutions in the New Commonwealth*, pp. 24–29, Leicester: Leicester University Press).
——————. 1983b. 'A Fragmented Nation', *Seminar*, 281: 24–29, January.
——————. 1988. *State against Democracy: In Search of Humane Governance* (Delhi: Ajanta Publications).

Kothari, Rajni (ed.). 1973. *Caste in Indian Politics* (Delhi: Orient Longman).
Krishna, Daya. 1979. *Political Development: A Critical Perspective* (Delhi: Oxford University Press).
Krueger, Anne. 1974. 'The Political Economy of Rent-seeking Society', *American Economic Review*, 64 (3): 291–304.
Kuhn, Thomas. 1962. *The Structure of Scientific Revolutions* (Chicago: University of Chicago Press).
La Palombara, Joseph and Myron Weiner. 1966. 'The Origin and Development of Political Parties', in La Palombara and Weiner (1972, *Political Parties and Political Development*, pp. 3–42, Princeton, New Jersey: Princeton University Press).
———. 1972. *Political Parties and Political Development* (Princeton, New Jersey: Princeton University Press).
Lacy, Creighton. 1965. *The Conscience of India: Moral Traditions in the Modern World*. (New York: Holt, Rinehart and Winston).
Lakatos, Imre and Alan Musgrave (eds.). 1970. *Criticism and the Growth of Knowledge* (Cambridge: Cambridge University Press).
Lawson, Kay (ed.). 1994. *How Political Parties Work: Perspectives from Within* (Westport: Praeger).
Lewis, John P. 1962. *India: A Quiet Crisis* (Delhi: Oxford University Press).
———. 1995. *India's Political Economy: Governance and Reform* (Oxford: Oxford University Press).
Lijphart, Arendt. 1984. *Democracies: Patterns of Majoritarian and Consensus Government in Twenty-one Countries* (New Haven: Yale University Press).
———. 1996. 'The Puzzle of Indian Democracy: A Consociational Interpretation', *American Political Science Review*, 90 (2): 258–68.
Lipset, Seymour M. 1959. 'Some Social Requisites of Democracy: Economic Development and Political Legitimacy', *American Political Science Review*, LIII: 69–105, March.
Long, Norman. 1977. *An Introduction to the Sociology of Rural Development* (London: Tavistock).
——— (ed.). 1989. *Encounters at the Interface: A Perspective on Social Discontinuities in Rural Development* (Wageningen: Agricultural University).
Luthera, Ved Prakesh. 1964. *The Concept of the Secular State and India* (Calcutta: Oxford University Press).
Lyon, Peter and J. Manor (eds.). 1983. *Transfer and Transformation: Political Institutions in the New Commonwealth* (Leicester: Leicester University Press).
Madan, Triloki Nath. 1987. 'Secularism in its Place', *The Journal of Asian Studies*, 46 (4): 747–59, November.
Maheshwari, Shriram. 1963. *The General Election in India* (Allahabad: Chaitanya Publishing House).
Malenbaum, Wilfred. 1962. *Prospects for Indian Development* (London: George Allen and Unwin).
Manor, James. 1983. 'Anomie in Indian Politics: Origins and Potential Impact', *Economic and Political Weekly*, 18 (1–2): 725–34.
———. 1987. 'Appearance and Reality in Politics: The 1984 General Election in the South', in Brass and Robinson (1987, *The Indian National Congress and Indian Society, 1885–1985: Ideology, Social Structure and Political Dominance*, pp. 400–426, Delhi: Chanakya Publications).

Manor, James. 1991. *Rethinking Third World Politics* (London and New York: Longman).
Marsh, Alan. 1977. *Protest and Political Consciousness* (Beverley Hills: Sage).
Masterman, Margaret. 1970. 'The Nature of a Paradigm', in Lakatos and Musgrave (1970, *Criticism and the Growth of Knowledge*, pp. 59–89, Cambridge: Cambridge University Press).
Mehrotra, Nanak Chand. 1980. *Political Crises and Polls in India* (New Delhi: Deep & Deep).
Mehta, Vrajendra Raj. 1987. 'Political Science in India: In Search of an Identity', *Government and Opposition*, 22 (3): 270–81.
Merkl, Peter H. 1967. *Political Continuity and Change* (New York: Harper and Row).
Mitra, Subrata Kumar. 1979. 'Ballot Box and Local Power: Elections in an Indian Village', *The Journal of Commonwealth and Comparative Politics*, 17 (3): 282–99.
———. 1982. 'Caste, Class and Conflict: Organization and Ideological Change in Orissa', *Purusartha*, 6: 97–133.
———. 1988. 'The Paradox of Power: Political Science as Morality Play', *The Journal of Commonwealth and Comparative Politics*, 26 (3): 318–37, November.
———. 1990a. *Post-colonial State in Asia: Dialectics of Politics and Culture* (Hemel Hempstead: Harvester).
———. 1990b. 'Between Transaction and Transcendence: The State and the Institutionalisation of Power in India', in Mitra (1990a, *Post-colonial State in Asia: Dialectics of Politics and Culture*, pp. 73–101, Hemel Hempstead: Harvester).
———. 1991. 'Room to Maneuver in the Middle: Local Elites, Political Action and the State in India', *World Politics*, 43 (3): 390–414, April.
———. 1992. *Power, Protest, Participation: Local Elites and the Politics of Development in India* (London: Routledge).
———. 1994a. 'Caste, Democracy and the Politics of Community Formation in India', in Searle-Chatterjee and Sharma (1994, *Contextualising Caste: Post-Dumontian Approaches*, pp. 49–71, Oxford: Blackwell/The Sociological Review).
———. 1994b. 'Party Organization and Policy Making in a Changing Environment: The Indian National Congress', in Lawson (1994, *How Political Parties Work: Perspectives from Within*, Westport: Praeger).
———. 1996. 'India', in Almond and Powell (1996, *Comparative Politics Today*, pp. 669–729, New York: Harper Collins).
———. 1997a. 'Legitimacy, Governance and Political Institutions in India after Independence', in Mitra and Rothermund (1997, *Legitimacy and Conflict in South Asia*, pp. 17–49, Delhi: Manohar).
———. 1997b. 'Nation and Region in Indian Politics', *Asien Afrika Lateinamerika*, 25: 499–519.
———. 1999. *Culture and Rationality* (New Delhi: Sage).
Mitra, Subrata K. and Dietmar Rothermund (eds.). 1997. *Legitimacy and Conflict in South Asia* (Delhi: Manohar).
Mitra, Subrata K. and James Chiriyankandath (eds.). 1992. *Electoral Politics in India: A Changing Landscape* (New Delhi: Segment Books).
Mitra, Subrata K. and R. Alison Lewis (eds). 1996. *Subnational Movements in South Asia* (Boulder, Colorado: Westview Press).
Moddie, A.D. 1968. *The Brahmanical Culture and Modernity* (Bombay: Asia Publishing House).
Moore, Barrington. 1966. *Social Origins of Dictatorship and Democracy: Lord and Peasant in the Making of the Modern World* (Boston: Beacon Press).

Moore, Wilbert E. 1960. 'A Reconsideration of Theories of Social Change', *American Sociological Review*, XXV: 810–18, December.
Morris-Jones, William H. 1963. 'India's Political Idioms', in Philips (1963, *Politics and Society in India*, pp. 133–54, London: George Allen & Unwin).
―――――. 1987. *The Government and Politics of India* (Wistow: Eothen Press).
Mukherjee, N. *Decentralisation of Panchayats in the 1990s* (New Delhi: Vikas).
Myrdal, Gunnar. 1968. *Asian Drama: An Inquiry into the Poverty of Nations*, 3 vols. (New York: Pantheon).
Naipaul, Vidiadhar Surajprasad. 1964. *An Area of Darkness* (London: Penguin).
―――――. 1977. *India: A Wounded Civilization* (London: Andre Deutsch).
―――――. 1990. *India: A Million Mutinies Now* (London: Heinemann).
Nanda, B.R. 1995. *Jawaharlal Nehru: Rebel and Statesman* (Delhi: Oxford University Press).
Nehru, Jawaharlal. 1960. *A Bunch of Old Letters* (New York: Asia Publishing House).
Neiburg, H.L. 1962. 'The Threat of Violence and Social Change', *American Political Science Review*, LVI: 865–73, December.
Nelson, J. 1987. *Access to Power: Politics and Urban Poor in Developing Nations* (Princeton: Princeton University Press).
Nettle, John P. 1967. *Political Modernization: A Sociological Analysis of Methôds and Concepts* (London: Faber and Faber).
Nicholson, Norman K. 1968. 'India's Modernizing Faction and the Mobilization of Power', *International Journal of Comparative Sociology*, IX: 302–17, September–December.
North, Douglas. 1990. *Institutions, Institutional Change and Economic Performance* (Cambridge: Cambridge University Press).
Norton, Philip. 1991. *The British Polity* (London: Longman).
O'Hanlon, R. 1988. 'Recovering the Subject: Subaltern Studies and Histories of Resistance in Colonial South Asia', *Modern Asian Studies*, 22 (1): 189–224, February.
Omvedt, Gail. 1992. *Reinventing Revolution. New Social Movements and the Socialist Tradition in India* (London: Crofthouse).
Organski, Abramo Fimo Kenneth. 1965. *The States of Political Development* (New York: Alfred A. Knopf).
Pai, Sudha. 1996. 'Panchayats and Grassroots Democracy: The Politics of Development in Two Districts of Uttar Pradesh', in Blomquist (1996, 'Agora Project: Democracy and Social Capital in Segmented Societies—Working Papers from the Conference on Social Capital and Democracy' at Toshali Sands, Orissa, India. Unpublished paper, Uppsala, March).
Palmer, Norman D. 1975. *Elections and Political Development: The South Asian Experience* (Durham, North Carolina: Duke University Press).
Parekh, Bhikhu. 1989. *Colonialism, Tradition and Reform: An Analysis of Gandhi's Political Discourse* (New Delhi: Sage).
Parmanand. 1985. *New Dimensions in Indian Politics: A Critical Study of the Eighth Lok Sabha Election* (Delhi: UDH Publishers).
Philips, C.H. (ed.). 1963. *Politics and Society in India* (London: George Allen & Unwin).
Plamentaz, John P. 1960. *On Alien Rule and Self-Government* (New York: Longman).
Poplai, S.L. and **V.K.N. Menon** (eds). 1957. *National Politics and 1957 Elections in India* (Delhi: Metropolitan Books).
Poston, R.W. 1962. *Democracy Speaks Many Tongues* (New York: Harper and Row).

Powell, G. Bingham. 1982. *Contemporary Democracies: Participation, Stability and Violence* (Cambridge, Massachusetts: Harvard University Press).
Putnam, Robert D. 1993. *Making Democracy Work: Civic Traditions in Modern Italy* (Princeton, New Jersey: Princeton University Press).
Pye, Lucian and **Sidney Verba** (eds.). 1965. *Political Culture and Political Development* (Princeton: Princeton University Press).
Quigley, Declan. 1993. *The Interpretation of Caste* (Oxford: Clarendon Press).
———. 1994. 'Is a theory of caste still possible?', in Searle-Chatterjee and Sharma (1994, *Contextualising Caste: Post-Dumontian Approaches*, pp. 25–48, Oxford: Blackwell/The Sociological Review).
Ramannah Shastri, K.N. 1968. *An Analytical Study of 1967 General Elections in India* (Agra: Vishva Bharati Prakashan).
Ranade, Sudhansu. 1991. 'Competitive Democracies: The Case of Integrated Transfers in India'. Ph.D. dissertation, Woodrow Wilson School of International and Public Affairs, Princeton University.
Rao, B.S. 1960. 'The Future of Indian Democracy', *Foreign Affairs*, XXXIX: 117–35, October.
Ray, Ramashroy. 1972. *The Uncertain Verdict: Study of the 1969 Elections in Four Indian States* (London: Longman).
Reddy, Rama and **K. Hargopal.** 1985. 'The Pyraveekar: The Fixer in Rural India', *Asian Survey*, 25 (11): 1148–62.
Riggs, Fred W. 1961. *The Ecology of Public Administration* (Bombay: Asia Publishing House).
———. 1964. *Administration in Developing Countries: The Theory of Prismatic Society* (Boston: Houghton Mifflin).
Riker, William and **Peter Ordeshook.** 1973. *An Introduction to Positive Political Theory* (Englewood Cliffs: Prentice-Hall).
Robinson, Marguerite S. 1988. *Local Politics: The Law of the Fishes. Development through Political Change in Medak District, Andhra Pradesh (South India)* (Delhi: Oxford University Press).
Rosen, George. 1966. *Democracy and Economic Change in India* (Berkeley: University of California Press).
Rostow, Walt W. 1960. *The Strategies of Economic Growth: A Non-Communist Manifesto* (Cambridge, Massachusetts: Cambridge University Press).
Rothermund, Dietmar. 1962. 'Constitutional Reforms vs. National Agitation in India', *Journal of Asian Studies*, XXI: 505–22, August.
Rudolph, Lloyd I. and **Susanne H. Rudolph.** 1960. 'The Political Role of India's Caste Associations', *Pacific Affairs*, XXXIII: 5–22, March.
———. 1967. *The Modernity of Tradition: Political Development in India* (Chicago: The University of Chicago Press).
———. 1971. 'The Change to Change: Modernization, Development and Politics', *Comparative Politics*, 286–302, April.
———. 1987. *In Pursuit of Lakshmi: The Political Economy of the Indian State* (Chicago: University of Chicago Press).
Rushdie, Salman. 1982. *Midnight's Children* (London: Pari).
Rushdie, Salman and **Elizabeth West** (eds.). 1997. *The Vintage Book of Indian Writing, 1947–1997* (London: Vintage).
Saberwal, Satish. 1986. *The Roots of Crisis* (New Delhi: Oxford University Press).

Bibliography ■ 333

Sadasivan, S.N. 1977. *Party and Democracy in India* (New Delhi: Tata McGraw-Hill).
Said, Edward. 1978. *Orientalism* (London).
Sathyamurthy, Tennalur V. 1971. 'American Science of Indian Politics: An Essay in the Sociology of Knowledge', *Economic and Political Weekly of India*, 6 (23): 1131–33, 5 June.
——————. 1986. 'Contemporary European Scholarship on Political and Social Change in South Asia: An Essay in the Sociology of Knowledge', *Economic and Political Weekly*, 22 (11): 459–65, 14 March.
——————. 1989. *Terms of Political Discourse in India* (York: University of York).
——————. 1990. 'Indian Peasant Historiography: A Critical Perspective on Ranajit Guha's Work', *The Journal of Peasant Studies*, 18 (1): 90–144, October.
—————— (ed.). 1994. *State and Nation in the Context of Social Change* (Delhi: Oxford University Press).
Scott, James. 1985. *Weapons of the Weak: Everyday Forms of Peasant Resistance* (New Haven: Yale University Press).
Searle-Chatterjee, Mary and Ursula Sharma (eds.). 1994. *Contextualising Caste: Post-Dumontian Approaches* (Oxford: Blackwell/The Sociological Review).
Seligman, L.G. 1964. 'Elite Recruitment and Political Development', *Journal of Politics*, XXVI: 612–26, August.
Sen, Amartya. 1981. *Poverty and Famines: An Essay on Entitlement and Deprivation* (Delhi: Oxford University Press).
Sen Gupta, Bhabani. 1996. *India: Problems of Governance* (New Delhi: Konark Publishers).
Shah, A.B. and C.R.M. Rao (eds.). 1965. *Tradition and Modernity in India* (Bombay: Manaktalas).
Shepperdson, Mike and Colin Simmons (eds.). 1988. *The Indian National Congress and the Political Economy of India, 1885–1995* (London: Avebury).
Sheth, D.L. 1975. *Citizens and Parties: Aspects of Competitive Politics in India* (New Delhi: Allied).
Shils, Edward. 1961. *The Intellectuals between Tradition and Modernity: The Indian Situation* (The Hague: Mouton and Company).
——————. 1962. *Political Development in the New States* (The Hague: Mouton and Company).
Singer, M. 1980. *When a Great Tradition Modernizes: An Anthropological Introduction to Indian Civilization* (Chicago: University of Chicago Press).
Singh, V.B. 1992. 'Harijans and their Influence on the Elections in Uttar Pradesh', in Mitra and Chiriyankandath (1992, *Electoral Politics in India: A Changing Landscape*, pp. 241–60, New Delhi: Segment Books).
Singh, V.B. and Shankar Bose (eds.). 1984. *Elections in India: Data Handbook on Lok Sabha Elections, 1952–80* (New Delhi: Sage).
Sirsikar, Vasant Manjunath. 1995. *Politics of Modern Maharashtra* (London: Sangam Books).
Sisson, Richard and Stanley Wolpert (eds.). 1988. *Congress and Indian Nationalism: The Pre-independence Phase* (Berkeley: University of California Press).
Smith, Donald E. 1963. *India as a Secular State* (Princeton, New Jersey: Princeton University Press).
Srinivas, Mysore Narasimhachar. 1967. *Social Change in Modern India* (Berkeley: University of California Press).

Srinivas, Mysore Narasimhachar. 1987. *The Dominant Caste and Other Essays* (Delhi: Oxford University Press).
Suri, Surindar. 1962. *Elections: A Political Analysis* (New Delhi: Sudha Publications).
Thorson, Thomas Landon. 1962. *The Logic of Democracy* (Holt, Rinehart and Winston).
Tilly, Charles. 1985. *The Formation of National States in Western Europe* (Princeton, New Jersey: Princeton University Press).
Toennies, Ferdinand. 1971. *On Sociology: Pure, Applied and Empirical* (Chicago: University of Chicago Press).
Vanderbok, William and **Richard Sisson.** 1987. 'The Spatial Distribution of Congress Electoral Support: Trends from Four Decades of Parliamentary Elections', in Brass and Robinson (1987, *The Indian National Congress and Indian Society, 1885–1985: Ideology, Social Structure and Political Dominance*, pp. 373–99, Delhi: Chanakya Publications).
Varshney, Ashutosh (ed.). 1989. *The Indian Paradox: Essays in Indian Politics* (New Delhi: Sage).
Verney, D. 1986. *Three Civilisations, One State: Canada's Political Traditions* (Durham, North Carolina: Duke University Press).
Wagner, Rudolf. 1991. 'Political Institutions, Discourse and Imagination in China at Tiananmen', in Manor (1991, *Rethinking Third World Politics*, pp. 121–44, London and New York: Longman).
Washbrook, David A. 1989/90. 'Caste, Class and Dominance in Modern Tamil Nadu: Non-Brahminism, Dravidianism and Tamil Nationalism', in Frankel and Rao (1989/90, *Dominance and State Power in Modern India: Decline of a Social Order*, pp. 204–64, two vols., Delhi: Oxford University Press).
Weiner, Myron. 1962a. 'Political Parties and Panchayati Raj', *Indian Journal of Public Administration*, VII (4) reprinted in T.N. Chaturvedi and R.B. Jain (eds.) (1981, *Panchayati Raj*, pp. 93–98, Delhi: IIPA).
——. 1962b. *The Politics of Scarcity: Public Pressure and Political Response in India* (Chicago: University of Chicago Press).
——. 1966. *Modernization: The Dynamics of Growth* (New York: Basic Books).
——. 1967. *Party Building in a New Nation: The Indian National Congress* (Chicago: University of Chicago Press).
——. 1978. *India at the Polls: The Parliamentary Elections of 1977* (Washington, DC: American Enterprise Institute).
——. 1983. *India at the Polls, 1980: A Study of the Parliamentary Elections* (Washington, DC: American Enterprise Institute).
——. 1989. 'India in the Mid-seventies: A Political System in Transition', in Ashutosh Varshney (ed.). (1989, *The Indian Paradox: Essays in Indian Politics*, pp. 263–91, New Delhi: Sage).
—————— (ed.). 1977. *Electoral Politics in the Indian States: The Impact of Modernization* (New Delhi: Manohar).
Weiner, Myron and **Rajni Kothari.** 1965. *Indian Voting Behaviour: Studies of the 1962 General Elections* (Calcutta: Firma K.L. Mukhopadhayay).
White, Gordon. 1994. 'Civil Society and Democratization, I: Clearing the Analytical Ground', *Democratization*, 1 (3): 48–65.
——. 1995. 'Civil Society and Democratization, II: Two Case-studies', *Democratization*, 2(2): 56–84, Summer.
White, Gordon, Jude Howell and **Xiaoyuan Shang.** 1996. *In Search of Civil Society: Market Reform and Social Change in Contemporary China* (Oxford: Clarendon Press).

Wittfogel, Karl August. 1957. *Oriental Despotism: A Comparative Study of Total Power* (New Haven and London: Yale University Press).
Wood, John R. 1985. *State Politics in Contemporary India: Crisis or Continuity?* (Boulder, Colorado: Westview Press).
Woodley, Heather. 1990. 'The Press during the Emergency'. Unpublished undergraduate Honours dissertation, University of Hull, Great Britain.

Index

AIADMK, 173
accommodation scale, 274–77, 299–300
Ahmed, Bashiruddin, 30
Asian Drama, 62, 187
Asoka Mehta Committee, 224
Asom Gana Parishad (AGP), 171–73

Babri mosque demolition issue, 22, 145–46, 256, 260, 263, 266, 276
Badal, Prakash Singh, 172
Bage Subcommittee, 230
Bahujan Samaj Party, 90, 135–36, 146–50, 269
Bailey, Frederic G., 32
Bajrang Dal, 145
Balwant Rai Mehta Committee, 224, 226, 260
Bardhan, Pranab, 187
Basu, Jyoti, 174
Bengal famine of 1943, 65
Beteille, A., 31
Bharatiya Jan Sangh, 25, 63
Bharatiya Janata Party (BJP), 64, 68, 72, 133, 135–37, 140, 146–50, 171–73, 175, 220, 264, 276
Bhattacharya, Dwaipayan, 232–33
Bhattacharya, Harihar, 233–36
Bihar famine of 1960, 65
Bose, 213
boycott, concept of, 26–27
Brass, Paul, 242
Butler, David, 159
Byres, Terrence J., 33

CPM, 171, 229, 235–36, 238, 244
chakka jam, concept of, 26

Chandra Shekhar, 137
Chatterjee, Partha, 276–77
Chenery, Hollis, 206
Citizens and Parties, 36
Civil Code for every community, 150
civil society, building from below, 211–13
class-caste relationship, 188–89
class-education relation, 189–90
Communist Party of India (CPI), 24, 63, 66, 171
competitive politics: primordial identities and, 268–70; social change and, 23–26
Constitution of India: 73rd Amendment, 74, 225, 227, 236, 245; article 40, 224; article 352, 130
cooperatives, effectiveness of, 233–34

DMK, 171
Dahl, Robert, 122
Davis, Hugh, 185
democracy: central tendency of, 273–78; Constitutional design, 22–23; electoral, 20–21; elite, non-elite and, 238–41; fragmentation and anomic violence, 229–31; growth of, 254–59; historical context, 20–22; liberalisation politics and, 199–202; mobilisation from above, 228; mobilisation from below, 228–29; multi-party democracy, 259–65;—, high trust in institutions, 260–61;—, efficacy and legitimacy, 261–65; panchayati raj and, 231–36; politics and ambiguity of identity in, 265–78; regional varia-

tion, 217–23; resilience of, 250–78; social change and, 250–78; social opportunity and economic security, 202–5; state formation and, 223–26; trust in local government by region and socio-economic strata, 236–38; trust in local, regional and national government, 226–31
democratic politics: ambiguities of identity 265–78; caste, 270; central tendency, 273–78; community, 270–73; primordial identities, 268–70
democratic social change, 38
democratic transitions in societies, 22
deprivation: attitude towards government policy, 203–5; combined measure of, 193–96; limits of land ownership and, 197–98; objective and subjective measurement of, 188–93;—, class, caste tabulation, 188–89;—, class education tabulation, 189–90;—, perception of financial satisfaction by socio-demographic groups, 190–93; politics of redistribution, 196–99; social profile of the most and least deprived, 195
Deve Gowda, 48, 68, 103, 174
developmental paradigm, of state-society interaction, 28–32
dharna, concept of, 26–27
Drèze, Jean, 181–82, 186, 278
Dumont, Louis, 32, 38
Dutt, Rajani Palme, 33

economic security, and democracy, 202–5
Eldersveld, Samuel J., 30
Election Commission, 63, 75, 244, 256, 260–61
election study: construction of scales and variables of,—, accommodation, 299–300;—, campaign exposure, 296;—, deprivation, 298;—, economic class, 297;—, elite status, 297–98;—, financial satisfaction, 296–97;—, political information, 296; field staff training, 294–95; methodology for, 283–95; questionnaire, 302–23; research instruments for, 294, 302–23; sample units and distribution of respondents, 284–85; sampling procedure, 285–95; selection of Lok Sabha constituencies, 286–93;—, polling booths, 293;—, respondents, 293–94;—, Vidhan Sabha constituencies, 287–93
elections; Assembly, 40–41; electoral participation in, 39–43; Parliamentary, 39–40, 47–48, 158–77; post-poll survey and, 47–48
electorates: background characteristics of, 87–90; communal accommodation, 169; ideological voices, 25; level of concern and information about central and state government, 160–61; loyalty to region, 161–64; methods of state integration, 169–70; opinion and attitudes of, 160–77; participation in elections, 39–40, 63; partisan preferences, 170–73;—, parliamentary elections, 170–71;—, regionalism effect, 171–73; political aggregation in. 87–90; political participation, 90–117;—, act of voting, 99–102;—, advice on vote, 99–102;—, attending election campaign, 92–94;—, campaign exposure, 94–95;—, financial prospects, 112–13; house to house contact, 95–96;—, improvement in financial situation, 110–11;—, index of financial satisfaction, 114–17;—, index of political information, 105–7;—, information about chief minister, 105–5;—, information about local M.P., 102–3; information about Prime Minister, 103–4;—, interest in campaign, 91–92;—, interest in election campaign, 92;—, main issues during election, 109–10;—, opportunities for children, 113;—, perception of economic conditions, 110;—, political information, 102–5;—, problems facing the country, 107–9;—, satisfaction with present financial situation, 111–12;—, voting decision, 90–91; profile of, 86–117; regionalisation conjecture reformulated, 164; regionalists, 165–67; sense of efficacy, 167–

68;—, financial, 168;—, political, 167–68; social diversity, 87–90; trust in capacity of regional parties, 162–64
elite status: local government and, 238–41; social construction of, 240

Field, John O., 30
Foreign companies, free trade of, 199–200
Foucault, 79
Frankel, Francine, 30, 33, 36, 43
Functional paradigm, of state-society interaction, 32

Gandhi, Indira, 20, 47, 72, 77, 103–4, 121, 130–31, 161, 224, 242, 257, 259, 261
Gandhi, Mahatma, 63, 210, 212, 226, 253, 258
Gandhi, Rajiv, 131, 224
garibi hatao concept, 26
Geertz, Clifford, 24
gherao concept, 26–27
Ghose, Atulya, 174
Gilmour, Ian, 38, 215
governance concept, 187
government companies, privatisation of, 201–2
growth, stage of, 29
Guha, Ranajit, 33
Gujral, I.K., 48
Gurr, Ted Robert, 184–85, 187, 211

Hardgrave, Robert, 30–31
Harrison, Selig, 39, 62, 124, 206
Harriss, John, 33
Hobsbawn, Eric J., 38
Hume, Alan Octavian, 123
Huntington, Samuel P., 22, 30, 39, 45, 62, 79, 83, 125, 184–85, 187, 211

Inden, Ronald, 79
India: A Million Mutinies Now, 20
India: A Quiet Crisis, 206
India: A Wounded Civilisation, 21
India: An Area of Darkness, 21
India: The Most Dangerous Decades, 62, 124

Indian National Congress, 61, 123–24, 126–37, 146–50, 171–72, 174–76, 214, 266
Indian politics, central tendency of, 273–78
India's Political Economy, 206
Indo-Pak relations, 148–50, 170
Integrated Rural Development Programme (IRDP), 206

Jai Prakash, 213
jail bharo concept, 26
jajmani system, 42–46, 126
jajmani vote bank, 42
Janata Dal, 91, 137, 171
Janata Party, 133, 137, 186, 213, 224, 259
Jawahar Rojgar Yojna, 231
Jayalalitha, 173
Jinnah, 210
Justice Party, 126

Kanshi Ram, 257
Kashmir problem, 147, 170
Khanna, Bhim Sain, 224, 228–30
Khilnani, Sunil, 186
Kochanek, Stanley, 30
Kohli, Atul, 33, 183–84, 186–87, 214, 242
Kothari, Rajni, 22, 36

Lahiri, Ashok, 159
Left Front, 146–50, 220–21, 224, 229, 231
Lewis, John P., 186–87, 190, 206
Lewis, R. Alison, 37
liberalisation politics, and democracy, 199–202
Lijphart, Arendt, 214
Little Buddha syndrome, 35
loan melas concept, 26
Lohia, 213
Lok Sabha elections, 39–40, 47–48, 158–77;—, electorate preferences, 170–73;—, opinion and attitude of electors, 160–77;—, vote and seat shares of national parties, 158–60

Index ■ 339

Madan, Triloki Nath, 31
Mandela, 246
Manor, James, 214–15, 242
Mayawati, 253, 257
Mehta, Asoka, 224
Mehta, Balawant Rai, 224, 226, 260
Midnight's Children, literary and political etymology, 58–60, 69, 71, 77, 79, 196
Mitra, Subrata Kumar, 32, 37
Moore, Barrington, 33, 37–38, 62, 125, 187, 211, 226
Morris-Jones, William H., 32, 242
multi-party democracy, 127, 129, 131–32, 259–65
Muslim League, 124, 126, 210, 266
Myrdal, Gunnar, 30, 39, 62, 125, 187

Nadar, Kamaraj, 253
Naidu, Chandrababu, 241–15, 257
Naik, V.P., 224
Naipaul, V.S., 20–21, 83–84
Narasimha Rao, 48, 183, 199–200
National Front, 68, 78, 132–33, 135–36, 146–50
Nehru, Jawaharlal, 17–18, 22, 31, 39, 60–61, 63, 82, 84, 87, 161, 180–81, 206, 210, 212, 224, 253, 259, 266, 273
Nelson, J., 31
non-elite, and local government, 238–41

Palmer, Norman D., 30
panchayati raj, 225–26, 230–36;—, CPM and, 235–36;—, Communist Pradhans and non-party ordinary members of panchayats, 234;—, cooperatives effectiveness, 233–34;—, political social dynamics of, 231–36;—, in West Bengal, 231–36
Pant, Gobind Ballabh, 253
paradigms of state-society interactions: competing, 37–47; developmental, 28–32; functional, 32; Indian model, 36–37; modernisation, 31; revolutional, 32–36
Parekh, Bhikhu, 263
Parsons, 30

participation concept, 180–85
party system: competitive elections, 123–27;—, evolution of, 123–31;—, interest articulation, 131–45; cross cutting value conflict, 145–50; during 1952–77, 128–31, 264; during 1977–98, 127, 129, 131–32; efficacy of vote, 140–41; empirical context, 121–23; in India, 123–27; interest articulation, 131–40; multi party system, 127, 129, 131–32; one dominant party system, 127–31; partisan competition, 145–50; political competition, 118–51; political efficacy, 140–41; political legitimacy, 141–45; since Independence, 127–31; social bases of, 134–35; social change and, 118–51; social cleavages and, 131–40; transformation of, 118–51
Patel, 225
polarisation model, 184–85, 187
political change, in context of structural continuity, 78–79
political culture: among post-Independence generation, 62–78; citizenship, 64–65; growth and redistribution, 65; institutionalisation of authority in post-colonial setting, 61–62; law and order, 65–67; political participation, 63–64; salient elements, 61–67; self-conscious and polarised, 67–78
Political Order in Changing Societies, 62, 125
political parties, *see*, party system; usefulness of, 141–43
politics of redistribution, and deprivation, 196–99
post-colonial society, institutionalisation of, 61–62
post-colonial state, 186–88
post-Independence generation, views on: age cohorts and economy, 75–76; age cohorts and liberalisation of economy, 76–78; analysis of data on, 80–84; attitudes towards the Ayodhya incident, 72; attitudes towards social conflicts and discrimination, 71–75; economic satisfaction, 76; effect of vote, 69; free

trade to foreign companies, 77; government better without parties, 77–78; importance of elections, 70–71; institutionalisation and participation, 69–71; level of education, 68–69; level of political information, 67–68; limited ownership, 77; need for atomic bomb, 73; need of Muslims neglected, 75; participation and partisanship, 77–78; parties attention to people, 70; party support, 77–78; policy towards Pakistan, 72–73; privatisation, 76; reservation for women, 74–75; resolution of Kashmir issue, 73; self conscious and polarised, 67–78; separate civil code, 74; Shah Bano incident, 74; trust in institutions, 71
poverty alleviation programme, 224
power, 180–85
primordial identities, and competitive politics, 268–70
protest concept, 180–85
Putnam, Robert D., 211, 216, 245

Ranade, 206
Rao, M.S.A., 30, 36, 43
Rashtriya Swayamsevak Sangh, 63
rasta roko concept, 26
Redistribution with Growth, 206
reform, concept of, 187
region, link between nation and locality, 213
regionalism, concept of, 156
regionalists: attitude towards, communal accommodation, 169;—, Kashmir issue and friendship with Pakistan, 169–70; by caste, 165–66; by education, 166; by religion, 166; partisan preference, 171–72; partisan stability and, 172–73; sense of financial efficacy, 168;–, political efficacy, 167–68; social profile, 165–67
Republican Party, 269
revolution, paradigm of, 32–34
Rostow, Walt W., 29
Roy, Prannoy, 159
Rudé, George, 38

Rudolph, Lloyd I., 26, 32, 42–43, 46, 126, 213–15, 274
Rushdie, Salman, 58–60, 80, 83

SSP, 137
Said, Edward, 79
Samajwadi Party, 91
Savarkar, 213
Scott, James, 211
Sen, Amartya K., 181–82, 186, 278
Seshan, T.N., 260
Shastri, Lal Bahadur, 103
Sheth, D.L., 36, 272
Shils, Edward, 30
Shiromoni Akali Dal, 172–73
Shiv Sena, 175
Singer, M., 31
Singh, Kalyan, 133
Smith, Donald E., 30
Social change: competing models of, 23–26; competing paradigms, 37–47; components of, 254–55; concept of, 24, 38; democratic, 38; developmental paradigm, 28–32; electoral politics and, 17–48; functional paradigm, 32; Indian model, 36–37; paradigms of politics and, 17–48; party system and, 118–51; patterns of, 26–28; resilience of democracy in India and, 250–78; revolution paradigm, 32–34
social dominance, pyramid of, 43–46
social opportunity, democracy and 202–5
Social Origins of Dictatorship and Democracy, 62, 125
Social Science Research Council, New York, 30
Srinivas, Mysore Narasimhachar, 43
States of India: local democracy and formation of, 223–26; per capita NDP, 219, 221; perception of conflict and social change by, 222–23; performance on various indices, 218, 220–21

Tamil Manila Congress (TMC), 171
Telugu Desam Party, 104, 171
Thorson, Thomas London, 110
Tilly, Charles, 38, 215

Toennies, Ferdinand, 30
two-nation theory, 274
Tyagi Subcommittee, 230

United Front, 103
universal adult franchise, principle of, 18
Untouchability Offences Act 1955, 268

V.P. Naik Committee, 224
Vajpayee, Atal Bihari, 68, 103
Viswa Hindu Parishad, 145

vote bank, 42

Washbrook, David A., 269–70
Weiner, Myron, 30
World Bank, 199

Yadav, Laloo Prasad, 91, 174, 246, 253, 257
Yadav, Mulayam Singh, 91, 133
Yadav, Yogendra, 41
Yeltsin, 246

About the Authors

Subrata K. Mitra is Professor and Head, Department of Political Science, South Asia Institute, University of Heidelberg and Visiting Fellow at the Centre for the Study of Developing Societies, Delhi. A Ph.D. in Political Science from the University of Rochester, New York, he has served at the French Institute for Public Opinion, Paris; Centre for Indian Studies, School of Social and Political Science, University of Hull; and as Visiting Professor of Political Science, Indo-US Community Chair at the University of California, Berkeley. Professor Mitra has been a member of the national executive of the British Association for South Asian Studies, and a Fellow of the Royal Society of Arts, London. He is also a life member of the Indian Political Science Association. Quantitative models of political behaviour, rational choice theory, state formation in postcolonial socieites, local elites and governance are among the main research interests of Professor Mitra.

V.B. Singh is Senior Fellow and Director, Centre for the Study of Developing Societies, Delhi. His main areas of interest are electoral studies, party systems and ethnic politics. Besides having contributed numerous research articles to national and international journals, Professor Singh has published a number of books, including: *Profiles of Political Elites in India*; *Political Fragmentation and Electoral Process: 1991 Elections in Uttar Pradesh*; *Elections in India: Data Handbook on Lok Sabha Elections, Between Two Worlds: A Study of Harijan Elites* (co-author); and *Hindu Nationalists in India: The Rise of the Bharatiya Janata Party* (co-author).